The Guardian Book of Obituaries

■ ■ ■

THE GUARDIAN BOOK OF OBITUARIES

Edited by Phil Osborne

The **Guardian**

Atlantic Books
London

First published in 2003 by Atlantic Books,
on behalf of Guardian Newspapers Ltd.
Atlantic Books is an imprint of
Grove Atlantic Ltd.

10 9 8 7 6 5 4 3 2 1

A CIP catalogue record for this book is
available from the British Library

ISBN 1 84354 195 5

Printed in Great Britain by MPG Books Ltd. Bodmin
Design by Lindsay Nash

Grove Atlantic Ltd
Ormond House
26–27 Boswell Street
London WC1N 3JZ

CONTENTS

POLITICS, PHILOSOPHY AND HISTORY

MOVERS, SHAKERS AND DOERS

THE MEDIA

THE GREAT AND THE GOOD

To you, and all you wish yourselves

INTRODUCTION

The most popular regular features of a British daily newspaper have always been reckoned to be the sports pages, the crosswords, the weather reports and the cartoon and comic strips. Tamper with them too much, move them around too often, omit vital statistics and the editor's postbag heaves, the e-mails zing. In the last twenty years, catching up fast on the rails has come the obituaries page. Of course, readers have always been attracted to the births, marriages and deaths column at regional and national level to spot who has 'come on' and 'gone on': a natural source of saloon-bar and dinner-table conversation. But not often were readers too interested in the surrounding text, unless the person was definitively famous or notorious.

The culture changed when the then editor of the *Daily Telegraph* obituaries page, Hugh Massingberd, began to solicit pieces which were more 'flavourful', seeking to present a more 'warts and all' treatment of a person's life. Previously, obituaries tended to be more prosaic and sometimes lacking in honesty. All obituaries editors, in one way or another, are indebted to Massingberd for paving the way for much more rounded insights into people's achievements – and their failures. Having said which, the aim should still be – and is – a celebration of a person's life and achievements, even if the disappointments cannot be ignored.

Widening the scope of what could be delineated in an obituary led to an extension of the breadth of the writing and spawned a succession of collections of obituaries in book form by the *Telegraph* (one entitled *Rogues*) and *The Times*. Both papers have been running dedicated obituary pages for many decades. This has not been true of the *Guardian*. Of course, major politicians, film stars, writers and academics have been acknowledged over the years, often with splendid displays and contributions by distinguished writers. But there had never been the resources or the inclination to translate this into a daily page, which could reflect not only the passing of the great and good but that of the ordinary people whose lives had illuminated specific areas of public life, and of the 'quirky' characters who belonged to milieus which highlighted a social aspect – however transitory – of contemporary life. An attempt was made to change this with the launch of the *Guardian*'s G2 tabloid section. Regular pages could now be devoted to obituaries, but the restrictions of the small format meant that brevity had to be preferred to breadth and depth. The late W. J. Weatherby, among others, wrote small gems, but the drawbacks were obvious and when lengthy contributions were necessary, they had to be accommodated in a small 'featurish' format or yanked out to appear in the main broadsheet paper. Eventually, in the 1990s, a dedicated broadsheet page became essential and space was found where the obituaries nestle today, running alongside the Comment and Opinion sections and the daily Editor page that collates news from around the world. The continuity and seamlessness of life and death, and the daily observations by commentators and writers, are pulled together in a series of pages.

So, we thought it timely to recognize the full flowering of the *Guardian's* obituaries page with a book incorporating the most important people and the best writing over the era in which the page became mature. Initially, since this is the first *Guardian Book of Obituaries*, we considered expanding the scope to take in personalities since the Second World War, but the more I delved the more this became truly daunting and it seemed best to concentrate on the last twenty years when we became more of an entity. Even then, the range of choice was akin to what I would imagine it to be like for someone asked to choose his or her desert island discs. We thought we'd start with a hundred, but it was soon obvious that to preserve the quality of the writing, always a prime *Guardian* consideration, we'd have to prune the numbers: after all they abridge the records in *Desert Island Discs* and we didn't want to fillet our contributors. So, in the end, this selection is nearer seventy and the choice was still invidious. Every time I thought 'I must have that one' along came another candidate in the same field who sat up and begged for inclusion. Then, overridingly, I tried to think of the excellence of the piece as well as the importance of the person and just as often I had to exclude people because the piece was too short to do justice to them, almost always because of the exigencies of the time at which they were prepared. The only really short item in the book is of the tennis player Fred Perry, and I felt he was needed to preserve the range of the sportsman.

In the end the picking and nit-picking left me with as broad, representative and well-written a selection as one book could hold. If you think some of your favourites should be here, I can only list a few of mine I would dearly love to have seen included for one reason or another: Ella Fitzgerald, Greta Garbo, Andrei Sakharov, A. J. P. Taylor, Aaron Copland, Graham Greene, Elisabeth Frink, Lew Hoad, Harold Acton and Jill Tweedie. I could go on, and no doubt there will be, in time, another book.

Finally, I would like to thank all the regular contributing writers to the obituaries page, some of whom are here, some not. They know who they are and without them the production of the page on many days would be well nigh impossible. Also grateful thanks to my predecessors in editing the page: W. L. Webb, Christopher Driver, Bill Smithies and Ian Mayes, who helped build it to what it is. And the present team: Nigel Fountain, Robert White, Polly Pattullo, John Shirley, Sarah A. Smith and Emma Hagestadt, who in many varied and creative ways help keep us consistently top of the form and as far as possible out of the Corrections and Clarifications column. And not least my publisher at the *Guardian*, Lisa Darnell, and Alice Hunt and Louisa Joyner at Atlantic Books, for their help and patience with a novitiate.

PHIL OSBORNE *Guardian* Obituaries Editor

THE ARTISTS

...

LAURENCE OLIVIER
Michael Billington

By any standards Laurence Olivier's list of achievements was incredible. He succeeded in a wider range of parts, classical and contemporary, than any British actor before him. He steered the National Theatre brilliantly through its first ten rock-strewn years. As a film director, he brought Shakespeare illuminatingly to the screen, while as a movie actor he enjoyed a fifty-year career that included superb performances in *Carrie* and *Wuthering Heights*.

In later years he also turned television producer, bringing a number of stage successes to Granada screens. He allied natural genius as an actor to unstinting hard work. He was not only the first theatrical Lord: in his chosen profession he was without peer.

Not the least extraordinary thing about Olivier (born in Dorking, the son of a clergyman) is that his talent manifested itself so early. At the age of ten he played Brutus in a production of *Julius Caesar* put on by All Saints Choir School, Margaret Street. Ellen Terry saw the performance, said to the overwhelmed young Olivier afterwards, 'Oh, don't you love the words?' and noted in her diary, 'The small boy who played Brutus is already a great actor.'

And five years later when he played Kate in a special matinee of *The Taming of the Shrew* at the Shakespeare Memorial Theatre, W. A. Darlington wrote, 'I cannot remember any actress in the part who looked better.' Indeed, pictures of Olivier in the part show him gazing at the world with an insulting hauteur.

Olivier was clearly born to act. From his Victorian clergyman father he may have derived his lust for language and his secret fury; from his mother, who died when he was thirteen, his clownish humour and feminine grace. For one of Olivier's extraordinary qualities was his ability to combine the male and female principles in a single performance: one moment as dangerous as a lion, the next as skittish as a gazelle. The qualities that most men hide and suppress, Olivier harboured and displayed; and that is one important source of his greatness.

Having trained as an actor with the redoubtable Elsie Fogerty at the Central School of Speech and Drama, then tucked away in the Albert Hall, Olivier's first extended opportunity came with Barry Jackson's famous Birmingham Repertory Company: in the 1927–8 seasons he played a wide variety of parts, including Tony Lumpkin, Uncle Vanya, Parolles, Malcolm in *Macbeth* and the title-role in Tennyson's *Harold*, which was seen at London's Royal Court. Already his name was being noticed. St John Ervine in the *Observer* marked him out as 'a distinguished romantic actor' of the future.

'Romantic' seems the word for Olivier's career in those early years. Sporting a Ronald Colman moustache and looking darkly handsome, he became from 1929 on a West End lead actor, playing Stanhope in *Journey's End*, *Beau Geste*, Prince Po in *The Circle of Chalk*, Victor Prynne with Noël Coward and Gertie Lawrence in *Private Lives*. Coward, Olivier has said, was a great influence at that time. 'He taxed me with his sharpness and shrewdness and his brilliance, he used to point out when I was talking nonsense, which nobody else had ever done before.' He also made Olivier read (Charlotte Brontë, Somerset Maugham, Arnold Bennett) and cured him of a bad habit of 'corpsing' on stage. It was a time when, as Sir Gerald Barry once remarked, conscience did make Cowards of us all.

For Olivier, these were heady years. In 1930 he married his first wife, Jill Esmond, and made his film debut in *Too Many Crooks*. In 1931 he first appeared in New York in *Private Lives*, returning there in 1933 to play in *The Green Bay Tree* under the iron direction of Jed Harris (on whom he part-modelled his Richard III).

But it wasn't until 1935 that he started his steady ascent of the classic repertoire. In a famous production of *Romeo and Juliet* at the New Theatre, he and Gielgud alternated the roles of Romeo and Mercutio with Peggy Ashcroft as Juliet and Edith Evans as the Nurse. Olivier's Romeo was slaughtered by the critics: he was accused (as Henry Irving had been before him) of butchering the verse, of playing Romeo as though he were riding a motor-bike, and so on. But in a TV interview with Kenneth Tynan many years later Olivier was unrepentant about his performance. He claimed that he was trying to sell realism in Shakespeare, and he made a classic distinction between himself and Gielgud as actors. 'I've always thought that we were reverses of the same coin … the top half John, all spiritual, all spirituality, all beauty, all abstract things, and myself as all earth, blood, humanity; if you like, the baser part of humanity, without that beauty.'

Whether or not Olivier was a great Romeo, his classical career was well and truly launched. He played Orlando to Elisabeth Bergner's Rosalind in a 1936 movie of *As You Like It* and at the Old Vic from 1937 to 1938 he had his first crack at many of the Shakespearean peaks: Hamlet, Henry V, Iago (to Ralph

Richardson's Othello), Macbeth (in an ill-fated Michel St Denis production) and Coriolanus.

James Agate, then the most powerful English critic, was often grudging in his praise; but, as Kenneth Tynan once remarked to me, that was probably because Olivier trod on memories of his beloved Henry Irving. Other critics, however, praised Olivier's speaking ('such attacks,' wrote Ivor Brown of his Coriolanus, 'as makes the syllables shimmer like a sword's blade') and the town flocked to see this rising star.

For Olivier, the years from 1939 to 1944 were largely occupied by films on both sides of the Atlantic (in the war he desperately wanted to be a fighter pilot but was consigned to training duties in the Fleet Air Arm, from which he was eventually released). These were the years of his Heathcliff, Maxim de Winter and Darcy in Hollywood (all capitalizing on his somewhat saturnine good looks) and of his legendary *Henry V*, which he produced, directed and starred in.

In *Henry V* he was, in Charles Laughton's phrase, quite simply England: instead of exploring the area of neurotic self-doubt that later actors (like Alan Howard) were to seize on, Olivier concentrated on patriotic fervour and crisp (even Crispian) humour. And to this day no one who has ever heard it can forget his delivery of 'Cry God for Harry, England and St George', which turned the final vowels into a spine-tingling affirmation of national heroism.

In a strange way, Olivier's career often went in great spurts, and he followed *Henry V* with two immortal years from 1944 to 1946 at the New Theatre. Olivier (by now married to Vivien Leigh), Ralph Richardson and John Burrell were appointed co-directors of the Old Vic, and the result was a string of legendary performances.

In September 1944, Olivier for the first time played Richard III and established seigneurial rights over the part for generations to come. 'A door opened,' a director told me recently, 'and round it came this great, black evil thing.' Even Agate was moved to talk of 'mounting verve and sustained excitement'. And Olivier himself has memorably described the feeling at the matinee the next day, knowing that at last he had won full-throated recognition. 'There is a phrase – the sweet smell of success – and I can only tell you (I've had two experiences of that) it just smells like Brighton and oyster-bars and things like that.'

They were legendary seasons at the New: Richardson as Falstaff and Peer Gynt, Olivier as Hotspur, Shallow, Astrov and (in one astonishing evening) both Oedipus and Mr Puff. 'A panther amongst doves,' someone called the *Oedipus*. And it is fascinating to note how often critics resort to animal-imagery in discussing Olivier; there was always something dark, predatory and dangerous about his acting, suggesting some beast of the field for whom all the world's a cage.

But those great years at the New ended curtly and shamefully, with Olivier being told in 1949 in the middle of an exhausting Old Vic tour of the Antipodes that he and Richardson would not have their contracts renewed when they expired. The politicking behind this has never been made clear, but it was not the only time Olivier was to be dealt a savage blow by the Establishment boards who employed him.

In the six years after this, Olivier's career rarely burst into flame. He and Vivien Leigh became the Oliviers (he had been knighted in 1947): the undisputed monarchs of Shaftesbury Avenue and the source of endless theatrical gossip. Olivier made his flat-footed movie *Hamlet*. Together he and Vivien Leigh played Shakespeare's *Antony and Cleopatra* and Shaw's *Caesar and Cleopatra* in London and New York. But publicly it was suggested that he was dimming his own brilliance to accommodate her talent. And, privately, as several showbiz biographies have later revealed, he was having to cope with a manic-depressive, mentally strained wife. These were cruel years when Olivier had a lot of fame but earned little glory; though one should not overlook his best-ever screen performance in William Wyler's *Carrie* (1952) as a high-class restaurateur ruined by an obsessive passion.

The *annus mirabilis* for Olivier, however, was 1955 when he returned to Stratford-upon-Avon to play Malvolio, Macbeth and Titus Andronicus. The first was an odd performance: a Jewish arriviste who had trouble with his vowels. But the Macbeth was incomparable: ironic with the Murderers, frenetic when confronted by Banquo's Ghost and filled at the end with an appalling spiritual exhaustion – 'My way of life is fallen into the sere, the yellow leaf'. Harold Hobson noted how, when Olivier described the things he must not look to have, his voice achieved a soaring arc of lamentation when he came to 'troops of friends'.

And then came Titus in Brook's ritualistic production: a forgotten play was elevated to tragic status, and when Olivier cried 'I am the sea', it was like the sound of Atlantic breakers hitting the rocks. An astonishing year was crowned by the release of Olivier's film *Richard III*: his best Shakespeare film and one that allowed him, through the camera, to take the audience into Richard's malignant confidence.

Whatever the traumas in his private life, Olivier's public career in those years was amazing. In 1957 he joined forces with John Osborne at the Royal Court to play Archie Rice in *The Entertainer*: all leering, thick-eyebrowed innuendo in the front-cloth numbers, while filled with a soaring tragic despair in the domestic scenes. And two years later he returned to *Coriolanus* at Stratford, proving once again his ability to mix male and female in a single performance. When praised for his military exploits and forced to kiss his wife in public, Olivier rolled his eyes like a shy schoolgirl. Yet the performance was also compact with irony, vigour and athleticism, ending with the famous death in which Olivier's body seemed to be spewed off a high rock and left ignominiously dangling to be stabbed and maimed. 'A more shocking, less sentimental death,' wrote Tynan, 'I have not seen in the theatre.'

As a new decade started, both Olivier's life and career seemed to enter yet another new productive phase. In 1960 his unhappy marriage to Vivien Leigh ended, and a year later he married Joan Plowright, a delightful, charming woman who had progressed to stardom via the Royal Court.

Olivier also accepted new challenges. In 1961 he became director of the new Chichester Festival Theatre, England's first large thrust stage. And after a few initial hiccups, the venture took off with Olivier's own production of *Uncle Vanya,* starring himself and Michael Redgrave. Vanya nights came to be known as 'holy nights' at Chichester, such was the atmosphere front-of-house and backstage. And after his managerial success at Chichester, Olivier was in 1962 appointed the first director of the National Theatre. Given his unparalleled career as actor, director, producer, it seemed the obvious appointment.

Olivier's decade at the National had many ups and downs. But he got the show on the road and he also looked to the future rather than the past. He was sometimes criticized for trying to be trendy and with-it. But I would argue that one of his signal achievements lay in putting his trust in a new generation of actors and directors.

William Gaskill and John Dexter came from the Royal Court to be associate directors. Kenneth Tynan was levered out of dramatic criticism to be the first literary manager (according to Tynan it was on the principle that Olivier would rather have him on the inside pissing out than on the outside pissing in). And the first company included such fine young actors as Robert Stephens, Colin Blakely, Frank Finlay and Derek Jacobi – with Billie Whitelaw, Joan Plowright and Maggie Smith taking many of the prized female roles.

The early days of that company at the Vic vindicated Olivier's judgement: *The Recruiting Officer, Hay Fever, A Flea in her Ear, The Royal Hunt of the Sun, The Crucible, Trelawny of the 'Wells',* were all superlative productions. We had waited 148 years for a National Theatre and, under Olivier's stewardship, it turned out to justify the wait.

Olivier himself also turned in some sensational performances. His Othello was unkindly compared by some to Pearl Bailey, and would undoubtedly have benefited from a closer relationship with Iago. But as the Captain in Strindberg's *Dance of Death*, he was superb: bullet-headed, jack-booted and with lips that seemed to curl in snarling irony. He also once confided to a friend that he regarded his Solness in *The Master Builder* as one of his greatest performances. 'Why?' he was inevitably asked. 'Because,' he said, 'that man is me.' An interesting remark to make about a character terrified of a new generation knocking at the door and driven to acts of pinnacle-climbing desperation.

There was little evidence of this at the National. The simple truth is that its fortunes declined from 1968 to 1971 for a variety of reasons. Olivier himself was stricken by cancer and had to shed some of his responsibilities. The Dexter–Gaskill team broke up and was never satisfactorily replaced. And the company over-extended itself with seasons at the Cambridge Theatre and the New.

Indeed, a New Theatre season in 1971 faced mounting criticism with productions of Giradoux's *Amphitryon 38*, Adrian Mitchell's *Tyger*, Büchner's *Danton's Death* and Pirandello's *The Rules of the Game*. The chairman of the National Theatre Board confronted Olivier squarely and said he was worried: he had his reputation to consider. Olivier smiled to himself, thinking his own reputation might possibly outlast that of his chairman.

Then, in the winter of 1971, Michael Blakemore's production of *Long Day's Journey Into Night* with Olivier himself, Constance Cummings, Ronald Pickup and Denis Quilley, showed the National back on the very peak of form. Olivier himself was unforgettable as the old actor-manager, James Tyrone. In the scene with his wife, in which he pleaded with her desperately not to go on another of her morphine jags, the great Olivier jaw sagged, the eyes gazed heavenwards in despair and, burying himself in her dress, he uttered a spine-chilling cry of 'Won't you stop now?'

This once again was great acting. But even before Olivier led the National back from near disaster to total triumph, a search for his successor had started; and so it was that Peter Hall succeeded Olivier as director in April 1973. But not without Olivier giving two spectacular final performances: as an elderly hat-fetishist in *Saturday, Sunday, Monday*, and as a tough Glaswegian revolutionary in Trevor Griffith's *The Party* – a typically daring choice for our most daring actor.

Picking up the threads after the National must have been difficult, but Olivier turned, despite illness, to film and television work. On TV he was a memorable Big Daddy, coarse and rubicund, in *Cat on a Hot Tin Roof.* And in 1983 a frail, wizened, incredibly moving King Lear with sudden sparks of the old animal danger.

In the cinema he was a sinister, tooth-pulling old Nazi in *Marathon Man*, a lecherous boardroom tycoon in *The Betsy*, a whimsical, Chevalier-like con-man in *A Little Romance*, trailing across Europe with two children. Not all his later films seemed quite worthy of his own mountainous talent. But for Olivier there was no question of a docile retirement. Like a Chekhov character, he believed in the sanctifying power of work. And one recalled him as Astrov musing of the indolent Elenya that such a life cannot be 'pure' – a word he used to hit with a hammer-blow.

To sum up such a career is difficult: it was too rich, too diverse, to be contained within a few phrases. I can only be grateful to have seen every performance he gave on stage or screen over the last thirty-five years. And I shall never forget the imprint made by that dark, brooding presence, the laser-like ability of that voice to cut through steel and that great gift for vulgar, mischievous comedy.

Future generations will be able to judge his performances on film. But they are no substitute for the thrill of his presence on stage: the pawing of the ground like an angry bull in *Macbeth*, the great wounded, indignant cry of 'Boy' in *Coriolanus*, the hand-on-hip Boyars' Dance in Strindberg's *Dance of Death*, the light, graceful backward step off a table in *Long Day's Journey Into Night*. Olivier has left the playgoer with a theatreful of memories; and one will be able to tell one's grandchildren that one saw, at his perihelion, the greatest actor of the twentieth century, maybe even the greatest in recorded history.

LAURENCE OLIVIER · *born* 22 May 1907 · *died* 11 July 1989 ·

17 July 1989

HERBERT VON KARAJAN
Edward Greenfield

Few conductors have ever dominated a whole generation in the music world so completely as Herbert von Karajan over the last thirty years. In that period it became almost axiomatic to nominate him as 'top conductor' over any possible rival. He has died at the age of eighty-one with his supremacy still maintained.

The very completeness of that supremacy has at many periods fanned the flames of hostility. The coolness of his manner, his seeming indifference to audiences and to the feelings of musicians alike, coupled with the glossy public image, for long fostered in the media, of a musical playboy figure, an athlete who loved flying his private aircraft, sailing his yacht and driving fast cars, provided fuel for his detractors. He has been described as the 'conductor you love to hate', and critics, particularly in Germany, were consistently reluctant to accord him the accolades he plainly deserved, whether for his records or his performances with the Berlin Philharmonic and the Vienna Philharmonic. It says much for the quality of his music-making and the charismatic power of his personality that the detractors had no effect whatever on the adoration of the public. He remained top conductor and that was it.

For many years the high polish of his performances with the Berlin Philharmonic, the orchestra of which he was music director for over thirty years, regularly attracted the criticism that he was superficial in the greatest masterpieces. There was fair justification for that in some of the performances he conducted on foreign tours, not least in London. Then, with his health undermined by a serious back condition, when he was suffering much pain, the final period of his music-making transcended even what he had achieved earlier, not in polish, but in depth of expression.

Herbert von Karajan shared his birthplace with Mozart, Salzburg, the city where during the summer festivals and his own Easter Festivals, he later had many of his greatest triumphs. He was born there on 5 April 1908, the son of the chief surgeon at the local hospital, who was also a keen amateur clarinettist. Young Herbert was given a musical training from his earliest years, learning the piano from the age of four and playing at a charity concert when only five. When still only eight he played at a Mozart celebration at the Mozarteum, where he was studying with, among others, the conductor Bernhard Paumgartner, who encouraged the boy to train as a conductor. Completing his studies in Vienna over the years 1926 to 1929, Karajan graduated as a conductor at the Hochschule für Musik, but later always complained that with the poverty of the instruction he and his colleagues in effect taught themselves. It was at this period in Vienna that he first heard Toscanini conducting. Hearing the way that Toscanini, with the visiting La Scala company, transformed what he had always thought of as a banal piece, Donizetti's *Lucia di Lammermoor*, revealing it as a masterpiece, fired him with the ambition to succeed similarly. In 1931, just to hear Toscanini conduct Wagner's *Tannhäuser*, Karajan cycled all the way from Salzburg to Bayreuth and back, some 250 miles.

In 1929, with his training completed, he had no chance to demonstrate his prowess as a conductor to potential employers until – thanks to his musical connections in Salzburg – he hired an orchestra and sold tickets for a concert of his own. It included two virtuoso works that have remained Karajan favourites, Strauss's *Don Juan* and Tchaikovsky's *Fifth Symphony*. The concert was a great success and promptly won him his first conducting appointment. The Intendant of the tiny opera company at Ulm promptly hired him, and on 2 March 1929 he conducted an opera for the very first time, Mozart's *Le Nozze di Figaro*.

The very limitation of forces in Ulm challenged the ambitious young man to do the impossible, and even with the usual tiny orchestra augmented, it was an amazing achievement to present such operas as Wagner's *Meistersinger* and Strauss's *Salome* there. It was then that he learnt his craft, enjoying himself and having great success, until after five years he was suddenly fired.

Only later did he discover that the Intendant felt that his brilliant young conductor needed, for his own good, to venture elsewhere. During his last year in Ulm he was looking hard for another post, and had almost given up hope, when the post of Kapellmeister in Aachen fell vacant. In 1934 he was made responsible for opera performances and symphony concerts there, and the following year he was appointed Generalmusikdirektor, the youngest in Germany. Years later, when challenged about his membership of the Nazi party, he was quite open that to obtain the Aachen post he had joined solely out of expediency.

His reputation then began to extend through Germany and Austria, and it says much for his unswerving standards in music, whatever his approach to politics, that when asked to conduct the Vienna State Opera for the first time, he insisted on its being a major work, Wagner's *Tristan ünd Isolde*. He also insisted on having adequate rehearsal time, which notoriously in Vienna the authorities never allowed to young conductors. When asked by Heinz Tietjens to conduct the Berlin State Opera, his attitude was similarly uncompromising. He conducted Beethoven's *Fidelio* there on 30 September 1938, and the following month sealed his triumph with *Tristan*, all this in the same year as his first Berlin Philharmonic concert. A much-quoted notice referred to him as 'Das Wunder Karajan', and by this time he was coming to be regarded as the young whizz-kid rival of the great Wilhelm Furtwängler, music director of the Berlin Philharmonic and Germany's leading conductor. It was a rivalry that the Nazis fostered, anxious perhaps that Furtwängler should never feel really secure, often defiant as he was of their authority.

In 1941 Karajan left Aachen to concentrate on working in Berlin, mainly at the State Opera, and from then to the end of the Second World War the only

Berlin symphony concerts he conducted were with the Staatskapelle, not the Berlin Philharmonic. He narrowly missed being called up for the army, but through a chance contact (his dentist's daughter was Goebbels' secretary) managed to have the order rescinded. Though his career flourished under the Third Reich, he certainly had his enemies. In 1945 Karajan and his family spent the closing months of the war in Italy. Then in Vienna, after the war, he had no chance to conduct, until he had been investigated by a denazification court.

It was largely through the advocacy of the English impresario and recording manager Walter Legge, anxious to sign up German and Austrian artists for his company, EMI, that Karajan returned so quickly to active performance. That was early in 1946, when on 18 January he conducted the Vienna Philharmonic once more.

He also made a series of what became historic recordings, of Mozart, Brahms, Strauss and others, and Legge promptly hired him to conduct the orchestra he had formed in London, the Philharmonia, which was already demonstrating its new supremacy. From then until 1955, when Karajan became music director of the Berlin Philharmonic in succession to Furtwängler, Karajan's close relationship with the Philharmonia produced a series of EMI recordings of supreme quality, including important opera sets with Legge's wife, Elisabeth Schwarzkopf, culminating in a recording of Strauss's *Der Rosenkavalier*, which has become a classic. For EMI he also made recordings with the company of La Scala, Milan, two of them with Maria Callas.

In 1951 he conducted for the first time at the Bayreuth Festival, returning there the following year, but never again. Karajan had already decided that as far as possible he would insist on acting as his own stage director, and that was to be impossible when Wagner's grandsons Wieland and Wolfgang were intent on being stage directors themselves.

After 1955, with his Berlin appointment, he made the greater number of his recordings for Deutsche Grammophon (DG). The late 1950s brought halcyon years for him, when in addition to his Berlin Philharmonic post he held the artistic directorship of the Vienna State Opera (1957–64), the artistic directorship of the Salzburg Festival (from 1957) and had a regular collaboration with La Scala. Quite apart from the attitude of the Wagner brothers, Karajan's Salzburg duties effectively prevented him from ever conducting Wagner again in Bayreuth. In 1967 he founded his own Easter Festival in Salzburg, where over the first few seasons he conducted his own production of Wagner's *Ring* cycle, which he subsequently recorded for DG.

In 1962 he recorded the nine Beethoven symphonies for DG with the Berlin Philharmonic, the first time that a Beethoven cycle had been recorded and issued as a single project, and over the years both for DG and EMI, he made an extraordinary range of recordings, returning to his favourite works many times over, not least when the potential of video recording fired him. He was always a lover of technical innovation and of gadgets. In the 1980s his encouragement and enthusiasm did much to promote development of the new medium of the compact disc.

He was also concerned to develop new talent, and would specially foster young artists, of whom the most strikingly successful was the violinist Anne-Sophie Mutter, who appeared in Mozart concertos with him in Berlin when only thirteen. Later it was his enthusiasm for the playing of the young clarinettist Sabine Meyer which prompted a serious rift with the Berlin Philharmonic. For some time it looked as though his insistence on having her as principal clarinet in his orchestra would completely rupture his relationship, and even after the wound was healed – and Miss Meyer, a natural soloist, left the orchestra – the old warmth did not completely return. Though in rehearsal Karajan was something of a dictator, it was remarkable during most of his career how devoted his Berlin players were. The Irish flute-player James Galway, unexpectedly chosen as principal in the orchestra, has regularly paid the warmest of tributes.

Though he was totally supreme in Europe, Karajan never fostered close contacts with the world of American music. He conducted the Berlin Philharmonic, and earlier the Philharmonia, on a number of successful tours, but as he grew older, so he was increasingly reluctant to conduct the orchestras that knew him intimately, above all the Berlin Philharmonic and Vienna Philharmonic, the resident orchestra each summer in Salzburg. It was a limitation, but his many records ensured that in America too he was counted a top conductor, even if latterly Sir Georg Solti with his Chicago Symphony Orchestra provided the keenest American rivalry. Just where Karajan's ultimate reputation will stand alongside those of his greatest predecessors, above all Toscanini and Furtwängler, remains to be seen, but at least he has an enormous advantage in the wealth of recordings that he has left. He may have preferred to return to his favourite works, but he was often at his most illuminating in rarer repertory. He made a superb set of recordings for DG of major orchestral works by Schoenberg, Berg and Webern, and early in his career he recorded a performance, both polished and passionate, of Balakirev's First Symphony.

He was also a tireless advocate of twentieth-century composers not especially popular on his home ground of Germany and Austria, above all of Sibelius and Bartók. Outstanding among his many opera recordings were not just those he made of the masterpieces of Mozart, Wagner, Strauss and

Puccini, but of Debussy's *Pelléas et Mélisande*, which he once counted his favourite among his own recordings. Latterly his recordings often fell short of perfection on technical grounds, when he was such a dictator in the studio and control room, and stringent schedules allowed little time. At least that latter-day haste, and his love of linking audio recording with video, brought extra spontaneity. No conductor has left so rich a legacy of his work behind him.

HERBERT VON KARAJAN · *born* 5 April 1908 · *died* 16 July 1989 ·

16 October 1990

LEONARD BERNSTEIN
Edward Greenfield

In an age when specialization is the norm, in music as elsewhere, Leonard Bernstein, who has died aged seventy-two, dared to be versatile. Here was a superstar conductor who was also a gifted pianist and an expressive composer, not just in the regular symphonic and choral repertory, but in popular music, above all the American musical (*Candide* and *West Side Story*). He also broke barriers in American television by talking about music to the millions without trivializing his thought.

His personal relationships were as warm as his music-making. In any party he was always performing, but unlike many extroverts he showed individual concern for all he met, even casually. As Clive Gillinson of the London Symphony Orchestra said: 'If you spent time with him, you seemed to grow yourself.'

Earlier this year he was conducting the Vienna Philharmonic in Bruckner's Ninth Symphony for a concert and recording. By then he was perceptibly tired. His punishing schedule was catching up with him. But in July he spent three weeks at the Pacific Music Festival in Japan, not only conducting the LSO in concerts but working with young conductors and the players. His last appearance was at the Tanglewood Festival where he had been a familiar figure for half a century.

Although Bernstein called himself a late developer, the breadth of his musical gifts was widely appreciated when he was still in his early twenties. He always counted the twelve months from 14 November 1943 as his *annus mirabilis*, for which, as he said, 'I've paid in blood.' At twenty-four hours' notice he had to deputize for Bruno Walter and had such a spectacular success that even in wartime it was front-page news. The following January Bernstein conducted his First Symphony (the *Jeremiah*) in Pittsburgh. In April at the Met he conducted his first ballet, *Fancy Free*, another hit, and at the end of the year came his first Broadway show, *On the Town*.

As though without trying, he immediately made his mark and when he discussed it at the time with his friend and mentor the composer Aaron Copland, the reply came, 'It's only what everyone expected.' Yet he came from an unmusical family, the son of an immigrant Jewish businessman in Boston. His first musical memory was being taught to play the ukelele by his aunt, who later left her piano for storage with the Bernsteins. Music became Leonard's obsession. Despite the active hostility of his father, who wanted him for his hairdressing supply business or else to become a rabbi, the boy took odd jobs to get better piano lessons.

His father did send him to neighbouring Harvard and there Leonard had his first formal lessons in harmony, counterpoint and musical theory, but not composition or conducting. As an undergraduate at a party in New York he met Aaron Copland, whose rigorous criticism became the nearest thing he ever had to a composition teacher. It was later, only after graduation, that he met Dimitri Mitropoulos, who put him on the road to becoming a conductor himself. Mitropoulos not only secured his entry into the Curtis Institute in Philadelphia where he was taught by the stern technician Fritz Reiner, but helped him financially. They were joined by another mentor, Serge Koussevitzky, music director of the Boston Symphony, and Bernstein became an assistant from the founding of the Berkshire Music Center at Tanglewood in 1940. Bernstein himself always paid the highest tributes to his own teachers, and though he was always viewed as an artist relying (perhaps too much) on his spontaneous response to the moment, he was rigorous in his preparation.

After his initial successes of 1943–4 his career flourished on every front. In 1945 he became Music Director of the New York City Symphony, and in 1957 returned to the New York Philharmonic as co-conductor with Mitropoulos, becoming Music Director in his own right the following year, the first American-born conductor to hold that post. In 1947 he visited Israel for the first time and conducted the new nation's Philharmonic. His Jewish roots were always a source of inspiration to him, though he firmly refused to compartmentalize the idea of Jewish and non-Jewish music. His composing career developed too, with his Second Symphony ('The Age of Anxiety'), inspired by W. H. Auden, in 1949. In the mid-1950s he wrote memorable music for the film *On the Waterfront* (turned into an orchestral suite), as well as *Candide* (1956) and *West Side Story* (1957), the latter an instant popular and cult success.

The 1960s brought more large-scale works, including the Third Symphony (*Kaddish*), and the *Chichester Psalms*, Hebrew settings written for Chichester Cathedral, another demonstration of confident barrier-crossing. Then in 1971 he wrote Mass for the opening of the Kennedy Center, an all-embracing act of celebration, not just Catholic or even religious, with Bernstein at his most vigorous, eclectic and contentious. The American bicentenary celebrations in 1976 prompted perhaps the most individual of Bernstein's later works, *Songfest*, a collection for six solo voices and orchestra of settings of American poems, depicting individual Americans.

Bernstein's conducting was caught on record at all stages in his career and conveys the voltage which marked his work in the concert hall. Over the years with CBS he came to feel that studio sessions were uncongenial. I remember a *Rite of Spring* where session time ran out until nothing could be done except to give a straight performance. It was a great success and such experiences led him over his later career with Deutsche Grammophon to opt for the recording of live performances, which were then edited together with a few studio 'patches'. Latterly he was eccentric in his preference for slow speeds, as in Tchaikovsky's *Pathetique* and Dvořák's *New World*, or 'Nimrod' from Elgar's *Enigma Variations*. Yet the passionate warmth of Bernstein's conducting comes out on most of his records. He did some outstanding operatic recordings too. Verdi's *Falstaff*, recorded with the Vienna Philharmonic, for example.

Last Christmas morning in Berlin, he celebrated the destruction of the Berlin Wall with a historic performance of Beethoven's Ninth Symphony. It was televised live, with musicians drawn from many orchestras both east and west, and will remain a remarkable memorial, even though he scandalized some by substituting 'Freiheit' for 'Freude' in the choral finale, which he claimed fitted Beethoven's true intention as well as the occasion.

In Britain, Bernstein's closest relationship was with the London Symphony Orchestra, which at the Barbican in 1986 presented the first wide-ranging retrospective of his music.

His great disappointment as a composer was his failure with his one grand opera, *A Quiet Place*. An American domestic drama with a limp libretto, it incorporates material of his early one-act piece, *Trouble in Tahiti*. That underlines the differences between the snappy memorability of early Bernstein and the later work, not helped by a weak libretto. Bernstein's last musical, *1600 Pennsylvania Avenue*, written for the American bicentennial, also failed at the libretto hurdle. But with these exceptions, Bernstein's career was a success story and few figures in music have generated such intense affection and envy.

His devotion to his wife Felicia Montealegre was intense too, though his marriage was rocked when in the 1960s he 'came out' in declaring his bisexuality, a facet of his personality he had never concealed from her. In spite of the malicious stories, Felicia remained unique for him, and he suffered deeply at her early death.

LEONARD BERNSTEIN · *born* 25 August 1918 · *died* 14 October 1990 ·

15 June 1991

PEGGY ASHCROFT
Michael Billington

Dame Peggy Ashcroft, who died yesterday at the age of eighty-three, was not only the finest English actress of her generation, she was also, in Trevor Nunn's words, 'a born campaigner'. She fought tirelessly for the cause of human freedom outside the theatre and for the idea of permanence and adventure within it. Look through her sixty-year-plus career on the British stage and you will find she was always in at the beginning of new ventures: the legendary Gielgud seasons at the Queen's in 1937–8, the Royal Court in 1956 (where she played Brecht), the RSC in 1960 and the National Theatre in 1976, where one March afternoon she spoke the first words to be publicly uttered on any of the South Bank stages in Beckett's *Happy Days*: 'Another heavenly day.'

I had the privilege of getting to know her well while working on a TV profile of her in 1986 and I was struck by many things: her passionate belief in the company ideal, something dating back to her first encounter with Stanislavsky's theories as a young actress in the 1920s; her extraordinary modesty and nervousness: having committed herself to a week-long series of interviews, she went through with it but she really didn't relish talking about herself and resisted any attempt to pluck out the mystery at the heart of acting. She disliked cant and hypocrisy, directors who did anything to cheapen her beloved Shakespeare, politicians who diminished human freedom. We often seemed to meet in her Hampstead home at times of political crisis; she was an avid listener to Westminster debates and had an actress's infallible ear for any touch of panic or insincerity in our elected leaders.

Peggy was, for all her innate courtesy, a woman of considerable determination: she needed it to become an actress in the first place. She was born in Croydon in 1907. Her father (killed in the First World War) was an estate agent; her mother, part Danish, part German-Jewish, had studied under the voice coach Elsie Fogerty. But Peggy, already in love with language and the plays of Shakespeare, bulldozed her reluctant mother into letting her leave school at sixteen so that she too could study with Miss Fogerty at her Albert Hall drama school. She even resisted her Croydon school's bribe of being allowed to play Hamlet if she stayed on in order to pursue her chosen vocation.

Peggy's major contemporary at drama school was Laurence Olivier ('…rather uncouth, his sleeves were short, his hair stood on end but he was intensely lively and fun.'); and her first professional job, while still a student, found her playing Margaret in Barrie's *Dear Brutus* opposite her idol, Ralph Richardson, at Birmingham Rep in May 1926. She told me she was 'absolutely hopeless' in that, but it was clear from the start she was destined for the top: contemporaries testify to her virginal beauty, vocal clarity and strength of spirit.

Starting out in London in 1927, she enjoyed a range of work any young actress today would give her eye-teeth for: she once pointed out to me that she did fifty-six productions in her first ten years. She played Naemi in Ashley Dukes's *Jew Suss* in 1929, Desdemona to Robeson's Othello in 1930 (an event that led to her political awakening since she and Sybil Thorndike received hate-mail for appearing with a black actor), Juliet in a 1932 Oxford University Dramatic Society production directed by Gielgud, with Edith Evans as the Nurse, George Devine as Mercutio, Terence Rattigan as a minor reveller and with Motley as the designers: part of 'the family' (as she called them) who were all to weave their way through Ashcroft's subsequent professional career.

In 1932 Peggy was also recruited by Lilian Baylis's Old Vic for a fantastic run of parts: Imogen, Rosalind, Juliet, Portia, Perdita, Miranda, Shaw's Cleopatra and Sheridan's Lady Teazle. Pay was awful ('Dear God, send me good actors and send them cheap,' was Baylis's prayer), standards were often low (the actor playing Leontes came on with book in hand) and Peggy herself said: 'It was always like running for a train – I could never catch up.' But at least she got a crack at the titles and was able to return to many of the roles later on: most famously at the New in 1935 when she played her third Juliet with Olivier and John Gielgud alternating as Romeo and Mercutio – Philip Hope-Wallace found the way she listened to Gielgud's Romeo 'absolutely heart-rending'. Peter Fleming wrote: 'She does more than make Shakespeare's expression of Juliet's thoughts seem natural: she makes it seem inevitable.'

What is crucial to an understanding of Ashcroft's career, however, is her desire to be part of a company rather than a blazing individual star, something fuelled by her brief second marriage in the 1930s to the emigré Russian director Theodore Komisarjevsky (she had been married previously for a short time to a young actor and later publisher, Rupert Hart-Davis) and by the visits to London of Jacques Copeau's *Compagnie des Quinze*. She was a vital part (along with Michael Redgrave, George Devine, Alec Guinness, Anthony Quayle and Glen Byam Shaw) of Gielgud's attempt to create a West End ensemble at the Queen's in 1937–8 with a repertoire of Shakespeare, Chekhov and Sheridan. She pursued the same ideal with Michel Saint-Denis in a short-lived venture at the Phoenix in 1938. 'From then onwards,' wrote Richard Findlater, 'Peggy Ashcroft was an actress in search of a company.'

She did, however, break away from the classic repertoire in 1947 as a woman drifting into alcoholism in *Edward, My Son* by Noel Langley and Robert Morley (he once told me that in the Manchester try-out she was so nervous she locked herself in her dressing-room) and as the plain-Jane Catherine Sloper in *The Heiress* in 1949. But at Stratford in the 1950s (often making her way up the Avon by canoe) she returned to the classic repertoire in the Quayle–Byam Shaw years. I first saw her on stage at Stratford in 1953 as a voluptuous, witty, 'proud-chinn'd' Cleopatra and later in that decade as a vibrantly youthful, ardent, passionate Rosalind and Imogen. She was fifty at the time but age could not wither her.

The 1950s were a decade that proved Ashcroft – by now the mother of two young children by her third husband, Jeremy Hutchinson – was an actress for all seasons, capable of plumbing the deepest emotions: any hint of *ingénue*-gentility had long been thrown off. In 1952 she created the role of the destructive, possessive Hester Collyer in Terrence Rattigan's *The Deep Blue Sea*. In 1954 she was a legendary Hedda Gabler ('as near perfection as you are likely to see in an imperfect world,' wrote T. C. Worsley): a production which, she told me, the actors pulled together during a six-week tour after a Dublin audience treated it as the funniest play they'd ever seen. And in 1956 she played both the mysterious governess in Enid Bagnold's artificial comedy, *The Chalk Garden*, and the dual role of the golden-hearted prostitute and her invented male cousin in Brecht's *The Good Woman of Setzuan* at the Royal Court. Her old friend George Devine had created a writer's theatre: she wanted to be in at the beginning.

Peggy's idealism made her a pioneering actress: her constant quest for truth made her a great one. In 1960 she became a founder-member of Peter Hall's RSC, playing Kate, Paulina and the Duchess of Malfi: to her it was the fulfilment of a long-cherished dream. It also, in 1963, gave her the chance to play what I consider the greatest performance I saw her give: Margaret of Anjou in *The Wars of the Roses*. Spanning some thirty-five years, the role took her from a flirtatious, youthful princess to a straggly haired, barbarous crone: none who saw it will forget the moment when she smeared the Duke of York's face with a cloth dipped in his son's blood. She told me that Peter Hall at that point gave her a superb piece of direction: to remember that York is the power in the scene, Margaret the weak and hysterical one. She also revealed that she argued with Hall over the use of a French 'r' sound throughout the trilogy because she wanted us never to forget she was an alien figure in the English court. What emerged, in Robert Speaight's words, was 'a great tragic creation'.

Ashcroft's commitment to the RSC merged during the 1960s and 1970s with a fascination with the challenge of new writing: she played in Duras's *Days In The Trees*, Edward Albee's *A Delicate Balance* and *All Over*, Harold Pinter's *Landscape* and *A Slight Ache*, Günter Grass's *The Plebeians Rehearse the Uprising*. It was partly a reaction to the drying-up of roles in the Shakespearean repertoire, partly a sign of her radicalism of spirit. And when Peter Hall took over the running of the National Theatre company, she was there to support him playing Ella Rentheim in *John Gabriel Borkman* and Winnie in *Happy Days*. I wrote at the time of her Winnie that 'Ashcroft, buoyant in floral green dress, knitted hat and gash of lipstick, was at her radiant best, phrasing the text like music.' And I shall not quickly forget her in *Tribute to the Lady* on the last night of the National Theatre at the Old Vic, playing the dumpy, bustling Lilian Baylis and then throwing off her wig, pebble-specs and MA gown to transform herself in a split second into a youthfully radiant Beatrice to Gielgud's Benedick.

Only once in later years did she return to Shakespeare: as the Countess in Trevor Nunn's 1981 *All's Well*, set in a world of timeless Edwardiana. I still remember the moral grace and vocal beauty of that performance, in particular the warmth of her relationship with the clown Lavache, played as an old retainer, and her quasi-maternal love for Helena. Peggy pointed out to me there are lots of father–daughter relationships in Shakespeare: very few mother–daughter ones. She discovered that in the play and lent it all her poetic instinct.

In later years Peggy won a whole new universal audience through her work in films and television. Once again, though, you find she was actually in at the beginning. In 1933 she was in one of the early British talkies, Maurice Elvey's *The Wandering Jew*, and in 1935 she had a famous scene, as a crofter's wife, in Hitchcock's *The 39 Steps*: it only lasts five minutes but she endows it with the pathos of a young woman married to a surly, suspicious man. In the late 1930s she was also in one of the first-ever transmissions of Shakespeare, *The Tempest*, from Alexandra Palace. But for a long time she avoided film and television cameras: 'I was rather busy elsewhere, I suppose: anyway, it wasn't a magnet that drew me.'

Fortunately she conquered her dislike in later years to produce some thrilling work. She was unforgettable as an imperious Austrian aristocrat (she got the voice from records of Lotte Lehmann) in the 1980 TV film of Stephen Poliakoff's *Caught on a Train*. But the summit of her TV work was the creation of Barbie Batchelor in Granada's *The Jewel in the Crown*: she actively sought the role and played this unregarded outsider, this Croydon-voiced missionary adrift in the collapsing world of the Raj, with infinite compassion and understanding. She capped her Indian summer (and won a Hollywood Oscar) with her portrayal of Mrs Moore in David Lean's *A Passage to India*: another Christian woman who goes to India and, in the course of the experience, loses her faith. She herself found it ironic that, after sixty years in the theatre, she was discovered by a larger audience than she had ever had. She remained active in films, radio and television: a lifelong CND supporter, she supplied the voice of a South London suburbanite for Raymond Briggs's anti-nuclear animated film *When the Wind Blows*.

She also shared a Venice Festival Best Actress Award in 1989 for her breathtaking performance as an old woman emerging from sixty years in a mental asylum in Peter Hall's film of Stephen Poliakoff's *She's Been Away*. And in April this year she was heard as a forthright, bruisingly candid octogenarian in Tom Stoppard's Radio 3 play about the legacy of Empire, *In the Native State*. It was somehow fitting that her final appearance should be in a play about the India that in later life she came to love so much.

But there was another vital dimension to Peggy Ashcroft and that was her commitment to a wide range of causes. In 1943 she founded the Apollo Society, which blended poetry and music and toured initially to military camps. In later years she was involved with Amnesty International, Index on Censorship, Equity's International Committee for Artists' Freedom and many other causes supporting individuals against tyrannical regimes, a commitment dating back to 1933 when she had witnessed first-hand the persecution of Jews in Berlin, and also to a speech she made on the first night of *Before Sunset* at the Shaftesbury in defence of a German actor in the company. (One of her more unusual jobs was to be conscripted by her friend, Lord Rothschild, to teach his bright young things in the first think-tank how to move an audience of ministers and permanent secretaries with their arguments.)

To me, however, Peggy Ashcroft's political views were indivisible from her career as an actress: both represent a belief in the indomitability of the human spirit. She was a great actress not merely because of her technical polish or her vocal beauty but because of some inner toughness of character and because of her refusal never to take the easy route: she and George Devine had a wonderful phrase for the business of searching for the truth of a character, which was 'digging potatoes'. She dug a lot of potatoes in the course of an outstanding career and she died secure in the knowledge that one of the major causes for which she fought – the establishment of permanent companies – had come about. She also embodied David Hare's extremely astute remark that 'acting is a judgement of character'. Her character shone out of all she did; and I, along with millions of others, will remember her with unstinting affection.

EDITH MARGARET (PEGGY) EMILY ASHCROFT ·
born 22 December 1907 · *died* 14 June 1991 ·

30 June 1992

JOHN PIPER
J. M. Richards

[Our obituary of John Piper was written by the late Sir James Richards two years ago.]

John Piper, who has died at the age of eighty-eight, was known on both sides of the Atlantic as one of Britain's outstanding painters, but in this country he was far more than that. He will be most affectionately remembered also as a designer of sets for opera and ballet; for his stained glass – an art he did much to revive – he designed numerous memorial windows and the grand baptistery window in Coventry cathedral; as an editor of guidebooks to English counties and their buildings; and as a writer on art and architecture. To all these must be added his perceptive influence over the many people – especially young people – whom he encouraged to visit him in the Oxfordshire farmhouse where he and Myfanwy lived for fifty-five years.

Nevertheless he regarded himself first of all as a painter. As such he found himself bracketed in the 1930s with Ben Nicholson, Graham Sutherland and Henry Moore. The association with Nicholson is significant because Piper passed through – and learned much from – an abstract and constructivist phase and with his wife edited a now largely forgotten magazine, *Axis*, devoted to abstract art here and abroad.

The discipline of this experience laid many of the foundations of Piper's later work, but as his painting became more romantic and representational another of his lifelong obsessions began to take charge: his passion for architecture, which had been present in him since he had toured the countryside by bicycle as a schoolboy, looking at old churches. In fact many people admire his art most when architecture has a predominant place in it, whether in the series of watercolours of Windsor Castle he was commissioned to paint in 1941, the dramatically evocative oil-paintings of bombed buildings he made while serving as a war artist, or his subsequent paintings of buildings in their settings, ranging from Caernavon Castle to Harlaxton House. He was, too, a masterly topographical draughtsman, continuing the tradition of Girtin, Cotman and – a special favourite – William Gilpin.

Piper was always fascinated by the techniques which he employed – new or old – with impressive mastery: collage in the 1930s, for example, and soon afterwards the almost extinct art of aquatint, which he revived to produce an elegant volume of views of Brighton (1939). His sense of craftsmanship was evident in everything he did, whether driving a car or tying up a parcel.

He was born at Epsom in 1903, the son of a solicitor, and educated at Epsom College. He then entered the family firm, but on his father's death he broke away from the law. He studied at several art schools and had one exhibition in London in 1925, but made no real mark until ten years later when, after a failed marriage to a fellow student, Eileen Holding, he met and married Myfanwy Evans in 1935 and moved with her to the farmhouse near Henley-on-Thames. They had two sons and two daughters.

Another landmark in Piper's career was his meeting, in 1936, with John Betjeman, who became a close friend and enlisted his help over the *Shell Guide to Oxfordshire*. When Betjeman retired from editing the county series, Piper established more firmly its very individual mixture of topographical and architectural description, guided the authors of subsequent volumes and illustrated them with his own evocative photographs. His travels in connection with the *Shell Guides* enlarged Piper's architectural range still further. No one can have had deeper knowledge of the parish churches of every corner of England.

Articles written for the *Architectural Review*, again with his own photographs, dealt with subjects few had yet begun to value, like lighthouses as well as Nonconformist chapels. The first of these articles, written in 1936, was on

Anglo-Saxon figure sculpture, which he photographed in dark corners of country churches with Myfanwy holding a lantern. Such sculptures were so little appreciated then that Professor Clapham, the authority on the period, was heard to call them 'young Mr Piper's golliwogs'.

With his acute and educated eye, Piper was a highly valued member of the Royal Fine Art Commission for the unprecedented span of nineteen years. When he retired in 1978, he was found to be irreplaceable. His advice about old buildings was sought in many other quarters; for example he served – and enjoyed serving, for he was a sincere churchman – on the Oxford Diocesan advisory committee from 1950 till almost the end of his life. He served the fine arts in similar ways, being a trustee for many years of both the National and the Tate galleries.

Like Betjeman, Benjamin Britten became both a close friend and a part of his career. Piper had his first contact with the stage as early as the 1930s when he worked with the Group Theatre, which produced plays by Auden and Spender, but the connection became closer when, through Britten, he designed opera sets. The one for *Death in Venice*, based on Thomas Mann's story, is especially memorable, with the libretto by Myfanwy. Piper was a skilful pianist and would entertain friends after dinner by playing from memory pieces ranging from Mozart to 1920s jazz.

Piper was appointed Companion of Honour in 1972. He declined other honours, except the honorary degrees bestowed on him by universities. He was a man of strongly held opinions and not easy to argue with, but that did nothing to diminish the devotion of his friends.

JOHN RUSSELL adds:

> I shall remember for the rest of my days the moment in 1943 at which the postman's knock brought me a letter, unprovoked and not at all expected, from John Piper. Piper at that time was probably the person in all England whom I most wanted to meet. He had liked something I had written. And now we corresponded. We met. Though abated by my removal to New York in 1974, our dialogue was dear to me.
>
> On my rare visits to England, I am intensely aware of that dialogue. Passing the New (now Albery) Theatre, I remember the blinding clarity of the set that Piper designed for *Oedipus*, in which Laurence Olivier loosed off his legendary howl. Walking along the Chelsea Embankment, I remember Battersea Park as John Piper refashioned it in 1951 in terms of a post-war Vauxhall or Ranelagh. Many is the second-hand bookshop in which I had looked without success for

Buildings and Prospects (1949), the book of his reprinted essays on the English environment that went out of print many years ago. Not even the author had kept one.

Gigantic beyond all imagining are the firework displays put on above New York harbour, but power and precision are not the whole of that particular art, and John Piper brought to it a poetry all his own – above all, reportedly, when he and John Mortimer marked a happy occasion near Henley-on-Thames.

Piper's genius was in all things a libertarian, inclusive, non-hierarchical genius. As much as anyone, he taught us to see England and Wales in a new way. As much as anyone, he responded to the great classic sights and the great classic houses. But he responded just as much to the unacclaimed look of English provincial harbours, the unspectacular architecture of Romney Marsh, the lettering on Welsh Nonconformist chapels and the dumpy tumbledown habitation to which no one else had turned an affectionate eye.

He could paint and draw all these things in a way that delighted a large public, and he could photograph them, too, using for many years the cheapest known box camera in one of its earliest forms. Those photographs could make us say, at once, 'That's by John Piper' and they perfectly complemented the spry, succinct, unsentimental entries that he wrote for the *Shell Guides*.

He loved working for the stage, and I remember the happy time when he and John Cranko thought they could make a go of the tiny Kenton Theatre in Henley. For twenty good years, he made magic on the stage, from Britten's *The Rape of Lucretia* and *Death in Venice* to Walton's *Façade* and Mozart's *Don Giovanni* at Glyndebourne. (He would dearly have loved a second shot at *Giovanni*). But he came to realize that, second only to a firework display, stage design is about the most ephemeral thing there is.

In all that he did he was sustained by Myfanwy, one of the great women of her generation. A playwright, librettist (*Owen Wingrave* and *Death in Venice*), anthologist and first-rate judge of art, she showed a sense of quality that equalled his own. The laconic, understated character of their exchanges on matters of importance was a lesson in life to those who witnessed it.

John Piper very much enjoyed working with others – with Patrick Reyntiens in stained glass, with Adrian Stokes on an illustrated edition of passages from Stokes's classic book on Venice, and with unnamed printmakers and publishers and potters. Long before 'the print industry' assumed its present proportions, Piper confided to his friends that he planned to make prints that could be sold for £4 or £5 to people who could not afford his paintings.

Piper never spoke of 'myself' or of 'my work'. When his eightieth birthday was marked by a dinner at the Tate Gallery, he behaved as if we, not he, were the persons most worthy of honour. When finally forced to his feet, he said 'Well, thank you all very much' and sat down as fast as he could. In this, as in all things he was completely himself. Thinking of him, I remember what he pencilled long ago into an edition of C. R. Leslie's life of Constable. 'Please return,' he wrote. 'Always needed'. John Piper is beyond recall now, but for those who knew him he will always be needed.

JOHN EGERTON CHRISTMAS PIPER · *born* 13 December 1903 · *died* 27 June 1992 ·

3 July 1997

JAMES STEWART
Ronald Bergan

There was the unmistakable rangy figure and the forthright eyes, but you hear first in your head the immediately recognizable, most impersonated voice in the history of Hollywood – the languid yet adenoidal drawl.

It was a woodwind instrument able to express a wider range of emotions than most film stars: there was his euphonious high-tenor singing of Cole Porter's 'Easy to Love' in *Born to Dance*; the excitement as he feels a scream coming on in *You Can't Take It With You*; and the celebrated climactic filibuster from *Mr Smith Goes to Washington*, when the voice becomes raw and husky without ever losing passion or conviction.

More emblematically, James Stewart, who has died aged eighty-nine, was the voice of a certain kind of America. He was able, better than any other American screen actor, to express what was decent, honest and unpretentious about the US of A. 'He grabbed you as a human being,' Frank Capra remarked. 'You were looking at the man not an actor. You could see this man's soul … When you're dealing in the world of ideas, and you want your character to be on a higher intellectual plane than just a simple man, you turn to persons like Jimmy Stewart because he has the look of the intellectual about him. And he can be an idealist … a pretty fine combination.'

This quality was used in different ways by the three most important directors in his career – Frank Capra, Alfred Hitchcock and Anthony Mann. For Capra, he represented simplicity and rugged worth, while Hitchcock utilized his 'familiarity' – because 'the moment he gets into jeopardy, the audience reaction is much stronger than it would be if the actor were a character man, who might be right for the part. It made him the perfect Hitchcock hero, because he is Everyman in bizarre situations.' Anthony Mann, in his westerns, discovered a grittier, more uncompromising and bitter Stewart than the charmer of the pre-Second World War pictures.

There is some truth to the legend that James Stewart was a hick, born and brought up in a small town, where his father owned a hardware store. Except that Stewart's grandfather had built the store in Indiana, Pennsylvania, into a thriving business, so that he could afford an imposing house, and was able to send his son to Princeton. That son in turn sent his son Jimmy there.

As an Ivy-Leaguer, Jimmy played football and joined the Triangle Club, Princeton's best theatre group, while taking his degree in architecture. His taste for acting was then developed with the University Players, a summer stock company at Falmouth, Massachusetts, led by Joshua Logan, Margaret Sullavan (with whom Stewart made three pictures) and Henry Fonda. He and Fonda remained good friends over the years, despite being on different sides of the political spectrum. Stewart was a lifelong Republican.

Although he was put under contract to MGM, the studio, at its peak during the 1930s, was so well supplied with top stars that it failed to appreciate his talent. So he was first noticed on loan-out to RKO, as a biology professor who marries a nightclub singer (Ginger Rogers) in *Vivacious Lady* (1938), and as the non-violent deputy sheriff in *Destry Rides Again* (1939), dousing Marlene Dietrich with water.

But it was his pre-war collaboration with Capra at Columbia that brought out his unique qualities. Capra had spotted him in *Navy Blue and Gold* (1937) in which Stewart, as a naval cadet, defends his father, an officer who had been unfairly court-martialled. 'When I saw him, I thought, oh my lord, there's a guy,' explained Capra, who cast him as the banker's son in love with a woman (Jean Arthur) from an eccentric bohemian family in *You Can't Take It With You*. Then came *Mr Smith Goes to Washington* (1939), one of the most memorable performances of his career.

'You fight for the lost causes harder than for any others; yes, you even die for them,' is the apogee of Jefferson Smith's twenty-three-hour filibuster. The idealistic senator set Stewart's image firmly in the public's mind, and after the film the star vowed: 'A James Stewart picture must have two vital ingredients. It will be clean and it will involve the triumph of the underdog over the bully.'

It was strangely ironic, many years later, to see Mr Stewart go to Washington to support Richard Nixon. When asked about this, Stewart replied: 'I was raised in a very definite conservative Republican philosophy. I suppose, in *Mr Smith*, the film could be on the side of the common man and against big business, but to me it was only a matter of right and wrong.'

In 1940, nobody was more astonished than Stewart when it was announced that he had won the Academy Award – for his performance in *The Philadelphia Story*. He felt he was the winner of the Holdover Award, for having lost out the previous year for *Mr Smith*. There is no doubt that as Jefferson Smith he had a more demanding assignment than his role as the reporter sent to cover the marriage of spoiled socialite Katharine Hepburn. But his elegant playing of the cynical journalist, smitten with the bride, proved he was a light comedian of the highest calibre, able to hold his own with Hepburn and Cary Grant. On the night he received his award, Stewart's father called him from Pennsylvania. 'You'd better send the trophy back to the store,' he advised Jimmy. The statuette remains in a glass case there to this day. But Stewart never added another to it.

In the same year, he was the reserved shop clerk in Ernst Lubitsch's classic romantic comedy *The Shop Around the Corner* (1940). Samson Raphaelson, who wrote the screenplay, said: 'Stop and contemplate the lanky, drawling young American playing a Hungarian clerk so flawlessly that no one seems to realize it is one of the great performances of cinema history. If you saw the picture ten times, and studied it, you would get a glimmer of the fine sense of detail, the capacity for controlled artistry that resides in Stewart.'

As soon as America entered the Second World War, Stewart joined the Army Air Corps as a private, returning four years later a lieutenant colonel. He had flown twenty missions over Germany as a bomber pilot, winning the Air Medal and Distinguished Flying Cross.

Once more in civvies, stirred by his war experiences, he seriously considered quitting Hollywood and going back to Pennsylvania to run his father's hardware store, when Capra called him to say he had an idea for a movie. It was *It's A Wonderful Life* (1947). As George Bailey, a man driven to suicide unaware that he had touched many lives for the better, Stewart demonstrated his range from hopeful youth to desperate middle-age. During the shooting, when

Stewart told Lionel Barrymore (playing a wicked banker) that he didn't think acting was 'decent', the veteran actor asked him 'if he thought it was more "decent" to drop bombs on people than to bring rays of sunshine into their lives with his acting talent'. This shook Stewart, and he resumed his career with zeal. *It's A Wonderful Life* was an ending for Capra, but a new beginning for Stewart.

In 1949 he returned to the stage in *Harvey*, as Elwood P. Dowd, an alcoholic who believes he is being accompanied everywhere by a giant rabbit. He repeated the Broadway performance in the 1950 screen version and in London as late as 1975. It was, with the title role in *The Glen Miller Story* (1954), his most lovable role. But, in the early 1950s, Stewart decided that 'I couldn't go on hemming and hawing – which I sometimes overdid. I had to toughen up.'

This roughing up happened mostly in the five westerns Stewart made with Anthony Mann. They are key films of the genre. Grizzled and stern, he tracks down the man who stole his gun in *Winchester '73* (1950), shoots the man who betrayed him in *Bend of the River* (1952) and seeks revenge on the man who killed his brother in *The Man from Laramie* (1955). He fights both Robert Ryan and the brutality in himself in the Rockies in *The Naked Spur* (1953), and he is provoked into violence in *The Far Country* (1954). But the hardness of the character does not disguise the pain behind the eyes, and the tenderness within.

With *Winchester '73*, Stewart became one of the first Hollywood stars to work for a percentage of the profits – a 50 per cent share of the takings – instead of being paid a flat fee. This decision made him millions, especially as he appeared in several box-office hits, including the three pictures he made for Hitchcock in the 1950s.

Although he was miscast as a college professor whose ideas on free will have a corrupting effect on two of his students in *Rope* (1948), this was his first opportunity to work with Hitchcock. He was a middle-class middle-American caught up in an espionage plot, in a picaresque pursuit (one of Hitchcock's favourite themes) in *The Man Who Knew Too Much* (1955). And then he was the immobilized voyeur hero in *Rear Window* (1954), the audience's surrogate, watching murder helplessly. In *Vertigo* (1958), his righteous persona makes his agoraphobic detective drawn into a world of fantasy and fetish compelling. It is also one of his rare demonstrations of sexual desire, with Kim Novak as the object of his attentions.

Stewart's wife Gloria, the wealthy divorcée whom he married in 1949, mother of their twin daughters, once said: 'I can honestly say that in all the years we've been married, Jimmy never once gave me cause for anxiety or jealousy. The more glamorous the leading lady, the more attentive he would be to me. He knew the insecurities I was going through and made sure they were totally unfounded.' There was never a whiff of scandal; the marriage lasted forty-five years until her death.

Stewart's post-Hitchcock films were less interesting. Among the best was Otto Preminger's *Anatomy of a Murder* (1959), in which, as an attorney defending a rape case, he had to use the words 'sperm' and 'contraceptive' and hold up a tattered pair of panties. He was much criticized by those who thought he had betrayed family values.

There was a contrast between his liberal, often pacifist screen persona and his hawkish stance on the Vietnam war, a view he shared with his friend John Wayne, with whom he appeared in John Ford's *The Man Who Shot Liberty Valance* (1962), and in *The Shootist* (1976). Even when Stewart's stepson was killed in Vietnam, there was no softening in his attitude. 'People say, what a terrible tragedy that he had to die. We never look on it as a tragedy. It's a loss, not a tragedy. He had a useful life. He graduated from college, and his country was at war. He became a marine and when he got on the battlefield he conducted himself with gallantry. What's tragic about that? What's tragic is boys giving their lives without having a unified country behind them. That's what's tragic.'

Until his retirement from the service in 1968, Stewart, who was a brigadier general in the Air Force Reserve, the highest ranking entertainer in the US military, made three trips to Vietnam.

Yet stars' real lives are far less real to audiences than those they live on screen, and Stewart's backing for the Vietnam war, Nixon and Reagan will be long forgotten while Jefferson Smith and George Bailey go on moving and entertaining us.

JAMES STEWART · *born* 20 May 1908 · *died* 2 July 1997 ·

10 January 1998

MICHAEL TIPPETT
Meirion Bowen

For a long time, Sir Michael Tippett, who has died aged ninety-three, languished under the shadow of Benjamin Britten. Britten, eight years his junior, was a musical prodigy, lauded in his teens, widely appreciated after the success of his opera *Peter Grimes* in 1945, and remaining prolific and popular up to his death in 1976. By contrast, Tippett, a late developer, was a slow, deliberate composer who won acceptance gradually. International fame came only in his late sixties. What distinguished the rest of his career was a prolonged Indian summer: for Tippett continued to write major new pieces until he was almost ninety, breaking new ground, moreover, with each one. Blessed with seemingly unremitting physical, creative and intellectual vitality, he became an almost legendary figure on the musical scene. His oratorio, *A Child of Our Time* (1939–41) – a moving assertion of humanitarianism in an epoch of catastrophe – acquired eventually the status of an icon.

Throughout his long life, Tippett ran against the grain of received British opinion. He early concluded that music and the arts were fundamentally international, and rejected (as did Britten) the then prevalent mode of nationalist folk-music-based composition championed by Vaughan Williams.

Tippett was a pluralist: a humanist who eschewed dogma; a socialist and pacifist; a Jungian who felt art was basically collective and archetypal; a visionary with a capacity to blend the most disparate ingredients – Beethoven, pre-classical counterpoint, jazz and gamelan music – within a single work, be it his exuberant First Piano Sonata (1936) or his bitter-sweet Triple Concerto (1979). Thus, his largest-scale compositions – notably, the five operas and three major choral works – were all attempts at creative synthesis at different points in his career. Prefiguring these summatory pieces, or developing out of them, were Tippett's four symphonies, five string quartets, five piano sonatas, concertos, songs and numerous shorter instrumental and choral works. Taken as a whole, however, this *œuvre* had a consistent and distinctively modern stamp.

Tippett wrote little that could be called 'experimental'. His friend and mentor, T. S. Eliot, said that for him, as a poet, 'the words come last'; likewise with Tippett the notes came last, following upon a lengthy period of gestation and structural planning. His sense of the line and shape of a piece was such that in his maturity he invariably wrote from beginning to end in sequence, sending each completed section to his publishers, confident that there would be no need for significant revisions. Tippett's quirky, maverick musical personality sometimes distracted attention from his assured craftsmanship.

Tippett was never a member of any artistic coterie, nor the centre of one. He stood aside from trends and fashions. As a student, he was overpowered by the humanistic idealism of Beethoven's music; and he took structural models from Beethoven's compositions throughout his career. A second strand in Tippett's musical make-up derived from his early discovery of polyphonic music, especially Elizabethan madrigals. A linear aproach to composition became a distinctive trait in his work. Although unsympathetic to nationalism, Tippett delighted in all kinds of vernacular music, utilizing it often to enrich his own style. The folk songs of his early (unpublished) ballad operas were later put to good use in his lively, tongue-in-cheek *Suite for the Birthday of Prince Charles* (1948); in his fifth opera, *New Year* (1985–8), he embraced the sonorities and rhythms of rap and reggae. His early encounter with jazz and blues, above all, convinced him that music retained a universal expressive potential, albeit tinged with irony. In his Third (and longest) Symphony (1972), Tippett polarized Beethoven and the blues: the work quotes the Ninth Symphony within a sequence of searing vocal blues, sketching a journey from innocence to experience in a world of concentration camps and atom bombs.

Tippett was born in London and grew up in Suffolk. His intellectuality was nurtured in early childhood by his highly articulate, well-read (and equally long-lived) parents. From his lawyer father, Tippett inherited a fascination with languages. As a child, he quickly became fluent in French and taught himself Italian and German as a student. From his mother – a nurse, active Labour Party member and a suffragette (for which she was imprisoned) – he derived notions of collective social responsibility, humane values and ultimately pacifism. Tippett's musical awareness, however, was negligible until his teens.

He was sent to board at Fettes School, Edinburgh, where he led a successful crusade against bullying, then to Stamford Grammar School. Holidaying in Germany in the 1920s, he observed the 'progressive' methods of schools for destitute children; decades later, this experience was reawakened when he came to write his opera *New Year*, in whose plot the problems of orphaned, uprooted young people are in the foreground.

His parents found incomprehensible his determination to become a composer, prompted by a concert he attended in Leicester conducted by Malcolm Sargent. Having persuaded them to support him at the Royal College of Music, however, Tippett came to London in the summer of 1923. But he lacked the fluency and versatility of his fellow-students, and his teachers, who included Malcolm Sargent and Adrian Boult, often despaired. Tippett got his degree at the second attempt and then left London for the country to have peace to compose. This became a rule thereafter, despite the public appearances and jet-setting of later years.

Conducting the Oxted and Limpsfield Players in Surrey, and teaching French at Hazelwood Preparatory School, where he met and worked with Christopher Fry on school operas and plays, Tippett accumulated enough compositions for a concert at the Barn Theatre, Oxted, in 1930. But this only convinced him that he needed more training in order to exorcize other composers' influences and discover his own voice: so he undertook a further eighteen months' tuition with the noted counterpoint expert, R. O. Morris. The rigorous discipline this entailed and a first, passionate love-affair, combined to draw from him the first work he would later regard as entirely his own – String Quartet No 1 (1934).

During the Depression, Tippett worked among the unemployed in the north of England, galvanizing a mixture of out-of-work miners and their families, students and friends for performances of *The Beggar's Opera* and a specially composed ballad opera, *Robin Hood.* Subsequently, he conducted a London orchestra formed mainly from theatre and cinema musicians made redundant by the talkies. They raised money for the needy and appeared at Labour Party rallies.

The climax of Tippett's extra-musical commitment – which had included brief membership of the Communist party – came in July 1943, when he served a three-month sentence at Wormwood Scrubs for failing to comply with the conditions of service as a conscientious objector. This, in his mother's view, was his finest hour. Over the years, Tippett became one of foremost leaders of the British pacifist movement – president of the Peace Pledge Union and a CND supporter. His identification with human rights causes in general was ultimately crystallized in the rhetorical cry of the Present, 'One humanity, one justice,' at the end of *New Year.*

As a student, Tippett accepted his homosexual leanings without qualm. By this time, his family life had disintegrated. His parents – unable, during the First World War, to draw upon the revenue from the hotel his father owned in Cannes – went to live on the Continent; and his elder brother Peter went into the Navy. Thereafter, Tippett yearned for the warmth he observed within the families of working-class friends. With his charm, charisma and good looks, Tippett attracted many female admirers. Two became very close friends: Evelyn Maude, an older married woman and a regular source of wise counsel (in prison, allowed to write letters to only one person, Tippett chose her); and Francesca Allinson, a choral conductor, folk-song researcher and puppeteer, with whom he considered starting a family. The latter's suicide in 1944 prompted one of Tippett's most poignant compositions, the song-cycle *The Heart's Assurance.*

Tippett's lifeline through this tangled web of personal relationships and the difficulties caused by his devotion to creative work was the writings of Jung. Briefly he underwent Jungian analysis and continued analysing all his dreams for about nine months. Just before the outbreak of war in 1939, with a dream of death by strangulation, he thought the analysis had achieved its goal. Few of Tippett's close relationships survived his ruthless creative obsession: one of the longest lasting, with painter Karl Hawker, ended with a contrived separation and the latter's suicide.

Tippett's personal turmoil coincided with the rise of Nazism in Central Europe and Stalinism in the Soviet Union. Following Jung, he interpreted the violence of the period and the war that followed as projections of one society's 'shadow' onto another: a view he held to, later, in the context of the Cold War. Tippett identified strongly with those made scapegoats by intolerance and self-righteousness. That was the inspiration underlying his oratorio, *A Child of Our Time*, which had begun as an opera about the Easter Uprising in Ireland, but gelled as a protest against the 1938 Kristallnacht in Nazi Germany. Tippett asked Eliot – whom he had recently met – to write the text, but Eliot, having looked at Tippett's draft libretto, advised him to construct his own text in full, as the poet's literary flights might conflict with the composer's musical concepts. After that, Tippett always fashioned his own libretti. Aiming for directness and lucidity in *A Child of Our Time*, Tippett took Handel's *Messiah* and Bach's *Passions* as his main models. Clinching the emotional impact of the work at five key stages, he incorporated Negro spirituals (replacing the Lutheran chorales Bach would have used): and this proved a brilliant ploy, helping to give the work great expressive breadth.

At its première in 1944, *A Child of Our Time* was understood primarily as a response to the Nazi persecution of the Jews. But its message – summed up in the final ensemble in characteristically Jungian language: 'I would know my shadow and my light/So shall I at last be whole' – suits all situations where intolerance has thrown up victims and outcasts. *A Child of Our Time* was the first work of Tippett's to be heard outside the UK: now it is constantly per-formed worldwide.

The oratorio's success in the mid-1940s helped Tippett's reputation to prosper. Meanwhile, he was attracting attention by making Morley College – whose musical director he had become in 1941 – the most lively concert-giving organization in wartime London. The Morley College Choir was broadcast by the BBC and (under Tippett) made a historic recording of Tallis's forty-part motet *Spem in Alium* for EMI. During Tippett's period at Morley, the Amadeus Quartet was formed and the countertenor Alfred Deller emerged from obscu-rity. Instigating a Purcell revival, Tippett found kindred spirits in Britten and Peter Pears, who had just returned from the US. They premièred Tippett's cantata, *Boyhood's End* (1943), and participated in other Morley concerts.

After the war, Tippett's priority was his first opera, *The Midsummer Marriage*, which absorbed his energies completely for six years (1946–52). Gradually relinquishing his Morley College duties, he finally resigned in 1951. When, unexpectedly (for he had no commission to write it), the opera was premièred at Covent Garden in 1955, audiences and critics, though baffled by the libretto, were bowled over by the score's unfettered lyrical ardour and radiance. In 1963 the BBC broadcast *The Midsummer Marriage* with a cast that included the young Janet Baker as Sosostris. A new production at Covent Garden followed in 1966 with Colin Davis as conductor, leading eventually to a bestselling recording. There have since been more than a dozen productions at home and abroad, all of which have attracted varying mixtures of praise, scepticism and scorn.

The main gibes against Tippett's operas have always been directed at the libretti – quirky, magpie-ish mixtures of references and quotations (emulating *The Waste Land*) – despite the composer's insistence that they were meant not to be read as 'literature', but as 'gestures for music'. Tippett brought to the opera house something of the innovatory zeal associated with contemporary playwrights and novelists. All his operas are studies in the nuances of human behaviour: there are never any standard heroes and villains, rarely a straightforward story-line. The masque-like interaction of mortals and immortals in *The Midsummer Marriage* is continued in different ways in Tippett's subsequent operas. Techniques absorbed from television and film helped Tippett control the pace and focus of this multi-level cross-cutting between the actual, the imaginary and the symbolic.

The path to the international fame Tippett enjoyed in his late years was fraught with difficulties. As well as *The Midsummer Marriage* a number of Tippett's compositions in the 1950s had troublesome premières. His Piano Concerto was rejected as unplayable by its designated soloist, Julius Katchen; his Second Symphony broke down under Boult: and the Fantasia Concertante on a Theme of Corelli was dismissed as cerebral by Malcolm Sargent (now there are fourteen recordings of it). Eventually Tippett was to find more sympathetic interpreters – conductors such as Colin Davis, David Atherton, Andrew Davis and, among the most recent generation, Paul Daniel; his piano sonatas were championed by Paul Crossley (who premièred the third and fourth and recorded them all); the Lindsay Quartet proved staunch advocates of his string quartets.

It was a brilliant production by Sam Wanamaker at the 1962 Coventry Festival of Tippett's second opera, the epic-style *King Priam*, that began to turn the tide in his favour, though its abrasive Brechtian dramaturgy and

mosaic orchestration initially disconcerted those won over by the lyrical efful-
gence of *The Midsummer Marriage*. In the mid-1960s, Tippett inherited the
Bath Festival from Yehudi Menuhin, saved it from bankruptcy and widened
its scope and audience appeal. Honours began to flow in: a CBE in 1959, and
knighthood in 1966; he was made a Companion of Honour in 1979 and
received the Order of Merit in 1984. He valued most of all the Gold Medal of
the Royal Philharmonic Society (1975) and awards such as that of the
Association of British Orchestras (1966) which, he felt, came from 'my colleagues in the profession'.

Tippett was always strongly committed to musical education and his stint
as guest conductor with Leicestershire Schools Symphony Orchestra
(1965–70) proved exemplary. Right into his eighties, he conducted or attended
concerts by other youth orchestras. An extension of this was the setting up of
Tippett's own charitable foundation – to support education projects and contemporary music tours – in 1979, funded then and after from the sale of his
musical manuscripts to the British Library.

Tippett's first visit to the US in 1965 as composer-in-residence at the Aspen
Festival, Colorado, was a major turning-point. He fell in love with the land-
scapes of the far west and identified with the polyglot culture of the cities.
America also took to Tippett in a big way. American commissions followed:
the Fourth Symphony (1977) and *Byzantium* (1989) were premièred by Georg
Solti and the Chicago Symphony; *The Mask of Time* was premièred by Colin
Davis in Boston; and Boston, together with the Toronto and London sym-
phony orchestras, jointly commissioned *The Rose Lake* (1993), while Houston
Opera, Glyndebourne and the BBC commissioned *New Year*.

Tippett's success in America led to numerous invitations elsewhere, and in
his seventies and eighties he undertook three world tours, conducting and
attending festivals of his music all over the Far East, Australia and Brazil.
Belatedly, his music began to attract real attention in Europe. All this activity
provided him with opportunities for exotic holidays; and right to the end, his
delight in exploration and adventure abroad remained insatiable, his travel
stories proving one of the great attractions of his autobiography, *Those
Twentieth Century Blues* (1991).

Tippett's 'discovery' of what he called 'a Newfoundland of the spirit' in
America also permeated his music from the mid-1960s onwards. Immediately,
his third opera, *The Knot Garden* (1970), uncovered a new toughness and
irony in his music, its harmonic character bluesy, its orchestration coloured by
electric guitar sonorities. The scores and libretti of *The Ice Break* (1977) and
New Year went even further. All three operas are explicitly about people of

today, grappling with contemporary problems and leaving at the end to begin new lives. There are parallels to these operatic endings in those of Tippett's abstract works, in which he eschewed bombastic perorations, instead favouring throwaway gestures.

Tippett was a mixture of seer and dreamer. Both are encountered in the two great choral compositions of his maturity, *The Vision of St Augustine* (1966) and *The Mask of Time* (1983). The former brings to the fore Tippett's fascination with concepts of time – above all, with the possibility that art is concerned with experiences in a virtual time-continuum, detached from everyday clock-time. Setting Latin texts from Augustine's Confessions, Tippett produced a typically unclassifiable work, whose three movements unfold with complete organic freedom and inward momentum. *The Mask of Time* was even more ambitious, a musician's answer to the scientific account of the development of civilization in Jacob Bronowski's celebrated BBC film series, *The Ascent of Man* (1973). An awesome conception, its ten movements, lasting altogether ninety-five minutes, depict, in broad chronological leaps, the evolution of the universe and mankind's constant defiance of destructive forces, ending with a wordless song of survival and hope.

Observing often – notably in his first volume of essays, *Moving into Aquarius* (1959) – that the artist is relatively powerless in a society that invests the greater part of its resources in technology, Tippett drew strength from a sense of belonging to a tradition, age-old and ever-present, which is (he wrote, memorably) 'to create images from the depths of the imagination, and to give them form whether visual, intellectual or musical ... Images of the past, shapes of the future. Images of vigour for a decadent period, images of calm for one too violent, images of reconciliation for worlds torn by division. And in an age of mediocrity and shattered dreams, images of abounding, generous, exuberant beauty.' Tippett's integrity as an artist and his humanitarian commitment made him one of the most esteemed figures in present-day culture. His absence from the musical scene leaves behind, in consequence, not merely an artistic vacuum but a moral and spiritual one as well.

MICHAEL KEMP TIPPETT · *born* 2 January 1905 · *died* 8 January 1998 ·

FRANK SINATRA
Richard Williams

The popular music of this century is too vast to be embodied by one man, but Frank Sinatra, who has died aged eighty-two, probably contained more of it than any other single figure. He was the first teenage idol, and the last of a line. He preceded Elvis and the Beatles, yet outlasted them. He began with Bing and ended with Bono.

His exit is what concerns us today, but Sinatra specialized in entrances. The orchestra would be tuning up, the audience finding their seats; and suddenly, with the house lights still on, in the midst of the noises of preparation, there he would be, on the stage, without fuss or announcement, as though he had just stepped off the street. Such underplaying was characteristic of his art, if rarely of his life. A concern for the nuances of that art made him the singers' singer, but the more garish aspects of his existence – the alleged underworld connections, the fist-fights with gossip columnists, the whole overbearing ring-a-ding-ding macho thing – made him human. And, when all is said and done, he bequeathed us definitive versions of some of the century's greatest songs: 'What's New', 'Angel Eyes', 'Violets For Your Furs', 'I've Got You Under My Skin', 'You Go To My Head', 'Someone To Watch Over Me', 'Guess I'll Hang My Tears Out To Dry', 'Laura', 'Come Rain or Come Shine', 'My One and Only Love', 'My Funny Valentine' and a hundred others. These are his monument.

Today's pilgrims will find only a parking lot on the site where he was born, 415 Monroe Street in Hoboken, a small New Jersey port standing across the Hudson river from lower Manhattan. He weighed an enormous 13.5lbs at birth, requiring the energetic use of forceps. His eardrum punctured and the skin of his face and neck torn by the implements, he showed no immediate sign of life and, believing the worst, the doctor turned to save the mother; but the infant was held under a cold-water tap by his grandmother until he wailed into life.

His genes were a blueprint for a refusal to take life as it came. Both his parents had been brought to America from Italy as children. His Sicilian father, Martin Sinatra, worked as a boilermaker and then as a fireman; he also boxed, under the name Marty O'Brien, and occasionally appeared as an extra in silent movies. But it was Martin's wife, Dolly, who exerted the stronger influence on their only child. Born Natalie Garavente, the daughter of a Neapolitan lithographer, she became active in Democratic politics in New Jersey.

Sinatra left Demarest High School at sixteen, having demonstrated no particular academic talent; his destiny had been determined a year earlier, when an uncle bought him a ukelele. Under the spell of Bing Crosby, he was singing in local clubs at the age of seventeen, aided by a $65 sound system bought with a loan from his doting mother. In the autumn of 1935 he auditioned for a New York radio show called *Major Bowes and his Original Amateur Hour*. Bowes put him together with a vocal trio called the Three Flashes, rechristened them the Hoboken Four, featured them in two short films (one involving a blackface performance, to the embarrassment of Sinatra, a lifelong anti-racist) and sent them on a national tour.

After three months on the road, sensing the onset of internal jealousies created by the attention he was already getting from their female listeners, he left the group and went home. For two years he hustled, singing in neighbourhood social clubs and pestering music publishers, until in 1938 he auditioned for a job at the Rustic Cabin, a roadhouse in Alpine, New Jersey. For $15 a week he sang and waited on tables between performances, the bonus being a nightly radio broadcast to New York. It paid off when the trumpeter Harry James heard the show and travelled to Alpine to hear and see the singer for himself. 'He'd sung only eight bars when I felt the hairs on my neck rising,' James recollected. That night he offered Sinatra $75 a week to join his new band.

A season at the celebrated Roseland Ballroom, one block away from the jazz clubs of 52nd Street, brought him his first review. During the engagement he made his first recording with the band, *From the Bottom of My Heart*, for the Brunswick label. In the same month that he joined the James orchestra he married Nancy Barbato, whom he had met as a teenager on holiday with their families on the Jersey shore. She went on the road with him, cooking spaghetti for the financially pressed band. To his credit, James did not stand in Sinatra's way when, early in 1940, Tommy Dorsey made a bid for the singer's services. Dorsey's trombone-playing had been one of the principal influences on Sinatra's vocal style. Singing while swimming underwater was a favourite exercise, giving him the breath-control to sing 'through' the breaks between the lines of a song, avoiding ruptures that could damage the meaning. 'It's always been just this little guy telling this story,' Ella Fitzgerald said of him, capturing the essence of his ability to get beneath the superficial design of a song. He had learned how to phrase a lyric from two other women singers: Mabel Mercer, the Staffordshire-born star of 1930s' café society in Paris and New York, and Billie Holiday, whom he heard on 52nd Street in the 1930s. Sinatra was with Dorsey from 1940 to 1942, earning $150 a week. He had his first hit, 'I'll Never Smile Again', with the band, and thanks to exposure to radio and dancehall audiences, and to his first feature films, the musicals *Las Vegas Nights* and *Ship Ahoy*, he was soon topping the polls in the music trade papers.

His efforts to enlist in the armed services after the Japanese attack on Pearl Harbor in December 1941 were thwarted by his punctured eardrum, which gave him an automatic 4-F health rating. But throughout the war he did what he could as a non-combatant, notably making efforts to publicize Nazi crimes against the Jews – it was on a Dorsey date that he attacked a fan who made an anti-Semitic remark.

There are many colourful accounts of the circumstances surrounding Sinatra's escape from his contract with Dorsey, which gave the bandleader 43 per cent of the singer's earnings for life. One of them formed the basis of an episode in Mario Puzo's novel *The Godfather*, but according to the singer's own testimony it was not his Sicilian friends but his civilian lawyers who persuaded Dorsey to accept a settlement of $75,000.

An audience made up of delirious bobbysoxers greeted the launch of his solo career on 30 December 1942 at the Paramount Theater, New York. Slim and debonair, a couple of inches under six feet tall and weighing a couple of pounds under ten stones, Sinatra redefined the appeal of the male pop singer, consigning the competition to instant obsolescence. He was being called the Lean Lark and the Sultan of Swoon; eventually these were distilled to an irreducible sobriquet: the Voice. Within a month his income rocketed from $750 to $25,000 a week; not long afterwards he moved from New Jersey to a house on Lake Toluca in southern California, with a ten-foot fence to keep his fans at bay while Nancy brought up the first of their three children, Nancy Jr.

With the help of the arranger Axel Stordahl, and despite the interference of Columbia's recording boss, the dim-witted Mitch Miller, he was making some wonderful records. His own explanation for his popularity is probably the most acute: 'It was the war years, and there was a great loneliness. I was the boy in every corner drugstore, the boy who'd gone off to war.' There is some evidence that his shrewd press agent, George Evans, was already devising schemes to maximize the phenomenon: fans were paid to scream, and Sinatra sometimes took the stage wearing suits with weakened seams. At any rate his return to the Paramount Theater in 1944 precipitated an event which became known as the Columbus Day Riot after 30,000 fans, unable to gain admission, ran amok in Times Square.

That year he sang at Ebbets Field, the home of the Brooklyn Dodgers, in aid of the Red Cross, and was received at the White House by President Roosevelt. His movie career advanced in 1945 when he co-starred with Gene Kelly in *Anchors Aweigh* and appeared in *The House I Live In*, which carried a civil rights message. But in the aftermath of the war, when the shrinking economy was putting an end to the swing era, a slow decline began. Perhaps it can be dated from the day in 1947 when he was forced to settle after a newspaper columnist, Lee Mortimer, had sued him for assault, following an incident at Ciro's nightclub in Hollywood, which Sinatra claimed Mortimer had started by calling him a dago.

Soon it was open season. The California state senate committee on un-American activities accused him of having 'followed or appeased some of the Communist Party line over a long period of time'. Another columnist, probably tipped off by a government agency, revealed that he had been seen socializing with the mobster Lucky Luciano in Havana, during a convention of Mafia heads. His abrasive response to these and other stories antagonized many gossip columnists.

What hurt more was that his vocal approach had been supplanted in the affections of teenage audiences by the likes of Frankie Laine and Johnnie Ray. This led to difficulties with Miller, who tried to revive his appeal by forcing him to record novelty songs. And in 1950 the death of Evans, his consigliere, left him directionless.

His personal life, too, had slipped its moorings. There were affairs with actresses and singers, including Lana Turner. He was dancing with her one night in 1947 at a club in Palm Springs, California, when he met Ava Gardner, who was in the arms of the tycoon Howard Hughes. Two years later Sinatra and Gardner began an affair which culminated in their marriage in Philadelphia in November 1951, a week after his divorce from Nancy had been finalized.

By the time they married, Gardner was already the bigger star of the two. This created tensions and led to rows. During an engagement at the Copacabana in New York, he lost his voice for the first and last time. But out of it came artistic capital. 'It was Ava who taught him how to sing a torch song,' the arranger Nelson Riddle said many years later. 'She was the greatest love of his life, and he lost her.' Sinatra's emotional turmoil is preserved in his recording of 'I'm a Fool to Want You', in which the listener seems to be eavesdropping on a private and painful battle between ecstasy and tragedy. Their wedding was still eight months away.

When they separated in 1953, his fortunes were at a nadir. His Columbia deal was over, and so, apparently, was his movie career. Determined to resurrect himself, he signed with a new label, Capitol Records, on terms which clearly indicated the company's lack of confidence: this was a mere one-year contract, with no advance payment against future royalties.

Sinatra wanted to play the lead in *On the Waterfront*, but was beaten to it by

Brando. So he pleaded with Harry Cohn, the head of Columbia Pictures, to give him the part of Angelo Maggio in Fred Zinneman's *From Here to Eternity*. As with the Dorsey deal, there were rumours that outside assistance had been necessary to secure Cohn's assent, but the result was a best supporting actor Oscar in 1954, and a relaunched career.

There was a change of visual image, too. His boyishness had gone. The figure slumped on a bar counter or leaning against a lamp-post on the covers of his new Capitol LPs was clearly a mature man. Wearing his new wardrobe of dark single-breasted suits, white shirts and snap-brim hats, he was in tune with an audience of young adults who were enjoying the Eisenhower-era prosperity and found his music the ideal soundtrack to the new world of G-Plan furniture and menthol cigarettes.

Between 1953 and 1960, he created a sequence of albums which remain definitive statements of twentieth-century American song, each devised as an informal song-cycle exploring a particular emotional climate, taking advantage of the great range and depth that experience had brought to his interpretations. Of all his arrangers, Nelson Riddle displayed the clearest understanding of the singer's altered temperament, a rare gift for orchestral colour, enabling him to locate the precise settings for the finger-snapping optimism of *Songs For Swingin' Lovers* and the elegant melancholy of *In the Wee Small Hours*. These classic albums were followed in 1958 by *Only the Lonely*, an astonishingly complex and assured meditation on emotional loss.

In Hollywood Sinatra broadened his range by playing a heroin addict in *The Man With the Golden Arm* in 1955, followed by the successful musicals *Guys and Dolls* (also 1955), *High Society* (1956) and *Pal Joey* (1957), and *The Manchurian Candidate* (1962), John Frankenheimer's atmospheric Cold War drama. Thereafter, disappointingly, his filmography consisted of little more than action and adventure films.

Divorced from Ava in 1954, he romanced Kim Novak, Marilyn Monroe, Lauren Bacall, Shirley Maclaine, Dorothy Provine, Jill St John, the heiress Gloria Vanderbilt, the dancer Juliet Prowse and many others. He was also gathering around him a group of male friends who became known as the Rat Pack, comprising the singer Dean Martin, the entertainer Sammy Davis Jr, the actor Peter Lawford, and the comedian Joey Bishop. Associate members included his close friends Jilly Rizzo, owner of nightclubs in New York and Miami, and Jack Entratter, operator of the Sands Hotel in Las Vegas, where Sinatra appeared regularly. This only child was clannish by nature, and in the early 1960s he built a spread of de luxe bungalows in Palm Springs, as a base camp for himself and his entourage.

At the dawn of the 1960s he left Capitol to form his own label, Reprise Records, in partnership with Warner Brothers. By this time he was rich, earning around $4 million a year, and powerful, with links to a variety of worlds, notably John F. Kennedy's Camelot. He produced Kennedy's inauguration gala in 1960; two years later, during the Cuban missile crisis, he was tipped off in time to plan his family's evacuation in advance of an expected Soviet nuclear attack. But his relationship with the White House cooled under the influence of Bobby Kennedy, the Attorney General, who was conducting a war on organized crime and felt that Sinatra's links with the gambling world could damage the administration. In 1963 Sinatra's licence to operate the Cal-Neva Lodge, his $4 million casino hotel at Lake Tahoe, was taken away after the Nevada Gaming Commission uncovered his relationship with Sam Giancana, a Chicago Mafia boss. He had appeared at Giancana's nightclub in Northbrook, Illinois, as a thank-you for contributions to JFK's campaign; he had also entertained Giancana at the Cal-Neva. Subsequently the singer, the mobster and the president were said to have shared a mistress, Judith Campbell Exner. That was as close as anyone ever got to putting the finger on Sinatra's rumoured mob connections. In 1981, after gaining access to his personal files under the Freedom of Information Act during a long legal battle, he won his casino operator's licence back.

The advent of the Beatles aged a lot of singers overnight. Sinatra responded with a bout of introspection, the 1965 album *September of my Years*. Yet only a few months later he married a nineteen-year-old actress, Mia Farrow, and demonstrated his continuing artistic virility by winning Grammy awards – the US music industry's Oscars – for an album, *A Man and His Music*, based on a successful TV special, and a hit single, 'Strangers in the Night'. And at the end of the 1960s he had an even greater success with 'My Way', a lush French ballad with an English lyric by the singer Paul Anka, which gave Sinatra the opportunity to explore some of the more rebarbative facets of his own character. The combination of cockiness and vulnerability that once seduced the bobbysoxers had decayed over a quarter of a century into a defiantly maudlin solipsism.

By now the voice which had bloomed in the 1940s and ripened in the 1950s was starting to wither as the 1960s wore on. In March 1971 he announced his retirement, taking his final bow at a gala performance in Los Angeles. But no one was very surprised when he revoked his decision two years later, releasing an album with a typically self-mythologizing title: *Ol' Blue Eyes is Back*.

The remainder of his career gradually assumed the air of a twenty-year farewell tour. Despite the occasional success with congenial material (such as

Sondheim's 'Send in the Clowns'), the later recordings were generally uninspired. The stage shows, scheduled with an impressively reckless disregard for his age, were eventually marked by a reliance not just on Frank Jr, who conducted the orchestra, but on large teleprompter screens at all corners of the stage, feeding him lyrics and patter. Even as his powers waned there was the occasional hallucinatory glimpse of the slim, youthful figure perched on a bar stool, a jacket over his shoulder and a cigarette between his fingers.

Many of his later appearances were charitable fund-raisers. Politically he had long since eased away from the Democrats, transferring his allegiance to the presidencies of Nixon, Bush and his old friend Ronald Reagan, whose inauguration he hosted. Personally he remained on good terms with his former wives, particularly Nancy, the mother of his children, and was successfully married for a fourth and last time in 1976 to Barbara Marx, the former wife of Zeppo Marx.

Gradually, he was transformed from a singer into a symbol. In the mid-1980s, with a suite of dances titled *Nine Sinatra Songs*, the American choreographer Twyla Tharp showed us that even his lesser creations – 'Strangers in the Night', 'Softly As I Leave You', 'Somethin' Stupid', 'Forget Domani', 'My Way' – had a special value of their own and a place in our collective consciousness. In 1993, astonishingly, he topped the charts again with an album called *Duets*, in which he was joined by singers both obviously compatible (his old friends Tony Bennett and Liza Minnelli) and staggeringly improbable (Bono and Gloria Estefan). The partners, often thousands of miles away from the studio at the time of recording, were linked by fibre-optics and digital technology, and by a collective reverence for the old man whose world they were entering.

Early in 1994 Sinatra faltered on stage at Radio City Music Hall while making a speech in acceptance of a lifetime-achievement Grammy award. Long-standing rumours that he was suffering from the onset of Alzheimer's disease gathered force. A week later, performing in Richmond, Virginia, he collapsed in front of 3,600 people while singing 'My Way'. After being taken to hospital, he swiftly discharged himself and flew home to Palm Springs and a real retirement.

All that remained was the following year's celebration of his eightieth birthday, its highlight an internationally televised party at which he was serenaded by the surviving giants of American popular music. The guest of honour chose not to sing. His work was done.

FRANCIS ALBERT SINATRA · *born* 12 December 1915 · *died* 15 May 1998 ·

JOHN GIELGUD
Nicholas de Jongh

Sir John Gielgud, who has died aged ninety-six, blazed a glorious trail through the English theatre of the twentieth century and left an indelible imprint upon it. He was the first classical actor of his generation to discard antique modes of Shakespearean interpretation and performance. His Hamlet, Richard II, Leontes, Angelo, Lear and Prospero were acclaimed as thrilling recoveries and discoveries of roles on which the dreariness of convention had long since settled. 'You have to spin it out of yourself, like a spider. It is the only way,' he said in 1961, and not until extreme old age did he lose that air of effortless spider-like facility.

After hesitations and doubts, he rode the surges of the New Wave theatre, and revealed himself a remarkable character actor in the plays of Harold Pinter, Alan Bennett and Charles Wood. In 1970 his desolate inmate of a mental institution in David Storey's *Home*, tears coursing down his face while he maintained a stiff-lipped façade, marked the full flowering of his theatrical Indian summer.

He was not, however, just the starriest actor for highly strung, tragic heroes half in love with painful suffering, deploying that famous tenor voice, which Alec Guinness once apostrophized as being 'like a silver trumpet muffled in silk'. He set new standards in the playing of the artificial high comedy of Congreve, Wilde and Sheridan, to which he brought the breath of natural-ness. He revelled in suave villainy and hauteur, in the drawn-out repartee of these periods, sometimes deliciously parodying aspects of his tragic demeanour and voice. He was in his glorious element playing doomed heroes and dandies, neurotics and aesthetes.

As a source of inspiration and influence on his profession, he was unrivalled by any actor in his time except for Laurence Olivier. For, in youth and middle age alike, Gielgud was a modern pioneer seeking to fulfil the actor's dream of working in a permanent ensemble, performing classic plays of high quality, where profit was neither motive nor stimulus. The famous companies he assembled in his historic seasons in the 1930s, 1940s and 1950s became blue-prints for the RSC and National Theatre decades later.

The other astonishing aspect of Gielgud's career, which spanned more than seventy-five years, lay in his ability to recreate and extend himself as fashion and circumstance demanded. He was socially and politically conservative. As a raconteur and conversationalist, scattering his indiscretions and gossip with gay abandon, he may have been the acme of unconventionality. But, theatrically speaking, the shock of the new often shocked him. Since he was also a restless seeker, he learned to rise above the prejudice of his first impressions and to cast aside hidebound convictions. In the 1950s, when the new wave of dramatists broke excitedly upon the London theatre, when Brecht and the Theatre of the Absurd threatened the hold of the upper middle-class drawing-room comedy and the regimen of the well-made play, Gielgud was at first left bothered and bewildered, though his astonishing, oriental King Lear at Stratford for George Devine in 1955, in which the Japanese sculptor and designer Isamu Noguchi enveloped him in a mane and head of horses' hair, proved he did not lack the spirit of wild adventure. Yet, unlike Peggy Ashcroft and Olivier, he did not join the avant-garde at the Royal Court in the 1950s and, by the early 1960s, he was beginning to look a thoroughly traditional figure.

This isolation from the new did not, however, last that long. Gielgud adjusted, adapted and learned. Critics have suggested he discovered an ideal point of mediation between the old theatre and the new with Alan Bennett's *Forty Years On* (1968), a revue-like play which regards the totems of England's early twentieth-century society with a mixture of mockery and nostalgia. But in fact his Broadway performance four years earlier, as a lay brother laid low after being persuaded to marry the richest man in the world, in Edward Albee's mystifyingly symbolic *Tiny Alice*, marked the point at which he threw in his lot with the *nouvelle vague.*

From then on, Gielgud's career revived. He began to disprove the old slur that he was only able to give a single performance in one voice. In *No Man's Land,* his sly literary vagrant in search of a billet – the model of bohemian seediness with a cigarette forever between his lips – cast off the familiar Gielgud persona as thoroughly as he did for his 1936 *Merchant of Venice* and the 1961 *Othello.*

When his ability to memorize parts for the theatre began to falter in his mid-seventies, while playing an archaeologist disturbed by excavations into his own past in Julian Mitchell's *Half Life*, Gielgud turned to the world of film. He adapted and fashioned a late career – notably as the conductor-hero of Alain Resnais's *Providence* (1977), and an ancient, naked Prospero in Peter Greenaway's astonishing version of *The Tempest, Prospero's Books* (1991).

He delighted in the suave malice of the narrator's father in the television version of *Bridehead Revisited* (1981). He won an Oscar for his performance as Dudley Moore's butler in the Hollywood comedy *Arthur* (1980). There was even a last stage performance. At the age of eighty-four, he took on the role of

Sir Sydney Cokerell, the museum curator in Hugh Whitemore's *Best Of Friends*, and had a field day with the character's mellow urbanity. Even in his nineties, he capered nimbly through the musical reaches of *Shine* (1996).

The essential Gielgud did not greatly change from first maturity to old age – he was all quick-silver and mercurial intelligence. In rehearsals and life alike, he was impulsive and master of the never-made-up mind. His tongue and ideas for altering performances often ran away with him. His capacity for speaking his mind at the wrong time in the wrong way was a lifelong joy – for all except those who suffered the cold blast of truth.

Gielgud may have been born into the heart of the conventional upper middle classes of Edwardian England, but this third child of an Edwardian stockbroker had the theatre in his blood. Ellen Terry, Henry Irving's leading lady, was a great aunt. His grandmother, Kate, played Cordelia at fourteen and became an instant star. His great uncle, Fred Terry, made his name with the *Scarlet Pimpernel*. Some have argued that his acting and looks bore no trace of his Terry ancestors. They suggest that his style bears the imprint of his father's Lithuanian forbears, and of his thespian Polish great-grandparents, who were renowned for their Shakespearean acting. Even in his thirties – and remarkable for his great, domed forehead and aquiline nose – he did not look English. Ronald Harwood has suggested that 'the fusion of the Anglo-Saxon and the Slav to be one of the clues to understanding Gielgud's qualities, both as an actor and as a man'.

Educated at Westminster school, Gielgud was stage-struck in childhood, during which the adjectives 'nervous, frail and sensitive' were attached to him. He became a willowy young man – quick and sharp, with a butterfly mind, who liked to dress in silk socks and broadband black hats, and with fluffy hair which barbers used to wave. He played no school games and walked in stiff self-consciousness – 'like a cat with rickets', said one of his first drama teachers. In a theatre which celebrated bluff maleness and matter-of-fact understatement in its leading actors, he seemed the man least likely to take the West End theatre at all, let alone by storm.

When Gielgud played his first leading role in London, as Romeo to Gwen Ffrangcon Davies's Juliet in 1924, the critics were loud in their scorn. 'Scant of virility,' accused Ivor Brown, 'with the most meaningless legs imaginable.' But perhaps the 'orange' make-up or coal-black, centre-parted wig and white tights did not help much. It may have been his Slavic heritage that saved him from sinking after this. For it was in the then almost unknown Anton Chekhov that Gielgud made his name. 'Perfection itself,' said James Agate, the most influential critic of the period, about his Trofimov, the young revolutionary in *The Cherry Orchard*. His Konstantin in *The Seagull*, and the doomed Tusenbach in the first English production of *Three Sisters*, were almost as eye-catching.

So it was that the twenty-five-year-old Gielgud arrived at the Old Vic at the end of the 1920s as leading man – and walked almost straight into theatrical history. In the next nineteen months, he took on more Shakespeare leads than any subsequent actor has attempted in twice the time. He was all ages and all types – Romeo and Lear, Orlando and Prospero, Macbeth and Malvolio, Antony and Benedick. One of these roles, his Richard II – 'A tall willowy figure in black velvet … the pale agonized face set beneath a glittering crown' – was the making of him.

Critics had already commented on Gielgud's voice, that fabulous piece of machinery which a few detractors have claimed to be capable of making flamboyant music with elongated vowels and little more. The old records of his stage roles disprove that charge. They reveal Gielgud as master architect, building and shaping character minutely. In Shakespeare, he composed a serious intellectual music. His grief-struck Richard, seething with hauteur, anger, self-pity and vulnerability, displayed both his Slavic and Anglo-Saxon aspects – his doomed king exuded emotion that he struggled to keep in check.

The Hamlet that followed was more remarkable still – a prince for all seasons, contemporary in its sense of disgust and outrage, instead of traditional ponderous nobility, fresh in its Oedipal stresses and strains. For an age accustomed to mature forty-something Hamlets, it was disconcertingly young; for an age familiar with understatement, it was riven with emotion, 'hysteria and self-lacerating sensitivity'. James Agate called it 'the highwater mark of English Shakespearian acting in our time.'

Four years later, Gielgud's second prince – bringing Shakespeare daringly into the West End – was less hysterical, more thoughtful and prone to flashes of humour. It was even more feted. The critic J. C. Trewin said it was the best of the seventy princes he had seen and, even when Gielgud played the role in his forties, the likes of the youthful John Mortimer were bowled over all over again. It was, however, in a new, slight costume piece about Richard II – Gordon Daviot's *Richard of Bordeaux* – that Gielgud really became a star. 'Yes, I know it's vulgar, but I can't resist,' he said to a friend, as he sat signing picture postcards of himself after a performance. But it was a mark of Gielgud's essential seriousness that he did not succumb to the frippery and shallowness of the 1930s West End. Instead, supported by the impresario Bronson Albery, he set about creating his own company of players in classical drama in St Martin's Lane.

It was typical of his eagerness to encourage the new that he cast the young Olivier to alternate with him the roles of Romeo and Mercutio to Peggy Ashcroft's Juliet. It was not supposed to be a theatrical contest. But so it proved, and Olivier, unsurprisingly perhaps, was a love-possessed Romeo from the fingertips to the heart, while Gielgud's Romeo was all surface and no sensuality. When it came to Mercutio, however, Olivier was second-bested. 'John's extraordinary darting imagination made him the better,' Ashcroft said. Gielgud may have felt pangs of jealousy but they never loomed large – he was always far more of a team player than Olivier, and far more willing to test himself against his best contemporaries.

His famous 1937 season at the Queen's, with Peggy Ashcroft as his leading lady, and a repertoire of *Richard II*, *The Merchant of Venice*, *The School For Scandal* and *Three Sisters*, directed by Michel St Denis, marked his first attempt to create an ensemble of classical players. But then, tiring of the producer's role, Gielgud was diverted by Binkie Beaumont, who was about to become the most powerful of London impresarios, into a Dodie Smith drawing-room romance. Beaumont, the canniest of producers, was a conservative influence in Gielgud's theatrical life, ranged against the likes of Komisarjevsky, St Denis, Guthrie and Peter Brook, who inspired him to new challenges and to new styles of performance. At least under Beaumont's aegis he was given the chance of launching a bold 1945 season at the Haymarket, which might have been designed to show the ease with which he scaled both the heights of tragedy and comedy. There was his fourth Hamlet, and the abominably cruel Ferdinand in *The Duchess of Malfi*, ranged with what the fledgling critic Kenneth Tynan delightedly called his 'tongue-in-cheek and hand-on-heart Valentine in *Love For Love*'. In 1953 Beaumont gave him another chance – at the Lyric, Hammersmith – to run his own classical company again. Astutely choosing Paul Scofield as his co-star, Gielgud resuscitated Thomas Otway's tremendous Restoration tragedy *Venice Preserv'd*, playing the role of the wracked Jaffier in a dazzle of torment and nobility.

In the 1940s Gielgud consolidated more than he advanced. He was more larch than oak when he played an admired, too youthful Lear, an unwarrior-like Macbeth and a new Italianate Prospero. But there were people who criticized what someone called his 'divine coldness' – it was as if there were something remote and aloof about his acting.

These reservations were set aside in his *annus mirabilis* at Stratford-upon-Avon in 1950, when he seemed to shed a sense of inhibition and restraint. His Angelo in *Measure For Measure*, for Peter Brook, marked a new immersion in wickedness. He discovered 'a dark and chilling urgency that froze the blood'. He was no longer courting sympathy or exuding an easy romanticism. He and Peggy Ashcroft turned *Much Ado About Nothing* into an exquisite war of words.

Anthony Quayle, directing him as Cassius in *Julius Caesar*, persuaded him to do away with lyricism and softness, and Gielgud achieved a pugilistic fury that astonished the critics. His Leontes, in Peter Brook's *A Winter's Tale*, confirmed his newfound confidence in playing unsympathetic roles. 'Dressed in hectic red, tall and tortured and rigid, he commands the bare black stage like a fury,' John Barber wrote. A year later, in the Coronation honours, Gielgud was awarded a long-delayed knighthood, for which Olivier and Richardson had had to lobby the prime minister, Winston Churchill; Gielgud's homosexuality had been the bar to this honour. Then irony and disaster struck in a double action. Just a few months later, when the government was in the midst of a witchhunt against homosexuality, Sir John was charged with persistently importuning for immoral purposes. He admitted his guilt and was fined.

The repercussions were great and awful for a man of Gielgud's temperament and character. It was said that he briefly contemplated suicide. 'You can't imagine what it was like,' he said to me years later. But in his weeks of stress and humiliation, much of the generosity and kindness that he had shown to his fellow actors was returned in full measure. Sybil Thorndike, who was acting with him in *A Day by the Sea*, led those determined to give support. A move by a minority on the Equity council to have him expelled from the union – and barred from acting – was defeated by a large majority.

For a time, the case may have turned Gielgud back to the safe, reassuring world of Binkie Beaumont and H. M. Tennent. But not for long. In 1957 his 'grizzled ascetic' Prospero, in whom the fires of revenge and recrimination still blazed, brought an outburst of applause. 'It's the best Shakespearean acting I have seen,' Richardson wrote to him. And even though miscast as Othello, in Zeffirelli's 1961 RSC production, with a first night rich in falling scenery and collapsing reputations, Gielgud emerged to play a delectable Gayev in *The Cherry Orchard* – all wistful solemnity, lightly mocking his own pompousness.

This ability to ignore setback and disappointment, to rise to new challenges, characterized the last twenty years of his life in the theatre. He may have had too few chances to play the classics – his last Lear was given when he was little more than fifty; his final, necromancing Prospero was something of a come-down. His Julius Caesar and Sir Politick would be unremarkable. But there were at least two great performances. In *Home*, Gielgud was sheer magic. His Spooner, in Pinter's *No Man's Land*, was even more of a departure.

It marked a feat of self-disguise and impersonation that he had not attempted since his early acting days.

Gielgud served the stage unstintingly. No actor was more adored in his time. Indiscreet, self-deprecating, avid for gossip, he strode poker-backed, immaculately dressed, witty, generous and endearing, through thousands of private lives. To listen to him talk in uncensored private was to enjoy a one-man festival of sharp, quaint indiscretions. All his yesterdays seemed to have been such fun. He lived for forty years with Martin Hensler, and when Martin died a little while ago, the life-force seemed to drain away from him. He wanted to see few people, though he longed for a glimpse of Maggie Smith again.

He was a master of acting in an age of great English actors. He encompassed everything from the tragic to the comic ridiculous. He was so old, and had worked for so long, that there will be hardly anyone left alive who can remember our theatre without his magic presence. Those who knew him even a little will lament the passing not just of an actor but of a man who was such infinite, mischievous fun.

SIR ARTHUR JOHN GIELGUD · *born* 14 April 1904 · *died* 21 May 2000 ·

1 July 2003

KATHARINE HEPBURN
David Thomson

Long before the end of her rich and irrepressible life, Katharine Hepburn, who has died aged ninety-six, had gone beyond the level of mere movie star, and won a public affection granted to few people. She would sometimes marvel at the warmth with which strangers wrote to her, and she could discuss the phenomenon of herself in ways that left no doubt about her steely, serene ego, but which never jeopardized her charm. Though 'charm' is not quite the word. She had an authority, a natural eccentricity and the spunky good sense of a magnificent aunt. So many who never met her must feel her loss in those terms.

From start to finish, Hepburn was a family person. The years of fame and Hollywood never matched her loyalty to Fenwick, the family property at Old Saybrook on the Connecticut coast, where she was raised. She was not just a fond daughter; she was deeply influenced by the life and work of her parents – the father a doctor, the mother a leader in the drive for women's suffrage and family planning. She took it for granted that one grew up striving for 'character', shouldering responsibility and finding strength in family ties and good work.

Kate Hepburn was very New England. She swam in the cold Atlantic ocean; she was a fanatic for exercise; and she enjoyed the long, severe winters and short, stunning summers, to say nothing of muddy spring and flaming fall. The US constitution came from her corner of the country, along with granite humour and equal respect for morality and privacy.

So she was vigorous and independent in thought and action, while part of an informed and opinionated family that talked about everything except feelings. With that, there was a pervasive mystery. There was some history of mental illness in her family, and suicide. At the age of thirteen, it was Hepburn who found the body of her older brother, who had hanged himself. This left her tomboyish, feisty, scornful of fuss, yet always curious about emotions and their secrecy.

Her character and her intelligence were never simple or superficial, and that prickly edge kept her from being a popular favourite for many years. Indeed, in the late 1930s – her finest years – she was sometimes called box-office poison, a wounding badge that she wore with defiance.

If acting had not worked out, Hepburn would never have moped. She would have played golf and tennis, travelled, driven and flown, perhaps; and she would have devoted herself to feminist causes long before they became fashionable. She would have had enduring friendships with women, and a string of bantering relationships with strong, tough men of the world.

Of course, she did most of those things anyway, while making some fifty films that got her twelve Oscar nominations and four of the statuettes – both records. She acted on the stage, too, but without either the assurance or the vulnerability she had on screen. She wrote a couple of books, including an enormously successful, blithely selective, autobiography, which she titled – simply, boldly, yet reasonably – *Me* (1991). Who else?

Hepburn was educated at the elite women's college Bryn Mawr, in Pennsylvania, and graduated with a major in history and philosophy. She went straight into the theatre, where she earned a reputation for being headstrong and undirectable. She was smart, and she mixed profound reticence with abrupt surges of outspokenness. Fighting her own reserve made her impulsive and perilous. She seemed mannered sometimes, but rather more in a social than a theatrical sense.

It was in line with her kind of American classiness that, in 1928, she married Ludlow 'Luddy' Ogden Smith, a Philadelphia stockbroker. The union did not last (they divorced in 1934), but she never lost her fondness for him. But she would not marry again; she had learned that she was too much 'me' for that.

By the time she went to Hollywood in 1932, Hepburn was regarded as difficult and lofty. Her first employer, David O. Selznick, was horrified: she wasn't beautiful, she wasn't sexy, she talked back, she didn't flatter fools. How could she survive?

Years later, Selznick denied her one role she longed for – that of Scarlett in *Gone With the Wind*. But in her first film, *A Bill of Divorcement* (1932), she had George Cukor as her director and John Barrymore playing her father – and she was extraordinary. Cukor saw a young woman anxious to seem sophisticated, yet often making a fool of herself, and then recovering. She was like a heroine from Jane Austen: she had a moral being, a mind and a conscience, and she was trying – in the words of *The Philadelphia Story* – 'to behave naturally', with grace.

She was perfectly cast as Jo in Cukor's *Little Women* (1933), and she won her first Oscar as the young actor in *Morning Glory* (1933). But she was not an established figure in the 1930s. She made several flops; she went for adventurous but misbegotten roles; she was under contract to a small studio, RKO; and she never let herself be cute or adorable. She played an aviatrix in Dorothy Arzner's *Christopher Strong* (1933) – so often she wore slacks. She was a strange tomboy in *Spitfire* (1934), and not too credible at genteel romance in *The Little Minister* (1934), *Break of Hearts* (1936) or *Quality Street* (1937). She was an early feminist in *A Woman Rebels* (1936).

None of those films did well, and Hepburn sometimes seemed stilted or querulous. But beginning with the pretentious show-off who learns better sense in *Alice Adams* (1935), she had an extraordinary run. She was dressed as a boy in parts of Cukor's risky *Sylvia Scarlett* (1936). For John Ford, she gave perhaps her most romantic performance, as *Mary of Scotland* (1936). In *Stage Door* (1937), she had wonderful battles of repartee with Ginger Rogers.

Then she did three films with Cary Grant – as the spirit of liberating disruption in Howard Hawks's *Bringing Up Baby* (1938); as the rebellious rich girl who wants a more decent life in Cukor's *Holiday* (1938); and as Tracy Lord in *The Philadelphia Story* (1940), in which emotional pride and coldness give way to a deeper understanding.

That last film was of her own choosing. Aware that she was not easily cast, Hepburn encouraged the playwright Philip Barry to write the play for her

(Howard Hughes loaned her money to buy the rights). She played it on Broadway, and then sold it – and herself – to Metro-Goldwyn-Mayer. If she had only ever made *The Philadelphia Story*, *Holiday* and *Bringing Up Baby*, her place in the comedy of manners and feeling would have been secure. The wary, very clever and teasing Grant was the greatest screen partner she ever had – more stimulating and testing than Spencer Tracy to come.

Hepburn met Tracy on the set of *Woman of the Year* (1942), a very effective comedy until its end, when the woman meekly adopts the man's demeaning rules. On screen and off, she deferred to Tracy. Still, it was the beginning of a partnership that made her a sentimental favourite. Though she revered health, in life Hepburn accommodated herself to all of Tracy's neuroses – he was an alcoholic and depressive, unhappily married, guilt-ridden over a son's deafness, and not in her class as a mind or a talker. But tough, bitter men gave her a thrill. There had been a romance with Howard Hughes, and a near marriage to her agent Leland Hayward. According to Barbara Leaming's 1995 biography (though this was disputed by family members), John Ford had been the love of her life.

At the same time, there were rumours – and evidence – that Hepburn preferred the company of women, especially Irene Mayer Selznick and the American Express heiress Laura Harding, her friend for more than sixty years. The truth may be that she always enjoyed friendship more than sex; she never quite lived with anyone, though she was a heartfelt care-giver to so many.

The Tracy films were often very good, even if they were not as piercing as the late 1930s movies – *Keeper of the Flame* (1942), Frank Capra's *State of the Union* (1948), the excellent *Adam's Rib* (1949) and *Pat and Mike* (1952) were the best, and three were by George Cukor. But if one film was the pivot of Hepburn's popularity, it was *The African Queen* (1951), where she and Humphrey Bogart made a salty, romantic coupling, like kids let out to play. On that dangerous African location, she won the love and admiration of director John Huston, by hunting with him and generally roughing it. In return, years later, in her book about the film, she described him as a pagan god.

There were also bad and inane films – playing Chinese in *Dragon Seed* (1944); helpless in *Without Love* (1945) and *The Sea of Grass* (1947), both with Tracy; trying to be Clara Schumann in *Song of Love* (1947); and in Vincente Minnelli's neurotic *Undercurrent* (1946).

As she neared fifty, and stayed resolute about acting her age, Hepburn was the schoolteacher plunged into late love in Venice, in David Lean's *Summer Madness* (1955), a spinster refreshed by Burt Lancaster in *The Rainmaker*

(1956), and a very creepy monster mother in *Suddenly, Last Summer* (1959). She did not overwork in those years, and when one considers the number of poor films she accumulated, her stature is all the more remarkable. It owed something to the 1971 publication of *Tracy and Hepburn*, by Garson Kanin (the scriptwriter on so many of their films). That book romanced the Tracy relationship and sweetened up its tough spots (including the moods and affairs of Tracy, and Hepburn's dogged independence) enough to be a best-seller. But she spent a lot of time looking after the ailing Tracy, even on screen in the woeful *Guess Who's Coming To Dinner?* (1967), for which she won her second Oscar.

That statuette should have melted like wax next to the exposed pain of *Long Day's Journey Into Night* (1962) – her best late film by far, and a rare but complete adoption of tragedy. There was another Oscar for *The Lion in Winter* (1968), and by then she was playing old ladies – sometimes in abject ventures – from *The Madwoman of Chaillot* (1969) through a fourth Oscar in *On Golden Pond* (1981) all the way to her aunt in *Love Affair* (1994), smiling on Warren Beatty and Annette Bening, and trying to restrain her palsy.

It is a life we may never plumb – just because she did not intend us to find out everything. Her own book, and Barbara Leaming's, leave so much out, and so much that we do know does not fit our image of a movie star. It surely helped her reputation as much as her life that she was brave, robust, loyal, edgy, and a survivor. She had been Hollywood in her time – and she was one of the few stars who liked Louis B. Mayer, her boss at MGM – but she never went Hollywood, or gave up New England habits.

To the end, her bright eyes and her large mind were filled with thoughts of other things to do besides having her picture taken. Maybe that is why, in enough movies, she looks like a newborn creature and one of the great American ladies. On *The African Queen*, John Huston had a brainwave – 'Do it like Eleanor Roosevelt,' he said. And she grinned and advanced. There was always a lot more there than just Me.

The mere wondering about who could take her place is enough to establish her rarity, and our final removal from the golden age of Hollywood. Golly, is she really gone?

KATHARINE HOUGHTON HEPBURN · *born* 12 May 1907 · *died* 29 June 2003 ·

...

THE SPORTSMEN

JOHN ARLOTT
John Samuel

John Arlott, who died on Saturday aged seventy-seven, was born in the Old Cemetery Lodge, Basingstoke. He never thought he would make old bones, but not for this reason. His beloved father, Jack, had no especial love of cricket, although later on his son delighted to recall that when cricket began to seek better playing surfaces it found them in the graveyards. His mother, Nelly, stuffing Liberal tracts into envelopes long into the night, was his induction into radicalism, so often at odds with his Hampshire traditionalism. 'The bastards are closing the "Watercress Line" forever...'

It was sometimes hard to find the right thing to say. His instant emotion was the actor-manager's: theatrical cordite. As you scrambled for a response the philosopher took over. Often you could wish you were an audience of millions instead of one. The mildest remark about an honest Dao enjoyed in an Algarve beach café could draw a withering response: 'The most evil colonial power the world has known.'

The MCC were to reel under a similar onslaught on the matter of South Africa. One visit in 1947 persuaded Arlott of the rightness of multi-racialism and the wrongness of apartheid. It was typical of him to find a place for Basil D'Oliveira in English cricket after the South African had written to him in desperation that his talent would ever find outlet.

Cyril Connolly had offered a similar generosity and recognition to the young Arlott, then a police sergeant in Southampton. His poems in *Horizon* and elsewhere, collected in book form in 1944 and 1945, led to his appointment by the BBC as a staff producer and then an instructor in broadcasting technique. As head of poetry in the early days of the Third Programme he grew to know Dylan Thomas, Roy Campbell and the postwar generation of poets and writers. They influenced him for a lifetime, though he would sometimes grump, 'I write like a copper, dun I?'

Sport, and especially cricket, projected him into a much wider domain, though it came about over the dead bodies of some BBC stuffed shirts who thought his Hampshire burr 'vulgar'. Arlott knew plenty about pusillanimity and meanness in high places. At best it was a snobbery which wholly overlooked his timing, eye and exactitude of judgement and imagery. Throughout the land listeners could feel the lethal pace of Lindwall or Miller running in to bowl at Hutton, Washbrook or Compton in that Ashes summer of 1948. Arlott's punctuation remains as evocative as the smell of linseed oil on willow. His voice was heard wherever on the earth cricket is played. Small boys swaying on the branches of trees overlooking Bridgetown, Kingston and Port-of-Spain sought to imitate him. But to others who knew nothing of cricket he sounded like home and no one could match his poetic gift for the right image. Asif Mahmood reminded him of Groucho Marx pursuing a pretty waitress. The South African Van de Buyl, bowling for Middlesex, was like a younger Lord Longford, 'though not nearly so tolerant'.

Nostalgia and sentiment helped him to his living but the road accident which cost him his son Jimmy at the age of twenty-one all but destroyed his religious faith. The hurt never left the depth of his eyes and each day of his life he knotted a black tie. A second son, Tim, to his great pride became a television executive. Valerie, his second wife, bore him a third son, Robert, a difficult birth presaging troubles which eventually cost her life in her forties. It was a deeply unhappy time. The BBC had turned from county commentaries to one-liners. A presenter who gabbled the Hampshire score switched to Arlott at Bournemouth for an update. 'You've given it,' said Arlott. 'Back to the studio.'

Test match broadcasting and his writing helped to bind many personal wounds. In the 1950s he wrote about soccer for the *Guardian* as 'Silchester'. Only the last-minute availability of 'Old International' – Donny Davies, his soccer senior – saved him from the Manchester United catastrophe at Munich airport. To his grief, Donny's widow could not find it in her heart to speak to him again.

For a while he was active in politics, twice standing as a Liberal. He described himself as a passionate Liberal, not a radical one. In 1970 he refused to broadcast the proposed South African tour. Persisting with the tour, he said, was a social, political and cricketing error. It brought him abuse from the Tory press and suspension from *Twenty Questions*. It was an issue on which he never bent. When he filled in a South African immigration questionnaire in 1947 he wrote 'Human' in the space marked 'Race'. He lived to see South Africa and the sports pages bend instead.

After writing for the *Observer* and *The Times* he returned to the *Guardian* as cricket and, subsequently, wine correspondent in the late sixties. For a dozen years it was a vintage period in all respects. His books ranged from his early verses to *English Cheeses of the South And West* (1956), *Jack Hobbs: A Profile of the Master* (1981) and *Arlott On Wine*.

Lunch at the Old Sun, his temporal and spiritual home at Alresford in eastern Hampshire, would usually end with the lamplighter. Libation began in a vast library-living room, often the bottle a newly discovered château or domaine, gleefully introduced with the latest ripe tale. Much that was important in Arlott's life was in this room, lined with first editions: John Piper, John Betjeman, Hardy, Osbert Lancaster, Hogarth, Cobbett, Kingsley Amis, and so much more. The aquatints, the country house topographies, the ship's glass … No Arlott journey of the middle years was without a chart of second-hand bookshops.

On the last day of the Centenary Test of 1980, Arlott signed off as a commentator: '…and Boycott pushes this away between silly-point and slip; picked up by Mallett at short third man; that's the end of the over; it's 69 for two, nine runs off the over, Boycott 28, 15 Gower, 69 for two, and after Trevor Bailey it'll be Henry Blofeld.' A swig of claret, then, as the sweat ran he took a handkerchief to mop his brow. The Lord's public address announced that Arlott had finished his final stint. The huge crowd spontaneously broke into applause. Boycott dropped his bat to clap. Lillee waved a fisted salute. The players applauded. Arlott took another gulp and walked out of regular broadcasting forever.

His decision to retire to Alderney with his third wife, Pat, was never easy. The family had spent warm and happy holidays in the 1950s on this seagirt rock, one mile by three, a fortress over the centuries, now beckoning him with a fine house, the Vines.

At the last he could not bring himself to sign the exchange contract. In that frozen moment his adviser said, 'C'mon you bloody fool. Sign it and sell it if you must. You can't lose.' Sign he did, giving up his past at the Old Sun. Next day he broke out in a savage rash, but the move began to Alderney and the last comfortable, well-solaced years. He'd auctioned his wine cellar and chuckled at the £28,000 it made. 'Only the big money stuff I'd choke if I drank…'

He was honoured with a life membership – of Somerset. His best book, he once said, was about Maurice Tate (1951). He was a proud, caring president of the Professional Cricketers' Association, especially during the difficult Packer years, the implications of which he read better than any. Asked once how he would like to be remembered, he said 'for producing *Under Milk Wood* and getting Basil D'Oliveira a cricketing job in England'.

LESLIE THOMAS JOHN ARLOTT · *born* 25 February 1914 · *died* 14 December 1991 ·

21 January 1994

MATT BUSBY
David Lacey

Matt Busby, who won a unique place in football's heart, has died aged eighty-four of coronary thrombosis. Two other Scottish managers, Bill Shankly and Jock Stein, ran him close in terms of respect and affection, but the course of Busby's career, scarred as it was by the Manchester United air disaster of 1958, earned him a special sort of devotion.

From his appointment in February 1945 to his retirement as manager in the summer of 1968, when he received his knighthood, Busby did not merely run Manchester United, he was Manchester United. During this period the club won the League Championship five times and the FA Cup twice. Busby's crowning moment came at Wembley in the spring of 1968 when, after a thrilling final against Benfica, United became the first English team to win the European Cup.

Yet Busby's life in football is ill-served simply by quoting statistics, which also show that his Manchester United teams were seven times runners-up in the First Division and lost two FA Cup finals: the first when Ray Wood's injury deprived them of a proper goalkeeper for most of the match and almost certainly cost them the League and Cup double; the second after the Busby Babes had been destroyed at Munich.

Busby represented a belief in the way that football should be played and it is that faith which still makes Manchester United the best-supported team in the country. He believed that the qualities of individual play and the demands of teamwork could live in harmony provided you had the right talents. 'I always wanted creative football,' he said. 'I wanted method and I wanted to manage the team as I felt the players themselves wanted to be managed.'

This approach enabled Busby to create three Manchester United sides who, while different in character and characters, shared a common theme of positive, attractive play which drew enormous crowds to their matches and gave the club a worldwide following rivalled only by Juventus of Italy.

Immediately after the war, when United had to play at Maine Road while Old Trafford recovered from the Blitz, Busby moulded the likes of Johnny Carey, Jimmy Delaney, Stan Pearson, Allenby Chilton, Jack Rowley and Charlie Mitten into his first successful team. Manchester United won the FA Cup in 1948 – their 4–2 defeat of Blackpool continues to be regarded as the purest game of attacking football ever seen in the final – but took an unconscionable time to win the championship.

That side, good though it was, turned out to be merely the prelude to the Babes, the team that epitomized Busby's belief in a sound youth policy and which was adopted by the nation. If an amazing third round FA Cup-tie at Villa Park in 1948, won by Manchester United 6–4, said everything about Matt Busby's first great side, then a First Division fixture at Highbury on 1 February 1958 was the ultimate statement by his second.

United beat Arsenal 5–4 and started to prepare for their European Cup tie in Belgrade the following Wednesday. There they held Red Star to a 3–3 draw. The following day they began the journey home and their British European Airways Elizabethan had to refuel in Munich.

When it took off again, amid the snow and ice of a Bavarian winter, the plane crashed. Eight Manchester United players, among them Duncan Edwards, who had come to represent the new sinew of English football, died along with three Old Trafford officials, eight journalists, two members of the crew and two other passengers. Matt Busby was on the critical list for several days. For a time it was hoped that Edwards, too, would recover. When Matt heard of the player's death he wept.

Back in England Busby regained full health with remarkable speed. A Manchester United team, patched up with the help of other clubs, who let them have the players, and the League, who waived some of the transfer rules, completed the season and reached Wembley again – but the rebuilding process had hardly begun.

Yet by the early 1960s, following the glorious but relatively brief reign of Tottenham and with Wolves on the slide, Manchester United were again the most accomplished team in the land. Talk to anyone over thirty about the United side they remember most vividly, and the names of Denis Law, Bobby Charlton and George Best will be the first mentioned. During the 1960s, Busby was accused by some critics of being a poor disciplinarian. They noted the at times reckless tackles of Nobby Stiles, the fierce retaliations of Law and the erratic behaviour of Best – both on and off the field – and were eager for a few words of condemnation from the manager.

Busby loved his players too much for that. He had seen one team die and could not bring himself to criticize their successors in public. In addition, the harshness of his own upbringing had given him an immense sympathy for those who followed. Matt Busby was born in the Lanarkshire village of Orbiston, and began life in a dingy two-roomed miner's cottage. His father died in the First World War, killed by a sniper at Arras, along with three uncles. How ironic that years later Busby's life should be saved by the devoted efforts of German surgeons.

What was left of the Busby family decided to emigrate to the United States. While they were waiting for a ship, Busby worked in the pits and never forgot how harsh earning a living could be. While playing for Denny Hibernians he was spotted by Manchester City and, instead of crossing the Atlantic, travelled to Maine Road. There he became an accomplished wing-half and a regular Scottish international. Neville Cardus described him in the *Manchester Guardian* thus: 'At best Busby has no superior as an attacking half-back. It is his bewildering footcraft which most delights the crowds. His crouching style may not be pretty but the control is perfect, the effect akin to conjuring. His dribble is a thing of swerves, feints and deceptions. Few opponents are not hoodwinked by his phantom pass … Busby scorns the obvious. His passes not only look good, they sound good.' Cardus went on to criticize Busby's defensive technique – indeed, much the same was said about his later Manchester United teams – but concluded: 'Who would have him different? He laughs equally at his blunders and his triumphs … He would be a certain choice for that select eleven of Footballers Who Obviously Love Football.' Busby's make-up as a manager was conditioned by his early experiences as a player. 'I wanted a more humane approach than there was when I was playing. Sometimes lads were just left on their own. The first team hardly recognized the lads underneath. There never seemed to be enough interest taken in players. From the start I tried to make the smallest member think he was part of the club.'

This was Busby's attitude to people in general and, more than anything, earned him universal affection. The name might have been awe-inspiring, but he went out of his way to put strangers at their ease. You always came away from Matt's company feeling better for the experience.

After retiring as Manchester United manager, he became a director, then club president. An attempt to make Wilf McGuinness chief coach with Busby as general manager failed because, while the man had given up the day-to-day running of the team, his presence could not be dismissed at the stroke of a pen.

Many things have happened at Old Trafford since Matt chose his last team. A number of managers, deeply contrasting in personality and method, have come and gone. Yet the club has never lost the aura of the Busby years, and his basic advice to teams in difficulty remains as sound as ever: 'Keep playing football.' If Matt could only be remembered for one thing it is that win, lose or draw, those who played under him rarely tried to do anything else.

MATTHEW BUSBY · *born* 26 May 1909 · *died* 20 January 1994 ·

FRED PERRY
David Irvine

Age never wearied Fred Perry's love of tennis. Until his death, at the age of eighty-five, in Melbourne – where he had been attending the Australian Open – Britain's greatest player remained a passionate enthusiast for a sport he so often claimed had blessed him with 'the perfect life'. From his humble origins in Stockport, Perry was to emerge in the mid-1930s along with Henry Cotton and Stanley Matthews and become one of the three revered symbols of British authority and excellence on the sporting field.

Perry's contribution was immense. From 1934 to 1936 he dominated the Wimbledon scene – the first Englishman to win the singles three times in succession since Laurie Doherty. Over the same rich period he extended his sphere of influence to win the French, United States and Australian titles. No previous player had put his name on all four championships and only three men have matched that achievement since. Though Wimbledon was Perry's favourite setting and Centre Court his spiritual home – when he first won there in 1934 the newspaper placards merely said FRED – his successes in the Davis Cup gave him almost as much pleasure as his many individual triumphs. Having ended France's long domination at Paris's Stade Roland Garros in 1933, the British team – Perry supported by Bunny Austin, Pat Hughes and Harold Lee – then went on to successfully defend the title; twice against Australia and once against the United States.

By 1936, however, Perry had decided that he had achieved all that was possible as an amateur and turned professional. To many in the All England Club this merely confirmed their doubts about the man. And his membership was instantly rescinded. In his autobiography, published in 1984, the year a statue was erected to him in the club's grounds, he wrote: 'Looking back I have to concede that I was sometimes a little brash and aggressive about what I regarded as the class-ridden set-up there. But at the time a young man with my background was bound to feel that snobbery very keenly and I still get angry about the shabby way I was treated when I won Wimbledon in 1934.'

It is difficult to believe that Perry was a world champion before he took up tennis. Yet at Budapest in 1929, aged twenty, he won the world table tennis championship at his first and only attempt. But Perry's father, Sam, later to become a Labour MP, did not approve of his son playing table tennis in smoke-filled rooms and agreed to fund him for a year if he would exchange bat for racket. The boy needed no second bidding. Perry found the transition to tennis easy. He just used what he called 'the same hatchet grip'. In that year also began his great love affair with Wimbledon. As a qualifier he reached the third round, but in 1930, in the main draw on merit, he defeated the Italian No. 4 seed Humberto de Morpurgo right under the sniffy noses of the LTA selectors. Perry, with his working-class background, was not considered the right stuff, but his performance put him in the British team to tour America.

So began a lifetime of travel that ended in Melbourne. It was, he often said, a great life, especially his time when he gained admittance to the Hollywood set. Perhaps the greatest hurt came when he beat Jack Crawford – the Australian he denied what would have been the first Grand Slam at Forest Hills the summer before – for his first Wimbledon title. As he lay soaking in the bath he heard an All England committee member say to Crawford: 'Congratulations. This was one day when the best man didn't win.' Then a bottle of champagne was opened. Not a word was said to Perry. All he found was a member's tie draped over his chair.

Perry was married four times. His last wife, Bobby, whom he married in 1952, a constant companion on his travels, was with him when he died. He also leaves a daughter and an adopted son.

FREDERICK JOHN PERRY · *born* 18 May 1909 · *died* 2 February 1995 ·

18 July 1995

JUAN FANGIO
Richard Williams

Decades after their prime, the immortals can still change the mood of a room simply by their presence: Bradman, Pele, Ali. In motor racing it was Juan Manuel Fangio, who has died aged eighty-four. More than thirty years after he last acknowledged a chequered flag, fans who had never seen him in action would jostle to glimpse the unprepossessing little Argentine who, by most available yardsticks, had been the greatest racing driver of all time. During his occasional visits to Europe, to take part in anniversary celebrations, there were many who would rather watch Fangio in his eighties, the survivor of several heart attacks, tiptoe around a circuit in a restored museum piece than the present generation race at full throttle in their computer-designed super-machines.

For his admirers, the 'Old Man' symbolized the heroic age when racing drivers went about their business in cork helmets, polo shirts, string-backed gloves and suede loafers, forearms bare to the wind, their faces streaked with hot oil. It was an age in which chivalry still played a part, and when the physical danger was such that each race seemed to thin the ranks of the participants. Perhaps the two were not unconnected.

For all the affection lavished on him throughout his long retirement, Fangio was nevertheless a hard case, a professional in the postwar world of dashing amateurs. Although capable of kindness and consideration, he never allowed sentiment to obstruct his path. Sound judgement and mental tough-ness served him well throughout a career whose greatest triumphs – twenty-three grand prix wins in fifty-one starts, five world championships (still unmatched) in seven and a half seasons – were achieved in his fifth decade, and thousands of miles away from his homeland. But the bare statis-tics tell nothing of his extraordinary qualities – the combination of delicate virtuosity, carefully deployed aggression and mechanical sympathy that often allowed him to rise above unhelpful conditions, superior opposition, or faulty equipment. Sometimes, being Fangio, all three at once.

Fangio was born in Balcarce, a potato town in eastern Argentina, in 1911. Both his parents had their origins in the Abruzzo region of Italy. Juan's father, the accordion-playing Don Loreto, arrived in Argentina at the age of seven, becoming a stonemason and house-painter; his wife Dona Herminia, a seam-stress, produced six children, of whom Juan was the fourth. The young Juan was a good student, and loved boxing and football. An agile inside-right, he was nicknamed Chueco – Bandylegs – by his team-mates.

Argentina had held its first motor race in the year before Juan's birth. At the age of four, he was enthralled by a neighbour's single-cylinder machine. At ten, he was hanging around the garage of a Señor Capettini, fetching and car-rying tools for the mechanics, and driving a car – a chain-driven Panhard Levassor – for the first time. At his father's wish Juan was apprenticed to a local blacksmith, but he soon talked himself into a transfer to Capettini's premises. There, and later at Miguel Viggiano's Studebaker garage, he learnt the inti-mate details of the internal combustion engine: how to profile a camshaft by hand, how to use a stone to grind a cylinder head. At night, after work, he began to modify machines himself. By his mid-teens he was also volunteering to deliver cars to customers, and ascribed his famous skill in slippery conditions to his early experience of driving on muddy tracks, which encouraged him to acquire a delicate touch.

At sixteen he briefly ran away from home to Mar del Plata, thirty-five miles distant, but was recaptured by his father. Soon afterwards, without telling his parents, he took part in his first race, as the riding mechanic in a four-cylinder Plymouth driven by one of Viggiano's customers. He performed a similar role the following year, accompanying his brother-in-law in a Chevrolet during a closed-circuit race in Balcarce. In 1931, however, Juan contracted pleurisy, and needed a long convalescence with relatives in the countryside before, in 1932, he reported to the artillery barracks in Buenos Aires for a year's compulsory military service. When he was able to return home, he set up a garage with a friend, Jose Duffard – the first step in a long business career which ran in parallel with his life as a racing driver.

Races on the open roads were the highlight of Argentinian motor sport, and Fangio's first really significant result came with seventh place in the 1938 Gran Premio Argentino de Carreteras, over 4,590 miles. His potential was now so obvious that the people of Balcarce clubbed together to buy him a decent car, a six-cylinder Chevrolet coupe. His first great win with the Chevrolet came in 1940, in the Gran Premio Internacional del Norte, which ran from Buenos Aires through Bolivia to Peru and back, a total of almost 6,000 miles in a fortnight, up mountain roads reaching 13,500 feet. Exhaustion and altitude sickness were enemies as formidable as the unmade roads. 'In the mountains of Peru,' he recalled, 'we chewed coca leaves' to counteract the symptoms. Victory in this, plus another in the Mil Millas Argentinas, made him the country's 1940 road-racing champion. He won the title again the following year, and was beginning to grow accustomed to street parades in Balcarce when, in 1942, the war halted racing. He was thirty-one. For another sportsman, these might have been the lost years of his prime, but Fangio was only just beginning. He concentrated on his garage business, and made solo drives from one end of Argentina to the other. With the resumption of racing in 1947, he was ready.

That year, the Argentine Automobile Club invited two great Italian stars, Achille Varzi and Luigi Villoresi, to take part in races at Buenos Aires and Rosario. The following year they returned, together with a third Italian, Nino Farina, and the French champion Jean-Pierre Wimille. Fangio began this series, known as the Temporada, in an old Maserati, but for the third race, in Rosario, he was offered one of a pair of Simca-Gordinis brought from France by their maker, Amedee Gordini. Fangio comfortably matched the performance of Wimille, a European grand prix star, in an identical car.

When Fangio arrived in Europe in 1948 with a delegation from the Argentine Automobile Club, Varzi and Wimille were among those who welcomed him. Fangio's only appearance during that trip was at Rheims, driving a Simca-Gordini at the French Grand Prix meeting. He failed to finish, but the party returned home in possession of a pair of new single-seater Maserati grand prix cars. For Fangio, though, the year also held sadness: he had been at the Bremgarten circuit in Berne when Varzi died under his capsized Alfa Romeo; and back in Argentina while competing in the epic Gran Premio de la America del Sur, he rolled his old Chevrolet, killing his co-driver and friend, Daniel Urrutia. Only three months later, during practice for the Gran Premio Juan Domingo Peròn at Buenos Aires, Wimille was also killed.

That race was the first of the 1949 Temporada series, in which Fangio was to make his real impact on the Europeans. At the Grand Prix of Mar del Plata, driving the fast little Maserati 4CLT in front of 300,000 ecstatic fans, he beat Farina, Villoresi and Alberto Ascari in a straight fight. Now he was ready to take on Europe. Within weeks he was leading the little Argentine team to victory in a grand prix along the San Remo seafront. It was followed by wins at Pau, Perpignan and Marseilles. So enthusiastic were his home fans that Peròn's government bought him a new two-litre Ferrari, and he repaid his country's faith by winning his first race, the Monza Grand Prix, matched against Ascari and Villoresi in similar cars on a circuit that he had never seen before. It was enough to attract the interest of the Alfa Romeo management, then preparing a team for the first world championship, to be held over a seven-race series in 1950. Fangio, Farina and Luigi Fagioli were their drivers, and between them 'the three Fs' won all six European rounds in their crimson Alfettas, the Argentine gaining victories at Monaco, Spa and Rheims to take second place in the final championship table, just behind Farina. But the following season three more wins – in Switzerland, Spain and France (the latter shared with Fagioli) – plus two second places gave Fangio his first world championship. He was forty years old.

Alfa Romeo, though, decided to retire from racing, and during the winter Fangio accepted two offers: the first from Maserati, for whom he would drive in Formula Two races; the second from a new concern, known as British Racing Motors. The first turned out to be the better deal, since the 1952 and 1953 world championships were run to the two-litre regulations of Formula Two. As for the supercharged 16-cylinder Formula One BRM, it turned out to be one of the great motor-racing fiascos, a costly disaster made the more embarrassing by the fact that the project had been paid for by public subscription. Fangio raced the ill-handling beast six times, and the two second places which were all he had to show may, in the circumstances, be counted among his most heroic feats.

But 1952 was, in any case, his worst season. It ended on the weekend of 7–8 June. On the Saturday he was due to race the BRM in the Ulster Trophy race on the Dundrod circuit near Belfast, followed on the Sunday by his first race in the Maserati, in the Grand Prix of Monza. After the BRM's customary retirement he flew from Belfast to Paris, there to be told that bad weather had ruled out all flights to Italy. Undeterred, Fangio drove non-stop through the night to Monza, just north of Milan, arriving two hours before the race was due to start. Although he had not practised, and was therefore not qualified to race, his fellow drivers immediately voted to let him participate. 'You look a bit tired,' Ascari told him. 'Oh, it's nothing,' Fangio replied. But starting from the back row of the grid in an unfamiliar car, he misjudged the Seraglio curve on the second lap and woke up in hospital with broken vertebrae. It was the only serious accident he was to suffer in the whole of his European career, and it put him out for a year.

Three races into the 1954 season, Mercedes-Benz made their long-awaited reappearance in Formula One. Alfred Neubauer, their peerless talent scout, always hired the best – which meant Fangio. Together they reduced their Italian, French and British competitors to the status of also-rans, Fangio winning six of the eight European grands prix (the first two in a Maserati), and taking the championship with a points total almost double that of the runner-up. The arrival at Mercedes of the brilliant young English driver Stirling Moss, in 1955, at least gave Fangio some competition, although Moss was generally content to follow in the master's wheeltracks, learning the finer points of race-craft in a sequence of one-two finishes. Fangio took the maximum points in Argentina, Belgium, Holland and Italy.

By contrast, in the British Grand Prix, Moss 'won' by a tenth of a second after ninety laps of the Aintree circuit. For many years Fangio did not reveal that he had run the race to the orders of the team management – which was looking for a public-relations coup in Britain and had fitted Fangio's car with lower gear ratios, restricting his speed. In any case, the championship had already been decided in his favour.

Curiously, Fangio's finest drive of the season may have been among his least praised. In the Mille Miglia, the non-stop time-trial over public roads from Brescia to Rome and back, he finished second to Moss in a race that became recognized as the Englishman's greatest triumph. But whereas Moss had enjoyed the prompting of a well-prepared navigator in the passenger seat of his eight-cylinder Mercedes 300SLR, Fangio accomplished the drive single-handed. And, for more than half the distance, on seven cylinders.

At the Le Mans twenty-four-hour race though, Fangio's Mercedes was peripherally involved in the crash which saw the machine of his team-mate Pierre Levegh flying over an earth bank into a public enclosure, killing eighty spectators. Fangio and Moss, sharing a car, were leading the race when, at two o'clock in the morning, orders came from Stuttgart to withdraw the entire team – a gesture of respect which also served as a partial safeguard against the consequent storm of bad publicity. The disaster bore heavily on Mercedes' subsequent decision to withdraw from racing.

Fangio, now forty-four, was contemplating retirement when a call from Enzo Ferrari changed his mind. Although they carried off the 1956 championship, the relationship ended with a bitterness which was vented in their respective memoirs. Ferrari, typically acting the injured innocent, wrote that Fangio had portrayed that season 'as a sort of adventure story blending betrayal, sabotage, deceit and many kinds of intrigue, all perpetrated with the intent of making him eat the dust'. He summed the Argentine up as 'a truly great driver, but afflicted with a persecution complex. A strange man, that Fangio. A sort of mystery.'

For the following season Fangio moved back to Maserati, whose 250F model, introduced in 1954, was reaching the peak of its development. The loveliest of all front-engined single-seater racing cars, it now became the tool with which Fangio could demonstrate the most profound elements of his genius. Its superb chassis permitted the refinement of the high-speed cornering technique known as the 'four-wheel drift', in which the driver pushed the car just past the limit of its tyres' adhesion, setting the front wheels against the direction of travel and steering with small movements of the throttle pedal. It was a skill requiring enormous sensitivity, and its masters were Fangio and his pupil Moss.

Of Fangio's four grand prix victories in 1957, the greatest was undoubtedly the win at the Nürburgring, a fourteen-mile circuit around the Eifel mountains, whose innumerable corners provided a test that revealed the relationship between the world champion and his Maserati. After leading the race in its early stages, Fangio was delayed by a pit stop, which put him almost a minute behind the more powerful but less agile Ferraris of Peter Collins and Mike Hawthorn, with ten laps to go. Constantly pulverizing the lap record, he drove with a rare combination of raw ferocity and technical brilliance, astonishing the two young Englishmen with the intensity of his assault. He caught and overtook them both with a lap to go, in that moment setting the seal on his legend.

He had won five world championships, but at forty-six he entered 1958 with misgivings about prolonging his career. They were only reinforced by the first grand prix of the season, on his home ground in Buenos Aires, where the revolutionary little rear-engined Cooper-Climax of Moss, its undersized four-cylinder engine adapted from a fire-pump motor, defeated the might of the classical front-engined Ferraris and Maseratis. Fangio missed the opening three races of the European grand prix season, but returned early in July for the French Grand Prix at Rheims. As he went through his old preparation routine in his hotel room, he suddenly realized that 'racing had become an obligation. And when racing begins to feel like work, well…' And after dragging the outclassed Maserati around in fourth place, Fangio discovered that Luigi Musso, his former team-mate, was dying in hospital after running off the track.

It was one accident, one race, too many. Quietly, without fanfare, Fangio returned to Argentina, where he settled into the life of a garage owner-cum-national hero. His Mercedes-Benz dealership expanded, a museum of racing cars was built in his honour by the people of Balcarce, and he was often flown across the ocean to be the chief VIP at Mercedes functions in Europe. At home, his door was open; abroad, crowds attended him wherever he went.

His personal life was always something of a mystery: in his ghosted autobiography, published soon after his retirement from racing, he offered his thanks to 'my wife, Andreina, for all she has done for me and our son Oscar'. They had married, he wrote, in 1941: 'She has not left my side since.' In the early 1970s, though, he described the relationship differently: 'We were not married, but we spent twenty years together. Then one day we had a discussion and she said, "If you don't like being with me, you may leave." So I left.'

Was he, then, the greatest racing driver of all? His record says so, but in motor racing, as in any sport, it is impossible to draw exact comparisons between different eras. If we say, as some critics would, that he was merely the shrewdest (which is beyond dispute), and not as divinely gifted as Nuvolari, Rosemeyer, Moss, Clark or Senna, then how do we explain the incandescent virtuosity of his drive against the odds at the Nürburgring in 1957? All we can say for certain is that Fangio raced against the best of his time, and beat them. And became, in the process, the embodiment of his sport.

JUAN MANUEL FANGIO · *born* 24 June 1911 · *died* 16 July 1995 ·

BEN HOGAN
David Davies

Ben Hogan, who has died aged eighty-four, was one of the best golfers the world has ever seen. Many believe that he was the best, although others would nominate Jack Nicklaus and yet others Bobby Jones. Nicklaus has the best record in terms of championships won, Jones the best in winning percentages, but Hogan was unique in that not only did the Second World War take away some of the best years of his career, he was also involved in a horrific car accident that threatened first his life and then his career.

His comeback from multiple injuries later became the subject of a film, *Follow the Sun*. The accident, in 1949, was a head-on crash, in fog, with a Greyhound bus. Hogan saved the life of his wife Valerie by diving across from the driver's seat to protect her, but his injuries were such that the last rites were administered as he lay in a coma. When, almost a year later, he returned to competition, he played his first nine holes in a two under par 34, tied for the tournament, the Los Angeles Open, but lost the play-off to Sam Snead.

But he completed the fairy tale by winning the 1950 US Open, played at the Merion club in Pennsylvania, the second of his four wins in that championship, and he also won in 1951 at Oakmont. That was the year that the course was purposely made extremely difficult, so much so that on the last day the average score was 75. Hogan, however, got round in 67 for his triumph.

Two years later he became the only man in modern times to win three major championships successively in the same calendar year, the 1953 US Masters, US Open and Open championships. Having been told that he could not truly consider himself a great player unless he won the Open, he made a rare trip to the UK to play at Carnoustie in Scotland.

Typically thorough, he arrived two weeks early so that he could prepare, bringing with him, at his mother's insistence, not only an enormous camel-hair coat to keep out the cold, but plenty of American food. He was put up by an American company in Dundee, which chauffeured him daily to the course. He won with four rounds each of which was lower than the one preceding it. It was the first time this had been achieved and the Scots, glorying in his detachment and intense concentration, called him 'the wee ice mon'.

As the Open clashed with the start of the PGA, Hogan was unable to complete the professional Grand Slam of the three previously mentioned events, plus the US PGA championship in one calendar year, something never yet done. Nevertheless, he was one of only four players to have done the Grand Slam over the course of his career, the others being Nicklaus, Gary Player and Gene Sarazen. He won nine major championships altogether, putting him alongside Player in the all-time list, but behind Nicklaus (18) and Walter Hagen (11). He also won sixty-three US Tour events, but he was again third, this time to Snead (81) and Nicklaus (70).

Hogan was quite possibly the most reticent of all great sportsmen. He could rarely be persuaded to speak either to the press or even to his partners on the course. He once, in a burst of candour while describing a round, told a press conference that 'one day a blind man will win a championship and you'll have nothing to write about'.

Hogan did not go to functions either, refusing every year to attend the champions-only dinner that precedes the US Masters. He did make one exception a few years ago, when an American golf magazine ran a poll to decide upon the Golfer of the Century. The winner – Jack Nicklaus – was announced at the dinner, and while there are conflicting accounts of what happened next – some say Hogan rose briefly, others that he remained seated – he did not wholeheartedly join in the standing ovation. Nor did his tournament playing partners reckon on much more than the time of day. During the Masters, a partner holed-in-one at the 12th. Hogan had a two and, as they walked down the next fairway, all Hogan said was: 'That's the first time I've had a two at that hole.'

Another, perhaps more incredible instance of his on-course aloofness is recounted by Gardner Dickinson in his book *Let 'er Rip!* Playing companion George Fazio holed a six iron second shot from the fairway for an eagle at the fifth, and Hogan said not a word. At the end of the round Fazio, inspecting his card, was astounded to see that Hogan had marked down a four as Fazio's score for the fifth hole.

Fazio said: 'Ben, you've marked me for a four at the fifth; I made a two there.' Hogan said: 'Are you crazy? The fifth's a par four.' Fazio then said: 'Ben, don't you remember I holed a six iron?' and Hogan, looking blank, had to say: 'No, I don't remember that.'

There was, however, a less publicized side to Hogan. Dickinson remembers when, as a struggling young professional, he was following the great man in a tournament. The previous week Dickinson, in contention after two rounds, had been paired with Hogan in the third round and taken a hugely nervous 78, to Hogan's 68. Spotting Dickinson in the gallery, Hogan came over, slipped him a piece of paper and said: 'Gardner, I don't know what your financial situation is, but if you run out of money, don't quit. This is my unlisted phone number. You call me and I'll get you some money.' Dickinson never needed to, but he said 'it made a huge difference to know that I could'.

Dickinson's book also sheds some light on the reasons for Hogan's success. He never stopped practising and it was once claimed that without the introduction of steel shafts he would never have become a great player, because hickory would not have stood up to the battering Hogan would have inflicted. Dickinson recounts a story, almost certainly apocryphal, of how Hogan, when practising to a caddie who collected the balls, hit and knocked down the caddie. His next four shots, it was said, also hit him before he could get up.

Hogan was never the charismatic character that Snead was, or Jimmy Demaret, players who loved to entertain the galleries. Hogan, dressed almost invariably in grey, with his trademark white cap, reasoned that his golf was entertainment enough. When he came to England in 1956 to play in what was then the Canada, now the World Cup, at Wentworth, my father took me to see this legendary name. I came away with my boyhood eyes filled with the swing and the incredible elegance of his partner, Snead. It was, however, Hogan who took the individual prize for the lowest total of the week.

Hogan was universally revered by his peers for his sheer shot-making ability. His book, *The Fundamentals of Golf*, became the student's bible of the game. In it Hogan propounded his theories of how golf should be played, although he did not reveal the 'secret'. He always said that such a thing existed, but steadfastly refused to say what it was. Nevertheless he set standards in golf that may be equalled, but probably not surpassed. He was the first of the completely dedicated professionals, a man who, right up to his final illness, would go to the practice range every day.

His success, and the mystique that grew up around him as a 'cold-eyed golfing killer' in a success-oriented country like America, ensured that the game itself prospered, and no one so far in the sport has made a greater contribution to that process.

WILLIAM BENJAMIN (BEN) HOGAN · *born* 13 August 1912 · *died* 25 July 1997 ·

STANLEY MATTHEWS
Brian Glanville

Nicknamed the Wizard of Dribble in Britain, known abroad as Der Zauberer (the magician), Stanley Matthews, who has died aged eighty-five, was the first-ever European Footballer of the Year, and arguably the outstanding British player of his generation. His career stretched from well before the Second World War to the 1960s; he was still playing League football at fifty. At forty-one, at Wembley, he was capable of demolishing as famous a left-back as Brazil's Milton Santos. Afterwards, in the England dressing room, in a rare moment of spleen, he said that when he read that he was too old he was sometimes tempted to tear up the paper.

But the truth is that throughout his career, Matthews was constantly accused of being too this, that or the other. Too unpredictable. Too individualistic. Too slow to release the ball. In one wartime Wembley international there was a small scandal when it was alleged that he had deliberately been starved of the ball. At the end of the war, when football officially restarted, he was excluded from the England team for most of the 1946–7 season in favour of Tom Finney, an outside-right with almost as remarkable a body swerve – only to return in triumph in Lisbon, Matthews on the right, Finney on the left, Portugal routed, 10–0.

As early as November 1934, when England won the bruising battle of Highbury against an Italian team which ran amok when its Argentine captain, Luisito Monti, limped early off the field with a broken foot, Matthews was damned in the *Daily Mail*. Geoffrey Simpson, its sports columnist, wrote: 'I saw Matthews play just as moderately in the recent inter-League match, exhibiting the same slowness and hesitation. Perhaps he lacks the big match temperament.'

Matthews was born at Hanley in the Potteries, the son of a formidable boxer, Jack Matthews, 'the Fighting Barber of Hanley'. Jack encouraged all his children to keep physically fit, doing deep breathing exercises in front of an open window even on the coldest mornings. In later years, Matthews would devise his own regimes based on long runs across the Blackpool beaches. It used to be said that if you passed his house at 9 p.m., the lights of his bedroom would be out.

His swerve was something which defied analysis; just as it defied attempts to counter it. He would take the ball up to the opposing left-back who, even if he were mentally prepared for it, would still 'buy' the dummy when Matthews swayed slightly to the left, putting the opponent off balance, only to wriggle around to the right, flick the ball up the touchline with the outside of his right foot, and sprint away. Catch him if you could. Over those vital first ten yards or so, he was beyond pursuit. 'Don't ask me how I do it,' he once said of the swerve. 'It just comes out of me under pressure.' He would opine: 'You must have butterflies.' Butterflies in the stomach, he meant, before a game, building up adrenalin, anticipation. 'I'm not really with you,' he told a journalist in the Stoke City dressing room immediately before his 'comeback' game; a mere Second Division match; aged forty-six!

Having sped past his left-back and reached the goal line, Matthews would then pull the ball back into the goalmouth; the most effective pass in the game. He seldom scored himself, but he could do so when necessary. Not least when playing at Tottenham for England against Czechoslovakia in 1937. Injury reduced England to ten fit men, and their unbeaten home record against foreign teams seemed in jeopardy. But Matthews, moving to inside-right, scored three times, and England won, 5–4. Much later, in the 1954 World Cup in Switzerland, when England were struggling in their opening game against Belgium, Matthews moved to inside-forward, galvanized the team, and helped it to gain a 4–4 draw.

Over the years he would time and again fall foul of the England selectors, troubled by so maverick a talent. It is true that he began badly, a nineteen-year-old, in his first two internationals against Wales and Italy, but it wasn't long before the 'big match temperament' was asserting itself. In May 1939, in the Berlin Olympic Stadium, he had one of his finest games for England just when they needed it most. Forced to give the Nazi salute before they played the German international side, England proceeded to cut them to ribbons, with Matthews rampant, irresistible against a full-back who had played him out of the game when last the teams met. Muenzenberg could do nothing with him that day and England won, 6–3.

An outstanding schoolboy footballer, he once scored a dozen goals in a game from centre-half. He played for England schoolboys, joined his local club, Stoke City, straight from school, worked in the office, and made his league debut for them soon after he had turned seventeen. But even before the war, his relations with the club degenerated with the appointment as manager of Bob McGrory, a former Stoke defender. It has been suggested that McGrory was displeased by the fact that Matthews had replaced his friend Bobby Liddle on the right-wing. Relations didn't improve when Matthews returned to Stoke after the Second World War.

During the war, he had played as a guest for Blackpool, a town where he and his wife Jean had opened a small hotel. Things came to a climax early in the 1946–7 season when Matthews was kept out of the Stoke team by the young winger George Mountford. Eventually Stoke agreed to transfer him to Blackpool, for the sum of £11,500. Matthews would stay there happily, forming famous wing partnerships with Stan Mortensen and Jackie Mudie, until his romantic and belated return to Stoke in 1961.

The war ate up much of his 'official' career, but he found an ideal partner in the England team in Sunderland's Raich Carter, even though Carter once complained that when he gave Matthews the ball, he never got it back. Tactfully, his captain, Stanley Cullis, responded that having passed he should move into the middle. The England attack, which included Tommy Lawton and Denis Compton, was an outstanding one, with an 8–0 win over Scotland at Maine Road, Manchester, to its credit.

Losing, then regaining his place in the England team in the first official postwar season, 1946–7, Matthews excelled in Lisbon against Portugal and, a year later, in Turin, reducing poor, blond Eliani, standing in as Italy's left-back for Maroso, to tatters. England won 4–0.

But when it came to cup finals, a winner's medal persistently eluded Matthews. In the 1948 final, Blackpool lost 4–2 to Manchester United, despite taking the lead through a penalty kick by Eddie Shimwell. In 1951, two spectacular goals by 'Whor' Jackie Milburn enabled Newcastle United to win 2–0. It seemed that 1953 would almost surely be the last chance. Blackpool were to meet Bolton, and this time, luck favoured them when Bell, left-half – and thus a direct opponent for Matthews – was hurt and had to limp along the left-wing. Even then, Blackpool made very heavy weather of it. They conceded an absurd early goal when their Scottish international keeper, George Farm, pitifully misjudged a shot by Nat Lofthouse after a mere seventy-five seconds. Lofthouse hit the post, Bell tore a muscle and Bolton were already down to ten active men.

Stan Mortensen would later say that Bolton lost the game when they decided to move their English international left-winger Bobby Langton inside, rather than let him contest space with Matthews, on the wing. Blackpool's equalizer, ten minutes from the break, was a fluke, the ball going in off their emergency left-half, Harold Hassall. But Bolton gallantly hit back with two goals, one by Moir, with Farm at fault again, the second a brave header by Bell himself. There were only twenty minutes left.

It was now that Matthews, strangely obscure till then, at last came into the game. Tommy Banks, Bolton's left-back, was exhausted by his efforts to halt

Matthews, contracting cramp in his shins, and four times leaving the field for treatment in the final quarter hour. One more Matthews run, a cross which would have gone out of play had Hanson, Bolton's keeper, not flapped at it, reached Mortensen on the far post and went in; 3–2. Mortensen equalized breathlessly from a free kick.

Then, classically, Matthews got away again on the right, beat Banks, took the ball up to the centre-half, Barrass, and pulled back an exquisite cross, not to Mortensen but to the South African left-winger Perry, free on the far post. A right-footed shot and the Matthews final had been won by Blackpool.

Would England have prevailed in the most humiliating match of their history, that defeat by the United States at Belo Horizonte in the 1950 World Cup, had Matthews played? Perhaps; but he didn't. Indeed, it was only at the last moment that he was grudgingly recalled from an FA XI tour of North America to play in Brazil at all. He did play the last England game, lost against Spain in Rio 1–0, but the die was cast by then.

Matthews's long marriage to Betty ended in 1968. He remarried, this time to a Czech linguist, Mila Winter, cultural assistant at the US embassy. He and Betty had two children, Jean and Stanley junior. The latter became three times British junior tennis champion, and also won the Wimbledon junior invitation title. He never quite fulfilled his early promise, and eventually turned to coaching in the US.

Knighted in 1965, a month before his fiftieth birthday, Matthews altogether made 698 appearances in the Football League for seventy-one goals, and played fifty-four full internationals for England for eleven goals. In 1963 he had the great satisfaction of helping Stoke City regain the First Division. A period as manager of Port Vale, after Stoke had rather sullenly parted company with him, reducing his wages and refusing him complimentary tickets, was ill-starred. The club fell foul of regulations concerning the signing of young players and Matthews was unfairly found culpable.

He went on to live in Malta, where he played for the Hibernians team at fifty-five, and to coach widely abroad, especially in South Africa, where he had first worked in 1954, and in Canada. He later returned to the Potteries. His wife Mila died last year.

STANLEY MATTHEWS · *born* 1 February 1915 · *died* 23 February 2000 ·

DONALD BRADMAN
Matthew Engel

Sir Donald Bradman, who has died aged ninety-two, was the greatest cricketer of the twentieth century and the greatest batsman who ever lived. He was also arguably the most famous of all Australians – and among the most influential. Sport played a major role in giving the young nation of Australia global standing, self-belief and a sense of identity. The tragic boxer Les Darcy and the racehorse Phar Lap played a part in this process, but nothing could match the phenomenon of Bradman.

His batting statistics are indelible and incredible, incomparably ahead of everyone else who has played the game. Seventy-two other players – including some indifferent ones – have scored more runs in first-class cricket; his totals of Test runs and centuries have been surpassed. But in Bradman's time, a first-class match in Australia, let alone a Test match, was an event, and then the war intervened.

He thus went to the crease in major cricket only 338 times, but in 117 of those innings returned with a century – a strike-rate above one in three, better than twice the ratios achieved by such greats as Jack Hobbs, Len Hutton, Walter Hammond or Denis Compton. His first-class average was 95.14; his nearest rival is on 71.

Most famously of all, he went out at the Oval in his last Test innings needing only four to finish with an average of 100, and was bowled second ball by Eric Hollies of Warwickshire, for a duck. It was as though the gods of cricket had reclaimed the invulnerability they had loaned him – though his final average, 99.94, remains so resonant that the Australian Broadcasting Commission uses it as its post-office box number.

In life, as in cricket, he came closer to immortality, outliving his contemporaries, rivals and enemies; there were always plenty of those – despite the near-perfection of his cricket, he was a complex, often troubled, man. Though he achieved everyone else's fantasies, he never seemed to find true fulfilment.

Yet he embodied the Australian dream. He was a country boy, born in Cootamundra, in rural New South Wales; his father was a farmer and carpenter – not rich, not poor. None of his schoolfriends lived near him, so in solitary moments he invented a game which involved throwing a golf ball at the base of the family water tank; he then had to whack it with a cricket stump. Though the ball fizzed off the tank at high speed and unpredictable angles, by the time he was ten, Bradman could whack it with the stump more often than not.

When he was twelve, he made 100 for Bowral high school against Mittagong. For a while, he played more tennis than cricket and seemed to be settling for a career in estate agency. However, when he was seventeen, Bradman played for Bowral against Wingello, who had the ace leg-spin bowler Bill O'Reilly. Bradman was dropped twice early on off O'Reilly, who got him out first ball when the game resumed the following week. In between, he scored 234.

Next match, he scored 300. In October 1926, he was invited to Sydney to practise for the state squad; a year later, aged nineteen, he was in the New South Wales team, scoring a century on debut. The following year, he scored 1,690 runs, a new Australian record. By November 1928, he was in the Test team, and seared by a match which England won by 678 runs. Bradman made 18 and 1, and was dropped from the next game to be replaced by one Dr O. E. Nothling. He was soon back; no one ever thought of dropping him again.

England, at this stage, were in one of their rare intervals of superiority over Australia, and had the world's leading batsman in Walter Hammond. Bradman scored two centuries in the series, one in defeat, one in a consolation victory. No one had the faintest idea that England would not win the Ashes again by fair means for another twenty-four years, and that one man would be primarily responsible for this. They got an inkling in the first week of 1930, when Bradman scored 452 not out for New South Wales against Queensland. But he was still rated behind another youngster, the more stylish Archie Jackson. Bradman's unclassical backlift would, it was thought, find him out on soft English wickets. In the event, Jackson failed in England (he died of TB three years later) and Bradman's tour was a triumphal procession.

It might be easy to imagine Bradman from this distance as a dull and mechanical batsman, something of a Geoffrey Boycott. In fact, he scored his runs at a phenomenal rate; the 452 came in 415 minutes, barely imaginable today. When he got to England, the style became more firmly established. It was almost metronomic, starting with the push for one first ball.

He was the master of timing; his eye was so extraordinary that he could make up his mind what shot to play a micro-second later than anyone else; and his judgement was so impeccable that the decision was almost always right. He eliminated the risk that comes from lofting the ball, and hardly ever hit a six in consequence. His batting was both intuitive and intellectual; as Neville Cardus said, he was that rare and devastating combination, 'a genius with an eye for business'. A Bradman innings was not as beautiful as one by Trumper or Woolley or Jackson, but it was awesome, and he drew unprecedented crowds from people just anxious to say they saw one.

In England in 1930, he became a colossus. He began by inaugurating his tradition of an opening double-century at Worcester, and hit 1,000 runs before the end of May. In the five-match Ashes series, he scored 974, 69 more than the record set by Hammond eighteen months earlier: 254 at Lord's, 338 at Leeds, 232 at the Oval. At Leeds, he made 309 in a day; a modern Test batsman does well to score a century in that time. Cardus insisted that essentially this was a triumph for cricketing orthodoxy: 'He is a purist in a hurry: he administers the orthodox in loud and apostolic knocks.'

Hammond was displaced completely as the world's batting champion, and there are those who argue that he never recovered as a cricketer or as a man. There have been moments when other cricketers – Denis Compton in 1947, Brian Lara in 1995 – have been almost as dominating, and perhaps even more exciting. But for Bradman, this was just the beginning.

He returned to Australia a hero, and progressed east from Fremantle by train to be greeted rapturously at every railway halt along the Nullarbor Plain. His team-mates, meanwhile, were making the transcontinental journey by sea, and growing ever more jealous. Though Bradman was assiduous at giving credit where it was due, the classic cricket team dichotomy between the individual hero and the collective was now in place. Inevitably also, skirmishing began with the Australian cricketing authorities, who fined him £50 for writing a book about the tour.

These battle lines remained in place throughout the 1930s, and in 1931 he came close to accepting an offer to play Lancashire League cricket for Accrington. There was insufficient money in cricket to provide the income his celebrity demanded, and a hasty sponsorship deal had to be cobbled together. The wicket was made slightly higher and wider in 1930–1; still Bradman scored prodigiously with further double centuries against the West Indies and South Africa. Some in England thought they had spotted a weakness in him against top-class wrist-spin. But as England came to Australia in 1932–3, their new captain, Douglas Jardine, had other plans.

Thus began the most notorious Test series of all time, in which England regained the Ashes by unleashing their fast bowlers to bowl bouncers at the Australians, with a field (now illegal) concentrated behind the stumps on the leg-side; this meant the batsmen had no alternative but to fend the ball to the fieldsmen, or get hurt. Imperialist arrogance, and poor reporting of the tour, ensured that the English establishment and public were slow to realize the sheer degeneracy of this strategy. The initial reaction was that the Australians were whingeing, and that a way had been found to beat them again and blunt Bradman at last. Even in these circumstances, he averaged nearly 57.

When bodyline was repudiated, and normality restored, Bradman resumed his untroubled progress. He was a fraction less domineering in the remaining three Ashes series of the decade, but only a fraction. In 1934 he scored another triple-century in the Leeds Test; in 1936–7 he led Australia back from 2–0 down with triumphant performances in the last three matches; in 1938, as captain, he again scored 1,000 runs in May, and averaged more than 100 throughout.

It should have been the happiest, as well as the most triumphant decade any sportsman has ever had. It was never quite like that. After the 1934 tour, Bradman was taken ill with acute appendicitis and peritonitis; he missed the 1934–5 season while recuperating. He moved from New South Wales to South Australia to accept an offer from a cricket-loving stockbroker (later jailed for fraud), which left some ill-feeling. Even the travelling got to him; he was seasick and later airsick.

And the tensions within the Australian team worsened. Bradman, a per-nickety, near-teetotal Protestant (religion mattered in 1930s Australia) with a Calvinist work ethic, was not a natural soulmate of the witty, happy-go-lucky, left-leaning Roman Catholics like O'Reilly and Fingleton, both of them later journalists with a waspish turn of phrase, often used against Bradman. 'Fingleton,' Bradman complained later, 'conducted a vendetta against me all his life.'

Moreover, though his marriage to Jessie was a triumph – and was to remain so for sixty-five years until her death in 1997 – the Bradmans' eldest son was to live for only a few hours; their daughter, Shirley, developed cerebral palsy; and their surviving son, John, had polio as a child. He pulled through, but was often estranged from his father later. Son and daughter survive their father.

The whispering increased after 1939, when cricket became less relevant. While other Australians had daredevil wars, Bradman – bizarrely enough – was declared to have defective eyesight, and spent the time in Adelaide. He was apparently often unwell, and there was some doubt that he would ever return to play for Australia in the hastily arranged series of 1946–7. He did appear, though, and carried on where he left off, striding to 187 in the first postwar Test, more than England made in either innings, but only after refusing to walk for what England were certain was a perfectly fair slip catch by Jack Ikin when he had 28. In the next game, he scored 234. And so on. In 1948, pushing forty, he came back to England for his farewell tour.

By now he seemed a mellower figure, willing to return the adulation of the crowds. His enemies in the dressing room had retired; the newer generation were less inclined to question his deification; and when cricketing mortality finally seized him at the Oval, it was possible to see it in very human terms. John Arlott was commentating. 'I wonder if you see a ball very clearly on your last Test in England, on a ground where you've played out some of the biggest cricket of your life, and when the opposing team has just stood around you and given you three cheers, and the crowd had clapped you all around the wicket … I wonder if you really see the ball at all.' But, came the cynical riposte: if Bradman had a tear in his eye, it was for the first time.

He was knighted in 1949, then slipped easily into the role of cricketing elder statesman. He gave up stockbroking and became a selector and administrator, dealing firmly with the throwing crisis that convulsed the game at the end of the 1950s. He played golf, off scratch (of course), remaining rooted all the time to his marriage and suburban home in Adelaide.

With elaborate courtesy, Bradman replied personally to all his correspondents into his nineties. But the answer was nearly always 'No' if it was a request for an interview. He spoke about bodyline in 1983, the fiftieth anniversary. After that came near-total silence. Eventually, he stopped going to the Adelaide Oval and became reclusive, indeed a bit of a curmudgeon, boycotting the celebrations laid on for his own ninetieth birthday. However, when a Wisden panel in 2000 voted him the cricketer of the century, with 100 votes out of 100, he issued a statement of delight. His reputation as a cricketer has never been questioned; as a man, he remains enigmatic. Though his fame extended only to the cricketing countries, within its limits it far exceeded the transient public obsessiveness with a Gascoigne or a Beckham and, in his own buttoned-up way, Bradman found it desperately hard to cope.

'You can't tell youngsters today of the attraction of the fellow,' said one of his opponents, the England bowler Bill Bowes, in 1983. 'I mean, business used to stop in the town when Bradman was playing and likely to go in – all the offices closed, the shops closed; everybody went up to see him play.' 'Our Don Bradman' was a song of the 1930s. But he was always his Don Bradman.

DONALD GEORGE BRADMAN · *born* 27 August 1908 ·
died 25 February 2001 ·

EMIL ZATOPEK
Nick Mason

Emil Zatopek, who has died aged seventy-eight, was one of the outstanding athletes of the twentieth century. In the years following the Second World War, he lifted distance running to a new plane, dominating the discipline to a degree achieved only by Paavo Nurmi before him, while at the same time enjoying the awe, respect and affection of his opponents and a popular acclaim that has rarely been matched.

From the week he won his first Olympic title in London in 1948 until his last major race in Melbourne in 1956, he was the most instantly recognizable figure in world sport, sending the back-page colour writers deep into their simile banks as they struggled to describe his tortured running style. He ran 'like a man who had been stabbed in the heart', 'as if his next step would be his last', 'like a man wrestling with an octopus on a conveyor belt'. Yet when the races were won and the head stopped rolling, a very different Zatopek emerged – a relaxed, gregarious figure with a captivating boyish smile, an aptitude for languages and an infectious enthusiasm for his sport. And he sealed his place in history over eight unforgettable days at the Helsinki Olympic Games of 1952, when he achieved the unprecedented (and since unequalled) feat of winning gold medals in all three classic tests of endurance running – the 5,000 metres, the 10,000 metres and the marathon.

Zatopek was born in Koprivnice, in Moravia, the son of a Czech carpenter who had little interest in the boy's passion for running. Away from home, too, the occupying Nazi authorities positively discouraged organized sport; but running tracks were not closed, and in the early 1940s in the town of Zlin, where he worked in the Bata shoe factory, the young Zatopek began to progress slowly in the 1,500 metres.

Soon after the end of the war, by now drafted into the Czechoslovak army, he watched the great Swedish miler Arne Andersson compete in an invitation race in Prague. Andersson's physical condition, and an insight into the Swede's heavy background training, revolutionized Zatopek's own running. He had already trained long; now he trained hard. He stretched his body and stamina to the limits: on sentry duty he might spend an hour running on the spot, knees high, shoulders straight; in winter, when saner athletes gratefully took time off from training, he would put on heavy baseball shoes, or even army boots, and run through the snow-covered forests, sometimes bounding in long, looping strides for two or three minutes at a stretch.

It was a self-taught and self-imposed regime, which took no account of the niceties of style. But the hours of relentless self-punishment gave him the capacity for sustained speed and the priceless bonus of a reserve tank of energy that would eventually allow him to run flat out for a lap, even at the end of a long, draining race.

In 1946 he was selected for the 5,000 metres in the European championships in Oslo, an unspectacular but promising debut on the big stage, which saw him take fifth place behind another runner with a celebrated storming finish, Britain's Sydney Wooderson.

Two years later, in the build-up to the London Olympic Games of 1948, Zatopek's capacity for consistent, high-speed lapping had brought him noteworthy times in a number of invitation races, but the first track final of the Games, the 10,000 metres, was considered the bailiwick of the Finns (they had won five of the last six Olympic finals), and in particular of Viljo Heino, the current world record holder.

No one, certainly not Heino, had been prepared for Zatopek. He took over the lead from the Finn in the tenth of the twenty-five laps, and five circuits later unleashed a spurt that took him ten metres clear. Heino simply ground to a halt. Zatopek ran on, unchallenged, as if the devil were at his heels, shoulders hunched, head rolling, face contorted in apparent agony, to the insistent chant of 'Zat-o-pek, Zat-o-pek, Zat-o-pek' from his compatriots in the crowd, and won by three-quarters of a lap. It was the first track-and-field gold medal ever won by Czechoslovakia.

Next day he ran the 5,000 metres heats, and lined up for the final two days after that. For ten laps of the race, through one of London's midsummer downpours, he shared the lead with the Belgian Gaston Reiff and the Dutchman Willem Slijkhuis. Then, either the fatigue finally hit him or he simply lost concentration; he fell hopelessly off the pace and Reiff accelerated for home. On the penultimate bend Reiff was leading by a good twenty metres from Slijkhuis, with Zatopek a further twenty-five metres back, splashing doggedly through the puddles in Wembley's red cinder track, apparently without a chance. Suddenly he seemed to wake up, and began a frantic last-ditch sprint. Within 150 metres he had gobbled up Slijkhuis, and in the final straight he closed on Reiff, who was alerted to the danger only when the crowd's roar became hysterical. Reiff lunged desperately for the tape and won by a couple of feet; if the race had been ten metres longer, Zatopek would have beaten him.

Czechoslovakia had found a national hero, and life could hardly have been better. A few weeks after the Games he married the national javelin champion Dana Ingrova (who, by the most bizarre of coincidences, had been born on the same day as he had) – a stable and happy partnership, which visibly sustained both of them in the public years as sporting celebrities, and by all accounts made life a lot more tolerable when, in later life, they fell foul of the Czechoslovak political system. She survives him: they had no children.

For the next three years Zatopek was the undisputed master. From 1949 to 1951 he competed in sixty-nine long-distance races (a schedule that would be simply unthinkable for any elite runner today) and won every one of them. From his first race at 10,000 metres in 1948 to his thirty-eighth in 1954, he was unbeaten at the distance. He won the European 10,000 metres championship in Brussels in 1950 by a full lap, and the 5,000 metres by twenty-three seconds. He broke eighteen world records at distances from 5,000 metres to thirty kilometres, and in 1951 he became the first man to run twenty kilometres in under an hour. He was, in short, a phenomenon.

Expectations for success at Helsinki in 1952 were naturally high, but the pressures on him mounted as the Games approached. He had run with a virus at a minor domestic meeting six weeks earlier, and became ill; he recovered, but the slow times in his build-up races were worrying. He also had his first serious brush with the communist authorities in Prague, when a young 1,500 metres runner, Stanislav Jungwirth, was dropped from the Czech Olympic team because his father had been jailed for political offences; Zatopek even threatened to pull out of the Games himself unless Jungwirth were reinstated, and the brinkmanship was successful, though hardly an aid to concentration.

Then there were reports, which he refused to confirm, that he might be persuaded to run the marathon rather than – or, conceivably, as well as – the 5,000 metres. Furthermore, he was in Finland, the land of Kolehmainen and Nurmi, where for the last forty years distance running had been meat, drink, mother's milk and a second religion; every step he took would be under the scrutiny of the most knowledgeable athletics audience in the world.

On the first Sunday he took the 10,000 metres gold medal more or less as he pleased, shaking off his opponents one by one with his unwavering pace to win by the length of the straight. On the Tuesday he was visibly relaxed, and came close to clowning his way through the 5,000 metres heats, dropping back down the field, cajoling and pacing lesser runners to qualification once the stragglers had been dropped. Two days later the Olympic stadium was full to bursting, with more than 66,000 spectators for the most eagerly awaited single event of the Games, the 5,000 metres final. The pace was fast, and no one had the courage to make a decisive break until, well into the final lap, Zatopek accelerated into the lead. In any race during the previous four years, that would have been decisive: if Zatopek led in the final lap, Zatopek won the race. But after a few strides in front he experienced something that had never happened to him in his career before, and which would have devastated a lesser spirit: with 300 metres to go, three men charged past him; the red-headed Christopher Chataway of Great Britain; the bespectacled Herbert Schade of Germany, who had been widely tipped to win the race, and the French-Algerian Alain Mimoun, who had followed Zatopek home in the 10,000 metres. Zatopek was left floundering in fourth place, seemingly out-paced and out of the medals. On the final bend, Chataway – who was to fall a few strides later – began to tire, Schade moved up to his shoulder, Mimoun pulled out to take them both on the outside ... and Zatopek pounced. With 150 metres to go, there were four men abreast on the crown of the bend, and the one in the red vest way out in lane two, his head rolling in agony, was going fastest of all; from that moment there was no question as to who was going to win.

Dana clinched the day's second gold medal for the family by throwing an Olympic record in the first round of the javelin to beat a powerful Russian trio into second, third and fourth places, and Emil, joking that a 2–1 score in the family gold count was too close for comfort, confirmed that he would indeed run in the marathon – the first of his life – the following Sunday.

The story of the Helsinki marathon has entered legend: how Zatopek intro-duced himself to the favourite, Jim Peters of Great Britain, at the start, and ran with him for the first hour; how – in a genuine search for information rather than a masterly piece of gamesmanship – he asked Peters if the pace was quick enough and, somewhat to his surprise, received the answer 'No, too slow'; and how he left Peters and all the other leaders behind him and drew steadily away. As he entered the stadium a full two and a half minutes clear of the field, the expectant buzz exploded into a single welcoming roar, and wave upon wave of cheering rang out across the Helsinki rooftops as he completed the last 300 metres to win his third gold medal in eight momentous days.

His career did not end in Helsinki; two years later he regained his European 10,000 metres title in Berne, but in the 5,000 metres he was beaten into third place by an even more hard-bitten, more relentless and infinitely less appealing competitor, the Ukrainian Vladimir Kuts, who was to assume Zatopek's mantle and win both long-distance track events for the Soviet Union at the Melbourne Games in 1956. Zatopek was at Melbourne to defend his marathon title, but he was hardly in the best shape to tackle it: one of his more outlandish training sessions, which involved running while carrying Dana on his shoulders, had resulted in a bad strain that had only just cleared up in time. He was never seriously in medal contention, but he trotted home in sixth place without seeming unduly bothered, only to break out in smiles and handshakes and hugs of congratulation when he realized that the winner was Alain Mimoun, the old adversary he had beaten in so many championships in the past.

He retired a national icon and a natural sporting ambassador for Czechoslovakia. He rose steadily to the rank of colonel in the Czech army, gave unstinting advice during coaching visits abroad, and unostentatiously enjoyed the resulting privileges at home, until 1968 and the Prague Spring, when he publicly welcomed the shift towards democracy promised by the Dubček regime, and roundly condemned the Soviet response as troops moved into Prague to re-establish communist control. He was expelled from the Communist party and dismissed from the army. He was consigned to a series of manual jobs for various state departments until, after seven years of this ritual humiliation, he was given a desk at the Ministry of Sport, employing his language skills to monitor and translate sports periodicals from the West.

Occasionally he was put on display at official receptions for visiting teams, when he would be seized upon by foreign journalists more eager just to shake his hand than to record the guarded answers he was obliged to give them. And towards the end of the 1980s, with the ice beginning to thaw and Zatopek long retired from the ministry, he would once in a while receive grudging permission to accept an invitation to an athletics event abroad. Invariably he would find himself at the centre of a crowd of foreigners who knew the face only from old newspapers or grainy archive film, but who had fallen under the spell of the legend; they would flock around him in unashamed awe, proffering scraps of paper for his autograph, hardly daring to offer a handshake in case it might be refused. It never was.

Zatopek's achievements in athletics are indelible, but bare statistics cannot reflect the genuine affection in which he was held by his fellow competitors, men with whom he chatted and joked as he ran them into the ground, men with whom he would willingly and honestly discuss race tactics even if he were due to run against them the next day, men whose insecurities and disappointments he could sympathize with and understand.

Late in 1968, another high-achieving record-breaker, the Australian Ron Clarke, left the Mexico City Olympic Games in deepest gloom: he had been the fastest long-distance runner in the world for a decade, yet in two Olympic Games fate, ill-judgement, altitude, or sheer bad luck had conspired against him, and his career was slipping away without a single gold medal to show for it. On his way home he stopped off in Prague to chat things over with his boyhood idol and long-time friend.

As they parted Zatopek gave the Australian a small parcel, and not wishing to embarrass his host, Clarke did not unwrap it until he was on the plane. It was one of Zatopek's Olympic gold medals, a gift from an athlete who had gloriously won four of them to a fellow athlete he just felt deserved one.

EMIL ZATOPEK · *born* 19 September 1922 · *died* 21 November 2000 ·

THE WRITERS

■ ■ ■

SAMUEL BECKETT
John Montague

Beckett is dead, a consummation he long claimed to seek. 'I have no bone to pick with graveyards' is one of the best of his bitter-sweet comments on the whole business. The world mourns the loss of a great writer, for whom recognition was almost a burden, and those of us who knew him will also miss a courteous, punctilious, faintly lunatic friend; a soft touch for a sob story or a permanent loan.

I floated quite naturally into his company in the early 1960s when we became Montparnasse neighbours. A. J. ('Con') Leventhal of Trinity was the catalyst, and if one was naturally wary of intruding on the great man, such caution was soon dissolved in cataracts of drink and good conversation.

We usually met about 10 p.m. in the Falstaff, an old watering hole of the 1920s still frequented by writers. Was that Sartre in the corner, or Ionesco? Probably, but after a friendly farmer's nod had been exchanged, we did not cross the lines, because that was the convention of our village. Sartre lodged with Simone de Beauvoir in the Rue Schoelcher around the corner, so everyone converged in the evening after the day's work to relax among friends. And relax Beckett usually did, the lined face suddenly crinkling with laughter, the seagull eyes sparkling. His bony reserve was daunting, but his beloved Con was a gentle subversive. Leventhal and I were discussing love in a leisurely fashion when Sartre saw a chance to shove in his oar. 'No love!' he said with satisfaction, 'only fuck.' Startled silence, as Beckett moves in again. 'Eat-drink-fuck, that's all!' he declared, unconsciously echoing Eliot. How a shocked Con recovered to discomfit Beckett is a longer story; but he succeeded because he knew his friend.

Friendship clearly meant a great deal to Beckett, and he was fiercely loyal; widows of his friends in particular can testify to his care and generosity. Although he was of the select company of those who, echoing Sophocles, would prefer not to have been born, he would do everything he could to ease a friend's suffering. Contemplating the cheerful grimness of his work and days, I once asked him if he had ever thought of ending it. 'Out of the question,' he said brusquely, 'but I have thought about disappearance.' His best plan, he elaborated, was a boat with a hole in the bottom, to be dredged up by the divers. Then a sigh. 'That's legally impossible too. The widow wouldn't inherit for seven years.' He lived without the protective outer skin of custom, and saw naked pain and suffering everywhere.

Chased out of a publishing party by a belligerent young Irish novelist, he first disappeared under the table, emerging at the other end to plead on his hands and knees for a kiss from a pretty young woman. In a taxi afterwards, he mutely pointed to the signs of various charities adorning the inside of the car: 'Help the blind', 'Save the starving', 'Mercy for the mutilated'; they seemed to sing an answer to his call. Over a cup of coffee, he confided: 'I see it everywhere. The human spirit is on its knees. Everything is on fire.' For him, only a few artists – the weeping canvases of Bram Van Velde, the ferocity of Celine's novels – were equal to the Goya-like darkness of our crematorium century.

Ireland was a sore subject, to be carefully handled: he had recognized Joyce's reservations and, though a firm Beckett family man and devoted to nephew or niece, he had no great desire to return. While he could speak with extraordinary fondness of the landscape, the land itself, and would praise books like Synge's *Wicklow Travels*, he suspected the inhabitants and their attitude towards art. The famous misquotation about our being driven into writing because we were caught between the English and the Church, was only partly right: we had also ruined ourselves. I had an early book savaged by an older Irish poet, and Beckett was relentless: 'Don't answer, they're not worth it.' He did not like bad manners, literary or otherwise, and regarded them as endemic to the great Hibernian bog.

Withal, he seemed to me deeply Irish, with his control masking volatile swings of mood from unshakable gloom about the human condition through ferocity at any surrender to lower standards; and underlying all, the quick redeeming flash of humour, the sudden surge of generosity.

We never mentioned Deirdre Bair's biography, not even my long, repentant review of it in the *Guardian*, but when I teased him about the confusions about his birthday, he still stuck to Good Friday, 13 April 1906, despite the birth certificate recording 13 May. 'I have it from a good source,' he said. 'Not the Dublin City Records,' I replied. 'A far better source,' he grinned, 'someone at the heart of the problem.' Then with one flat Dublin phrase, he swept my friendly prodding away: 'The mother!' His look dared me to contradict that authority.

I watched once as a crafty journalist, seeking his confidence, lightly mentioned that he had played rugby with Ollie Campbell. Beckett's eyes lit up, and all the weary embarrassment vanished. 'Do you really know Campbell?' he said excitedly. 'What's he like?' My cunning confrère confided that no more modest humble man ever pulled on rugby boot. 'He's a genius!' cried Beckett. 'But you're not supposed to have a television,' I reminded Sam. 'You're supposed to be against all that.' 'Only for the games,' was his furtive apology, 'and only when the Irish play.'

But the journalist had the hook in, and soon Sam was discussing with him a rugby team of Irish writers. Spoilers like O'Flaherty were easy to place, but the half-blind Joyce was a problem, and Beckett would not relegate his old master to the bench. 'Very crafty, very nippy, try him at fly-half. He might surprise you when the light is fading.'

When I moved back to Ireland, a decision about which he was mildly apprehensive, our meetings became rarer. In any case, his retreat for such occasions to the ultra-modern hotel opposite his flat was a sign not only of his advancing age but also of general change. We rarely discussed writing, except when some technical problem was involved, but he was complimentary when I needed support. Once when I lamented the fact that Irish literature seemed to have gone backwards and that there were no longer any links between French and English literature as in the great days of the Modern Movement, I was so eloquently gloomy that I finally let my head hang, declaring: 'There's no point in going on.' There was a sigh and a stir above me until I looked up into his concerned gaze: 'But John, you must go on.'

People sometimes wondered if Beckett's retiring modesty was genuine, considering his professional exactitude. In our second-to-last conversation, after we had moved away from that monstrous hotel to a little worker's café, he became his old relaxed self. 'What are you writing now, Sam?' 'Senilities,' he said with pleasant sharpness. 'But I'll manage something yet. Did you have that terrible choice at school between science and the Greeks? I wish I had read Sophocles…'

A phrase from our differing backgrounds intrigued him suddenly. 'John, what do you mean by a spoiled priest?' I explained, and there was a wry pause. 'Well, I suppose that I'm a spoiled hermit,' he said reflectively. 'My father was always worried about me and wanted me to do a Guinness Clerkship. I'd be retired by now.' 'And unknown,' I said. 'Ah yes,' he said with a genuine sigh. 'Never heard of.' He sounded as if he meant it.

Samuel Beckett died on 22 December and was buried yesterday in a secret ceremony at the Montparnasse Cemetery. The son of a surveyor, he was brought up in Dublin as a Protestant, and studied modern languages at Trinity College, Dublin. He first came to Paris in 1928 to lecture in English at the

Ecole Normale Superieure. After his father William Frances Beckett died in Dublin in 1933, his mother tried to persuade Beckett to curtail his literary ambitions. In 1937 he escaped his middle-class family and settled in Paris.

He married Suzanne Deschevaux-Dumesnil, six years his elder, in secret in 1961. She died in Paris on 17 July at the age of eighty-nine. They had no children.

SAMUEL BECKETT · *born* 13 April 1906 · *died* 22 December 1989 ·

17 July 1995

STEPHEN SPENDER
Frank Kermode

Stephen Spender, who has died aged eighty-six, achieved his first celebrity as a young man, and remained for some sixty years one of the most famous names in twentieth-century literature. His international fame may have owed something to his impressive appearance and his appetite for travel – abroad he was probably best known as a lecturer – but it was founded on his achievements as a man of letters in the old sense, prolific in almost every literary form: novelist, playwright, essayist, political commentator, editor, translator, literary critic, memoirist, occasionally a professor, and, always in his own mind, a poet before anything else.

Spender was born in London, the son of the Liberal journalist E. H. Spender. He was educated at University College School and University College, Oxford. At Oxford he began a friendship with W. H. Auden which lasted until Auden's death in 1973. It was founded on a true appreciation of Auden's qualities, and called for a degree of tolerance that only profound friendship and a dedication to genius could have maintained. When little more than a boy he printed Auden's first collection of poems and was thereafter always his champion. Their relationship changed, and Spender was not always to play his Oxford role as the gauche disciple. Auden might on occasion resume the role of guru to naive postulant, but he found in Spender much that he needed, including kindness, fun and common sense.

It was at Oxford that Spender came to know Louis MacNeice and, through Auden, Christopher Isherwood and Edward Upward. In the 1930s all felt compelled to take politics seriously, but Spender's reaction to communism and the world crisis was different from and probably better informed than those of the others. MacNeice was the coolest of them, the readiest to confess that he regretted the loss of class privilege that seemed imminent. The imaginations of Upward and Auden were strongly imbued by a private mythology; but Upward alone was to become, and remain, a committed communist.

Spender lacked MacNeice's resigned elegance, and had little taste for 'Mortmere' fantasies as described by Isherwood in *Lions and Shadows*. His feeling for politics was surer and more genuine than theirs; his copious writings on the subject, and on the relation of artists to politics, remain the most considered and the most serious of any by the young writers of the period.

He was briefly a member of the Communist party and wrote on behalf of the Spanish Republican cause, but his defection from communism – described both in his autobiography, *World Within World* (1951), and in his contribution to the celebrated mass palinode *The God That Failed* (1949) – was far from frivolous or unconsidered. He had taken communism as a call upon his bourgeois conscience, but in the end the demands of the party came to seem conscienceless. Certainly, they meant telling lies, and telling lies was a disagreeable duty to any artist – certainly to Auden, who came to deplore his poem about Spain as a lie, and even to Upward, who was to leave the party on the ground that it had broken faith with true Marxist-Leninism. When Auden told Spender that 'Exigence is never an excuse for not telling the truth,' he was preaching to the converted.

His play *Trial of a Judge* may have been meant to demonstrate the conflict between communist truth and fascist lies but, as MacNeice remarked, it was really about abstract justice – not a communist theme. Spender came to recognize it as a failure but he also thought of it as having a place of peculiar importance in his work; in his later years he worked hard at revising it, trying to get at the truth it contained; but his final version has not been published. Like Rex Warner's novel *The Professor*, also published in 1938, Spender's play is a clear expression of the problems afflicting the rentier conscience in those days of war and the threat of war.

When the war came, Spender joined Cyril Connolly in editing *Horizon*, a periodical notable more for liveliness and variety than for responsible political commitment. He then, like Henry Green, became a London fireman; this unusual extra-curricular experience is described in his autobiography. Having been ridiculed by Orwell as a pink poet, he was now ridiculed by Evelyn Waugh as a fireman poet. He was quite used to a certain amount of literary teasing; but some of the poems which were favourite targets were meanwhile becoming famous anthology pieces.

That so many stories were told against him – not least by himself – was testimony to his fame and also to the security of his sense of himself as writer and poet. It is worth remembering that his wholehearted admiration for the seductive voice of Auden never prevented him from developing his own poetic voice, which was in quite a different register, and although he was saddened when it seemed that his juniors sometimes undervalued his verse it would never have occurred to him to cultivate a manner more acceptable to current fashion.

He was a persistent and austere reviser of his own work; indeed his latest *Collected Poems* probably leaves out too much, but some of its changes are certainly evidence of a continuing self-critical power. Spender omitted from that collection some poems from *Ruins and Visions*, one of his finest books, which contained a series of beautiful meditations on the breakdown of his first marriage.

Before the war he had come to know Europe well, especially Weimar Germany, and Spain left a deep impression on him. In the postwar years he travelled more extensively – to India and China as well as Europe and the United States – and wrote a great many books, notably *The Struggle of the Modern* (1963), *Love–Hate Relations*, about England and America, and a book with David Hockney about China. He was co-editor of *Encounter* from its foundation in 1953 until 1967, when he severed connection because of the revelation that the journal had been funded through 'front' foundations by the CIA. The story of his relations with his co-editors, and with the Congress for Cultural Freedom, will be a large knot for his biographer to unravel. More recently he had been associated with *Index on Censorship*, a journal devoted to the struggle for intellectual freedom. His *Journals 1939–1983* – an ample selection from records even more interesting and ample – give an account of his interests, friendships and travels over these years. In the same year (1985) were published the *Collected Poems* and the abbreviated translation of Sophocles' *The Oedipus Trilogy*; earlier in life he had made many effective translations from Schiller, Rilke, Lorca and others.

Spender's second marriage was with the pianist Natasha Litvin; they had two children, Matthew and Lizzie. His friendships were extraordinary in number and variety – they included poets and painters and musicians, dancers and actors, politicians and dons, journalists and clubmen. Though delightfully clubbable, and a superb companion at lunch, he was never in danger of surrendering to the temptation of idle afternoons. An editor of vast and various experience, he never fell into routine or into corruption; though famous for his vagueness he was scrupulous about deadlines; as a friend he never forgot a favour and never forgot to confer one if it was in his power. He was an absolutely distinctive figure, distracted yet accurate, funny yet serious. He was for so long – and without willing it – the unofficial ambassador of English letters, that to nominate a successor seems simply out of the question. To the poetry he valued above all his other achievements time will attend. His charm, civility and wit we shall remember with warm affection in our own time.

STEPHEN HAROLD SPENDER · *born* 28 February 1909 · *died* 16 July 1995 ·

4 August 1997

WILLIAM S. BURROUGHS
James Campbell

William S. Burroughs, who has died aged eighty-three, was the hard man of Hip. His aims as a writer were traditional, to entertain and instruct, but the means he chose to express them were unclassifiable, sometimes indescribable, occasionally unspeakable.

Some of Burroughs's books, his first, *Junkie*, and *Cities of the Red Night*, are recognizable as novels in the ordinary sense; but his most original work came in the form of what he called 'routines': short, surreal sketches which sometimes include real characters, but more often involve the products of Burroughs's weird imagination, such as Spare Ass Annie (who 'had an auxiliary asshole in the middle of her forehead') or the Lobotomy Kid.

All his energy went into a battle with the agents of 'control' – call it 'police' in every form, including the thought police – and his strategies ranged from drugs to the notorious cut-up technique. Norman Mailer said of Burroughs that he was 'the only American writer who may conceivably be possessed by genius', but the compliment which he treasured above all others was an austere remark of Samuel Beckett's: 'He's a writer.'

Burroughs was born in St Louis, Missouri, into a family that was well off but, as he repeatedly insisted, 'not rich'. His grandfather, after whom he was named, invented the adding machine, but the family had lost its connections to the company by the time of the Depression. None the less, Burroughs senior was sufficiently comfortable to allow his wayward son a monthly stipend of $200 from 1938 onwards.

Burroughs read English at Harvard but his real studies began when he reached New York in the early 1940s and met the young men who would later be grouped as the Beat Generation: Jack Kerouac, Allen Ginsberg and Neal Cassady. Other members of this circle were David Kammerer and Lucien Carr, old friends from St Louis. Kammerer was stabbed to death by Carr in 1944, and Burroughs, as the first person to whom Carr turned, was held as a material witness to the crime – neither his first nor last encounter with the law. Another close friend of those days was Herbert Huncke, an old-time crook who later became a writer, under Burroughs's influence. From Huncke's circles Burroughs learned the art of rolling drunks and picking pockets in the New York subway.

Burroughs was extremely sober in manner and appearance; his dress typically consisted of a grey three-piece suit, tie and fedora hat. 'His whole person seemed at a glance completely anonymous,' he wrote about himself. 'Sometimes his face looked blurred...' When Huncke first met him, he mistook Burroughs for an FBI agent, but was soon turning him on to hard drugs. As reported by Huncke, Burroughs's response to his first shot of morphine was, 'That's very interesting ... that's very interesting indeed.'

In the late 1940s, he tried his hand at farming in Texas and Louisiana, growing tomatoes as a useful cover for his marijuana and opium crops. By this time he had met Joan Vollmer who, though he was homosexual and she was not, became 'Mrs Burroughs' (they were never formally married). Burroughs had previously wed a German Jewish woman, Ilse Klapper, in Europe, so that she could emigrate to the US and escape the Nazis. They divorced amicably some years later.

The bond with Joan was close, but troubled. From her he received a sympathetic understanding probably never reproduced in a relationship with a man. She was a highly intelligent, attractive woman, brought low by a dependence on Benzedrine and drink. She had a daughter by a previous marriage and a son with Burroughs, William Burroughs III, also a writer, who died in 1981. Joan's life ended on a September afternoon in Mexico City in 1951. The couple had joined a drunken party in a flat above a bar. Burroughs was carrying a gun, and at some point said to Joan: 'It's time for our William Tell act. Put that glass on your head.' She did, and Burroughs fired an inch too low, killing her. He was bailed after a week in jail and when his Mexican lawyer skipped the country, having killed someone himself, Burroughs followed.

He was never tried for the shooting but, according to his biographer Ted Morgan, entered 'a nightmare that he would live for the rest of his days'. Ostensibly, Joan's death was an accident, but Burroughs was harried by the dreadful thought that, subconsciously, he had meant to kill her. In the introduction to the novel *Queer*, written in the 1950s but not published until 1985, he wrote with candour about his feelings:

> I am forced to the appalling conclusion that I would never have become a writer but for Joan's death, and to a realization of the extent to which this event has motivated and formulated my writing ... The death of Joan brought me in contact with the invader, the Ugly Spirit, and manoeuvred me into a lifelong struggle, in which I had no choice except to write my way out.

Burroughs began writing much later than Kerouac and Ginsberg. He was thirty-nine when his autobiographical account of being a drug addict in New York and New Orleans, *Junkie*, was published in 1953 under the pseudonym 'William Lee' (a name he retained when referring to himself in his later work). *Junkie* is written in a straightforward prose reminiscent of Dashiell Hammett. Its first edition counts as one of the great curios of modern literature. Aimed at the popular markets, the book came out back to back with another, *Narcotic Agent*, whose moral tone the publisher hoped would offset the scandalous *Junkie*. The law took no notice and neither did the reviewers, but it sold more than 100,000 copies. (It was later retitled *Junky*.)

After two expeditions into the jungles of South America in search of the vegetable drug Yage, which he had heard bestowed telepathic powers on the user (it didn't), Burroughs moved to Tangier, intending to stay only a few weeks but remaining for several years. Drugs and sex were cheap. Burroughs met Paul Bowles and Brion Gysin, with whom he would later form an uncompromising avant-garde partnership in Paris.

Skulking through the back alleys of Tangier, seeking a connection, Burroughs became known to locals as 'el hombre invisible'. His most famous book, *The Naked Lunch*, was written there, fuelled by heroin and kif; but anyone who believes Burroughs glamorized drugs should be persuaded otherwise by reading the introductory 'Testimony concerning a sickness': 'I had not taken a bath in a year nor changed my clothes or removed them except to stick a needle every hour in the fibrous grey wooden flesh of heroin addiction ... I did absolutely nothing. I could look at the end of my shoe for eight hours.'

Burroughs told Kerouac that the writing he was doing in Tangier – apocalyptic, absurdly pornographic, comically violent – represented the act of 'shitting out my past'. Some of the routines are horribly funny, such as 'Displaced Fuzz', which features a pair of redundant policemen repossessing people's artificial kidneys. *The Naked Lunch* is something of a cooperative enterprise: many of the routines emerged from letters to Ginsberg; Kerouac supplied the title; the manuscript was typed by these two and other visiting Beats, while the order of chapters came about by random selection. For Burroughs, the extreme edge of art, as of life, was the only place to be. 'The only way I can write narrative is to get right outside my body and experience it,' he told Ginsberg. 'This can be exhausting and at times dangerous. One cannot be sure of redemption.'

Sections of the 'dangerous' book were published in the *Chicago Review* in 1958, leading to the suppression of the magazine by the university that sponsored it, and to a prosecution on the grounds of obscenity (the last major case of its type in the US). Meanwhile, the Olympia Press in Paris had published the entire novel. Olympia's rascally owner, Maurice Girodias, later admitted failing to pay Burroughs his royalties, but the author typically forgave him, pointing out that Girodias had published *The Naked Lunch* at a time when no other firm would touch it. The book was published in Britain in 1964 by John Calder. Shortly before that, a protracted correspondence took place in the *Times Literary Supplement*, following a review of the Olympia edition under the headline 'Ugh…' Calder and the critic Eric Mottram defended the novel, but they were outnumbered by the disgusted, including Dame Edith Sitwell: 'I do not wish to spend the rest of my life with my nose nailed to other people's lavatories. I prefer Chanel Number 5.'

By this time, Burroughs had moved even further out. He had discovered a new method of writing, which, he told Ginsberg imperiously, could not be explained 'until you have necessary training'. Gysin had stumbled on the cut-up technique while playing around with old newspapers and a pair of scissors in his room at the Hôtel Rachou in rue Git-le-couer in Paris, thereafter known as 'the Beat Hotel'. Burroughs, also a resident, extended the experiment, and soon the Olympia Press had published two cut-up novels, *The Soft Machine* (1961) and *The Ticket That Exploded* (1962). The trilogy was completed by *Nova Express* in 1964. As entertainment, the cut-ups are hard going, but seen in the context of Burroughs's obsessive desire to free his mind from 'control' – in this case, the control of 'word locks', or rigid conceptual structures governed by language – the experiments make more sense.

Burroughs was off hard drugs by then (though still using cannabis and hallucinogens). He had been trying to kick the habit since the late 1940s. With the help of Dr John Dent in London, who administered an apomorphine cure, Burroughs finally freed himself from the biggest control agent of the lot. New experiments included the use of a dream machine, invented by Gysin, and Scientology, which Burroughs discussed in a book-length interview with Daniel Odier, *The Job* (1970).

In the 1960s, Burroughs moved to London, where he lived in Duke Street, St James's. He contributed to publications as uncool as *Mayfair* and the hippy magazine *International Times*. He was prolific and generous.

Another drug addict and Beat, Alexander Trocchi, gave me a copy of a short unpublished piece by Burroughs *circa* 1972 and suggested I call the author and ask for permission to use it in a little magazine I edited in Glasgow. Burroughs agreed readily, without mention of payment. The only word he spoke was 'Yeah', which he drawled in response to everything I said.

He returned to the US in 1974, living first in New York, in 'the Bunker', a disused locker room without windows on the Bowery, and then, from 1982 on, in Lawrence, Kansas. The books continued to flow – *Cities of the Red Night, The Place of Dead Roads, My Education, Ghost of Chance* – mixing science fiction, the western, the travel book, the dream journal and other genres. His publisher, Grove Press, has just completed a manuscript of Burroughs's previously unpublished writings to be released in 1998.

Burroughs was also a painter, and his efforts in that medium are as idiosyncratic as in any other. He held several exhibitions of paintings on wood riddled with bullet holes ('shotgun art', he called it; he was also a member of the National Rifle Association). In 1996 a catalogue of his involvement with the visual arts was published, *Ports of Entry: William Burroughs and the Arts*.

In Lawrence he was looked after by his long-term secretary James Grauerholz and a team of assistants. There was no other woman in his life after Joan. Her death continued to haunt him, and in 1992, with Ginsberg present, he underwent an exorcism ceremony at the hands of a Sioux medicine man to evict the Ugly Spirit, which he believed had entered him at the time of Joan's death. His main affection in later life was reserved for his cats, and he published a small homage to his feline friends, *The Cat Inside*.

Like many artistic revolutionaries, Burroughs became an icon late in life. Among rock stars, it became fashionable to seek him out. David Bowie, Mick Jagger, Frank Zappa and Patti Smith all sang for their supper at the Burroughs table in the Bunker, and he became an honorary godfather to the New York wave of punk.

Less accessible than that of his Beat colleagues, the work of William Burroughs is likely to prove at least as enduring. He was modern man in extremis, an exemplar of alienation, constantly subverting his targets with satire. His extreme individualism never wavered. His first piece of writing, as a child, was called 'Autobiography of a Wolf'. When grown-ups pointed out that the correct word was 'biography', Burroughs replied: 'No, I meant "autobiography".' And, he told his own biographer seventy-five years later, 'I still do.'

WILLIAM SEWARD BURROUGHS II · *born* 5 February 1914 · *died* 2 August 1997 ·

15 May 1997

LAURIE LEE
John Ezard

April Rise

If ever I saw blessing in the air
I see it now in this still early day
Where lemon-green the vaporous morning drips
Wet sunlight on the powder of my eye.

Blown bubble-film of blue, the sky wraps round
Weeds of warm light whose every root and rod
Splutters with soapy green, and all the world
Sweats with the bead of summer in its bud.

If ever I heard blessing it is there
Where birds in trees that shoals and shadows are
Splash with their hidden wings and drops of sound
Break on my ears their crests of throbbing air.

Pure in the haze the emerald sun dilates,
The lips of sparrows milk the mossy stones,
While white as water by the lake a girl
Swims her green hand among the gathered swans.

Now, as the almond burns its smoking wick,
Dropping small flames to light the candled grass;
Now, as my low blood scales its second chance,
If ever world were blessed, now it is.

From *Laurie Lee: Selected Poems,* published by Penguin Books

One of the earliest memories of Laurie Lee was of a small boy sitting in the village street at Slad, Gloucestershire, surrounded by attentive old men. He was reading aloud news of the First World War. 'This boy and I were of one generation and we shared the same trick of enlightenment,' Lee wrote. 'We were both the inheritors, after centuries of darkness, of our country's first literate peasantry.'

It was a gift and a background to which Lee, who has died aged eighty-two, remained faithful while growing into one of the most treasured prose writers of his age. His return to Slad, after the success of *Cider with Rosie*, crowned a hungry Bohemian life in London and the Mediterranean, and made the village into a fabled place. It was extraordinary, as Philip Oakes wrote, 'rather like Dickens watching tourists invade the blacking factory or Hardy steering visitors around the D'Urberville acres'. In old age Lee would bump into tourists who had come to see his grave. But he trod humbly and did not allow his birthplace to be spoiled. He spent some of his last years, although he could feel death approaching, in a struggle to save one of its meadows from property developers.

The scope and form of his work was slender: the autobiographical sketches for which he is famous, early poems that are now little read, essays which at their old-fashioned worst verged on the *belle-lettres*. Yet he had a nightingale inside him, a capacity for sensuous, lyrical precision rare in writers ten times more grandiose. Although he claimed hardly to have read Dylan Thomas, the comparison was often made. Lee's prose imagery is more measured and much more relaxed; he created, through craft and intensive revision, the illusion that he could stroke language into life. One of his most compressed, often-quoted sentences is half a joke: 'Quiet incest flourished where roads were bad.' His work is inlaid with such phrases: 'I began my tale at the age of three, when I was no taller than grass' (of *Cider with Rosie*). 'Wild parsley sprouts head-high, garlic sprawls rank and oniony in the woods, orchids and fungi smoulder among sweating roots' (of the valley around Slad).

His stock-in-trade was a lost rural world and he was promoted as part of the nostalgia industry. But the six million readers who bought *Cider with Rosie* did so for reasons more personal than that. He managed to offer them his eyes, to transfer to them his own exactitude and intensity of seeing as a gift they could use after they had closed his books. No one ever faulted him in the integrity of that transaction, though he was a deliberate charmer and sometimes wrote glutinously.

Lee's mother, Nancy, was a coachman's daughter, his father, Reg, a sailor's son. Reg was a Stroud widower with four children when she became his housekeeper. Laurie, whose birth was never registered, was one of four further children they had. While he was a child, his father decamped, joined the Civil Service and formed a threesome with a couple in Morden, south London. Each week he sent his Slad family £1: 'Dear Nance, Herewith the usual. Yours Reg.'

The son was brought up by his mother and his elder sister Marjorie inside the warm, sometimes hungry family in the village of twenty to thirty half-hidden hovels, which he later memorialized, where 'everybody minded everybody else's business', where cows walked sideways along old Ice Age flood terraces.

His schoolteacher, the 'Old Crabby' of *Cider with Rosie*, jeered at his essays as high flown. He hit back by winning a competition with an essay on the dabchick, a bird he – wrongly – thought he had invented. From the village school he went to Stroud Central School, leaving at fourteen to be, briefly, an office boy. His father sent him £1 to buy a bow for an old violin he found. With it he formed a dance band when he was sixteen and toured Gloucestershire.

In 1934, at nineteen, he left Slad and walked to London. He stayed away twenty years. He worked as a builder's labourer, wrote poetry and joined the Communist party. In 1935 he took his violin on the first of two walking trips to Spain, finding it still a semi-feudal country where a youngster who played lively music could live on his wits, financially and sexually. He left with £2, was rescued by a Royal Navy destroyer when Malaga fell to Franco, and returned with £18. In 1936–7 he trustingly returned to a grimmer Spain; the lone stroller carrying only a violin, frying pan and poetry books was arrested twice as a suspected spy and shot a soldier dead while fighting for the Republic. Spain, after Slad, formed his sensibility and eventually generated two of his most praised books, *As I Walked Out One Midsummer Morning* (1969) and *A Moment of War* (1991).

During the war he got jobs with the GPO, Crown and Green Park film units and as publications editor for the Ministry of Information, making documentaries in Cyprus and India. His first book of poems, *The Sun My Monument*, came out in 1944; his final output totalled four volumes containing only sixty-seven poems. His last recorded employment was as Caption Writer-in-Chief and Curator of Eccentricities for the 1950–1 Festival of Britain. He detested working for others.

Through the 1950s he was a small, affable, hard-up figure in the Fitzrovia of the Chelsea Arts Club and the Soho Colony Rooms. The columnist Jeffrey Bernard used to say that you could date events in that decade by trying to remember whether they were before or after 'the last time Laurie Lee wrote a drink'. He turned to prose after becoming convinced he had lost the passion needed for poetry. *Cider with Rosie* – which he once summarized in the words, 'There's nothing more glorious than tickling a girl under a haystack when you're not taking love that seriously' – took four years to write. It brought instant hosannas, led by the *Observer*'s fastidious chief critic Harold Nicolson, a Bloomsbury veteran, who spoke of its 'rapturous beauty' and declared it a first-rate work of art.

Lee said at first, 'The only difference it has made to me is that there is more whisky in the house.' But the breadth of his readership is indicated by the Freedom of the City of London he received in 1982, an exceptional award for a writer. His subsequent books, all written slowly with the same scrupulously revising disregard for publishers' pressures, include *A Late Fall* – about Jessy's birth – and a collection of essays, *I Can't Stay Long* (1975).

In his long old age, back in Slad, he was a contented, immensely approachable figure, who to interviewers talked almost as beautifully and sensibly as he wrote. In conversation, he was sometimes close to heartbreak at the thought of young generations growing up without the sense of organic community he had known. He said: 'My books are not scandalous, not sexy, and the story waves about from place to place – and yet much to my surprise, they are still in print … I stumbled on a form of writing that sets off recollections.'

In 1950 he married Catherine Polge, a niece of the sculptor Jacob Epstein, whom he first met on the way to Spain in 1936 when she was five. They were as close as two shoes.

LAURIE LEE · *born* 26 June 1914 · *died* 13 May 1997 ·

17 February 1998

MARTHA GELLHORN
Veronica Horwell and Julia Pascal

The streetcars of her hometown of St Louis, Missouri, shaped the life of Martha Gellhorn, who has died aged eighty-nine. Her suffragette mother and doctor father had raised her to confidence and campaigning, and, as a child, she had freedoms her peers did not; she roamed the city alone on those cars, looking in on lives unlike her own. 'One bends one's only twig and it stays bent,' she drawled long after.

She was briefly collegiate at Bryn Mawr, she was a cub reporter surviving on a diet of doughnuts. Then at twenty-one, in 1930, her life began with a steerage-class passage to Europe, $75 and a suitcase. She went to Paris to become a foreign or, better still, a roving correspondent. Just like that.

Even for a girl who looked, as she once remarked, like the cartoon character Betty Boop – all batted eyelashes – and had limitless insouciance, it did not happen quite like that. Gellhorn sold any old writing she could and got a 'very high-class education – standing room at ground level to watch history as it happened'. Her learning process involved European poverty and politics and an affair, later a short marriage, with the radical journalist Bertrand de Jouvenal, who, as a youth, had been the lover of a middle-aged Colette. She innocently took a room in a bawdy-house and knowingly bought absurd Parisian couture cheap at the end of the season. She was also introduced to her first Nazis, 'scrubbed and parrot-brained'. They didn't teach a girl any of that at Bryn Mawr.

The process also covered returning to – and crossing – America, walking in on an oil boom and on the great Russian film director Sergei Eisenstein, who was failing to film in Mexico, and writing her first novel. It took her on to the payroll of the Federal Relief Agency, for which she filed reports on the lives of the forgotten poor, which read like epic captions for Depression photographers: she was sacked for inspiring local revolutions.

It allowed her the naivety to cadge room and board from H. G. Wells in London, where she wrote a vivid eye-witness account of a southern lynching she later admitted that she had never seen; and to accept the offer of President Roosevelt and his wife Eleanor – her mother's campaigning friend – to stay in the White House, which was pretty homey then. She was put up there in Abraham Lincoln's bedroom and was fed regular meals during an awkward patch, when her furious moral righteousness made her otherwise unemployable. There she finished *The Trouble I've Seen*, fiction based on her underclass investigations. It was published in 1936, with her portrait, blonde and elegant, on its dustjacket: this was a titillating combination and a success. She was immediately celebrated, but fled the hoopla by holidaying in Florida.

At a Key West bar called Sloppy Joe's, she ran into Ernest Hemingway, bulky in his 'odiferous Basque shorts'. Two big celebs in a small town. His books had been her models. She said so. He had seen her face on Troubles. All afternoon and evening, they drank Papa Dobles, two-and-a-half jiggers of white Bacardi rum, juice of two fresh limes, swirled in a rusty electric blender. It sounds like a Hollywood 'meet-cute' – she walked into the bar in a black dress and high heels, with her terrific mother in tow. The Bacall and Bogart versions were merely remakes. She seems to have thought she had found the partner her nerve deserved. Hemingway was hooked. He was also married and off to cover the Spanish Civil War. She decided to join the fight and him (perhaps not in that order), this time with a rucksack and $50, a letter of introduction from *Collier's Magazine*, and a notion that the 'correct response to a war against fascism was simply to be present on the right side'. She thought that war correspondents reported the battlefield, and was surprised, but willing, when one suggested that a description of ordinary life in besieged Madrid was worth sending home.

Collier's printed the piece, put her name on their masthead, and there she was, a war correspondent and Hemingway's lover – and under his patronage, eating his tinned supplies and sharing his mattress on the road, yet still stubbornly independent. Her reports from Spain were more candid than his. The ration portion of dried salted cod weighed as heavily as the shells. She did not have to pretend to be an authority. One editor at *Collier's* appreciated and trusted her copy and, for eight years after that, she could go where she wanted and write what she saw. 'I had the chance to see the life of my time, which was war': the British unprepared for total war; the Czechoslovak army walking home after the German land-grab; the Finns democratic but frozen, fighting the Russians; the Chinese, in hunger and filth, out-enduring the Japanese invaders. Her base was a house outside Havana, which she had made over for Hemingway and herself. They married and settled in. They worked on fiction. But Gellhorn wanted to be in on the war at last breaking out in Europe, and a crazy Caribbean sea-hunt for U-boats (with a resulting, unpublished, extremely funny piece) was not enough. She was drinking daiquiris in a bar on the Mexican border when the newspaper boy hawked her the edition reporting Pearl Harbor.

Hemingway was having a fine time with his sporting Cuban buddies chasing phantom Nazi subs. He had already done global conflict. Gellhorn failed to persuade him to engage with the world at war a second time around. The marriage fractured. She reached London and followed the action in Europe and North Africa as closely as she could, with, or usually without, official permission, and with directions from friends in useful places. She advanced recklessly up through Italy with the Allies. Hemingway's telegram to her there read: 'Are you a war correspondent or my wife in bed?' This time, he eventually came after her. Their rivalry was not friendly anymore. She seems to have been Hemingway's personal bullshit-detector, especially when she coldly watched him holding court in a London hospital after a drunken accident. Gellhorn stowed away on a D-Day hospital ship and went ashore at Normandy. Hemingway crossed the Channel as officially as possible, but did not land.

In a hotel in free Paris, Gellhorn was advised by her old buddy the photographer Robert Capa to demand a divorce. She did, then loosely attached herself to the 82nd Airborne through the bitter 1944–5 winter of the Battle of the Bulge, and also to its leader, the heroic General James Gavin. She was present when the chaotic mass of the Russian army swarmed up to the other Allies. She was in newly liberated Dachau, at the apex of her anger, when peace was declared. What the inmates told her there – that it had been useless to protest or weep about what happened to them – was the antithesis of all she had believed in; she mistrusted Germany ever after. Her St Louis ancestry included both immigrant Germans and Jews.

About all of these places and people she wrote simply. An American prose style of Shaker plainness was laboured at by many of her contemporaries. To Gellhorn, it seems to have come naturally. She spoke that way. She believed real reporters did not take notes, but knew instinctively what remained forever important – trivia, the tone of the times. This might include a GI toasting himself a frontline cheese sandwich from K rations, or a Dutch slave labourer, recently freed, buying tulips in the ruins of a German city. It seldom included any utterance, or even mention, of a politician. 'All politicians are bores and liars and fakes. I talk to people,' she said. To read her dispatches (collected as *The Face of War* and *The View From the Ground*) is to be granted instant access to where she was, whenever it was.

The business in peace was to settle down. As a woman divorced on the grounds of abandonment, Gellhorn made some random gestures to pacification. These included acquiring a decrepit property in London, returning to Washington – only to find herself in solo outrage against McCarthyism – trying fiction and playwriting, and adopting a fifteen-month-old Italian orphan, Sandy. She brought him up, supporting their life together in cheap places like Mexico by journalism and writing potboilers for women's magazines – novellas differing from her own taste in their happy endings; and from her own life too, for General Gavin had married a nice young girl.

Gellhorn's next love, David Gurewitsch (a protégé of Mrs Roosevelt) could barely cope with her. She was courted by Tom Matthews, a recently retired editor of *Time* magazine, with a Mount Rushmore profile and a sound mind, and they married. But he wanted an urbane life in Britain, and she missed the excitement, and even more the whole-soul engagement, of the fight against fascism. 'I am a loner. I am not a team player,' she said once – she could certainly be unsociable, abrupt and grand – and 'The ideal is to live five blocks away from a man who makes you laugh and is wrapped up in his work'. The marriage petered out after nine years.

And so, by the 1960s, she was wandering again, observing more of the fifty-plus countries of her travels. She knew a lot about how people respond to place, especially when they respond by misbehaving: in that honestly funny book *Travels With Myself and Another*, she confessed how she misbehaved herself, how she was revolted by stench in west Africa and daunted by dengue fever going upriver by canoe. She repeatedly fell in love with countries, affaires which led her to hang curtains in impossible shacks. Her long-lasting final devotion was to a cottage on the Welsh borders, which had demanding vegetables in the garden.

Her association with *Collier's* had lapsed with her editor's death in the 1940s: thereafter, she had often to give herself assignments, and pay her own expenses, to satisfy her curiosity. For one long period, she had writer's block; for another, there was an editorial block against her copy – she was no longer a sexy novelty nor yet venerable, and the robustness of her New Deal attitude was out of fashion. Nevertheless, with help – which she remembered as rather minimal – from the *Guardian*, she reached Vietnam in 1966 to report the war (of which she was ashamed) that confirmed America as a colonial power.

Her long perspective eventually became valued again, when she returned to Madrid at the time of Franco's death, or to Castro's Cuba, where she saw, in the splendour of the full-grown trees now filling the garden of her old home, 'the years of my life made real'. At eighty, she took off to enquire into the US invasion of Panama, supple of spine and mind, stroppy as ever. *Granta* took her up as a sibyl; its editors and writers longed to have lived as she had done.

Gellhorn stayed flexible, except, notably, in her attitude to Israeli–Palestinian relations; she saw Israel always as the defiant David of its founding battles. She planned to go snorkelling with Paul Theroux well into her eighties. When surgery on her eyes went awry, she had the doctor professionally cursed by a Malagasy medicine man.

She dined with the BBC's John Simpson on his way to Bosnia. She saw off the East–West nuclear confrontation she most feared. She became part of the century's image bank. And to the end, this fierce pacifist reported drinking pitchers of red wine, or iced Scotch, with the children and the grandchildren of fighters she had known.

JULIA PASCAL writes: I was writing a play set at the Nuremberg Trials. Martha Gellhorn had been there. I wrote to her London publishers, she called me and in the next post came an American edition of her report. I rang to thank her and suggest lunch. In her strong St Louis voice she rasped, 'I loathe lunch. I drink'.

In her Eaton Square flat, she took whisky on the rocks and offered me 'a very good vodka someone gave me for Christmas'. At eighty-two, Gellhorn was sharper than almost anyone I had ever met. Slim, well made-up, elegant, she obviously cared about her appearance. She was quick to tell me mine needed improvement. 'You ought to put your hair up,' she said, examining my long hair with disapproval. 'Looking good isn't just vanity. It's a public service.'

The hair-up obsession was linked to her past. As a young woman, she was always chignoned, 'until the Nazis ruined my ear'. She had contracted an infection in Germany in 1933. Doctors in Nazi armbands botched her ear operation, so, with a huge bandage around her ear, without money or passport, she fled to Paris, ending up in the American Hospital. She never wore her hair up again.

We spoke about Nuremberg and I told her how watching hours of celluloid archive gave me the feeling that the trials only existed on film. 'Don't forget I've been to Dachau,' she replied. 'I've seen Germany flooding with a mad stream of slave labourers. For me, the unreal people were the people on trial. I looked at them day after day and was forced to think about what crimes those men had committed.' She talked of sleeping in a makeshift dormitory in a disused factory. 'I came back from the trials and vomited night after night. It was impossible to hear all the testimony without a violent reaction. Then I thought, if this is what I feel hearing this, what was it like to live it?'

She spoke easily of the ageing process and blamed the onset of her arthritis on the British damp. Always spoilt by male attention, she noticed her 'invisibility' with advancing age. 'But,' she announced, 'there are advantages. Nobody is jealous once you get to seventy or seventy-five, and then there is always the companionship of darling young men … Why do people talk of the horrors of old age? It's great. I feel like a fine old car with the parts gradually wearing out, but I'm not complaining. Those who find growing old terrible are people who haven't done what they wanted with their lives.'

MARTHA GELLHORN · *born* 8 November 1908 · *died* 15 February 1998 ·

TED HUGHES
John Redmond and Alan Sillitoe

Edward James Hughes, who died yesterday after a long battle with cancer, was, after W. H. Auden, arguably the finest English poet of the century. To the public he was best known for being Poet Laureate (the post he held from 1984 to 1998), as the unlucky husband of the American poetess Sylvia Plath, as a writer for children, and as a poet who had an unusual gift for evoking the natural world, especially the lives of animals. But his public image, if any-thing, tends to underestimate his actual cultural importance. He was a writer of very wide sympathies and a huge influence on other poets, from Seamus Heaney to R. S. Thomas. Beyond his surface subject material, any first reader of his work is most likely to be struck by its extreme intensity, a quality which it shares with the work of Plath.

Unlike Plath, however, Hughes worked on a much grander canvas. He is perhaps best seen as a critic of the mainstream of western culture, particularly of the utilitarian rationalism arising from the Enlightenment. In this he is in line with such writers as William Blake, W. B. Yeats and D. H. Lawrence. Although his sharp sense of humour has often been insufficiently acknowl-edged, this owes a lot to the uncompromising texture of the poetry, the sense in which in each poem, it is more than England, more than the West, which is at stake – it is existence itself.

Such an all-embracing, ambitious vision of poetry is easily derided. When he was parodied, affectionately and in a very English way, by *Private Eye* or Wendy Cope, the parodists would usually draw attention to how, in a Hughes poem, a simple act like drinking a cup of tea would be transformed into an event of shattering, cosmic significance. Nothing could just be casual. But then Hughes, as a young man, was reacting to a poetic generation who wanted to render everything in a casual manner. The Movement writers who pre-ceded him, such as Donald Davie and Kingsley Amis, had embraced a poetry of deliberately limited aims. Having experienced, as they had seen it, the worst consequences of irrational forces on the loose – romantic nationalism, group hysteria, charismatic dictators – during the Second World War, they had nat-urally sought a more sceptical, commonsensical mode of expression.

Hughes, with some sympathy, describes that exhausted generation as having returned to England, wanting little more than 'a nice cigarette and a view of the park'. But whatever sympathy, on a personal level, he had for their feelings, he did not extend it into his work, where everything, as he put it, 'was up for grabs'. While the Movement could blame the rampant phantasmagoria of the unconscious for the war, phantoms which now ought to be repressed, Hughes saw the war as a consequence of the inner warps and wounds of the western mind, damage he felt ought to be faced and healed. As a poetic force, Hughes emerged in 1957 with the publication of the much-lauded, prize-winning collection *The Hawk in the Rain*. Like the work of the Angry Young Men writers, such as John Osborne, Hughes's debut criticizes the lack of vitality in postwar English society. While the book shows some traces of being influenced by writers like Hopkins, Auden and Graves, it was a confident and original beginning. Its harsh, sharp, Anglo-Saxon-sounding rhythm and diction, its vivid, grandiose imagery and its sheer energy immediately set it apart from contemporaneous work, a feature recognized by its enthusiastic reviewers.

The landscape of Hughes's early work, which remained a major inspiration throughout his career, was that of the Yorkshire Pennines where he grew up. Hughes was born in the Calder Valley, in a town with the evocative name of Mytholmroyd. Later he wrote of the bald, unforgiving expanse of the Moors as 'a stage/ For the performance of Heaven./ Any audience is incidental'. In a manner reminiscent of Wordsworth, his childhood was shadowed over by a 600-foot-high scoop face, known as Scout Rock. Hughes, together with his older brother Gerald, used to explore the region around the rock and it quickly came to dominate his imagination. Later he wrote how this looming presence, visible from the house, seemed to represent a Gateway to Liberation. Beyond it was the south of England and 'the world'.

Hughes nevertheless immersed himself in this industrially scarred land-scape (he speaks of its peculiar 'purplish light'), studying the natural rhythms and closely observing how man and all his works interacted with the plants and animals. As he later pointed out in his homage to the area, *Remains of Elmet*, he was conscious of how he had grown up in a grievously damaged place: 'You could not fail to realize that cataclysms had happened to the population (in the First World War, where a single bad ten minutes in no man's land would wipe out a street or even a village), to the industry (the shift to the East in textile manufacture), and to the Methodism (the new age). Gradually it dawned on you that you were living among the survivors, in the remains.'

This survivor ethos Hughes would also encounter, in an extreme and troubling form, in Sylvia Plath, his first wife. Hughes met her at a Cambridge literary party in February 1956 and, after a sizzling romance, they were married four months later. It was Plath's drive and organizational abilities, together

with the faith that she had in his work, which hugely contributed to the publication of *The Hawk in the Rain*. A brilliant student, troubled by the early loss
of her father, and by the high but confused expectations of those around her,
Plath had been fortunate to survive a previous suicide attempt. Initially the
stronger poetic force, Hughes made his wide, esoteric reading and his poetic
theories and processes available to her. Their inner worlds, to a large degree,
converged.

At Cambridge University, Hughes had begun his degree in English, but
after two years, discouraged by the course's limited horizons, he switched to
anthropology. During his third year, Hughes read much about the role of
poetry in primitive societies and immersed himself in folklore. His exposure to
such sources remained a very significant influence on all his writing, sometimes accounting for its beguiling obscurity. Hughes was especially fascinated
by the animism of early cultures, their recognition and characterization of the
spirits immanent in things – animals, stones, rivers, trees – an animism which
he felt would be a corrective to the damagingly functional western view of the
environment, a view he blamed for the ruined landscape of his childhood.

Such themes and influences began to emerge in his second book, *Lupercal*,
published in 1960. Although not the most ambitious of his books, Hughes
emerged in it as a fully mature and powerful poet. In *Lupercal* one finds many
of the animal poems for which he is best remembered, his much anthologized
evocations of the jaguar, pike and otter, as well as his menacing, mesmeric
identification with the hawk roosting high in a tree:

> The sun is behind me.
> Nothing has changed since I began.
> My eye has permitted no change.
> I am going to keep things like this.

With the success of *Lupercal*, Hughes was now recognized as one of the
major poets of his generation. He continued to read into ever more exotic literary territory. He was a counter-culturalist *avant la lettre*, embracing Zen
and Sufi literature, later turning to Tamil and Taoist writings. Hughes was also
one of the first English writers to appreciate the growing importance of
Eastern European writing, which had a severe, existentialist quality agreeable
to him, and he was one of the main channels for bringing its influence into the
country.

While his literary career was going from strength to strength, the same
could not be said of his personal life. Although Plath had borne him two chil-

dren, he had gradually become alienated by her mood-swings and jealousy. After beginning an affair with a married woman, Assia Wevill, he separated from Plath. Left in her London flat to bring up two children alone, Plath became increasingly depressed during the unprecedentedly harsh winter of 1962–3. It was in this period that she wrote her deeply pessimistic, poetic masterpiece, *Ariel.* She committed suicide in February 1963.

Hughes now entered a somewhat rootless period, with his two children, moving back and forth through the 1960s from Ireland to Devon. The experimental volume *Wodwo* consolidated the success of *Lupercal,* but Hughes's personal life was to undergo further trauma with the death of the woman for whom he had left Plath, Assia Wevill, and her daughter Shura, in 1969. It was also the year his mother died.

These tragedies heavily scorched the poems of his fourth book, the one which is most likely to endure, and for which he is most famous, *Crow.* Drawing on native American Trickster myths, a character reappears throughout this slangy, crazy and violently irreverent book. Crow is capable of extreme cruelty, but he is also something of a child, ambiguously embodying the twisted side of twentieth-century psychology and history. Often he engages in banter with an ineffectual God:

> When God went off in despair
> Crow stropped his beak and started in on the two thieves.

The spiky consonantal language, the surreal, cartoon-like situations, and the super-brisk tone, as here, are typical of the collection. The book was hugely successful, sharing something of the extremely dark humour of such modern classics as *Catch 22* and *Slaughterhouse Five.*

In 1970, Hughes married his second wife, Carol Orchard, and finally settled in Devon. From this point on his personal life became more peaceful, and the work began to lose a little of its intensity. He bought the relatively secluded Devon farm and effected something of a withdrawal from the literary circuit. At the same time, he continued to produce work of the highest standard, and after 1975's ambitious, experimental narrative *Gaudete,* his experiences working on the farm were captured in the somewhat underrated 1979 collection, *Moortown.*

Hughes was, along with Philip Larkin and Seamus Heaney, one of the presiding poetic geniuses of the British literary scene. His continuing interest in children's literature, which was a symptom of his belief in educating the whole person, led to his collaboration with Heaney on two anthologies for young readers, *The Rattle Bag* and *The School Bag*, as well as his support for new creative talent through the Arvon Foundation.

After becoming Poet Laureate his collections in the 1980s seem to fall off from his earlier heights. Most of the poems that he wrote as Laureate are unlikely to be remembered for literary reasons. But there are many who regard his more recent books, *The Birthday Letters*, his unexpected poetic memoir of his marriage to Plath, and especially his translations in *Tales from Ovid*, as close to his best work. As a poet there is no denying his immense significance. Hughes completely transformed the postwar scene in Britain. He expanded its range of subject matter and lent it several new styles through which it could catch up with the modern world. He renewed its confidence in itself, and encouraged poets to look for universal values in their local landscapes, armed with the vigour of an honest simplicity:

> The farm-roots sink in the welter again, like a whale's fluke.
> Sheep fade humbly.
> The owl cries eerily, breaking parole,
> With icicles darkening witness.

He is survived by his wife Carol, and a daughter and son from his first marriage.

ALAN SILLITOE writes: It was always my notion that Ted would have been doing this for me, but these days God seems to have got his hands on a machine-gun, and is no respecter of a few years between contemporaries.

When I received the Hawthornden Prize for *The Loneliness of the Long Distance Runner* it was the custom that the winner would be present at the ceremony of whoever was awarded it the following year. This happened to be Ted, for *The Hawk in the Rain*, and we met on the steps of a house in St James's Square, in summer 1961, which makes him one of my oldest friends.

Sylvia Plath was there, as was Ruth Fainlight (our wives), both poets and American. Ted and myself were – although it is stretching a point for me – from 'the North', and in the following weeks we ate dinner in each other's flats. Ruth and I must have been among the first to call on them when they bought Court Green a couple of months later.

Ted was diffident and modest, even taciturn, but what enlivened our gatherings was a sense of humour, laughter almost taking up as much time as speech, as if we were plugged into the same vein. In 1962, Ruth Fainlight and I went away for the year with our baby son David, and at the end of that time, after Ted and Sylvia had split up, Ruth arranged to stay with her for a month while I was in Russia. Sylvia killed herself, and we often wonder whether she would have done so had we returned to England in time.

Our friendship with Ted lasted. One night at Court Green, with Ted's sister Olwyn, we deplored the fact that poetry wasn't cheaper and more widely available, and spent the time over a long dinner working out details of the Give Away Press. Poems would be printed on the cheapest paper and sold at street corners for very little. The result, after a couple of years, was the Rainbow Press, each plush and boxed volume costing about £75! On another convivial evening, Ted and I worked out a trip to the beaches at Gallipoli. His father had been a soldier there in 1915, and had told Ted that the winnings of a pontoon school among the troops, amounting to hundreds of sovereigns, had been buried in the sand and must still be there. We opened maps and reckoned up distances, calculated the number of days to drive there, and the supplies to take. That did not materialize either, all of us having more important things to do. Ted retreated more and more into himself as the years went by, which was understandable, but to me he wasn't the silent ox-like creature many people imagine. The closeness and rapport remained, in that he always sent copies of his books to me, and I reciprocated with copies of mine, both of us offering comments in our letters. In later years we could be relied on to leave each other alone because, as Ted said in a letter: 'As you get older, guarding your time has to be the greatest aim,' as indeed it always had been and still is with me.

On the first day of January last year he called at our place in Somerset on his way to London. In those few hours, the mood was as open and free as at any time before. Why he was going to London I didn't know, though it may have had something to do with his illness, about which I had only heard rumours. Whatever it was, Ted would never tell, being reticent about such things, but I didn't imagine, as we waved him off at the door, that I wouldn't see him again. It's as if he has taken a large slice of my past with him.

TED HUGHES · *born* 17 August 1930 · *died* 28 October 1998 ·

IRIS MURDOCH
Peter Conradi

Iris Murdoch, the novelist and philosopher, who has died aged seventy-nine, was one of the best and most influential writers of the twentieth century. Above all, she kept the traditional novel alive, and in so doing changed what it is capable of. She was not the heir – as she early and wrongly imagined – to George Eliot, but to Dostoevsky, with his fantastic realism, his hectically compressed time-schemes, his obsessions with sado-masochism and with incipient moral anarchy. Her best novels combine Dostoevsky with Shakespearean romance and love-comedy. When asked by whom she had been influenced, she was wont to reply she would like to have been influenced by Homer, Shakespeare, Tolstoy, Dostoevsky and Proust. This is not a modest list, and nor is her achievement a modest one.

Iris Murdoch was born in Blessington Street, Dublin, an only child. Her father, Hughes, Murdoch was a minor civil servant – a 'gentle, bookish man' she later called him – who came from County Down Presbyterian stock. He had served in King Edward's Horse in the First World War and, being a cavalryman, had escaped the holocaust of the trenches. Iris described him as a really good man, something whose rarity she only later came to be impressed by, not a religious man in any ordinary sense, a 'great inspiration to me and certainly the greatest influence in my life'. The influence was literary as well as moral. 'He was a very literary man, he loved books and tales. I could read at an early age. He wanted to discuss books with me, so I was reading *Treasure Island, Kim* and the *Alice* stories. These were the first books I remember enjoying, and I discussed them with my father.'

One day on the way to church he had met a pretty, eighteen-year-old girl. Irene Richardson wanted to train as a singer, and had a wonderful voice. They married, and the singing career languished. Iris inherited a somewhat more uncertain version of her mother's 'shebeen soprano', loved a sing-song, and on a small number of public occasions in later life was capable of breaking into song.

Though they all moved to London in her first year, her Irish origins mattered to her. Her only relatives lived in Dublin and Belfast, there were summer holidays in Ireland, and she would claim to feel Irish, even Anglo-Irish, all her life. Her mother could make some claim to be Anglo-Irish in the Ascendancy sense. An early Richardson is recorded in O'Hart's Irish Pedigrees as possessing

Crayhallock in 1619 – the large property now known as Drum Manor Forest Park. Iris put echoes from her own family history into a few novels. Murdoch lovers will, for example, recall the name Grayhallock, with its County Tyrone connections, from *An Unofficial Rose*. The first name of Effingham Cooper in *The Unicorn* – which is set in a mythicized County Clare – was that of her maternal grandfather. Nolan, in the same novel, was the grandmother's maiden name. Iris wished to identify with both Protestant and Catholic elements in her family background – one cousin had purportedly become Catholic. The family included another very distinguished woman writer, who wrote under the name of Henry Handel Richardson. In *The Red and the Green*, set in Dublin around the time of the Easter Rising, partly in Blessington Street, and involving a good deal of original research on her part, she invented a mythologized Whig Ascendancy past for herself.

After the Troubles began again in the late 1960s, Iris would say that 'one's heart is broken over Ireland'. She saw the activity of the IRA, like that of the Communist party – with which she was briefly involved – as an example of how a few ruthless, opinionated and evil people can maim a whole society. She felt passionately that Irish Protestants had an incontestable right to call themselves Irish. She tried to write about Ireland later, for example while composing *The Book and the Brotherhood* (1987), but found she could do so only partially. Perhaps the twin veins of fantasy and puritanism in her owed something to her Irishness.

Family life at home was a 'happy trinity'. Iris ascribed to her lack of siblings both a happiness that she only later came to understand to have been exceptional, and also an inspiration to write, as a way of inventing imaginary brothers and sisters: twins abound in the early books. She later said she would not have tolerated a sibling: by then she was cooking up the plot of *The Green Knight* (1993), which depends upon a murderous sibling rivalry, a theme at which she excelled.

She was happy at Badminton, the progressive girls' boarding school which she described as left-wing and high-minded. One contemporary recalled her there as an adolescent, pretty and serious, pricking out seedlings. She learnt Latin and Greek and acquired a love of languages. In later life she would read poetry in French, German, Italian, Spanish and Russian. Indira Nehru (Gandhi) was among her friends: there were scholarships for Jewish girls, so she knew about refugees before the war.

Between 1938 and 1942 she was up at Oxford reading Greats. Kingsley Amis and Roy Jenkins were contemporaries. She went to Eduard Fraenkel's lectures, the great Agamemnon class which went on for years. 'She was absolutely captivating,' another contemporary, M. R. D. Foot, recorded. 'She had personality and that wonderful Irish voice. Practically everyone who was up with Iris fell for her.' She briefly flirted with the Communist party – enough to have her entry to the US on a Rhodes scholarship refused.

Ten days after she had finished her exams she was conscripted as an assistant principal at the Treasury. It was the second part of the Blitz, and Iris, on occasion, took refuge during the bombing in her bath – and listened to the sound and the fury outside. Like William Golding, and perhaps Muriel Spark, the Second World War made her think anew about human wickedness and irrationality.

From 1944 to 1946 she worked for the United Nations Rehabilitation and Relief Association in camps in Belgium – she met Sartre briefly in Brussels, and not long after published the first study of his work. She was also in Austria, helping displaced persons. Work meant finding food and blankets, and sometimes a new nationality, for people who were lost and destitute. Some feeling about homelessness and exile, and 'an utter breakdown of society', came out of that experience.

Then she was in love with two victims of Hitler. The first was Frank Thompson – E. P. Thompson's older brother – whom it was assumed Iris would marry. He was parachuted into Macedonia during the war, and marched with the partisans towards Sofia, Bulgaria. He was captured and executed by the Nazis. A volume of poems by Catullus, and a Byzantine coin found in his pocket, were later presented to Iris by the Bulgarians. The second, the poet and anthropologist Franz Steiner, a scholarly Czech-Jewish refugee, lost both his parents through death in a concentration camp, and suffered a coronary in 1949 from which he never fully recovered. He died in November 1952. 'I loved him greatly,' Iris later said. 'I was with him on the evening before his death. We parted happily in the expectation of meeting again soon. I still miss him.' The gentle Peter Saward in *The Flight From the Enchanter* (1956) would seem to owe something to Steiner. That book was completed before the publication of *Under the Net* (1954) and has as much claim to be her Ur-novel. It is full of refugees, and meditates on displacement and uprooting. What are good and evil, what is courage? How is it that a few fanatics – Nazis in Weimar Germany, communists in postwar Europe, the IRA – can drive their cultures mad?

This is an obsession which connects the very earliest of Iris's novels to those novels that were written forty years later, for example *The Good Apprentice* (1985) and *The Message to the Planet* (1989), with their own Holocaust meditations. The enchanters and maguses of her fiction belong on an international stage, and have always a political dimension.

Had the war not supervened, Iris might have continued her studies as a Renaissance art historian. With her first degree she got a post in Cambridge for a year and then in Oxford, where she taught philosophy from 1948 to 1963. She is remembered as a generous and brilliant teacher – very beautiful, with great big eyes and striking dresses. There was a brief period teaching philosophy at the Royal College of Art in London in 1963–7. She found the wildness of the students picturesque, and this gets into the novels of that decade.

In 1952 John Bayley, a humble junior instructor, saw Iris from his Oxford window pedalling past on her bicycle, and fell in love with her at first sight. Even from a distance, he insists, he could tell that she was 'mature, sensible, mysterious and humorous'. Two weeks later they met at a party, found they both lived in the same street, and bicycled home together. They married in 1956. She cooked for the first fortnight, not well, then he took over.

It was a famous literary partnership. He rose to become Warton Professor of English, published *Romantic Survival*, *The Characters of Love* and books on Tolstoy and Pushkin. He is also a novelist and an energetic reviewer. Marriage made it easier for Iris to write, because all the events of her imagination were free and tumultuous, whereas her ordinary daily life could now be calmer. They toured the world, often for the British Council, giving joint lectures. There was a big rambling house in Steeple Aston, succeeded from 1989 by a Betjeman villa in north Oxford, but in a don-free area, quiet and easy for shopping. She sewed like mad, and wore plimsolls to ease the pressure of arthritis, not least when she went to the Palace to collect her DBE.

Under the Net, her first published fiction, was her fourth written one. T. S. Eliot at Faber had refused a predecessor on grounds of paper-shortage, in terms just sufficiently cold to make her decide not to send him any of the successors. This must count as one of Eliot's less far-sighted critical – and financial – judgements. The rhythm of around eight months' gestation – 'a time of awful torment, when you're dealing with a lot of dead pieces and you have to wait for some kind of animation', followed by about six months' writing, once established, did not often vary – unless there was some big piece of philosophy or a play on the way. 'No more novels, no more philosophy', she would despairingly cry to friends during the composition. This was a ritual cry, which only turned true towards the end, when her memory started seriously to let her down with the onset of Alzheimer's disease. She seemed proud that she could not type or use a word-processor. She used a fountain pen for two drafts – 'One should love one's handwriting', she used to say – and took the second draft in a plastic bag in order personally to deliver it to her publisher.

She was loyal to Chatto, with whose redoubtable Norah Smallwood she worked for many years. Carmen Callil called her the queen of Chatto. Once Callil cut one of her books. 'Please restore everything', said Iris. She would rather be read by fewer readers who were more intelligent. Callil obliged.

What was she like? There are myths here, as well as truths. She created, in Rozanov in *The Philosopher's Pupil* (1983), one character who feared that after his death he would be wrongly praised as a saint, and seems to have meant this as a whimsical warning about being turned into the Abbess of north Oxford herself. Yet she would answer all fan-mail by hand, with no help from a secretary, who – this was her fear – would eat up further time. As a result she was plagued by bores who returned for more. 'Pals for life' she once despairingly complained. There were often twelve letters per day, and then 200 at Christmas. She helped her mother's window-cleaner publish a detective novel. When A. S. Byatt's son was killed, Iris listened to her and wept, and let her say the things that no one else would.

It may have been a myth that Bayley was wholly uninvolved in her work during composition. He certainly proposed at least some of Charles Arrowby's whimsical and disgusting recipes in *The Sea, The Sea*. She claimed never to paint from life and would not accept sub-editing. Dogs at least were certainly lifted from life – our blue-eyed collie is immortalized as Anax in *The Green Knight*. She wished to keep herself out of the novel. Yet in Bradley in *The Black Prince* she created one ironic and very un-self-flattering self-portrait. It was said that she would never talk to journalists about her love-life or her kitchen: she did both.

She is read in Japanese and Russian and French, and belongs to her world-wide readership as much as she does to us. The British notoriously underestimate their great artists. We see them as smaller than they are, needing them explained to us by those from outside, and this is one true measure of our provincialism. A train story: travelling between Paddington and Oxford, she once sat out the hour watching a hungry reader of one of her own novels turn the pages with obvious fascination, oblivious to its author sitting opposite. 'Say what you like', she reflected: 'I can at least tell a story.'

Iris could do more than that. We can now see that, in *A Severed Head* (1961), she prophesied the dionysiac 1960s before they happened: the 1960s seem to have been as colourful and experimental a decade for her as for any of us. But she had something important to say about desire in human life generally, and its relationship with goodness. She wrote well about the rivalry between men, and about the Oedipal conflict between strong-willed mothers and their Nietzschean offspring. She could capture those moments of startled vision when we see our world without preconception. She could describe the ordinary and make it magical. *A Fairly Honourable Defeat* (1970) marvellously retells the story of *Much Ado About Nothing* with a modern-day Christ and Satan added, in South Kensington. *The Black Prince* (1973) is by far the most self-revelatory and yet also the most artificial of all her dark comedies, with its meditation on *Hamlet* and on the black Eros. *The Sea, The Sea*, which won the Booker prize in 1978, is enabled by *The Tempest*, just as *The Good Apprentice* (1985) is by the parable of the Prodigal Son and *The Green Knight* (1993) by *Sir Gawain*. All these combine myth with realism, and are built to last.

Iris wrote Gothic twelve years before Angela Carter, and romance years before David Lodge. It is striking to read the latter's strictures, in a review of *A Fairly Honourable Defeat* as a romance, fifteen years before he turned to explore the same sub-genre himself. She helped pioneer writing about homosexuality as merely one part of human life. It is typical of her quiet subversiveness that it is only the gay partnership that survives in *A Fairly Honourable Defeat* – the heterosexual relationships all fall apart under the strain of a typical Murdoch plot. Apart from Mary Renault, few women novelists write with as much conviction from the point of view of male homosexuals, and no other woman writer so well impersonates men.

Indeed, she kept a debate about human difference alive, through the bad years when the fools of both extreme right and left had sheepishly pretended that it did not matter, or even did not exist anyway. Human difference also meant moral difference. How is it that some human beings are morally better than others? What is it that might make a man good, even in a concentration camp? Consider Korczak, who gave his life in Treblinka, or Kolbe in Auschwitz, or, indeed, Frank Thompson. How did it come about that in the epoch of greatest political evil, the century of Stalin and Hitler, moral terms had simultaneously been evacuated of any absolute significance by philosophers?

The Sovereignty of Good (1970), *The Fire and the Sun: Why Plato Banished the Artists* (1976) and *Metaphysics as a Guide to Morals* (1992) have been important to theologians, to aestheticians, and moral philosophers, and seem likely to remain so. She could not believe in a personal god demonic enough to have created the world whose sufferings are so clear to us, yet wanted religion to survive, too. She took confession once, and alarmed the priest concerned with her moral passion and her vehemence. She was taught a form of Buddhist meditation also, and wanted Buddhism to educate Christianity, to create a non-supernatural religion. God and the afterlife were essentially anti-religious bribes to her. Her vision of the world as sacred looks forward to ecology and the Green movement.

Visiting a cottage I share in mid-Wales in 1995, a cottage which abuts a graveyard, Iris Murdoch asked happily and with much interest: Do you know many of the dead people in your cemetery? Dying was, for her, not simply the intensely significant Wagnerian last moment that Christianity can make of it, but rather an undramatic part of everyday moral life. Redemption meant for her the Buddhist hope that one might gradually, moment by moment and day by day, learn to perceive less selfishly. Such a process of learning is necessarily a calling-into-question of what is normally meant by 'identity'. Indeed, she would often speak of herself as having no strong identity. And yet the capacity so to forget herself depended equally on an unusually strong sense of who she was. In the bar of a train in 1981, an enthusiastic lady greeted Iris Murdoch as Margaret Drabble. 'How can you tell,' Iris quizzically and patiently enquired, 'that I'm not Doris Lessing, Iris Murdoch, or Muriel Spark?' 'I'd know you anywhere Margaret,' cried the enthusiast.

She connected goodness, against the temper of the times, not with the quest for an authentic identity so much as with the happiness that can come about when that quest can be relaxed. We are fortunate to have shared our appalling century with her. I count myself among the many who hope to have been taught by her, and who will miss her terribly.

IRIS MURDOCH (DAME JEAN IRIS BAYLEY) · *born* 15 July 1919 · *died* 8 February 1999 ·

30 March 2000

ANTHONY POWELL
Norman Shrapnel

Anthony Powell, who has died aged ninety-four, is inevitably regarded as the English Proust on the strength of the massive novel sequence *A Dance to the Music of Time*, twelve volumes and a million words, that became his central life's work. The Proust impact was more dominant and more obvious than that of other great European novelists and assorted influences from Petronius to modern Americans. Yet he will stand as essentially a comic writer in the English tradition – comic in the least uproarious way imaginable, reflective and often melancholic, the strong social spine to his work being the one distinctively uncommon feature in a branch of writing remarkable more for eccentricity than togetherness.

In fact, Powell has a measure of both. He goes in for no deep psychological dredging, yet his novels rest on a firmer base of instinct and belief than is usual among English comedians. He is fascinated by the play of time and chance on character, and it is by no means time and chance that always win. His narrating hero and anchorman, Nicholas Jenkins, is constantly being mildly surprised by the way things and people turn out.

The unpredictability of life, as Powell himself described, is built into his structure as an essential part of it. Coincidences, so irritating to some readers, often happen in life, so why should they be forbidden to fiction? They are not excluded from Powell's novels, nor are all manner of trivia other writers might scorn or mishandle. It was his belief that with the right cook in charge anything could go into the cauldron. A novelist never lacks material – only the capacity and energy to handle it.

Silver spoons, in the Powell kitchen, were never in short supply. The world he deals with, upper middle-class life from the 1920s onwards, is his own world. The son and grandson of distinguished soldiers, he spent part of his childhood with his mother in rented accommodation in the home counties following his father, a lieutenant-colonel in the Welsh regiment. He was at Eton, where he was a contemporary of Orwell and a founding member of the Eton Society of Arts, and then at Balliol College. After Oxford, he got a job with Duckworth, a small London publishing house, but left after nine years to write scripts for Warner Brothers, even paying a six-month visit to Hollywood.

His first novel, *Afternoon Men*, appeared in 1931 and there were several others by way of prelude, followed by a long silence through the war – when he joined his father's regiment before being transferred to the Intelligence Corps – and for some years after it. Then, in 1951, came the start of *The Music of Time* sequence, the title deriving from Nicolas Poussin's allegorical painting. The books emerged at roughly two-yearly intervals.

The sequence, stretching across a quarter of a century from *A Question of Upbringing* (1951) to *Hearing Secret Harmonies* (1975), is more than a successful fictional marathon. It achieves a coherence, a central vitality which runs sluggishly at times but is never extinguished. His vast army of characters, clubmen all, pursue their power games through peace and war, marriage or divorce, in sickness and in health. War – as memorably described in the ninth volume, *The Military Philosophers* – is for Powell-people an extension of ordinary life; the flow is diverted but not stemmed, and rank is merely a crude token of what always existed in this elegantly competitive world. Some characters may only be glimpsed before disappearing from view, perhaps springing up like blades of grass in another volume years later. But nothing is lost or without its effect on the total pattern, while the allegorical master of the dance – as in the Poussin picture – smiles a shade malignly. Other characters are as perennial as the unreliable Dicky Umfraville, often in hot, or at least very warm, water, first noted leaving school under a cloud (not actually expelled, it was insisted) and last seen masquerading as an octogenarian drug-addict. Or the ever-indulgent Lady Molly, whose house in South Kensington, more than the Ritz, is really open to all.

With Powell's known writing method and this roving cast of hundreds there was naturally much speculation about who were the originals, in whole or more usually in part, of the characters appearing in the *Dance*. Sometimes the guess-who game was easy, as with the well-known Fitzrovian writer and reviewer Julian Maclaren-Ross who became the character X. Trapnel. He appears as a novelist who holds forth at length about the art of the novel to the narrator Jenkins, also a novelist. He insists, and Jenkins doesn't contradict, that naturalism is only natural in the right hands and that reading novels takes almost as much talent as writing them. It can hardly be carrying presumption too far to assume that some of these ideas, as from novelist to novelist, are shared by the club's founding member, Powell himself.

Others are more mysterious. Above all – literally so, if he had his way – there is the preposterous, the ever-haunting Widmerpool. Writhing with self-contradiction – a shade pathetic, a little absurd, more than a little sinister – he pervades the book, occupying a full half-century even of Powell's ocean of time. Where can this strange creature have sprung from? 'I am perpetually badgered about Widmerpool,' Powell said when he was being interviewed for his eightieth birthday. All sorts of originals have been suggested, from a recent Lord Chancellor down. Actually, so far as the character was drawn from life, 'he was drawn from somebody I served under during the war'. Powell tells us, in *Journals 1982–1986* (1995), that he first came across Widmerpool as a Cromwellian Captain of Horse in Hutchinson's *Memoirs of the Life of Colonel Hutchinson* (Lucy Hutchinson, 1670). Further volumes of the *Journals* were to appear, covering the years 1987–9 and 1990–2. If any character was going to beat time you felt it would have to be the apparently indestructible Widmerpool, but he goes in the end – suitably weirdly, collapsing (it seems) on a ritual jog at dawn.

The inextricable mingling, in such a world as Powell's, of life and literature is made doubly apparent in the memoirs, *To Keep the Ball Rolling*, which

Powell brought out in four volumes between 1976 and 1982. So happily do fact and fiction marry that it is easy to forget at times that you are reading about a real character in an actual place, and imagine you have slipped back into one of the novels. This reaction is particularly strong in the account – laconic and uninhibited like the fiction – of the early days in London when Jenkins is finding his feet in the literary world. The real-life memories develop, as the novels do, a sense of the significance of trivial and seemingly casual events, while large ones may pass invisibly by. Real people surge on to the scene like figures from a fantasy world: Augustus John, J. C. Squire, Rosa Lewis of the Cavendish, Maclean and Burgess ('a notorious scallywag'), the seedy diabolist Aleister Crowley at Simpsons, Tallulah Bankhead in a nightclub. We watch him becoming a Territorial recruit in the Royal Artillery ('I felt that if the gunners were good enough for Tolstoy they were good enough for me') and, rather more dangerously, pursuing a friendship with Evelyn Waugh. There are drinks with the Sitwells. The air of clubbishness, a cool, bookish intimacy, persists. Most of the way, that is. Just once in a while togetherness fails: 'In the flat below mine lived E. M. Forster (a writer whose books have never greatly appealed to me), but we never met.' The trivia of the memoirs can be as funny as anything in the novels, and that means very funny indeed. Powell was of the opinion that most important writers, unlike most critics, have been well equipped with resources of humour; he even seems to have regarded it as a touchstone in evaluating them.

Powell began as a writer for addicts – clubmen too, members of the Powell Club – but they increased rapidly. Or was it more like an open prison, in which Powell was governor and his readers were condemned to life sentences? They never wanted to be anywhere else for long, and they always came back at call.

For a single writer to have put such a stamp on his day, and against the pre-vailing mood and style of the time, is a huge achievement. Powell didn't stand quite alone. Kingsley Amis was with him, dealing bold strokes in defence of the comic spirit; but the Amis comedy, though by no means all belly-laughs, was of a rougher order and failed to carry the approval of the bookish estab-lishment. While Amis sold books, Powell won praise. It was ungrudging and well earned. Largely it was a triumph of tone. A fastidious satirist, he never shouts and seldom mocks – or (except in the physical sense) moves very far. Powell's ideal hunting-ground seems a mile square and an inch deep, and there are bound to be some – particularly when so little, for such long spells, manages to happen – who get to find the inflexibly well-bred narrative voice a shade wearing. This is surely part of the fun. Powell's descriptive powers are clinically accurate and searching, and he is constantly putting himself in the way of good material.

He is a conscientious mixer in the interests of his profession. It goes beyond clubland and the haunts of off-duty politicians, bureaucrats and important artists, though even lower life has its standards and good manners survive in unlikely places. Powell's world is well supplied with pubs without being beery, and there are times when the streets are thronged with well-born paupers conscientiously dodging their creditors. In taxis, of course. Violence, public and domestic, in peace and war, is muted by the modulated tones of civilized life. This relentless gentility would risk serious tedium without that sharpness of eye and wit. The head, you could say, remains as cool as the heart. He lacks what Amis and most of the later English humorists have possessed – sentimentality. That would have destroyed the work.

He has a strong indulgence towards fantasy and eccentric behaviour, always with the assumption that it is observed and not invented. He can be ruthless, not always in expected settings. There are funerals, not necessarily particularly mournful occasions; death seems no more serious than life, which is indeed serious enough in so inflexible an English comedy world. There is an inclination for ritual, with serious sacrificial moments such as the drowning of a key manuscript in the Regent's Park canal (*Books Do Furnish a Room*), or the death – could it be possible after all? – of Widmerpool in the final volume of the sequence.

The fiction adds up to a marvel of skill, originality, patience and sheer longwindedness. Technically the challenge, brilliantly met, must have been the handling of that enormous flock of free-range characters and the disposing of the maddening, mysterious, apparently indestructible Widmerpool. No wonder the face in Poussin's ritual dance came to look more malign than ever, for the Powell version must have called for a kind of anti-choreography remote from dancing. These hundreds of performers had to be trained to collide with each other as much as possible for fear that they might otherwise stray off and never be seen again.

There must have been many who wished that for Widmerpool. Did Powell ever wish he had never created the man, if man it was? Keeping track of Widmerpool through twelve volumes and a million words, not really knowing whether he was ink or flesh, whether his true existence was inside the book or out, could have been a lifetime's job in itself. He popped up everywhere: something in the City, something in the army, employed in many an advisory capacity. He was a Labour MP under Attlee, an admirer of Mrs Ernest Simpson. Hugh Gaitskell – though nobody seems quite sure about this – was thought to have been instrumental in getting him a peerage. He influenced people's lives though not in the traditional way; more a kind of one-man quango. He would always be in touch. There was no danger of his getting lost.

After the *Music of Time* sequence Powell continued to write – he had also been literary editor of *Punch* after the war and a long-time book reviewer for the Daily Telegraph – until immobilized by a series of strokes in the late 1980s. There was a short novel in 1983 dementedly entitled *O, How the Wheel Becomes It!* (Ophelia's mad scene, it fittingly turns out, provides the clue). And in 1986 he published *The Fisher King*, an elegant modern version of an ancient myth. He was made a Companion of Honour in 1988.

Powell had married Violet Packenham, sister of Lord Longford, in 1934 after a brief acquaintanceship. For many years they lived in a handsome regency house near Frome in Somerset. He is survived by Lady Violet and two sons.

ANTHONY DYMOKE POWELL · *born* 21 December 1905 · *died* 28 March 2000 ·

POLITICS, PHILOSOPHY AND HISTORY

∎∎∎

ALFRED AYER
P. F. Strawson

Sir Alfred Ayer, Wykeham Professor of Logic at the University of Oxford and Fellow of New College from 1959 to 1978, was the most celebrated British philosopher of his generation. Though he was widely known outside academic circles for his anti-religious views and his advocacy of liberal causes, his lasting reputation will rest securely upon his strictly philosophical publications.

By the age of twenty-five he had published what is still one of the best known and most widely read philosophical works of the century: *Language, Truth and Logic* (1936), a work of uncompromising philosophical iconoclasm which, in clear and incisive prose, introduced the full-blooded doctrines of logical positivism to the English philosophical world, scandalizing the more conservative, and impressing the more discerning of his seniors, and delighting and enthralling his juniors. This was but the first of a series of twelve philosophical books which appeared over the succeeding decades and in which many of the implausibilities or crudities of the original position were corrected or tempered as Ayer's empiricism assumed increasingly undogmatic, increasingly flexible and increasingly subtle forms. Outstanding among these many works are *The Foundations of Empirical Knowledge* (1940), *The Problem of Knowledge* (1956), *The Origins of Pragmatism* (1968) and *The Central Questions of Philosophy* (1973). Significant changes in Ayer's position included the abandonment of phenomenalism in favour of a sophisticated form of realism and the adoption of the view that some basic ontological questions were to be settled, if at all, by pragmatically inspired choice or decision.

Throughout his career, however, Ayer remained firmly in the British empiricist tradition of Locke, Berkeley, Hume and Russell. The last two of these Ayer acknowledged as his masters; and it is appropriate that his most recent works included two brief but brilliant studies of Russell (1972) and of Hume (1980). Ayer concluded his autobiographical *A Part of my Life* (1977) with the modest remark that he would consider it 'glory enough ... to be thought even to have played Horatio to Russell's Hamlet.'

Though Ayer could not, and made no attempt to emulate Russell in logic and logical theory, the area in which Russell displayed his peculiar greatness, he was at least Russell's equal in the wider field of theory of knowledge and general metaphysics. Ayer's philosophical output as a whole, though not marked by the greatest originality, is exemplary in clarity of exposition and conciseness and elegance of expression. His replies to his critics and colleagues in the Festschrift, which appeared in his honour in 1979 under the title *Perception and Identity*, showed an undiminished vigour and forthrightness. Ayer always directed a sustained attention to the central questions of major philosophical importance, remaining indifferent to intellectual fashion and impervious to the seductions of the merely technical. This fact, and the brilliant clarity of his style, will ensure the continued relevance and accessibility of his work.

Born in 1910, of a Jewish mother and a French-Swiss father, Ayer was educated at Eton and Christ Church. He gained first-class honours in *Literae Humaniores* in 1932, and in the same year married and went to Vienna, where he was invited to attend the meetings of the celebrated Vienna Circle. From 1932 to 1944 he held, first, a research lectureship and subsequently a research studentship at Christ Church, and in 1944 was elected to a fellowship at Wadham. From 1940 to 1945 he served in the Welsh Guards, attaining the rank of Major. He left Wadham in 1946 to become Grote Professor of the Philosophy of Mind and Logic at University College London, a post he held until his return to Oxford in 1959. He found the London department moribund and left it flourishing.

Among other academic honours, Ayer was elected a fellow of the British Academy in 1952 and was invited to deliver the William James Lectures at Harvard and the John Dewey Lectures at Columbia in 1970, the year in which he was knighted. He was president of the Humanist Association from 1965 to 1970, and honorary fellow of Wadham and an honorary student of Christ Church. On his retirement from the Wykeham Chair he was elected to a fellowship at Wolfson College, Oxford.

The regular and even tenor of Ayer's writings, philosophical and autobiographical, is in contrast with the style of his unstudied speech and of his life. The former had an impulsiveness, even an explosiveness, which reflected the extreme quickness of his mind and his impatience with anything that struck him as obscurantist or as otherwise wrong-headed. His life reflected a need for stimulation and applause which nevertheless co-existed with a considerable objectivity about his own achievements, talents and personality. He was vain, but not conceited. He had great powers of enjoyment and great vitality. He was completely without pretence. Thrice married, he neither concealed nor paraded his taste for amorous adventure. He faced death with the imperturbability which he admired in Hume (and which so shocked Boswell).

ALFRED JULES AYER · *born* 29 October 1910 · *died* 27 June 1989 ·

10 October 1992

WILLY BRANDT
Hella Pick

For Willy Brandt, who has died aged seventy-eight, the 1971 award of the Nobel Peace prize was one of the high points in his life. 'After the ineffaceable horrors of the past,' he wrote later, 'I had the privilege to reduce the words of "Germany" and "peace" to a common denominator.' The other emotional Everest in Willy Brandt's life came with the collapse of the Berlin Wall and the unification of the two Germanys. Widely regarded as the 'father of German unity', he had lived to see a seemingly impossible dream turn into reality.

Unhappily, in his last few months, he also had to watch, too ill to intervene in public, as the unification process soured and right-wing extremism surfaced again. He had yearned to use his great moral authority to make one last personal appeal for moderation but was too weak to attend last month's congress of the Socialist International in Berlin's Reichstag. Instead he sent a message, exhorting them to remain true to the ideals of democracy. It brought all the delegates to their feet in tribute to the man they knew would soon be gone. Willy Brandt was one of the handful of political giants to emerge in the postwar world. With his humanity and unswerving commitment to freedom and democracy, Brandt did more than any other German to change the moral climate and restore the good name of Germany. But he achieved far more: he engraved himself on the popular awareness around the world as one of those rare statesmen who combined compassion, humour and deep humility with great vision and at critical times, political courage. He communicated an enduring belief in the essential goodness of man.

At times this blurred his judgement. When people or events disappointed him, it affected him deeply. But such were his popularity and influence that he survived his resignation as Chancellor in 1974, when one of his closest aides,

Gunther Guillaume, was revealed to be an East German spy. By his later admission, at the time of his resignation he was close to suicide. But with extraordinary resilience, he returned to the public stage, no longer seeking office. He took over the chairmanship of the SPD, allowing Helmut Schmidt, his successor as Chancellor, to concentrate on running the government. He also became the president of the Socialist International, travelling the world in search of a North–South dialogue to complement the East–West *détente*, which he had fathered. He headed an international commission, quickly known by his name, to advise how economic and political relations between rich and poor countries could be improved. Until he suffered a heart attack in November 1978, he was also widely encouraged to stand for the presidency of the first directly elected European Parliament. Throughout Europe, even in the communist bloc, countless people believed that Willy Brandt was still capable of converting lofty aims into political reality.

Brandt was so simple, direct and warm in his personal relations with all manner of people, that it was possible to forget that he had to surmount so many stiff obstacles on the road to power. Nor did he always find it easy to use power, once he had won it; his search for social justice and his enduring commitment to morality in politics often came into conflict with the ambitions of others.

As a young man, Brandt had almost everything against him. He was illegitimate; he fled Germany to Norway to escape the Nazis; after his return, at the end of the war, he settled in Berlin and began his political career in the one western city that was most exposed to the blasts of the Cold War. Yet this personal experience of a divided Europe led Brandt to the conviction that a *modus vivendi* must be found. He concluded that the Federal Republic could only regain its self-confidence and moral stature if it also led the way to understanding with the Soviet Union, and reconciliation with Poland and the other countries of Eastern Europe, which had all suffered so cruelly from Hitler. Equally, Brandt understood that it was both possible and essential to seek Jewish forgiveness: when he finally went to Israel, he was received with honour.

He was born Karl Frahm in Lübeck. His mother was a shop assistant. He never saw his father but he knew and loved his grandfather, who became the first member of the Social Democratic party in his village. Karl won a scholarship to a grammar school in Lübeck. Still at school he began writing articles for the Lübeck SPD paper. As in all German cities at the time, there were street fights between the Socialists and the Nazis. Karl Frahm became a marked man when the Nazis came to power and his life was in danger. He went to Norway and changed his name, later explaining that he kept this new name because in Norway he developed his ideas and principles and became the man, warts and all. Norway remained his second home.

He studied history at Oslo University, working part-time as a journalist, and became active in the Norwegian trade unions. In 1937 he managed to spend a short time in Berlin disguised as a Norwegian student with forged Norwegian papers. In the same year he spent five months in Spain, reporting the Civil War from the Republican side for several Scandinavian newspapers. For the rest of his life he enjoyed the company of journalists and recognized the importance to a democratic society of well-informed media. When the Germans invaded Norway, he put on the uniform of a Norwegian soldier and was taken prisoner. He was released and managed to get to Sweden where he took out Norwegian citizenship. In Sweden he worked as a writer and after the war he was sent to cover the Nuremberg trials. At the end of 1946, the Norwegian Foreign Office appointed him press attaché in Berlin.

In 1947 Brandt resumed his German citizenship. He also rejoined the Social Democratic Party, and at the request of its leader, Kurt Schumacher, represented the party executive in Berlin. His political career had begun. Brandt was first elected to the Bundestag in 1949. Next year he became a member of Berlin's Parliament, presided over it 1955–7 and then succeeded Ernst Reuter as Berlin's governing mayor.

Running West Berlin involved far more than managing a large conurbation. For almost forty-five years, until Germany's reunification in 1990, West Berlin remained as a surrounded symbol of the West's determination to prevent the Soviet Union from extending its grip. The mayoralty was one of the most sensitive political posts in Western Europe. Brandt had already established an unrivalled popularity in Berlin when in 1961, at a critical period of the Cold War, the infamous Berlin Wall rose up. His refusal to be intimidated, tempered by his habitual good humour, helped to keep up the morale of Berliners at that testing moment. It also brought him national and international fame. Two years later, he was elected chairman of the SPD.

Long afterwards, when he wrote his memoirs, he described the Berlin Wall as one of the defining events of his political life. Its presence convinced him that the Federal Republic must come to an understanding with its communist neighbours – including even the German Democratic Republic, whose very existence Bonn and its allies had persistently ignored. As he contemplated the Wall, Brandt concluded that the West was deluding itself. Its policies had proved 'unrealistic and ineffective'. Brandt, as head of the SPD, stayed in Berlin until 1966 – but not for want of trying. He was his party's unsuccessful candidate for the chancellorship in the Federal elections of 1961 and 1965. Brandt had to contend with personal smears about his illegitimacy (even Konrad Adenauer joined the chorus, to his everlasting shame) and Norwegian uniform.

Brandt suffered from one of his depressions after the 1965 defeat but in his memoirs he denied that he contemplated a return to Norway. Instead, he applied himself once again to the problems of Berlin, until in 1966 the SPD formed the Grand Coalition with the CDU. The CDU leader, Dr Kiesinger, became chancellor. Willy Brandt was named foreign minister and vice-chancellor.

Now he was at last in a position of significant influence on foreign policy, where he could lay the foundations of his Ostpolitik and simultaneously strengthen his party's domestic base. During his three years in this office, the Federal Republic established diplomatic relations with Romania and re-established relations with Yugoslavia, which had been broken off when President Tito had recognized the East German regime. These and other moves tacitly implied acceptance of divided Germany and did much to kill the Hallstein doctrine, under which Bonn had refused to recognize countries that established diplomatic relations with the GDR.

His period as foreign minister also made Brandt a wholehearted 'European', convinced that Germany's future lay with the European Community, an instrument for unity in the search for East–West *détente*. After the 1969 elections in Germany, the SPD formed its coalition with the small liberal party, the FDP, and Willy Brandt became Germany's first Social Democratic chancellor in more than thirty-nine years. Although he promised to devote much of his energies to domestic reforms, Brandt continued to concentrate on furthering his Ostpolitik, and transforming the Federal Republic into pied piper, leading the US and other western countries towards normalization of relations with the communist bloc.

The year 1970 was one of the most productive of his career. He negotiated two key treaties: one with the Soviet Union; the second with Poland. He twice met the East German leader Willy Stoph. Together, these treaties and the face-to-face meetings conclusively paved the way for the Federal Republic's *de facto* acceptance of East Germany as a separate state.

Reunification was never taken off the agenda. But in 1970 it seemed like an impossible dream. Brandt had to use great political courage to persuade German public opinion that the division of Europe, for the foreseeable future, had become a reality that Bonn could not continue to ignore. Germany should take the lead in promoting stability. Dialogue with the GDR was an essential prerequisite to an easing of tension in Europe, therefore in West Germany's best interests. Brandt had never forgotten a warning that John Foster Dulles had delivered in Berlin back in 1959. 'The United States and the Soviet Union can disagree about a thousand matters. But there is one subject on which there is no difference. We shall never permit a reunited, rearmed Germany to wander about a no man's land between the East and the West.' In 1970, few would have predicted that two decades later the Berlin Wall would be gone, and the two Germanys would again be reunited. Of all the events of that year perhaps the most poignant moment came on a cold December day, just after Brandt had signed the treaty with Poland and went to lay a wreath at the Warsaw ghetto. Instinctively he fell to his knees. His own explanation of an occasion that caught the world's imagination, came many years later: 'Oppressed by memories of Germany's recent history, I simply did what people do when words fail them. My thoughts dwelt not only on the fact that millions had been murdered, but that fanaticism and the suppression of human rights persisted … it was an attempt through the expression of fellowship to build a bridge to the history of our nation and its victims.'

During the remaining four years of his chancellorship, Brandt's international reputation continued to grow. But at home he came under mounting fire for neglecting domestic problems. It then took time not only for Brandt, but for the German nation, to erode the scars of the Guillaume affair. Yet it led to an extraordinary renaissance, which helped Brandt to acquire a serenity he had hardly anticipated for himself. A third marriage, to a much younger political aide, Brigitte Seebacher, brought him much happiness, and persuaded him to adjust his lifestyle to a touch more moderation. His own self-confidence and equanimity was fully restored and as his national stature grew he came to enjoy a rare respect across the German party spectrum, even while he remained active to the end within the SPD.

German unification rejuvenated Brandt. He had tears of deep emotion when he came to celebrate the first break in the Berlin Wall, on that tumultuous October day in 1989 with the whole of Berlin carpeted with cheering people. A few weeks later, he was out in the field, addressing rapturous crowds and campaigning vigorously and with all his old flair, in East Germany's first postwar democratic election.

In the first of his memoirs, *People and Politics*, Brandt has described (with humour, perception, generosity and a fair sprinkling of indiscretion) his encounters with postwar leaders and the events they had all helped to shape. Like the man himself, the memoirs are totally free of pomposity. So was his after-dinner speaking in English, well remembered by *Guardian* staff from their grand Dorchester celebration of the paper's 150th anniversary in 1971. His presence that day happened to coincide with a currency upheaval and after the festivities I had the opportunity to learn his interpretation of the crisis. That evening signalled the beginning of a much treasured friendship.

Perhaps only those who knew him well can fully appreciate what a staunch friend he could be; what a good story-teller he was, and just how deep his reserves of compassion were. But he summed up his philosophy in his own writings: 'We need more democracy; not less, in the sense of individual and collective responsibility. We need more civil rights, not less. We need more social justice, not less. We need more self-accountable freedom; not a diminution of freedom which may culminate in its abolition. My objectives have always been peaceful cooperation and a proper blend of freedom and justice.'

WILLY BRANDT · *born* 18 December 1913 · *died* 9 October 1992 ·

19 September 1994

KARL POPPER
Anthony Quinton

Sir Karl Popper, who has died aged ninety-two, was this century's most important philosopher of science in those parts of the world where that subject is taken seriously. Working from a few simple fundamental ideas, which turned out to be of considerable depth, he set himself to disencumber the prevailing conception of the nature of scientific knowledge from some old and tenacious empiricist errors. These ideas proved to be capable of wide application and were developed by him over half a century.

Science is not, he said, mechanically ground out by generalizing the findings of observation. Instead, it is a matter of weeding out falsehoods by empirical tests from the imaginative conjectures of theorists, so that there is a continuous, but never conclusively achieved, approximation to truth. His views were more attractive to people working in particular disciplines than to pure philosophers, but Popper did not think well of pure philosophy.

Popper was born in Vienna, the son of assimilated Jews – a lawyer of radical liberal sympathies, and a mother from whom he derived his love of music. Leaving school early amidst the post-First World War chaos, he educated himself at the university, in discussion amongst the young, hungry Viennese intelligentsia, in the Social Democratic Party and in social work under Alfred Adler's aegis. In 1928 he gained a doctorate with a thesis on the psychology of thinking, containing the first expression of his conviction that the mind does not acquire knowledge by the passive recording of impressions from outside it, but confronts the world with inborn expectations.

In 1930 he married Josephine Henniger and they worked as schoolteachers. Popper's main energies, though, were given to the writing of *The Two Fundamental Problems of the Theory of Knowledge*. He had come to know some of the scientifically minded philosophers of the Vienna Circle, the nucleus of logical positivism. Although never a member of it and critical of many of its beliefs, he was interested in the same problems and was well treated by the leaders of the group. Schlick invited him to abridge his manuscript as one in the series of books put out by the Vienna Circle and it was published in 1934 as *Logik Der Forschung* (translated in 1959 as *The Logic of Scientific Discovery*).

Nazism in Austria and the success of *Logik Der Forschung* led Popper to take a post at Canterbury University College in Christchurch, New Zealand, in 1936. There he remained until 1945 when he was invited by the distinguished economist F. A. von Hayek to the London School of Economics as reader in logic, becoming professor in 1948.

In New Zealand Popper produced two books he described as his 'war work': *The Open Society and its Enemies* (1945) and *The Poverty of Historicism*, first published in article form in 1944–5. Both argue that it is not the task of history and the social sciences to issue predictions of the general course of historical development. That idea encourages the view that society can be completely planned. Since it is an illusion, the failure of such total plans to get realized leads their totalitarian exponents to seek to enforce them by violence and to conceal their failures by systematic lying. The gospel in these books of rational moderation in politics is at least as important as their profound and imaginative contribution to the understanding of Plato and Marx. From 1945 until his 1969 retirement, Popper's activity was centred at the LSE where he built up a group of vigorous disciples; his seminars – a somewhat authoritarian undertaking for the prophet of the necessity of criticism – drew scholars from around the world. Two large essay collections came out. *Conjectures and Refutations* in 1963 developed and applied the doctrines of his earlier books, while *Objective Knowledge* in 1972 announced a major advance in his thinking, in which knowledge is seen as something public, not simply contained in people's heads, and as intelligible only in thoroughly evolutionary terms.

In retirement he was immensely productive. The intellectual autobiography he contributed to, a two-volume study of his work, edited by P. Schilpp, in

1974, was published on its own as *Unended Quest* in 1976. In 1977, in collaboration with his admirer, the Nobel-prizewinning biologist Sir John Eccles, he brought out *The Self and its Brain*, a defence of Descartes' thesis that mind and body, although utterly distinct in nature, nevertheless interact causally.

Popper was an excellent writer of lucid, colloquial, contemporary English. He regarded the clear expression of thought as a stringent moral obligation. But his hostility to obscurantism did not involve him in pedantic rigorism about language. He was wholly out of sympathy with the idea that philosophy is primarily concerned with meaning, an idea that in one way dominated logical positivism and in another the linguistic philosophy of the first two postwar decades in this country. Language, in his view, is inevitably imperfect. Instead of seeking an impossible final formulation of one's thoughts, one should simply try a number of different ways of putting them across. This commitment to clarity, distinguished with a slightly inconsistent exactitude from precision, was something Popper very effectively conveyed to his followers.

He was a compelling lecturer. In public discussion he was often fiercely combative; a tendency to take himself and his ideas, both serious things, with unrelenting seriousness was evident. But in private conversation an altogether more Viennese atmosphere prevailed, and he would be relaxed and entertaining. Few philosophers since Whitehead and Russell have combined such a vast breadth of knowledge with the capacity to produce important original ideas as he did. An essentially solitary person, he was happiest at home with his wife in Buckinghamshire, working prodigiously, but giving some time to music.

KARL RAIMUND POPPER · *born* 28 July 1902 · *died* 17 September 1994 ·

25 May 1995

HAROLD WILSON
Geoffrey Goodman

Lord Wilson of Rievaulx, as he came improbably to be called, will not go down in the history books as one of Britain's greatest prime ministers. But, increasingly, he will be seen as a far bigger political figure than contemporary sceptics have allowed; far more representative of that uniquely ambivalent mood of Britain in the 1960s; and a far more rounded and caring, if unfulfilled, person.

It is my view that he was a remarkable Prime Minister and, indeed, a quite remarkable man. Cynics had a field day ridiculing him at the time of his decline. Perhaps that was inevitable given his irresistible tendency to behave like the master of the Big Trick in the circus ring of politics – for whom there is nothing so humiliating as to have it demonstrated, often by fellow tricksters, that the Big Trick hasn't worked.

James Harold Wilson happened to be Prime Minister leading a left-wing party at a time when the mores of postwar political and economic change in Britain (and elsewhere) were just beginning to be perceived. Arguably it was the period of the greatest social and industrial change this century, even if the people – let alone the Wilson governments – were never fully aware of the nature of that change. Social relationships across the entire class spectrum were being transformed. What with the Pill, television, fashion, lifestyle, pleasure and leisure, there was a deepening uncertainty in the 1960s about what it all meant and where it was all leading. Harold Wilson's 'burning with the white heat of technology', and other famous phrases, sought to grapple with the era while never quite understanding what was happening to him or his government in a changing Britain and a dramatically changing world. He was blamed for things he never properly understood were happening. In that sense the Wilson of the 1960s was a victim far more than a hapless architect. He lacked the deep conviction of Thatcher or De Gaulle; he never possessed the philosophical and inspirational qualities of Aneurin Bevan – who, had he lived beyond 1960, would probably have been Labour's prime minister. Wilson often drifted. There was no compass, no weight of ideological baggage.

But Denis Healey is wrong in his assessment of Wilson as a man who had 'neither political principle' nor 'sense of direction'. Wilson did have both – embedded not in ideology but in his intuitive sense of decency and his powerful drive to try to spread that decency among his fellow citizens. Not classical socialist doctrine, but a profound belief that the Labour party was the instrument in his hands for the establishment of social decency.

There was another curious aspect to Harold Wilson – a strange modesty. Sometimes one had the impression that he never quite believed that he had arrived at the top of the greasy pole. Just before he was due to go to the Palace in 1964 after narrowly winning that memorable election, I interviewed him for the *Daily Herald*. We sat alone in Labour party headquarters at Transport House and I asked him how he felt. 'I still can't believe it,' he responded. 'Just think, here I am, the lad from behind those lace curtains in the Huddersfield house you saw – here I am about to go to see the Queen and become Prime

Minister ... I still can't believe it.' The cynics will dismiss that as an act. I am convinced it was genuine, vintage Wilson.

Not that those lace curtains concealed a working-class home of poverty and deprivation. He came from a lower middle-class family. His father, James Herbert, whom Harold later had pride in bringing to Labour party conferences, was an industrial chemist who worked for ICI. But in the slump after the First World War Herbert Wilson was made redundant. It devastated the family and shaped Harold Wilson's political mind for all time. He later confessed: 'Unemployment more than anything else made me politically conscious.' At Milnsbridge New Street council school he won a county scholarship to Royds Hall secondary school in Huddersfield. But when Herbert found a job as a chief chemist on the Wirral, Harold was transferred to Wirral grammar school – from where he won a history scholarship to Jesus College, Oxford. He was on his way.

One is tempted to say that he was the typical grammar school boy up at Oxford in the prewar 1930s. Almost working class; certainly lower middle class: no particular privileges in his background – unless you regard the nonconformist social and moral discipline as a privilege. Yet he wasn't typical. Unlike Denis Healey, from a roughly similar background in Yorkshire, Wilson did not dive headlong into Oxford politics or literary life. He was a swot. He spent his time almost exclusively on his studies – and did brilliantly. He won the Webb Medley economics prize as well as the Gladstone history prize. He gained an outstanding first-class honours degree in PPE and was elected to a junior research fellowship at University College, where he helped the master, Sir William Beveridge, in a study of unemployment and the trade cycle which had a clear influence on the great Beveridge Report.

Nor was Wilson a political lefty: his views were radical – but much more akin to the liberalism of Lloyd George than, say, the socialism of Stafford Cripps (Wilson's later hero) or even Clem Attlee. He regularly attended the Oxford Liberal Club in the mid-1930s and was hardly known at all to the band of student socialists like Healey or young socialist dons like Dick Crossman. But shortly before the war Wilson joined the Oxford Labour Club – largely, it is said, under the influence of G. D. H. Cole, economics fellow at University College and guru of Oxford socialism in the interwar years. There was another important influence developing – in the summer of 1938 Wilson become engaged to Gladys Mary Baldwin and they were married on New Year's Day 1940.

It was then that he began seriously to consider a political career, though he was still deeply attached to the academic lifestyle. When he registered for war service he was directed, as a specialist, to do government department work and this eventually led, through the War Cabinet secretariat, to Wilson's appointment as Director of Economics and Statistics at the Ministry of Fuel and Power. It was a critical turning point in his developing political awareness. Soon he came under the gaze of the redoubtable Hugh Dalton, in charge at the Ministry of Economic Warfare. Dalton chose Wilson to be secretary of an inquiry into the coal mining industry, which resulted in a book on the nationalization of coal. *New Deal For Coal* became a minor political classic, which provided the launch-pad for Wilson's leap into a parliamentary candidature. In the 1945 election he won Ormskirk, close by the Wirral, by a large majority and remained there till 1950 when redistribution took him to the nearby Merseyside seat of Huyton, where he remained until his retirement in June 1983. His rise to Cabinet office was exceptionally rapid. He was quickly appointed to a junior post in the Attlee administration. His feet had scarcely touched the back benches before he was made Parliamentary Secretary of the Ministry of Works and two years later, in March 1947, he was promoted to Secretary for Overseas Trade. By October he was in the Cabinet as President of the Board of Trade – at thirty-one one of the youngest Cabinet ministers of all time – succeeding Sir Stafford Cripps, who became the Government's economic overlord.

Wilson fell under Cripps's spell and continued to carry out many of the policies that Cripps had already laid down – especially the intensive postwar export drive. It was while at the Board of Trade that he first established a contact with the Soviet trade mission and with Stalin's shrewd and experienced trade minister, Anastas Mikoyan. Wilson's time at the Board of Trade is perhaps best remembered for his 'Bonfire of Controls' – when between November 1948 and February 1949 he removed hundreds of controls covering consumer goods, industrial equipment and the purchase of foreign supplies. Wilson's bonfire delighted the press and the public – but not many of his backbench MPs, particularly those on the left who regarded it as a clear sign that Wilson was really a right-winger at heart.

The real test of Wilson's political courage – or opportunism if one now reads his motives that way – came when he joined Aneurin Bevan in resigning from the Government in protest against the NHS charges in Hugh Gaitskell's 1951 budget. Gaitskell, a new Chancellor, was faced with the commitment to a huge rearmament programme (the outbreak of the Korean war), which Bevan opposed as fundamentally mistaken and because it meant the erosion of other spending plans, notably on the NHS. But Gaitskell was as stubborn as Wilson was flexible and, though no natural supporter of Nye Bevan,

Wilson followed Bevan's resignation a day later, along with another minister, John Freeman.

For a time Wilson went along with the Bevanites, participating in *Tribune* brains trust meetings throughout the country and campaigning on a broad left-wing platform. He was co-author of a famous *Tribune* pamphlet, *One Way Only*, a socialist argument against revisionist policies. Generally he identified himself with the anti-Gaitskell camp, which split the whole Labour party after the 1951 election defeat. Yet there was never a great deal of trust for Wilson among the proven Bevanites – and always some doubt in the mind of Nye himself, a doubt which became entrenched when Wilson took Bevan's place in the Shadow Cabinet in 1954 after Nye walked out over another policy rift. That gulf of distrust between Wilson and the left was never effectively healed.

Increasingly Wilson seemed to be grooming himself for a senior role in the Labour leadership. When Gaitskell became leader in 1955 Wilson canvassed and voted for Gaitskell – not for Bevan. In the late 1950s Wilson became a very effective Shadow Chancellor. He was also chair of an internal inquiry into organization, which produced a damning report on the party's cobwebbed methods and called for an end to the 'penny farthing' party machine. The legendary Morgan Phillips, party secretary, never forgave Wilson for that report.

Yet the 'Walter Mitty' label, which was to become the trademark of Harold Wilson's personality in his premiership years, was already being woven. He hovered between moderate left and moderate right throughout the late 1950s and into the 1960s. In 1960, the year Gaitskell was defeated over nuclear disarmament, Wilson actually challenged Gaitskell's leadership – but was heavily defeated, 166 votes to 81. It was Wilson's bid to try to rebuild a bridge with the left in the party, though it was regarded by the left as pure opportunism. The result of it all, ironically, was that he became Shadow Foreign Secretary.

Then came Gaitskell's sudden death. It found the Labour party completely unprepared, and the contestants had little time to develop their individual platforms. George Brown, James Callaghan and Harold Wilson went into the first ballot of MPs, which eliminated Callaghan, who polled 41 to Wilson's 115 and Brown's 88. In the run-off Wilson beat Brown by 144 to 103 – largely with the help of the old Bevanite left. So in February 1963 the little man from Huddersfield took over the Labour party and immediately began preparations for the general election that had to take place in 1964. At the Scarborough Labour conference of 1963 Wilson produced his famous speech on the 'white heat of technology' – from material provided for him by several committees in which Richard Crossman and Professor P. M. S. Blackett played a crucial role. And in the period between that conference and the election of October 1964

Wilson made six major speeches outlining the 'socialist alternative' to thirteen years of Tory rule and mismanagement. It was an unusually effective preparation in the country as a whole, while in Parliament Wilson dominated the House against the gentle but inadequate Alec Douglas-Home.

The surprise was to come: most pundits believed Wilson would secure a substantial majority in the October 1964 election: yet Labour won by a mere five seats, soon reduced still further by deaths. Even so, it was a remarkable victory. In the first hundred days of that first Wilson government there was genuine political excitement. The inheritance was a crippling one in economic terms. There were fearful problems with the balance of payments, the strength of sterling and the entire condition of the domestic economy. Lord Cromer, Governor of the Bank of England, told the Prime Minister that there would have to be severe cuts in government spending and fundamental changes in Labour's election promises. That was an outright and direct challenge to Wilson from the City establishment – within weeks of the election. Wilson's response was equally forthright. He told the Governor that his challenge was a threat to the government mandate and to democracy itself.

Wilson told Cromer that, if forced, he would 'go back to the electorate for a mandate giving me full power to handle the crisis'. Perhaps gamblers' talk, but also Wilson at his most audacious and courageous. He knew he must go to the country again before long. The counter-attack worked. Cromer retreated, though the City never forgot.

In fact none of the four Wilson governments was free from economic crises in one form or another. The 1966 election victory gave him a majority of 97, but by July the Government was plunged into its worst crisis of all: a seamen's strike exacerbated an already tense financial situation. Inflation at home led to a run on the pound and a severe strain on reserves. Devaluation was discussed and advocated by George Brown – but rejected by Wilson. Rumours spread about a Cabinet crisis and a possible putsch against Wilson. The Government scrambled through – far from the harmonious band their majority had promised.

What should have been the beginning of Wilson's most productive period as Prime Minister began in crisis and rarely moved away from that pitch. George Brown's National Plan was dumped. There were endless problems with the trade unions over incomes policy, culminating in Barbara Castle's White Paper on reform of industrial relations, *In Place of Strife*, which was undermined by union resistance and backbench MPs, as well as Cabinet divisions, where James Callaghan led the opposition. The retreat from *In Place of Strife* in summer 1969 contributed directly to the defeat of the Wilson government at the 1970 general election. Wilson's retreat in 1969 was seen by the press and public as capitulation to trade union power – which in many senses it was, though the issue was more complex than that.

On the overseas front there were few successes. Wilson's endless attempts to reach an accommodation with Ian Smith's Rhodesia ended in fudged deals culminating in UDI. Over Vietnam, Lyndon Johnson put increasing pressure on Wilson to provide a British contingent – which he resisted. But he also had to maintain the posture, which was costly window-dressing, of a significant British defence presence east of Suez. The devaluation of the pound in 1967 virtually destroyed what was left of the economic strategy. In November sterling fell to $2.40 and a badly shaken Prime Minister made an inept television address to the nation, arguing that the 'pound in your pocket' was unaffected – an extraordinary reversal of the euphoric days of 1964–6.

Most people, including Wilson, believed Labour would win the 1970 election. The polls were consistently in Labour's favour. The economy was showing distinct signs of improvement and Roy Jenkins's standing as Chancellor was regarded as a significant strength. Edward Heath was not rated as a dangerous challenger but turned a large Labour majority into an easily workable Tory one. Inside Wilson's Downing Street entourage there was a last-minute panic and much disagreement, especially between Marcia Williams (Lady Falkender) and other members of Wilson's 'kitchen cabinet'. These disagreements and personal animosities were to return and haunt the Wilson government of 1974.

In opposition the spark seemed to have been snuffed out of Wilson. It took him a long time to regain his confidence after the 1970 defeat. Yet he did so with, once again, unusual skill, holding the Labour party together and avoiding serious splits over the Common Market and defence policy. He was still a master at exploiting the theme of Labour unity and finding the compromise formulas. Indeed, it was during that period that Wilson picked up the theme of the 'Social Contract' – chiefly from Jack Jones, the Transport Union leader and Professor Tommy Balogh (Lord Balogh) – which provided the main platform when Labour returned to office in 1974. The Heath government blundered into a miners' strike after the oil crisis of 1973 and by the winter of 1973–4 appeared to offer no clearer solution to the 'trade union problem' than the Wilson governments of the 1960s. The February 1974 election was an extraordinary political event. The Heath government in effect abandoned ship. Wilson, to my own close knowledge at the time, did not expect to win. It was not so much an election victory for him as a defeat for Heath. No one had an overall majority, though Labour was the largest group. For several days the formation of a new Labour government remained in doubt as Heath sought a deal with the Liberals. Only when that failed did the Queen call on Wilson to form his third administration – a minority Labour government.

Immediately the Prime Minister turned to settling the miners' strike and the follow-through industrial problems. He appointed Michael Foot as Employment Secretary to orchestrate the Social Contract. It was a period of intense activity, a touch reminiscent of October 1964, albeit with the climate profoundly different. Former Cabinet ministers from the 1960s met in depressed mood, privately of course, to discuss what they regarded as the grim prospect of another Wilson administration. Men like Roy Jenkins – appointed unwillingly to the Home Office in 1974 – had already lost all confidence in Wilson's leadership and were actually looking for a defeat in the 1974 election. It was an unstable government – quite apart from whether a group of MI5 officers was busily trying still further to destabilize it. Yet in the few months between March and October 1974, when Wilson won his fourth term, the 'interim' government did actually perform rather well. Its very existence hinged on support from the Liberals, and the gamble that Scottish and Welsh Nationalists would not vote with the Tories. Healey's first budget was very tough, making no attempt to disguise the grave economic situation. Wilson began the process of trying to 're-negotiate' the terms of Britain's EEC membership. Michael Foot started to redraw the Heath government's industrial relations legislation. And the National Enterprise Board was established to help link the state and private industry in a redevelopment programme, while Wilson and Tony Benn fought their own ideological battle in the Cabinet about the degree of state intervention.

If the conspiracy theory of Wilsonia is to be believed, then it was about this time that, according to Peter Wright's book *Spycatcher*, a group of MI5 'dissidents' began to 'work' on the Government. Wilson himself, albeit later, as well as Lady Falkender, became persuaded that there was 'something in it'. At any rate those months between the two 1974 elections were certainly the time when Wilson pencilled a ring around the date of his resignation – to come shortly after his sixtieth birthday in March 1976. The great disappointment for him was the result of the second 1974 election. He hoped for a reasonable, if not large, working majority. In the event he secured a fragile overall majority of only three. He had achieved something no previous prime minister had done this century: he led four administrations, equalling the record of one of his old heroes, Gladstone. He had also kept the Labour party in one piece. Yet, somehow, real success evaded him.

Wilson began his final period as Prime Minister with an outward display of boldness. He helped Giscard d'Estaing, the French President, launch the concept of annual economic summit meetings; in the aftermath of the Arab–Israeli war and the huge increase in oil prices, the Wilson government managed another rescue operation to save sterling which Wilson described as 'the most hectic and harrowing month (December 1975) I experienced in nearly eight years as Prime Minister'. He brilliantly trumped Tony Benn's demand for a referendum on the Common Market by holding one; certainly an act, tactically, of political genius well in the tradition of Wilson. Domestic inflation, after its peak of 27 per cent early in 1974, was beginning to fall; the Social Contract, despite all the strains, was actually working; and Wilson pushed strongly for a new impetus to be given to regional policies in Scotland, Wales and the North. Quite remarkable for a man who was already tired, unwell and surrounded by personal uncertainties.

He resigned on 16 March 1976 – five days after his sixtieth birthday. I happened to be working for him at the time (though I had no idea of what was impending) and I knew how tired and ill he was. Some observers of that scene, like Len Murray (Lord Murray) the former TUC general secretary, still believe he could (and should) have continued. But I doubt it. He had had enough. He was not driven out by MI5 plots, real or imagined; there were no hidden mysteries about scandals, sexual or otherwise; it was not because Marcia Williams, Joe Haines and Bernard Donoghue were squabbling in an ante-room (though they were). His doctor – the late Joe Stone – had already detected problems which, later, became diagnosed as cancer of the colon. He was taking brandy to comfort the difficult afternoons and evenings. What I witnessed, first-hand, was the reality of a tired man, trapped by his own deep sense of uncertainty, which always lurked below the self-confident surface.

Yet after all criticism has been thrown at him, and the sneers and scepticism reduced to routine clichés, Harold Wilson, in my view, remains a remarkable man and a remarkable Prime Minister. He alone – other than Attlee in 1945 – was capable of making Labour the 'natural party of government' and maintaining a unity within such a disparate and warring coalition of ideas and ambitions. He failed to rise to greatness because he failed in the critical period after the victory of 1966. The final tragic years, in which the jewel of his extraordinary memory became increasingly destroyed by terrible illness, robbed him – and probably the nation – of an opportunity to demonstrate a matured wisdom that, undoubtedly, was there.

JAMES HAROLD WILSON, BARON WILSON OF RIEVAULX ·
born 11 March 1916 · *died* 24 May 1995 ·

FRANÇOIS MITTERRAND
Peter Morris

The death of François Mitterrand at the age of seventy-nine removes from the French, and European, political stage one of its most tenacious leading men. He will be remembered as the left-wing President of France, who in his two terms of office between 1981 and 1995 educated French socialism into an appreciation of the realities of power in a post-Marxist age, and who sought to convince his fellow citizens that European integration was the means to fulfil France's self-proclaimed mission to lead Europe.

His election to the presidency in 1981 was the culmination of a political odyssey that had started thirty-five years earlier and had survived setbacks which would have destroyed a less single-minded ambition. His career combined moments of great national popularity with long periods in which he was distrusted, and even despised, as a scheming and unprincipled adventurer. Towards the end of his second term, he became the most unpopular president in the history of the Fifth Republic. The publicizing of his links during the Second World War with the collaborationist Vichy regime, and even more of his enduring friendship with Rene Bouquet, who in 1942 had supervised the rounding up of the Paris Jews, caused utter dismay to those who had regarded him as the champion of Republican values. The verdict of posterity is likely to be kinder and to place him, alongside General de Gaulle, as a key figure in the creation of modern France.

The comparison with de Gaulle is one that never failed to infuriate the general's acolytes, for whom Mitterrand personified the corrupt political class which had done so much damage to France before the advent of the Fifth Republic and which understood nothing of national grandeur. Yet there are similarities between the two men. They shared an Olympian manner; a deep interest in literature and history; the capacity to behave with cold ruthlessness towards opponents; and a refusal to acknowledge the right of the United States to determine the foreign policy of its allies. Above all, Mitterrand taught the French left to accept the institutional order created by de Gaulle after 1958.

Little in Mitterrand's background suggested the future course of his career. Born in 1916 in the small village of Jarnac, near Cognac in the Charente department, he was one of eight children and grew up in a family that was bourgeois, conservative and Catholic. He did not rebel against this background either as a schoolboy or as a law student in Paris, and to the extent that he was involved in the frenetic politics of 1930s France his sympathies unquestionably lay with the nationalist right rather than with the left-wing causes of the Popular Front or the Spanish Civil War.

The Second World War was the making of Mitterrand. He fought, and was decorated for bravery, in the disastrous 1940 campaign that led to the fall of France. Like de Gaulle twenty-five years earlier, he was taken prisoner by the Germans. Unlike de Gaulle he managed to escape from captivity, aided perhaps by his unremarkable physical appearance, and returned to France. What happened next provides the background to the first great controversy surrounding his career. Mitterrand became an important resistance leader and took part in the liberation of Paris in August 1944. But he also accepted employment from Marshal Petain's collaborationist Vichy government and was awarded the regime's medal of honour, the Françisque. To his enemies this showed the duplicitous opportunism that characterized his whole career; to his supporters it demonstrated his intelligence in finding a cover for his resistance work.

Mitterrand emerged from the war with a wife, Danielle, daughter of a resistance leader, to whom he stayed married despite an almost legendary series of affairs and one-night stands, and with the determination to make politics his career. Crucially, the war defined Mitterrand as an opponent of the two principal forces of the New France – Gaullism and communism. At a memorably unsuccessful meeting with de Gaulle in Algiers, he refused to acknowledge the latter's authority over the resistance movement he ran, an act of insubordination that the general neither forgot nor forgave. At the same time, however, he resisted the smothering embrace of the French Communist party, which had emerged as France's largest and most politically correct political movement. This double refusal of allegiance gives a unity to the whole of his subsequent career.

By the age of thirty, Mitterrand was established as a drivingly ambitious, and independent-minded, professional politician. Elected to the National Assembly in November 1946 for the largely rural department of the Nievre, he retained his seat for all but three of the next thirty-five years and acquired the local power base – mayor of Château-Chinon, member of the departmental council – that all French politicians regard as a vital political resource. In January 1947, he became the youngest government minister this century and he subsequently served in eleven cabinets during the Fourth Republic. No one doubted his intelligence or his capacity for hard work; what was queried was the integrity of his convictions. He was a leader of a small centrist party, the

UDSR, that was more notable for the opportunistic bargaining of its parliamentary votes than for the solidity of its beliefs.

He was distrusted by the democratic left for his willingness to lock up Algerian nationalists once the war of independence began in 1954, and by the nationalist right for his Europeanism and his support for self-government for France's sub-Saharan colonies. To his immense chagrin, even Pierre Mendes France, the hero of progressive France, seemed willing as Prime Minister to give credence to unfounded rumours that his Interior Minister might be a communist agent. This period gave Mitterrand his reputation for Machiavellian cunning and the most enduring of his nicknames, 'the Florentine'. Yet to say that his name was made by the Fourth Republic is a dubious accolade, given the regime's collapse in the face of decay at home and insurrection in Algeria. With the exception of Mendes France, none of the politicians most identified with it was ever fully rehabilitated. What saved Mitterrand, apart from his youth and talent, was paradoxically his absolute refusal to compromise with the new political order established by de Gaulle in 1958.

He opposed de Gaulle's return to power and in a famous pamphlet, *Le Coup d'État Permanent*, denounced the authoritarian nature of the new Fifth Republic. In the short term, this opposition cost him dear. He lost his National Assembly seat in the 1958 elections; was refused entry to a new left-wing grouping, the Parti Socialiste Autonome; and was nearly destroyed in 1959 by a scandal in which he was accused, falsely as it – much later – transpired, of setting up a fake assassination attempt. He was to be out of office for twenty-three years. Yet his resolute opposition to de Gaulle's republic enabled him to drape himself in the clothes of French democratic republicanism and to begin the process of alliance-building with the left-wing parties and movements that had hitherto rejected him. He brought to the fragmented and dispirited elements of the non-communist left not only his own eloquence, energy and proclaimed commitment to France's republican traditions, but also a shrewd appreciation of the realities of power. Most important, he offered the left a strategy for winning power that required it to accept the directly elected presidency as the key political prize in the new institutional order and to unite its forces behind a single candidate. The aim was left unity, and he was to be its architect.

Mitterrand's long march to power through the institutions of the Fifth Republic began with the 1965 presidential contest. His very isolation made him an acceptable (because expendable) stalking horse for the big battalions of the communist and socialist parties, in a contest which everyone expected de Gaulle to win easily. And win he did – but narrowly. The 45 per cent of the vote that Mitterrand won in round two suggested that there might be political life after de Gaulle and he established his own position as the leader of the opposition to the regime. His subsequent strategy was dedicated to developing and consolidating his position as its guardian. In 1971 he engineered the sort of political operation at which he excelled by getting himself elected first secretary of the Socialist party, a position he held for ten years. Under his supervision, the party became the vehicle for a generation of political talents and ambitions, who fell under the spell of a leader who could combine inspirational warmth with chilling remoteness. In 1972 he negotiated an electoral and programmatic alliance with the still powerful Communist party. That enabled him to mount an impressive second bid for the presidency after Pompidou's death in 1974. In a thrilling contest, he lost by less than 1 per cent of the vote to the non-Gaullist conservative Giscard d'Estaing. When he told his voters that 'your victory is inevitable', he was also thinking of himself.

These high points were, however, matched by lows that on more than one occasion seemed to leave him politically dead. He came very badly out of the events of May 1968, being rejected by radicals as just another machine politician and denounced by constitutionalists for what looked like an illegal bid for power. Ten years later his entire strategy for gaining power – the alliance with the communists – collapsed when the latter took fright at the advance of their socialist rivals and sabotaged the expected victory of the left in the 1978 parliamentary elections.

For Mitterrand, 1978 was a catastrophic result. He was now over sixty; he had begun to look like a permanent loser; and his reputation as a political strategist lay in ruins. Within the Socialist party, he was challenged by the rising star of Michel Rocard. Though he managed to win the socialist nomination for a third bite at the presidency in 1981, some commentators even doubted that he would make it to the second round. That Mitterrand did not succumb can be explained by his strength of character, by his ability to keep control of the Socialist party and by the changing contours of national and international politics in the early 1980s. The incumbent president Giscard fell victim to the recession blues syndrome that had seen off Carter and Callaghan.

Mitterrand skilfully combined policy radicalism with personal reassurance; his almost Baldwinesque campaign posters placed him against a rural background, complete with church steeple, and the comforting message – 'la force tranquille'. What made the message work was the electoral decline of his old adversary/ally, the Communist party. Sixty years of right-wing propaganda disintegrated as the poor first-round performance of the communist candidate meant that a socialist president would no longer be at the mercy of the men with the metaphorical knife between their teeth. In round two Mitterrand swept to power at the head of a coalition of socialist enthusiasts, communist voters, and Gaullist and non-party malcontents. It was a sensational victory and one that Mitterrand immediately consolidated by holding fresh elections for the National Assembly in which the socialists triumphed.

Mitterrand's presidency can be divided into three periods. In the first, he and his governments sought to realize the economic, social and political reforms identified with French socialism. The guillotine was abolished; civil liberties and trade union rights were strengthened; local government was freed from the stifling embrace of centralization; and welfare benefits were increased.

The core innovation, however, was an extensive programme of nationalization and demand stimulation that set France on a course diametrically opposed to that being followed in the United States and Britain. It was small wonder that Mitterrand became a beacon of hope for the faltering European left who, like Michael Foot's Labour party, chose to overlook his resolute support for the introduction of Cruise missiles. Within two years of taking office, Mitterrand's recovery programme crashed against the harsh realities of low investment, soaring inflation and a depreciating currency. Thus in 1983 a second period began, as Mitterrand abandoned the dream of 'socialism in one country' and turned to the new 1980s orthodoxies of sound money, entrepreneurialism and company profitability. His conversion was probably made easier by the fact that his socialism had never been based on economics (critics like Lady Thatcher derided his ignorance of eternal economic verities) and by the ever decreasing credibility of the alternative strategy advanced by the communists and his own left-wing.

In the short term, employment and his popularity plummeted. But his control over his ministers and over the socialist majority in the National Assembly remained intact and gradually the French economy recovered its competitiveness and confidence. Even the more than honourable defeat of the Socialist party in the 1986 legislative elections was turned to his advantage. By staying in office and appointing the Gaullist leader Jacques Chirac as Prime Minister, he inaugurated the period of cohabitation. This enabled him to consolidate a highly effective profile as the venerable but vigilant guardian of constitutional proprieties and national solidarity against the aggressive neo-liberalism of Chirac. Potential embarrassments like the 1985 *Rainbow Warrior* scandal, in which French secret services blew up a Greenpeace boat in Auckland harbour, were shrugged aside.

The second period also saw the European Community move to the centre of his political agenda. As President, Mitterrand had always accepted the de Gaulle-inspired contours of French defence policy, symbolized by the independent nuclear deterrent, the ruthless pursuit of French interests in Africa, and the *entente* with West Germany. In 1984 he was photographed holding, rather than shaking, hands with Chancellor Kohl at Verdun – the site of the murderous First World War battle between France and Germany. More practically he played a major role in the mid-1980s relaunching of the European Community. He sent Jacques Delors, his former finance minister, to Brussels; worked to heal the running sore of Britain's Community contribution; and put his authority behind the Single European Act.

It was a tribute to his popularity and authority that by 1988 the Florentine was more commonly referred to as Uncle or God. He strolled to victory in the 1988 presidential election, standing on his record and personality and articulating a collection of liberal-sounding platitudes that bore little resemblance to the ambitious policies of 1981. Yet the sheer ease of his victory made it inevitable that the second term would turn sour. This was not because of any decline in Mitterrand's intellectual agility or zest for the game of politics. Despite an operation for cancer of the prostate in 1992, he experienced a last period of popularity in his skilful handling of the Gulf crisis. His problems originated in a series of domestic and international crises. The strong currency and business-oriented policies of his governments gave France one of the best balance of payments records in the industrialized world. But they were quite unable to prevent widening social inequalities in France and to slow the inexorable march of unemployment to the three million mark, an increase that proved a fertile recruiting ground for the extreme right politics of Le Pen's National Front. Neither reflected well on Mitterrand's complacent invocations of republican virtues.

Abroad, the collapse of the Soviet Union left France once again exposed to the power of its neighbour across the Rhine. Mitterrand strove energetically to organize the new European disorder by a series of diplomatic moves, of which the most substantial was the 1991 Maastricht Treaty, accelerating the process of Community integration. Governments throughout Europe were in trouble by the 1990s and the long-serving Mitterrand was now facing the same sort of voter fatigue that had contributed to de Gaulle's decline in the late 1960s. Increasing numbers of his fellow citizens came to believe that the arrogance of power had set in and Le Pen's denunciations of the caviare left struck a nerve that transcended their tainted origin. A series of corruption scandals involving the Socialist party and presidential associates did untold damage in a country which always wants to believe the worst of its rulers.

Mitterrand survived charges of personal corruption; but his haughty manner and his extravagant use of public money for public, and private, ceremony caused great resentment. This might have mattered less had Mitterrand not made the disastrous miscalculation of celebrating his tenth anniversary in office by sacking his respected Prime Minister (and intimate enemy) Michel Rocard and replacing him with Edith Cresson, of whom it might politely be said that she was a long-time political friend. Cresson proved totally unable to win the respect of the political nation, and of the nation *tout court*, and she dragged Mitterrand down with her. Less than a year later, in what was widely interpreted as a sign of declining presidential authority, Mitterrand was forced to replace her with another long-time associate, the Finance Minister Pierre Bérégovoy. By now it was too late to restore the authority of the sober-suited socialism that Mitterrand had come to symbolize. Despite an effective television intervention, Mitterrand was unable to achieve more than the narrowest of majorities in the referendum on Maastricht in September 1992.

Six months later, the Socialist party he had done so much to create went down to overwhelming defeat in the parliamentary elections and plunged into a period of recrimination that did not spare its erstwhile hero. In a melancholy epilogue, his last Socialist prime minister and devoted admirer Pierre Bérégovoy shot himself out of despair that he too was accused of financial malpractice – and, so some people said, that Mitterrand had done nothing to help him in his spiritual agony. Once again Mitterrand's sheer toughness and imperturbability came to the surface. He remained in office, reading, golfing and intellectualizing when there was nothing else to do – and emphasizing his continuing authority when, as in the case of Europe, there was. He collaborated closely with his conservative prime minister Edouard Balladur in the August 1993 crisis of the exchange rate mechanism and refused to accept that the European dream was dead.

His opponents continued to treat him with wary respect and his presidency did not suffer the fate of American equivalents like Carter. Machiavelli never became Lear, though the revelations of his Vichy past inevitably posed the question of what, apart from his own star, he had ever believed in. The monumental architectural projects he imposed on Paris – the Bastille Opera, the Louvre Pyramid, the Defence Arch – constitute one form of legacy. The reshaping, and perhaps ultimately the sabotage, of the political agenda of the

French left is another. But perhaps the most enduring legacy of all will be the memory of his extraordinary career.

FRANÇOIS MAURICE MARIE MITTERRAND · *born* 29 October 1916 · *died* 8 January 1996 ·

7 November 1997

ISAIAH BERLIN
Bernard Crick

Isaiah Berlin, most famous English academic intellectual of the postwar era, outstanding lecturer, peerless conversationalist and superlative essayist, has died at the age of eighty-eight. His career began in pure philosophy but he became interested in the history of ideas, especially those claiming to offer a comprehensive view of human purposes. He had a genius, in dazzling lectures and essays, for expounding empathetically the plausibility of such ideas and evoking the character of their principal exponents, but always with determination to expose the danger to freedom and human diversity of all such ideologies that claim to have, or be leading us towards, a single goal or truth. To Berlin, the plurality of human beliefs has to be accepted. Philosophy, no more than brute force, can resolve conflicts of values. His pluralism was not an uncritical exaltation of variety, still less the postmodern cynicism of 'anything goes'; rather he recognized the recurrent pain, at times tragedy, of knowing that whatever values we pursue are always at some cost to other values and other people. To be humane and tolerant and to act honourably, we must know our own limitations and appreciate the almost boundless oddity of others.

He was born in Riga, Latvia, the only child of Marie and Mendel Berlin, a prosperous timber merchant. His parents were secular Jews but his grandparents were pious Chabad Hasidim, the sect now known as the Lubavich. He grew up speaking Russian and German. The family moved in 1915 from Riga to Andreapol, and on to Petrograd in 1917, of which he had vivid memories. In 1921 his parents, finding conditions intolerable for them, left for England. Isaiah was put to school at St Paul's. He studied Classics and picked up French as well, achieving a greater linguistic ease and proficiency than most of his contemporaries at Oxford, where he read philosophy at Corpus Christi

College. In 1932 he won a prize fellowship to All Souls and became a Fellow of New College in 1938.

He quickly became famous as a great talker in that famously self-important small world. His conversation bubbled and fizzed at astonishing speed, with literary and philosophical speculation and illustrative anecdotes drawn from Russian, German and French authors of years gone by, often quite unfamiliar to his listeners.

Berlin's promise as a philosopher was clear in that he became one of a small circle, convened by the formidable J. L. Austin and including A. J. Ayer, who met to discuss the purest problems of the new philosophy at the highest possible level. Are there a priori truths? What is the logic of counter-factual statements? What is perception? Can we have knowledge of other minds? Berlin stayed with the circle until 1939, but after the war, as he recounts with good humour in his essay on 'J. L. Austin and the Early Beginnings of Oxford Philosophy', he realized this activity, while probably important and certainly exhilarating in its friendly zeal to refute each other's arguments (so that what was left was lean and true), was no longer for him.

So very English he sounded, as was Oxford philosophy itself, yet he never forgot, or let it be forgotten, that he was deeply conscious of Russian and Jewish roots and concerns. Even during the time of apparent total immersion in linguistic analysis, he wrote for the Home University Library a marvellously lucid and judicious *Karl Marx: His Life and Environment* (1939), almost the first remotely objective account of what Marx had said back then, who he was, why he said it, his Hegelian roots and Jewish background. This short book was, austerely and provocatively, about Marx and ignored Marxism and international communism. The critique of determinism was clear and firm, but not laboured. He had the good manners to enjoy unlikely company and to draw out, not to put down or caricature, interesting people, whether living or dead, whose ideas he thought quite wrong-headed.

With unusual imagination, the Ministry of Information sent him to New York in 1941 to show hesitant American intellectuals the honest face of an intellectual who was a belligerent English patriot, fiercely anti-Nazi but never anti-German, indeed even more than a little Zionist, which presumably helped. The Foreign Office soon brought him to the embassy in Washington, where he wrote weekly despatches on the state of American opinion in his vigorous, flowing, complex long sentences, as if dictated at great speed with perfect control. (Someone said: 'Like Gibbon on a motorbike.') Churchill said they were some of his favourite wartime reading. But, alas, the famous tale is not true that Churchill confused Isaiah with Irving Berlin.

He filled in for a few months at the end of 1945 in the embassy at Moscow. There he met, semi-clandestinely, Boris Pasternak and the great poet Anna Akhmatova, and later wrote a memorable account of their conversations about Russian literature and the condition of writers under Stalin. Akhmatova was, in her isolation, to attach an extraordinary, almost a crazed significance to their meeting: thus could art and intelligence rise above and annul political oppression universally. And it affected Berlin greatly. To his natural gaiety, literary facility and pyrotechnic intellectuality was added a great moral seriousness.

When he returned to Oxford, his interests quickly changed from pure philosophy. He had reread Tolstoy's *War and Peace* and plunged deeply into the Russian novelists, poets and social thinkers of the mid-nineteenth century. 'Their approach seemed to me essentially moral: they were concerned most deeply with what was responsible for injustice, oppression, falsity in human relations, imprisonment whether by stone walls or conformism – unprotesting submission to man-made yokes – moral blindness, egoism, cruelty, humiliation, servility, poverty, helplessness, despair, on the part of so many.' Thereafter he turned his back on analytical philosophy; but with a mind sharpened by those ultra-intelligent mental exercises, he evoked the dilemmas inherent in great or hitherto obscure but interesting figures in the history of ideas.

When Anna Akhmatova had told him everything she could about herself personally, as well as her views on all great questions, as people will when they fear not to survive and to be obliterated in memory, she had asked Berlin who he was. He tells us he replied in kind, but not, of course, what he replied. He is the least autobiographical of writers in any psychological sense. But by then he must surely have known or suspected that his grandfathers, an uncle, an aunt and three cousins had all perished in the holocaust in Riga. That may have helped make the old ways seem parochial, deeply though he loved Oxford, college life and Englishness. He married in 1956 a beautiful and rich woman, of Russian and French parentage, Aline de Gunzbourg. The following year he became Chichele Professor of Social and Political Theory, while remaining a Fellow of All Souls, to where he had been translated from New College in 1950. His inaugural lecture, 'Two Concepts of Liberty', made him instantly famous among intellectuals on both sides of the Atlantic and provoked lasting debate. Many called it at the time, 'a classic restatement of English liberalism'. But that was a two-edged judgement and few of us then knew anything of the more pessimistic tones of Russian nineteenth-century liberalism, quite different from J. S. Mill's optimistic rationalism.

Three things about the manner of his lecture became the hallmark of all his writing. He could be and was read by both academics and general intellectuals. He joked against himself that he was 'a general intellectual, by analogy to "general domestic"; will tackle anything', for he affably ignored disciplinary boundaries. He combined rhetoric with analytical rigour in an unusual but characteristic way. He was always excited by ideas but attached them to persons, rarely to periods, movements or general tendencies. He translated Turgenev's *First Love* and later *A Month in the Country*. The melancholy tone of old Russian liberalism appealed to him more than the English liberal tradition, still wedded to a belief in inevitable progress.

Essays flowed out and honours flowed in thick and fast. He was a director of Covent Garden from 1951 to 1965, then from 1974 to 1987, suppressing his dislike of Wagner but not his enthusiasm for early rather than late Verdi, and was a trustee of the National Gallery from 1975 to 1985. Through his friendship with Sir Isaac Wolfson, he was virtually founder as well as first president of Wolfson College in 1967. He was elected to the British Academy in 1957, the same year he was knighted, and was its president from 1974 to 1979.

But for all his fame and authority, he had a certain amiable *naïveté*. The story was that when he received a CBE in 1946, the King said, as he always did: 'A pleasure to meet you'; but when he took that as a conversational opener, he was cut short by an equerry, guiding him because he was almost blind without his thick glasses, removed in case the ribbon pulled them off: 'Bend your neck and stop talking.' Two things he never, to his honour, otherwise did.

In 1971 came the Order of Merit. He willingly served on numerous time-consuming scholarship, fellowship and award committees in Britain, the US and Israel, enjoying meeting the rising stars of each generation, asking them searching, interesting questions – and often generously answering them himself. He held twenty-three honorary doctorates (including Harvard, Yale, Oxford, London, Jerusalem and Tel Aviv) and several great prizes, including the Jerusalem Prize for services to freedom and the Erasmus Prize for the history of ideas, and was the first to gain the Agnelli Ethics Prize in 1987.

His bibliography is confused since he rewrote speeches and essays for different occasions, and published some in different collections with varying titles. But basically there are four books: *Karl Marx*, *Four Essays on Liberty*, *Vico and Herder* and *The Magus of the North*; six volumes of essays, edited by his friend Henry Hardy (trying heroically, like Zuleika Dobson's maid packing her trunk, 'to make chaos cosmic!'); and in 1997 a fine anthology of 'the best of Berlin', *The Proper Study of Mankind*. Letters have been prepared for publication and an authorized biography by Michael Ignatieff, but to appear only after his death.

He spoke with astounding rapidity and in that very low-pitched Oxford accent, swallowing many vowels, eliding like a Frenchman, not the high-pitched drawling Oxford. American audiences often found him difficult to follow, both the rapidity and the number of syntactically perfect sentences, always exciting to follow – what would come next, could he possibly regain the main subject, spoken two minutes and twenty dependent clauses ago, with an object sufficient for climax not bathos? Yes, always – often to mass sighs of relief and admiration. He was the most exciting and famously extempore of lecturers. I could never hear anything but Oxford in his voice, but the mother of an American friend, an uneducated woman born in Belarus, took a telephone call from him one day and, calling her son, remarked that a man with a very English accent was on the telephone: 'But he was born in Russia, Mel.'

He loved England, as often only emigrés can, and he appeared so very English. It was England almost too specifically – he never spoke or wrote of Great Britain or the United Kingdom, and had no interest in Scottish, Welsh or Irish literature. Well, he was aware that the Scottish enlightenment of David Hume and Adam Smith was part of the history of British empiricism, but on neither did he write, and there was no essay on Burke. Almost too English, but also naturally cosmopolitan, always introducing forgotten or misunderstood continental figures, especially those who had thought on a continental scale.

Only large themes interested him, even in obscure authors; but he was endlessly kind to individuals. A young man received a letter as short as this: 'I have not the pleasure of knowing you, but I have read and admired your book and I will shortly say so in the *Observer*.' The pride and delight that gave me was only mildly diminished by his not actually getting round to reviewing it for two years, and then in a series on 'Neglected Books' in a dying monthly. He always had so much on the go, including a vast correspondence. But to call him workaholic would be wrong. Mental work to him was pleasure, leisure – keen argument in good company.

The speed and restlessness of his thinking made the essay his *métier*, not the book, never the monograph. Most read as if dictated. Conclusions were not always as clear as they might have been had he written more slowly and with difficulty, but then the energy, facility, enthusiasm and the startling bursts of stimulating free-association, bringing unlikely figures together, might have been lost. There is a recording in the National Sound Archive of the Mellon Lectures he gave at the Kennedy Center, Washington, in which such runs and bursts are punctuated by the kind of applause that striking a six, or a home run, evokes from a partisan crowd. In 'Joseph de Maistre and the Origins of Fascism', he remarked on 'the peculiar characteristic of a time of transition between sharply divergent outlooks, of which such psychologically complex figures as Goethe and Herder, Schleiermacher and Friedrich Schlegel, Fichte and Schiller, Benjamin Constant and Chateaubriand, Saint-Simon and Stendhal, Tsar Alexander of Russia and indeed Napoleon himself are typical representatives'.

Useless to cry, in the voice of Oxford philosophy: 'Wait a moment, let us unpick quite what you mean by "peculiar" and "time of transition"' or to ask: 'Are all these twinnings apt?' for he then gallops on to a brilliant evocation of the mysterious-man-of-destiny myth, the 'l'homme fatal' as 'conveyed by the celebrated painting by Baron Gros, now in the Louvre, of Napoleon at Eylau'. To him, Carlyle's great-man theory of history was tosh, indeed dangerous tosh; but yet there was value in being reminded that some great figures had altered the course of history, even if not always for the better.

So brilliantly evocative. But often, at the end of the day, so much of his writing, like that 'celebrated painting', is dramatic evocation, a cascade of resonant proper names and adjectives, not explanation. The twists and turns of 'the crooked timber of humanity' (a phrase of Kant he used as the title of a collection of studies) are, he held, perhaps not capable of explanation, in any scientific or logical sense, only of understanding.

He is called a historian of ideas, but he showed little interest in either the pre-history of the ideas he discussed or the sociology of knowledge – the when and how ideas emerge from obscurity to centre stage. Weber and Mannheim interested him not at all. The history of ideas is now a specialized and method-conscious scholarly discipline, and its adepts look at Berlin with a mixture of both admiration and exasperation. But he wrote for intellectuals more than for disciplinary scholars. What he did do with unique brilliance was to evoke the plausibility of ideas, especially those that threaten freedom, and relate them to the character of particular thinkers. He was humanist through and through, sometimes in the almost reductionist sense that individuals alone move or personify events, but also in the moral sense that it is the happiness or dignity of individuals that counts, not the pride and power of nations or ethnic groups.

He was a Zionist, indeed, not because he was Jewish, but because Jews were persecuted and thus needed, contingently not in principle, the protection of a national home. He had a darker view of human nature than liberals who thought that goodwill and the UN could achieve a peaceful coexistence in the

Middle East without paying a heavy price. We cannot live without group identities, hence his interest in Herder and the German romantics, but individuals can and sometimes should take on other identities, or challenge dominant beliefs of the group in the name of freedom. All this made this larger-than-life man, or this mortal Isaiah, kindly and helpful to young scholars – many, many such letters as the one to me. Some colleagues shook their heads that all geese were swans, but he knew when to encourage, when to cut down or when to turn his massive back. He exemplified Ernest Gellner's maxim: 'Social tolerance always, intellectual tolerance never.'

He had blind spots. 'We seem to agree on most things. But I cannot share your enthusiasm for Baron de Jouvenal and Miss Arendt. Tell me what she is saying. Put it in a simple proposition. Fairy gold, Crick, fairy gold. Metaphysical free-association.' And occasionally he spoke as if his name did for argument. The *Observer* once had a foolish Christmas feature to designate the most overrated writer of the year. Other contributors mentioned a name with a sentence or two of explanatory denigration; but Berlin simply pronounced *ex cathedra*: 'Hannah Arendt.'

A famous essay, 'The Hedgehog and the Fox', was on Tolstoy's view of history. Many friends as well as critics see Berlin as a foxy essayist ('The fox knows many things,' the Greek poet said), but all through, there are two really big bits of hedgehoggery (who 'knows one big thing'): his defence of freedom and his account of pluralism. 'Two Concepts of Liberty' distinguished between negative and positive liberty, and argued that to seek to go beyond negative liberty, that is freedom from restraint, into positive liberty, that is freedom as achieving some positive good, is politically dangerous, morally dubious and logically self-contradictory. Positive liberty is when I feel more free when I know the truth or am serving a just cause. But all these 'freedoms' involve either restrictions on others, or a certainty that their values or views of truth are false, as in Rousseau's 'forcing people to be free'. There are often good reasons for restricting freedom, but let us recognize, he said, that to do so is not to increase freedom, otherwise the concept becomes simply a synonym for justified restraint. Freedom is a fundamental human value, but it is not the only value. It may be right and just that I should be taxed so that you do not starve; but do not say that either of us is then positively free, otherwise freedom to debate the justice, the degree and the results of such actions is denied.

If he was a libertarian, it was in the sense that the protection of negative freedom is a necessary condition of any just social order; but it is never a sufficient condition, as the market liberals tried to argue. Like Popper, his views on social policy were pragmatic, though both were misrepresented by socialist critics. It took a long time for British Marxists to realize that bourgeois liberties are liberties, and that social problems and conflicts of values have neither unique nor complete solutions. 'Where does he stand?' some of us asked impatiently, some contemptuously. But at the time he was writing, any British variations on freedom and justice paled into minor questions compared to the reality of the denial of anything sensibly called freedom by Soviet power; and Nazi marchers in the 1930s as well as German communists had cried 'Freiheit!'

To Berlin, it was not the business of political philosophers to endorse one party rather than another, but to defend a strong but minimal (or strong because minimal) concept of freedom. But perhaps this was a little austere and closer than often noticed to analytical philosophy, in its weakness as well as its strength, than to history. He was interested in the nature of freedom and passionate to defend it against persecution, obvious or covert; but had no interest in the social conditions of freedom, the appropriate institutions, nor in the history of citizenship, as in the work of those who in the last decades have revived the idea of civic republicanism and traced its history. He was a definitive critic of single-truth systems of thought, what he called systematic ideologies; but with their threat diminished, some of his finest writings may lose the bite of relevance that once they had.

More lasting will be his understanding of pluralism, but it is not a comfortable one. He was not a relativist. Some values are universal, like freedom and science; and some value systems threaten or distort both. Nonetheless we live in a world of diverse values, not all of them equally pleasing for good reason, but which we can, with knowledge and empathy, understand; and too often have to choose or compromise between them.

In 'The Pursuit of the Ideal', he said: 'The notion of the perfect whole, the ultimate solution, in which all good things coexist, seems to me to be not merely unattainable – that is a truism – but conceptually incoherent ... We are doomed to choose, and every choice may entail an inseparable loss. Happy are they who live under a discipline that they accept without question ... or those who have arrived at clear and unshakeable convictions about what to do and what to be that brook no possible doubt ... Those who rest on such comfortable beds of dogma are victims of forms of self-induced myopia, blinkers that may make for contentment, but not for understanding of what it is to be human.'

John Gray has well named this 'agonistic liberalism', the *agon*, the conflicts of character seen by Greek tragic drama as inherent and perpetual. Noel Annan saw Berlin's work as exhibiting 'the truest and most moving interpretations of life that my generation made'. Berlin's memory of Pasternak quoting Heine could be turned to himself. 'I may not deserve to be remembered as a poet, but surely as a soldier in the battle for human freedom.'

SIR ISAIAH BERLIN · *born* 6 June 1909 · *died* 5 November 1997 ·

3 November 2000

STEVEN RUNCIMAN
Nigel Clive

Sir Steven Runciman, the historian, aesthete and traveller, who has died aged ninety-seven, was the pre-eminent British specialist of the Byzantine empire and of the crusades. His three-volume *A History of the Crusades*, published between 1951 and 1954, set out to exemplify his belief that the main duty of the historian was 'to attempt to record, in one sweeping sequence, the greater events and movements that have swayed the destinies of man', and show that history's aim was to give a deeper understanding of humanity. He aimed as much at a non-specialist audience as at fellow academics. For Runciman, the crusades were the last of the barbarian invasions; their disaster was their failure to understand Byzantium. 'High ideals were besmirched by cruelty and greed, enterprise and endurance by a blind and narrow self-righteousness,' he wrote, 'and the holy war itself was nothing more than a long act of intolerance in the name of God, which is a sin against the holy ghost.'

Runciman was the second son of the 1st Viscount Runciman of Doxford, who was descended from the mid-eighteenth-century Scottish painter Alexander Runciman. His father was a member of Asquith's Cabinet and his mother was MP for St Ives. He himself always welcomed the fact that, as the younger son, he was not obliged to go either into politics or the family's shipping business. Indeed, an academic career was foreshadowed by his precocious ability to read French at three, Latin at six, Greek at seven and Russian at eleven.

He won a scholarship to Eton, where a combination of an early interest in Greece and medievalism led naturally to his study of Byzantium. His school friends included Cyril Connolly, George Orwell and 'Puffin' Asquith, the Prime Minister's son. In 1921 a further scholarship took him to Trinity College, Cambridge, where he began to demonstrate an elegant and fashionable aestheticism by papering his rooms with a French grisaille wallpaper depicting Cupid and Psyche, and being photographed by his friend, Cecil Beaton, with a parrot poised on his ringed finger. Through his school friend George Rylands, he was introduced to John Maynard Keynes, Lytton Strachey and Virginia and Leonard Woolf, and got to know the Bloomsbury group.

After taking a first in history, Runciman became a research student of the notoriously elusive J. B. Bury, the first British historian to take Byzantium seriously. He artfully discovered the Regius Professor's regular habit of taking an afternoon walk along the Backs, and was thus able to manoeuvre Bury into giving him unofficial tutorials. Following an attack of pleurisy – and his doctor's prescription that his best chance of recovery would come from a long sea voyage – he went to China, arriving in the middle of the civil war. But this did not prevent him from befriending the last Chinese emperor, with whom he played piano duets.

In 1924 Runciman made his first trip to Greece, was enchanted by the Byzantine town of Monemvasia and, later, by the old city of Istanbul. On his return to Cambridge, he concentrated on his Fellowship thesis, with pioneering investigations into Armenian and Syriac sources, which, in 1929, resulted in his first book, *The Emperor Romanus Lecapenus*. After that, in quick succession, came *The First Bulgarian Empire* and *Byzantine Civilisation*.

Runciman had gone back to Trinity in 1927 to teach and hold a Fellowship until 1938. His first pupil had been Guy Burgess, whom he remembered for his intellectual brilliance and his dirty fingernails. His last pupil was Donald Nicol, who became Koraes Professor of modern Greek and Byzantine history at London University. Meantime, his travels had taken him to Jerusalem and Thailand, with several more visits on foot and muleback to Greece and Turkey.

When his grandfather died in 1938, Runciman could afford to give up his Fellowship, and take George Trevelyan's advice to leave Cambridge and concentrate on his writing. By a happy chance, the war took him back to the countries of his choice, first as press attaché in Sofia in 1940, then to Cairo and Jerusalem for the Ministry of Information, and finally to Istanbul for three years as Professor of Byzantine art and history. This gave him the opportunity to follow the tracks of the crusaders and plan his *History of the Crusades* – as well as visiting Syria and becoming an honorary whirling dervish.

Immediately after the war, Runciman willingly accepted the offer to direct the work of the British Council in Greece. During the next two years, assisted by Paddy Leigh Fermor and Rex Warner, this remarkable triumvirate endeared themselves to the Greeks in a manner that has never been rivalled. In Athens, Runciman became a well-known figure in the smart Kolonaki set ('the good bandit families', as he characteristically called the descendants of the leaders of the Greek war of independence) and was a friend of George Sepheriades, the diplomat whose poetry, under the name of Seferis, later won a Nobel prize. In his spare time, he improved his collection of icons, tanagras (figurines) and Edward Lears.

After the publication, in 1947, of *The Medieval Manichee*, a still unchallenged study of the Christian dualist heresy, Runciman returned to Britain to start work on the crusades, dividing his time between his house in St John's Wood, London, and the Isle of Eigg, off the Scottish coast, which his father had bought in 1926. From 1951 to 1967, he was chairman of the Anglo-Hellenic League, which he nicknamed 'the Anglo-Hell'.

His reputation was triumphantly established when *A History of the Crusades* was published in three volumes, between 1951 and 1954. Praising the pace and style of its narrative history, some critics even compared its author to Macaulay. *The Eastern Schism* was published in 1955, and *The Sicilian Vespers* in 1958. This was the year in which Runciman was knighted, and in 1961 he was made a Knight Commander of the Greek Order of the Phoenix. As part of his continuing revival of interest in Byzantium, *The Fall of Constantinople 1453* appeared in 1965, *The Great Church in Captivity* in 1968, *The Last Byzantine Renaissance* in 1970, *The Orthodox Churches and the Secular State* in 1972, and *Byzantine Style and Civilization* in 1975.

When a street was named after him in Mistra, his expression of gratitude took the form of a book, published in 1980, about the Byzantine capital of the Peloponnese. Runciman had always found theology both fascinating and entertaining. Although he did not belong to the Orthodox Church, he had a profound commitment to orthodoxy and believed that it enshrined the future of Christianity.

When Eigg was sold in 1966, he quickly moved to Elshieshields, a border tower in Dumfriesshire. Indeed, throughout his long and peripatetic life, he had always known that his roots were in Scotland. This became his last home, where he happily entertained both old and new friends, introducing them to his collection of eighteenth- and nineteenth-century musical boxes, worry beads, a hubble bubble pipe, the Alexander Runcimans and Edward Lears, the limericks as well as the watercolours. Here, too, he could display his knowledge of the genealogical ramifications of European royalty, often flavoured by well-informed gossip. The year after his eightieth birthday he was made a Companion of Honour.

But although he settled in Scotland and made only irregular visits to London, Runciman still found time to travel abroad to lecture and discover new Coptic churches. In 1987, his name and fame reached a much wider audience when Channel 4 produced a well-directed verbal autobiography, *Sir Steven Runciman: Bridge to the East*.

Even in his middle eighties, there was no slackening of his energy or intellectual vitality, and his ability to charm his friends of all ages. Early in 1991, an exhibition of his collection of Lear's watercolours was held at the National Gallery of Scotland. The catalogue contained his introduction and comments on each of the pictures, as well as a photograph of Stephen Conroy's portrait of him, which hangs in the Scottish National Portrait Gallery. Soon afterwards, he published *A Traveller's Alphabet: Partial Memoirs*, which colourfully recorded in alphabetical form – A for Athos, Z for Zion – a lifetime of travels that had taken him round the world, and 'where a certain amount of serendipity had crept in'.

In 1992 Runciman rediscovered a short story or novella, written in 1935 and entitled *Paradise Regained*. This fictional account of an expedition to Iraqi Kurdistan, dedicated to George Rylands and revealing both his wit and sharp sense of humour, was privately printed and distributed to his friends in place of a Christmas card. In 1993, to celebrate his ninetieth birthday, dinners were given for him by the Old Collegers of Eton, by the British Byzantines and by Trinity College, Cambridge. The Cambridge University Press organized a reception for him, and the National Trust for Scotland gave him its guest flat at Culzean in Ayrshire. Finally, he invited some hundreds of friends to a lavish reception at Spencer House.

All the while, Runciman continued to travel. In September 1994, he took part in the ceremony on the island of Lemnos inaugurating the Aegean declaration, an agreement between Unesco and the Greek Ministry of Culture to turn the Greek archipelago into a European cultural park. In April 1995, in his capacity as president of the Friends of Mount Athos, he published a learned article in *The Times* deploring the fact that, on the Athonite peninsula, the tradition of faith transcending ethnic difference, which had been the practice for more than a millennium, was under threat.

As late as 1997, besides his regular visits to Bahrain and Greece, he contributed a sparkling review in the *Spectator* of a life of Marthe Bibesco, the Wallachian princess who was a confidante of countless heads of state. As recently as last month, he was in Athens to receive from the Greek President the international prize for culture (arts and humanities) of the Onassis Foundation. In addition to its silver trophy, he received $125,000, which he generously offered to Mount Athos.

Runciman was greatly distressed by the Kosovo war, where his sympathies lay with the Serbs. When well on in his nineties, he began writing his memoirs. He never married.

JAMES COCHRAN STEVENSON RUNCIMAN · *born* 7 July 1903 · *died* 1 November 2000 ·

4 May 2002

BARBARA CASTLE
Anne Perkins and Denis Healey

Barbara Castle, who has died aged ninety-one, was Labour's Red Queen, the woman Michael Foot called 'the best socialist minister we've ever had'. Clever, sexy and single-minded, author of some of the best political diaries of her time, she was the most important female politician the Labour movement has yet produced, a unique witness to, and participant in, the twentieth-century history of the left.

From the prewar unity campaign against fascism, via the early issues of *Tribune*, to the Bevanites in the 1950s, taking in Cyprus and the Hola camps in Kenya, and climaxing in the heart of Harold Wilson's government, she was an unflagging champion of an ethical socialism that she believed should shape every aspect of life. In one of the ironies of politics, she paved the way for Margaret Thatcher to capture the commanding heights of government.

Throughout her political career, Castle maintained a hard-headed pragmatism, without compromising a passionate belief in the transforming power of socialism. Her ambition, she said, was 'to inch people towards a more civilized society'. She was brave and determined, the heart-throb of the constituency Labour parties for nearly thirty years. Her career foundered on an inability to master the key political skill of building support where it counted, in the parliamentary party. She claimed to find making political alliances demeaning; her critics found her wearisomely egocentric. Even her friends distrusted her temper. The last five years brought her an Indian summer of popular favour, as her distaste for Blairism made her the heroine of the same right-wing press that had cheered her departure from the Cabinet in 1976.

Barbara Anne Betts grew up in Bradford, in the secure environment of a family with a need for belief. The socialism of the Independent Labour party (ILP) was the main, but not the only, religion of the household. Her mother,

Annie, a Labour councillor, was a devotee of the romantic William Morris; her father, Frank, a tax inspector, was a poetry-writing intellectual who filled the columns of the ILP journal, the *Pioneer*, which he edited in the late 1920s and early 1930s, with art, criticism and politics in equal measure. He nurtured young talent like Vic Feather, thus enabling the future TUC General Secretary to dismiss Barbara, when she was Secretary of State for Employment and Productivity – fighting her doomed battle for trade union reform – as 'a lass he knew when she was still in dirty knickers'.

Although she was never untruthful about her own past, it was rather less proletarian than she would have liked for a party suspicious of middle-class intellectuals. She toiled through Bradford girls' grammar school, and followed her older, more brilliant, sister Marjorie to St Hugh's College, Oxford, where she made the daring choice of sex and practical politics over economics and philosophy. She graduated with a third-class degree and a sense of intellectual inadequacy, which drove her to work with almost damaging diligence throughout her political career. She was determined to become a journalist and a politician, but the Depression forced her to briefly earn a living selling dried fruit from a mobile display in a Manchester store while, in her free time, setting out to save the Labour party from the betrayal of Ramsay MacDonald's national government.

Soon after Oxford, Barbara fell in love with the leading socialist intellectual and journalist, William Mellor. He was married with a young child, but for more than ten years they pursued a tempestuous, semi-public affair, their passion spent equally between each other and the politics of the left. But although his wife knew of the affair, Mellor could never bring himself to leave her. He died, suddenly, in 1942.

Barbara found other friends, notably her immediate junior at Oxford, Michael Foot. Later, he happily indicated they had shared more than Marx and Dickens in front of the gas fire of a small flat in Bloomsbury, but she angrily denied there had ever been an affair, and Foot, professing mild surprise, loyally retracted. Together, in 1937, they helped launch *Tribune*, which was edited by Mellor until he fell out with *Tribune*'s financial backer, Sir Stafford Cripps. The paper, whose declared mission was to recreate Labour as a truly socialist party, was also Cripps's personal contribution to the left's campaign against rearmament, and in favour of a united front against fascism. It was soon in conflict with the leadership, which, in turn, was increasingly making common cause with the Churchill wing of the Conservative party. Cripps sent Barbara off to Moscow, from where she reported, without irony, on the new assurance of Russian women in the age of Stalin.

Determined that not even war would interrupt her pursuit of a political career, she rejected more exotic offers to became a temporary civil servant while she hunted for a parliamentary seat. In 1943 she made her first speech to the Labour party conference, accusing the leadership – accurately – of preparing to compromise on the timing of the implementation of the Beveridge Report. 'We want jam today, not jam tomorrow,' she warned. It was a popular cry for the *Daily Mirror*. Its night editor was Ted Castle: he put the story on the front page. After a courtship of proselytizing together for Beveridge on street corners and in parish halls, they were married – and stayed so, through some rough times, for thirty-four years.

In 1944, after a mutiny by Labour women, who insisted that at least one woman candidate be interviewed, Barbara was selected for one of the two Blackburn seats, beating three men for a constituency she represented until her retirement from the Commons in 1979. As soon as she got to Westminster, Cripps asked her to become one of his parliamentary aides. Clement Attlee notoriously underpromoted young and left-wing politicians and, when Cripps moved on from the Board of Trade to take over as Chancellor, Castle was left behind to work for his successor, Harold Wilson. She often disapproved of Wilson's rapacious ambition, but it was the start of the most important political relationship in her life. She nominated him for the leadership when he challenged Hugh Gaitskell unsuccessfully in 1960, and again when he won, after Gaitskell's death, in 1963.

When Labour was finally returned to power in 1964, her reputation was for division within the party, and personal vituperation against enemies outside it. Probably the only leader who would still have given her a department to run was her old friend Wilson. He squeezed her into his first Cabinet at the Department of Overseas Development – a department whose creation she had often advocated – and gave her the opportunity to reinvent herself, at the age of fifty-three, as one of the most effective Cabinet ministers of her generation.

With no ministerial experience, and a department to be chiselled from the stony faces of the Foreign, Colonial and Commonwealth offices, Barbara sent her private office staff round to the Fabian Society to collect every available copy of a pamphlet she had written on international development, and instructed them to treat it as a blueprint. Within a year, she had established her department and secured its budget, and demonstrated a flair for the photo-opportunity desperately needed by a government already wracked by internal tensions and an economy in crisis.

Wilson promoted her to the Department of Transport (even though she couldn't drive), where her dominant traits as a minister became clearer: she demanded total support from her civil servants – in a very public battle of wills, much effort was devoted to trying to move her Permanent Secretary, Sir Thomas Padmore; she had a good eye for what was both desirable and achievable, and the left's unshakeable belief in the power of government to plan from the centre. In her two and a half years at Transport, she transformed the culture of motoring with the introduction of the breathalyser and the seatbelt. But with the economy still perilously fragile, despite the devaluation of 1966, Labour was locked in its long and, ultimately, failed attempt to control inflation while maintaining full employment. A pay policy was unavoidable, but equally unpopular.

Wilson wanted Barbara to bring her dynamism and popularity to selling the pay restraint to an increasingly nervous parliamentary party. He created a new department for her, Employment and Productivity. And she was brought into the heart of government as First Secretary, a title generously foregone by another political intimate, Richard Crossman. It was the pinnacle of her career, and from it she heroically flung herself, convinced of her own rightness, down into the deep gulley of union reform. Convinced that a statutory pay policy was an instrument of socialism – a brake on the industrial might that won inflationary pay claims at the expense of the economy and of weaker unions – Barbara was brought up short by trade unions totally resistant to any restraint on free collective bargaining. Under pressure from the Tories, and wrapped in an unshakeable confidence in the duty of government to bring order to the chaotic state of British industrial relations, she attempted to deliver a socialist solution – 'The trouble with Barbara is that she thinks anything she does is socialism,' sniffed a contemporary. *In Place of Strife* (1969) was the inflammatory title of a White Paper that proved to be the most divisive attempt at legislation for thirty-five years.

Although there were many worthy proposals intended to strengthen trade unions, all anyone saw were plans for compulsory strike ballots and a cooling-off period, both to be underwritten by sanctions. Barbara, who believed that given time she could make anyone love her, wanted a long, evangelical campaign to build up popular support. Roy Jenkins, the Chancellor, was desperate for some reassuring morsel to feed the bankers hungrily circling the floundering pound. She was forced to accept a short bill to enact only the penal clauses.

In the face of a campaign illuminated by the startling duplicity of senior colleagues, including the then Home Secretary, James Callaghan, and an entirely hubristic challenge from the unions, pathfinding for the Thatcher assault on trade union rights ten years later, Barbara and Wilson rashly made the legislation an issue of confidence. Egged on by an enthusiastic press (with the exception of the *Guardian*), Barbara took the battle to seaside resorts and spa towns around the country in a dramatic and hugely popular appeal, to individual union conferences. In barrister's black, the taut passionate figure aroused the admiration of millions.

But trade unionists, led by Vic Feather at the TUC, found her ignorant, inflexible and hectoring. Friends on the left could not understand why she was doing the Tories' work for them. And Wilson's more ambitious enemies planned for what they were sure was his imminent downfall. There were genuine fears the party could be split into union-sponsored and independent MPs, another 1931.

The Cabinet – and ultimately even the Chancellor – deserted the bill. Wilson and Barbara were forced into a humiliating defeat, behind a fig leaf of 'solemn and binding' agreements that the TUC and the unions would work together to try to restrain the unofficial strikes that were undermining economic recovery. Barbara's stock crashed to earth. But the ramifications went far beyond personal disaster. The episode accelerated a renewed alienation between party activists and the Labour leadership. Local parties became vulnerable to infiltration by Trotskyite groups, like Militant, preaching the politics of betrayal. The leadership of the left – never quite within Barbara's grasp – was now torn between Michael Foot and Tony Benn. The unions, after Edward Heath's failed attempt at union legislation, which was uncomfortably close to Barbara's own, agreed to the Social Contract, a promise of voluntary pay restraint in return for legislative favours from a future Labour government.

Back in power in 1974, Wilson loyally put Barbara – who had been thrown off the elected Shadow Cabinet in 1972 – into the Department of Health and Social Security. Here, in a period of government often overlooked, she launched a last effort to push back the frontiers of the welfare state. But although it was marked by notable achievements – like the introduction of SERPS, the scheme for second pensions which was intended to transform the old age of millions of low-paid – she squandered her last political capital on an ideological battle over pay-beds in the NHS. This time, the backbenches and the unions cheered her on. But it was at a heavy cost to the health service: at one stage, all hospital doctors, from the most junior to the most senior, were involved in industrial action, which closed accident and emergency wings, and tainted industrial relations for years afterwards.

Before she could bring in the legislation for which she had fought so hard, Wilson resigned. His successor, Jim Callaghan, sacked Barbara with unexpected brutality, and her pay-bed reforms ran slowly into the sand. By 1979 only a quarter of all pay-beds were phased out, while the private sector outside hospitals blossomed unrestrained.

There were other, more subtly achieved and lasting successes. Although she always rejected single-issue politics as a distraction from socialism (like Mrs Thatcher, she was a politician who was also a woman – tough, flirtatious, vain, often hot-tempered, capable of tears in moments of drama – rather than a woman politician), and she brutally dismissed recent attempts to make Westminster a kinder, gentler place, her most enduring achievements came on behalf of women. Equal pay was the most notable, slipped past a reluctant Roy Jenkins in a late-night bid in 1970 to avert a backbench revolt. She won other vital concessions for women in pensions reforms. She introduced child benefit, and insisted it went into the purse not the wallet.

Even when she gave up the Commons in 1979, she could not give up politics. After a lifetime's opposition to the European Union, she became the leader of the Labour group in the European Parliament, where, for another ten years, she harried Commissioners on the Common Agriculture Policy, before finally demanding a seat in the Lords in 1990 from the then Labour leader Neil Kinnock.

She remained an active and determined campaigner for pension rights – the Chancellor, Gordon Brown, called her 'my mentor and my tormentor' – and against animal cruelty until her final illness. Her passion for politics was given full rein in her final incarnation as national treasure. As the figurehead and part-inspiration for the 1990s campaign to restore the link between pensions and earnings (which she had introduced twenty years earlier), Barbara finally won the near-universal applause of which she had so long dreamed. Committed to the socialism of her youth, she hated what she thought Tony Blair was doing to the party. But her loyalty to the Labour movement was unfaltering.

Contemporaries, infuriated by her single-minded and relentless pursuit of her objectives in government, recalled, in the cosy glow of nostalgia, her huge appetite both for life and for the fight. She was a woman who delighted in dancing with the enemy at night, before spearing them with her invective the next day.

Barbara and Ted, who died in 1979, had no children, but were devoted to their nieces and great nieces and nephews.

DENIS HEALEY writes: Barbara Castle was an iconic figure in the postwar politics of Britain, personally attractive to friend and foe alike. Many found her energy and intelligence irresistible. She had red hair like other Labour women

– Ellen Wilkinson between the wars, and Patricia Hollis today. She was always concerned about her appearance, and even as a minister had her hair done every day.

Although we often disagreed on political issues, particularly when she was a member of the Tribune group, Barbara and I had a lot in common. I was a boy of eleven at Bradford grammar school when she was a prefect at Bradford girls' grammar school. As MPs, both of us worked as journalists, because in those days we could not live on an MP's salary alone. We served together on the national executive of the Labour party, and for many years in Labour Cabinets.

Her time as a civil servant during the war had given her experience invaluable for work as a minister. Yet she was one of the few leading politicians who kept an interest outside politics – particularly poetry and walking.

Both of us spent some years as members of the European Parliament. I always regretted that I was abroad when she was defeated in Cabinet on her proposals to strengthen control of the trade unions, though her White Paper, *In Place of Strife*, caused years of civil war inside the Labour party.

She told me she was glad I was a pugilist and not a patrician, and dedicated my copy of her autobiography, 'Affectionately to Denis, the man I love to fight'. When she once complained that I was crucifying her, I replied: 'Your hands do invite the nails.'

BARBARA ANNE CASTLE, BARONESS CASTLE OF BLACKBURN ·
born 6 October 1910 · *died* 3 May 2002 ·

26 February 2003

CHRISTOPHER HILL
Martin Kettle

Christopher Hill, who has died aged ninety-one, was the commanding interpreter of seventeenth-century England, and of much else besides. As a public figure, he achieved his greatest fame as master of Balliol College, Oxford, a post he held from 1965 until 1978. Yet it was as the defining Marxist historian of the century of revolution, the title of one of the most widely studied of his many books, that he became known to generations of students around the world. For all these, too, he will always be the master.

It would be a pardonable exaggeration to say that Hill created the way in which the people of late twentieth-century Britain – and the left in particular – looked at the history of seventeenth-century England. As he never tired of pointing out, some of the themes he illuminated so richly had already been explored by left-wing scholars in the 1930s. But from 1940, when he published his tercentenary essay, *The English Revolution 1640*, his own voluminously expanding and unfailingly literate work became the starting point of most subsequent interpretation, even for those who rejected his method and conclusions. No historian of recent times was so synonymous with his period of study; he is the reason why most of us know anything about the seventeenth century at all. He was, E. P. Thompson once said, the dean and paragon of English historians.

Hill was born in York, where his father was a solicitor. His parents were Methodists, a fact to which he attributed his lifelong political and intellectual apostasy. Though his life was to be the embodiment of a secularized form of dissent, his high moral seriousness and egalitarianism surely had roots in this radical Protestant background. At St Peter's school in York, his academic prowess was immediately evident. It is said that, when Hill was sixteen, the two Balliol dons – Vivien Galbraith and Kenneth Bell – who marked his entrance papers, agreed to award him 100 per cent, before travelling to York to capture him for the college and prevent him going any further with a Cambridge application. Galbraith, in particular, was to remain an immense influence.

Hill's association with Balliol was to continue, with only brief interruptions, from his arrival as an undergraduate in 1931 until his retirement as master forty-seven years later. Academic honours regularly fell his way, starting with the prestigious Lothian prize in 1932, and continuing with a first-class degree in 1934 and an All Souls Fellowship that winter. But he was a successful rugby player too, the scorer of a famous cup-winning try for Balliol. Even more lastingly, he had become a Marxist.

Exactly when and why this happened is uncertain, since Hill was always notoriously inscrutable about discussing his personal life. He once claimed it came about through trying to make sense of the seventeenth-century metaphysical poets, but although he read Marx as an undergraduate, the moment of his conversion to communism is elusive. His contemporary, R.W. Southern, once teasingly remembered 'a time when Christopher was not in the least bit leftish', but Hill was an undergraduate during the period of the Great Depression, the hunger marches, the New Deal, Hitler's rise (he visited the Weimar Republic before going up to Oxford), and the first (favourable) impact of Stalin in the West. He was a regular attender at G. D. H. Cole's

Thursday Lunch Club, where, as he once put it, 'I was forced to ask questions about my own society which had previously not occurred to me.'

Certainly by the time he graduated, Hill had joined the Communist party. In 1935 he spent a year in the Soviet Union, during which he was very ill, but also formed a lasting affection for Russian life – and a somewhat less lasting one for Soviet politics. After Moscow, he had two years as an assistant lecturer at University College, Cardiff, before returning to Balliol as a fellow and tutor in modern history. In 1940 he was commissioned as a lieutenant in the Oxford and Bucks Light Infantry, before becoming a major in the Intelligence Corps and being seconded to the Foreign Office from 1943 until the end of the war. This was, to put it mildly, an intriguing period, about which he rarely let fall much detail.

By this time he had begun to publish, at first pseudonymously, articles and reviews which, among other things, did much to draw attention to the burgeoning Soviet school of English seventeenth-century studies. Then, in 1940, arising out of intensive debate among a group of Marxist historians, who included Leslie Morton, Robin Page Arnot and – particularly influential on Hill – Dona Torr, came the decisive *The English Revolution 1640*. The essay was originally published as one of a collection of three reflections (the others were by Margaret James and Edgell Rickword). Hill's contribution, which was subsequently published alone, was a no-holds-barred assertion of the revolutionary nature of England between 1640 and 1660, and an assault on the traditional presentation of these years as an aberration in the stately continuity of English history. 'I wrote as a very angry young man, believing he was going to be killed in a world war,' Hill later told an interviewer. The book, he said, 'was written very fast and in a good deal of anger, [and] was intended to be my last will and testament'. It has rarely, if ever, been out of print since.

The discussions surrounding Hill's essay also produced, in 1946, the Communist Party Historians Group, an association he regarded as 'the greatest single influence' on his subsequent work. This formidable academy, which included Edmund Dell, Maurice Dobb, Rodney Hilton, Eric Hobsbawm, James Jeffreys, Victor Kiernan, George Rude, Raphael Samuel, John Saville and Dorothy Thompson, has a good claim to have redefined the study of history in Britain, especially after the launch, in 1952, of the journal *Past and Present*, of which Hill rapidly became the moving spirit and, later, the doyen. It also generated the path-breaking collection of documents, *The Good Old Cause*, that he edited with Dell in 1949.

The active, twenty-year involvement with communism, which also led to his short biography *Lenin and the Russian Revolution* (1947), came to a crisis after the Soviet invasion of Hungary in 1956. Along with many in the Communist party, Hill had become disenchanted with the party's lack of democracy and its reluctance to criticize the Soviet Union. Both issues came to a head in the late weeks of 1956, though his own break did not come until the following year. He was appointed to a Communist party review of inner-party democracy, but the rejection of the critical minority report, written by Hill (with Peter Cadogan and Malcolm MacEwen), precipitated his final departure.

These were watershed years in Hill's personal life too. A wartime marriage to Inez Waugh, the former wife of a colleague, produced a home life that combined the high seriousness of Balliol Marxism with an extravagant Bohemianism. It also produced their daughter, Fanny Hill, later a dashing figure on the Oxford scene, who drowned off the Spanish coast in her forties. The marriage collapsed early, and in 1956 he married again, this time to Bridget Sutton, then a history tutor with the Workers' Educational Association in Staffordshire. Turbulence was replaced by the single greatest happiness of Hill's life. With Bridget he had a son and two daughters, one of whom died in a car accident.

After 1957, Hill's career ascended to new heights as he began the remarkable output of books on which his reputation will rest, and which continued undiminished until he was well into his eighties. Hill always argued that the connection between leaving the Communist party and his wider fame was *post-hoc* rather than *propter-hoc*, and it is certainly true that 1956–7 caused no revolution (let alone a counter-revolution) in his analysis of the English revolution. On the other hand, the Bridget effect can hardly be underestimated.

If the steady flow of books which began with *Economic Problems of the Church* (1955) can, to some extent, be seen as a succession of more scholarly explorations of the themes sketched out in the early didactic essays, they also reflect the extraordinary sweep of Hill's interests and mind. Central to the whole project was a patient fascination with religion, represented, in particular, in his attempt to understand the revolutionary power of puritanism. But Hill's explorations were in no way bound by traditional or preconceived theories. The single, most striking and controversial aspect of his method was the way in which he subtly identified intellectual connections, currents and continuities between the most unlikely pieces of evidence – from scraps of court records to *Paradise Lost* and *The Pilgrim's Progress*. His use of literary sources was one of his most fascinating characteristics.

Many of the tasks he set himself were laid out in his next book, *Puritanism and Revolution* (1958). They were further explored in *Society and Puritanism in*

Pre-Revolutionary England (1964) and the remarkable *Intellectual Origins of the English Revolution* (1965, and extensively revised thirty-one years later), this last based on his 1962 Ford lectures. Alongside came more popular works of exegesis – a Historical Association pamphlet on *Cromwell* (1958), the best-selling (but not adulatory) biography *God's Englishman* (1970), the textbook *The Century of Revolution* (1961) and the hugely successful Penguin economic history, *Reformation to Industrial Revolution* (1967).

Those who heard Hill deliver the lectures on which it is based – lectures delivered in a nervous, slightly stuttering voice – will always reserve a special place for his 1972 study of radical and millenarian ideas, *The World Turned Upside Down*. Not only was this one of the very few history books to be turned into a play (at the National Theatre), it was also a work made more exciting by the time in which it was written, an era of counter-cultural energy which Hill observed (and quietly celebrated) from the Balliol master's lodgings.

This was a period of immense academic daring (and, thought some, of over-reaching) as Hill scythed through received tradition in his study of *AntiChrist in 17th-century England* (1971) and his controversial study of *Milton and the English Revolution* (1977), which, like many of his later works, was written at the plain but lovely house in Perigord which Bridget badgered him into buying in 1969.

Meanwhile, in 1965, Hill had defeated Ronald Bell in the election for Master of Balliol, a success which caused raised eyebrows (it was only ten years or so since academics with Hill's politics had been, to all intents and purposes, blacklisted from many posts) and much press attention. His tenure was deft and collegiate, and he tried to maintain his teaching and research amid the administrative and ceremonial duties. He never seriously hid his enthusiasm for the two main innovations of his mastership – the opening of male-only Balliol to women, and the representation of students on the college governing body. 'Common sense varies among the young,' he admitted, 'as among the old.'

Retirement found his productivity undiminished. He moved to Sibford Ferris in the Cotswold hills, and for two years worked as a visiting professor at the Open University, an entirely characteristic effort to bring his learning to a wider audience. Then he settled down to further books: *Some Intellectual Consequences of the English Revolution* (1980), *The World of the Muggletonians* (1983), and *The Experience of Defeat* (1984), an account of the Restoration made poignant by the reverses twentieth-century left-wing politics were suffering at the time. A marvellously vivid study of Bunyan followed in 1988, before *The English Bible in 17th-century England* (1993) and *Liberty Against the*

Law (1996). Three volumes of essays were published in the 1980s – throughout his life, Hill wrote some of his most challenging and original work in articles and reviews.

Hill was honoured by an OUP festschrift, *Puritans and Revolutionaries*, when he retired from Balliol in 1978, and Verso published a series of tributes and criticisms, *Reviving the English Revolution*, ten years later. Yet, for the last twenty years of his life, he became once again a more controversial figure. His methodology was famously assaulted by J. H. Hexter in a *Times Literary Supplement* review in 1975, and his assessment of Milton was powerfully denounced by Blair Worden. A reaction against his big reading of seventeenth-century history took root in the work of Conrad Russell, John Morrill and others. Yet Morrill's tribute in 1989 – 'If we can be sure that the seventeenth century changed England and Englishmen more than any other century bar the present one, we owe that recognition to him more than to any other scholar' – shows how, even in relative eclipse, Hill remained the central point of reference in seventeenth-century studies.

People always felt there was something enigmatic about Hill. Whether as a friend walking through Oxfordshire or the Dordogne, as a tutor hunched in his armchair discussing an essay – and still more on formal occasions – he kept his cards close to his chest, forcing you to do the talking, making you listen to what you were saying in the way that he was listening too. But then he would make a joke, often just a pointed ironic observation, that made you love him. As someone once said, although he affected to be severe, he could not help being benign.

But tough too. Always. Hill once gave a radio talk marking the centenary of the publication of *Das Kapital*. He ended it by telling how, in old age, Marx had bumped into a fellow revolutionary from the 1848 barricades, now prosperous and complacent. The acquaintance reflected that, as one got older, one became less radical and less political. 'Do you?' Marx replied. 'Do you? Well, I do not!' And nor, he clearly intended us to understand, did Christopher Hill.

JOHN EDWARD CHRISTOPHER HILL · *born* 6 February 1912 · *died* 24 February 2003 ·

MOVERS, SHAKERS AND DOERS

...

WILLIAM PENNEY
Christopher Driver and W. L. Webb

Go easy with Penney, Lord Cherwell advised Churchill prior to the first meeting of the policy committee before the 1952 tests in Australia that proved Britain's own atomic bomb: 'He is not always very tactful, but his heart is in the right place.' More importantly, 'he is our chief indeed our only real expert in the construction of the bomb, and I do not know what we should do without him'.

All the Harwell–Aldermaston–Risley Lords Cockroft, Penney and the engineer Christopher Hinton were among the 'New Men', to borrow the title of C. P. Snow's novel about the making of the bomb – scholarship boys from working-class or modestly middle-class families. Only Lord Penney, who has died aged eighty-one, was actually born into ordnance, the son of a sergeant-major in the Royal Army Ordnance Corps (RAOC). From the technical school in Sheerness, he rapidly progressed via London University and Cambridge, where he was an exhibitioner at Trinity. At twenty-seven he was assistant professor of mathematics at Imperial College, and by thirty-three he had two Ph.D.s and a D.Sc. for his theoretical work on molecular structure.

For most of the war he was a problem-solver for the Ministry of Home Security and the Admiralty on the effects of high explosives and of waves on Mulberry harbours, but in 1944, when work on the atomic bomb began in earnest at Los Alamos, Penney was sent there as the Department of Scientific and Industrial Research's Principal Scientific Officer. By the time that work came to devastating fruition in Hiroshima and Nagasaki, he knew more about its operational aspects than any other British scientist and more than all but a very few of the Americans. He saw the Nagasaki bomb dropped from an accompanying plane, and he was part of the team that visited both ruined Japanese cities to calculate the effectiveness of the blasts. 'In all the discouraging attempts in the early postwar years to secure Anglo-American cooperation,' writes Margaret Gowing in her magisterial history of the development of the British bomb, 'Penney was the British asset most coveted by the

Americans.' He got on 'extremely well' with them 'not only because of his brains, but also because he was entirely honest and unaffected'.

Many lucrative offers were made to him. Instead, in 1946, he accepted the offer (at the grand salary of £1,900) of the challenge of making a British bomb (without consulting Parliament), working closely with Cockroft, who was in charge of Harwell, and the sharp-tongued and formidable lanky giant Christopher Hinton ('Sir Christ' to his awed juniors), who was responsible for designing, building and operating the plants that would produce the necessary fissile material.

At Fort Halstead in Kent, the Ministry of Supply arms research department, where he began to recruit the team he would later take to Aldermaston, Penney was known as Caesar, from the acronym of his official title, but his managerial style was unstuffy, and on the surface very approachable, though later there were complaints that he was easily bored with things that didn't immediately take his attention, and apt to retreat into his private world of calculations. The only experience he had lacked, at the beginning of the project, was of administering a large and complex undertaking, but he was quickly respected for his scientific gifts, his commonsense, his remarkable capacity to synthesize, explain and simplify, and, as Margaret Gowing notes, 'for his simple but highly effective relationship with admirals and generals and, at the weapons trials, with able seamen and privates too'.

In 1953 he was appointed Director at Aldermaston, and his six years there covered the birth of CND and that wet Easter in 1958 when an organized march started in Trafalgar Square and ended, by a contemporary account, with up to 10,000 men, women and children moving 'between the regiments of sour and drab fir in a procession that was probably the longest that English roads have seen these centuries on foot, and was certainly the most purposeful'.

Aldermaston had most of its troubles after Penney had left to join the UK Atomic Energy Authority itself, initially as member for Weapons Research and Development, later chairman (1964–7). On his retirement he went into business with Tube Investments and STC. Throughout his career he firmly believed in the deterrent philosophy. Yet he was keenly aware of the cost of the programmes for which he was responsible, and used to look anxiously at new buildings and remark that it would be grand if they could be hospitals.

He scarcely ever ventured a public opinion on nuclear war and regarded himself as the servant of governments. But late in life, the shadow of the Monte Bello tests, hailed as a triumph by the British military-scientific establishment in 1952, came back to haunt him, when he was required, at the age of seventy-five, to give evidence and submit to cross-examination in the Australian government's commission of inquiry into the conduct and effects of those tests.

In particular, there was an unresolved question about a paper which Dr Headley Marston, director of biochemistry at the Commonwealth Scientific Industrial Research Organization, had not been allowed to publish. It suggested that there was a danger that particles of strontium 90 from the fallout might be carried by the wind to people living north of Adelaide. Had Sir William Penney, as he then was, vetted the paper? He had no recollection of that, he said. Asked again whether Dr Marston's evidence had been suppressed because it was feared the tests might be put in jeopardy if the press got hold of it, he replied: 'No. It was my view that Dr Marston could be defeated on scientific grounds.'

WILLIAM GEORGE PENNEY, BARON PENNEY OF EAST HENDRED · *born* 24 June 1909 · *died* 4 March 1991 ·

26 June 1992

JAMES STIRLING
Deyan Sudjic

The history of British architecture over the last forty years is, in truth, the history of James Stirling, who has died aged sixty-six. Since the architectural profession has pursued such a roller-coaster ride in public esteem, this hardly made for a comfortable career. But he enjoyed both an enormous critical reputation as well as suffering the indignity of seeing his largest single project in Britain, a monumental concrete housing complex in Runcorn, demolished: the victim of shifting fashions in housing management.

He handled both the praise and the occasional vituperation against him with an amused detachment. He refused to behave like a celebrity, he was never given to sweeping manifestos, or the opaque language that the architectural avant-garde favours. He never got involved in designing kettles or shopping bags, pitfalls that faced the rest of that small circle of celebrity architects who were such a feature of the 1980s. And Stirling was the only architect to politely turn down a request from the Disney organization to design them a hotel.

He continued to run his practice with the informal accessibility of an old-fashioned family solicitor. Whenever he was not commuting between Germany, America and Japan, he answered the telephone himself, and handled the most humble office chores. He was an architect who believed in drawing and thinking about architecture, rather than building a business or theorizing about it.

Stirling had a remarkable influence on his peers. In every case it is a building of Stirling's that sets the agenda for architecture. In the 1950s it was his disgust with the sentimentality of the Festival of Britain and what followed that helped to define the unfortunately named Brutalist school. In Stirling's hands this was not a deliberate onslaught on public sensibilities, but an aesthetic derived from Le Corbusier's late buildings, which valued bluntness in the use of materials over cosmetic camouflage. Thereafter he moved on, enthusiastically exploring different stylistic directions. He always claimed that even if he was not completely consistent in his output, he never turned his back on what he had designed at the earlier stages in his career.

Nevertheless his work certainly seems to be divisible into two radically different halves. In the 1960s and 1970s he worked his way steadily through the canon of modernism, from the mechanistic constructivism of the university buildings at Cambridge and Leicester, to the high-tech plastic-skinned Olivetti training centre in Haslemere and the prefabricated concrete of his halls of residence for St Andrew's University. He approached each with gusto but refused to allow them to typecast him and was always looking to explore new directions. The ten years of relative inactivity that followed the university buildings coincided with a general crisis in architecture, and the downturn in his own workload. That gave him plenty of scope for reflection, and a re-evaluation of the definitions of modern architecture. And by the time that Stirling won the Stuttgart Staatsgalerie competition at the end of the 1970s, he had shifted his attention away from the free plan and the abstraction of modernism, and towards a more catholic architectural approach, involving a whole range of revivalist imagery. It produced a building that turned out to be both a huge popular and critical success.

Until his death yesterday it looked as if there was going to be an exciting new phase, which achieved some kind of accommodation between the two earlier periods of his career. In the factory complex at Melsungen, Germany, that Stirling and his partner Michael Wilford designed with their former assistant Walter Nagerli, he had moved on again, this time redeploying some of the themes of his own work in the 1960s. It had all the hallmarks of being a building that was to take on the same significance in the 1990s that Stuttgart had had in the 1980s; hoping to shift the terms of the architectural debate.

James Stirling was born in Glasgow, the son of a ship's engineer, who moved his family to Liverpool. After distinguishing himself as a young lieutenant at the Normandy landings, he studied architecture at Liverpool University. his architectural career began in London with the firm of Lyons, Israel and Ellis before he began his own partnership with James Gowan in 1956, with whom he built the Leicester University engineering building. That partnership was dissolved in 1963, and he began a new partnership with Michael Wilford in 1971.

Something in Stirling's personality, perhaps a lack of enthusiasm for the social politicking needed to win architectural commissions in Britain, coupled with a peculiar antipathy to contemporary architecture in this country, curtailed Stirling's work here. In the last twenty years he built little more than two extensions for the Tate Gallery, one to house its Turner collection, the other to accommodate the Museum's northern outpost in Liverpool, neither of which can be counted among his best work. Bizarrely, both of Stirling's former students, Norman Foster and Richard Rogers, were knighted before he was finally named in the last Honours list.

Instead, Stirling has worked more and more outside Britain. He built a theatre for Cornell University, a research centre in Berlin and worked on a series of high-profile projects around the world. A major extension to the Stuttgart gallery is under way. It's a curious phenomenon, for Stirling remained a peculiarly English architect in his attitudes and his prejudices. The prejudices that saw certain of the dons at Cambridge attempt to demolish his history faculty library there rather than repair it tell us more about the nature of present-day Britain than they do about Stirling's qualities. One day they will evaporate and Stirling will be seen clearly as an architect of the same stature as his illustrious predecessors John Soane and Nicholas Hawksmoor.

JAMES FRASER STIRLING · *born* 22 April 1926 · *died* 25 June 1992 ·

DOROTHY HODGKIN
Guy Dodson

With the death of Dorothy Hodgkin aged eighty-four, chemistry, biochemistry and crystallography have lost a giant. She was a pioneer who solved the structures of cholesterol, penicillin, vitamin B12 and insulin. (All of these molecules are of key importance in biochemistry and medicine. For these contributions alone Dorothy would be recognized as one of the outstanding scientists of her time.) She influenced the course of modern chemistry and X-ray analysis, and with J. D. Bernal carried out the crucial experiments that started protein crystallography.

Dorothy was one of the very few figures who could keep contact between the scientific communities of the world. Her gently presented but uncompromising and humane views on such issues as nuclear and chemical weapons were a reminder of the responsibilities scientists have, and an example of how to meet them.

Dorothy's father, John Winter Crowfoot, and her mother, Grace Mary (*née* Hood), both had a Quaker background. Dorothy was born while her parents were in the Sudan, where her father was serving with the Egyptian Ministry of Education. During the First World War she returned to England and lived in Gelston in Norfolk, where she was educated locally. Dorothy went to Oxford to study chemistry, at which she excelled, and from there she moved to Cambridge to do a doctorate. Her supervisor was J. D. Bernal, already a legendary figure in X-ray structural research, and his laboratory was an exciting place to be. After completing her thesis, Dorothy immediately began organizing her own research laboratory in Oxford, with very limited funds and with no tradition of expensive research from which to draw upon.

Dorothy was a chemist, but her research into chemistry and biochemistry was carried out by X-ray crystallography – a discipline which is based on physics, and which makes it possible to see the individual atoms (as an X-ray image) of the molecules in the crystal. There is no doubt that the pleasure she had in growing them, and in their beauty and symmetry, were factors in Dorothy choosing this approach in her research. In the 1930s, when Dorothy began, X-ray crystallography was very primitive, but Dorothy was ambitious – she said it was simply chemical curiosity that drove her to determine the structures which mattered to chemistry, biochemistry and medicine. She was such a good crystallographer, however, that her chemistry could be overlooked.

Her grasp of chemical principles was such that she could discuss on an equal basis the problems associated with penicillin and vitamin B12 with synthetic chemists.

Dorothy remained at Oxford all her working life and was profoundly attached to the city, university and her college, an association strengthened by her marriage in 1937 to Thomas Hodgkin, a historian from Balliol College. They had three children, Luke, Liz and Toby, who helped make the Hodgkin household the friendliest and liveliest place. Thomas's vivid personality complemented Dorothy's quieter approach. Together they attracted to their house an extraordinary range of people, many of whom became lifelong friends.

Between 1934 and 1960, while her family grew up, she determined the structures of cholesterol, penicillin and vitamin B12 and many other molecules. All of these were solved by inspired crystallographic and chemical insight and by pushing the techniques to their limits. These achievements had immense impact and helped establish X-ray analysis as an essential component of modern chemical and biochemical research. Perhaps the most striking example of her scientific courage was in 1935 when, after moving to Oxford, she began X-ray studies on crystals of the hormone insulin, whose structure was finally solved thirty-four years later. From the early 1960s onwards, Dorothy concentrated on insulin, finally solving it in 1969. This research and her wide interest in proteins made her an important figure in establishing, with Max Perutz and David Phillips, a worldwide and successful protein crystallographic community.

Dorothy was regarded with enormous affection by people from all over the world and particularly from the Third World. She was interested in their work and always encouraging. Most important, she ensured the recognition of scientific work done in Africa, China and India and helped the scientists there to establish themselves. An example of this was the Chinese synthesis of insulin, a phenomenal achievement, and some years later, their independent determination of the insulin structure. Her laboratory was stamped by her personality; it got the best out of Oxford's wonderful scientific and intellectual environment, free of the usual tiresome formalities. It was surprising to many (including me when first I met Dorothy) that a person with such standing and such a large scientific commitment, who always had too much to do, could be so approachable. When I arrived to work with her, she told me that the laboratory followed the American custom and that everyone used first names. This helped create the happy and relaxed (some said too relaxed!) atmosphere.

But the most important influence was Dorothy's confidence in the value of crystallography and in the people doing it with her. It was this that gave her the quality of patience that is essential for long-term and fundamental research and which led to so many triumphs. She had remarkable concentration and could work with all kinds of distractions about her. She is most remembered by me, examining electron density maps, often humming a hymn as she identified the atoms and connected them together into a molecular structure. When interpreting the insulin maps from which the structure was solved, her ankles swelled so seriously she was unable to wear her shoes. She completely ignored this problem. During this time, a visitor from India, Vijayan – also working on the structure – arrived, as he was to be married that weekend. As Vijayan described his plans, Dorothy, anxious that he should not miss the fun and conscious he was needed, suggested the ceremony should be on Saturday and that he should have a nice honeymoon and join us again on Monday. It was typical of Dorothy that she helped find a fellowship for his bride to come to England and pursue her own research career.

Dorothy was physically slight and she became increasingly frail with advancing years. The rheumatoid arthritis, which she contracted after Luke's birth in 1938, became more and more serious over the years, giving her a great deal of pain and discomfort, though she never seemed to complain. Her hands were particularly affected. When Henry Moore was doing her portrait he was so struck by their appearance that he did some separate sketches of them, which are now exhibited in the Royal Society.

After her retirement, Dorothy continued her research unabated, publishing a comprehensive and definitive monograph on insulin, thus completing properly her researches into the hormone's structure begun fifty-three years earlier. She also travelled to all parts of the world to give lectures and to take part in discussions on scientific and political affairs. Remarkably, in spite of her great frailty, she decided to go to the International Union of Crystallography's Congress in Beijing last August. Good relations between communities were always important to her and it was logical that she should be active in the Pugwash movement (a fraternity of scientists dedicated to nuclear disarmament and improving life on earth) and finally become an extremely effective President.

Naturally, Dorothy received many distinctions during her life. They often provided an opportunity to meet friends or widen contacts, which she greatly enjoyed. The Nobel prize, awarded in 1964 for her studies on biologically important molecules, was very timely. It pushed her more onto the world stage where she was needed, and the Order of Merit, awarded in 1965, was another distinction she valued, partly because she was only the second woman to receive it, the first being Florence Nightingale.

The occasion when, as Chancellor of Bristol University, she made her final address to the graduates, gives a good picture of her on a formal occasion. Not many people knew she had only just returned from the US, where she had been lecturing at a large crystallographic meeting. Beneath the robes, originally designed for Churchill, she looked extremely frail. Her address began with a slow approach to the podium and opened with the words – 'I wish to speak to the graduates.' She spoke of the importance of education and research for modern life, in spite of a political and economic climate which could make their practice difficult. She said, reminding the graduates of the even larger difficulties of her early career: 'And I hope some of you too will live modestly and do serious things.' This is in some ways an epitaph, which describes her own picture of herself.

Dorothy will be deeply missed as a person and as a scientist. But there is consolation. She has left an example of generosity and seriousness which, through her countless friends, associates and students, is a legacy for science and human affairs.

DOROTHY MARY CROWFOOT HODGKIN · *born* 12 May 1910 · *died* 29 July 1994 ·

18 June 1996

FITZROY MACLEAN
Ed Vulliamy, Richard Norton-Taylor and Hella Pick

Brigadier Sir Fitzroy Maclean, one of the grand, romantic heroes of the wartime epoch, founder member of the SAS, covert pilot of Tito's partisans, and epic raconteur of his own adventures, has died aged eighty-five.

There was no greater account of Maclean's life than his own – *Eastern Approaches*, written in 1949 and republished to mark his eightieth birthday – and it is the version he stuck to in all the conversations and interviews as his old fighting ground of Yugoslavia burst into flames again. It is a titanic odyssey across the turbulent Balkans and the USSR, which combines all the dichotomous but quintessential urges of the *Boys' Own* hero, and more: a stiff upper lip in the face of extreme danger, a courteous and debonair manner, and an unquenchable thirst for action and adventure.

Fitzroy Maclean, from a military family, grew up commuting between

Cairo and Hampshire. He went to Eton and Cambridge, and entered the Foreign Service aged twenty-two, when it was made up of no more than 250 diplomats worldwide, in 1934. He first caused cocked eyebrows in Whitehall by making a forceful application to be despatched to what was regarded as the least enviable of postings: Stalin's Moscow. He arrived in Moscow in 1937, seeing the dictator on a parade past Lenin's tomb. He described him as 'a squat Asiatic figure, in a peaked cap and drab semi-military greatcoat, narrow eyes, close set'. Maclean became famous almost immediately, and later came to be denounced by Moscow's *Literary Newspaper* as a bourgeois, drunken murderer. He travelled famously and often illicitly, taking a train across Siberia and moving far beyond the Urals, into Samarkand, Mongolia and Turkestan, writing a glorious account of the world he uncovered – *The Back of Beyond*. Maclean had no intention of being bound by the rules that governed diplomats of the day. After official approaches had failed, he joined a queue of Tartar workmen waiting for rail tickets and got aboard a train bound for the Asian part of the Soviet empire that had been part of the 'Great Game' between the British and Russian empires of Kipling's time. Using such tactics, and often coming within an ace of being arrested or shot by the more vigilant functionaries, he came by a unique first-hand knowledge of the eastern Soviet Union.

There were other adventures in the Caucasus mountains, and another book, *To Caucasus: the End of all the Earth*. But Maclean was also one of the few – and by far the most lucid – witnesses to Stalin's show trials of 1938. During the trial of the Trotskyite rebels of Shakhty, he noted – by the glow of an arc light – the drooping moustache of Stalin himself.

When war came, Maclean had but one idea: 'to get into it'. He was told that the only way he could leave the Foreign Service was to become a Member of Parliament, which he duly did almost at a stroke, coupling his election for the seat of Lancaster with the uniform of his father's regiment, the Cameron Highlanders. Churchill once introduced his friend to General Smuts, and later recalled the line he used to do so: 'Here is the young man who used the Mother of Parliaments as a public convenience.' The regiment was also a piece of dressage for Maclean's real area of interest. In Egypt he had already met David Stirling, a relative of Maclean's wife Veronica and founder of the SAS. Stirling said: 'Why not join the SAS,' to which Maclean responded, as he later wrote: 'I asked what it was. Stirling explained, "It was a good thing to be in … We could operate in the desert first of all, then in Southern and Eastern Europe." There were endless possibilities, it sounded promising. I said I'd be delighted to join.' Brigadier Maclean proceeded to the Special Operations

Executive, Britain's elite grouping set up by Churchill to propel resistance movements in Nazi-occupied territories. Maclean was despatched to Yugoslavia, where the British had initially opted to back the Chetnik Royalist movement of Colonel Draza Mihailovic, extreme Serbian nationalists. Churchill recognized the authority and claim of a rival movement, Tito's communist partisans.

Maclean was despatched on Churchill's personal authority, literally parachuting into the savage Yugoslav interior. Although the SOE was his organization, Maclean's brief came from the Prime Minister himself, and was – as he later put it – 'to find out who was killing the most Germans, and to help them kill some more'. The answer ascertained, he became Churchill's 'personal liaison officer' to Marshal Tito, with Churchill providing the job description: 'daring ambassador-leader to these hardy and hunted guerrillas'. Maclean had been assigned the mission on account of his experience of communism, and now raised doubts about how far he was to assist the Soviet-backed Comintern in its westward struggle against Hitler. Maclean wrote later: 'Mr Churchill's reply left me in no doubt as to the answer to my problem. So long, he said, as the whole of Western civilization was threatened by the Nazi menace, we could not afford to let our attention be diverted from the immediate issue by considerations of long-term policy.' The two met in Cairo in December 1943, when Churchill, now wary of Maclean's enthusiasm for the cause, asked: '"Do you intend to make Yugoslavia your home after the war?" "No, Sir" I replied. "Neither do I," he said, "and the less you and I worry about the form of government they set up, the better."'

The victory of the partisans, and the SOE's pivotal support for it, became one of the legends of the Allied victory. Maclean was immersed not only in Tito's strategy, but in the SOE's direct contribution of helping to blow up bridges in the cradle of the war, Bosnia-Herzegovina, and devising manoeuvres to hamper the Nazi occupation and later harass the retreat. Maclean's campaign was a clear inspiration for the greatest war thriller of them all, Alistair Maclean's *Guns of Navarone*. It was also a bloody affair, as the partisans took revenge upon their Croatian opponents (Tito was himself a Croat) with the massacre at Beliburg in 1945. Maclean took his place beside Tito in the parade that followed the battle of Belgrade, one of the very last that witnessed – as did Maclean himself – a charge by the mounted Soviet horse artillery. While Maclean always denounced Mihailovic's Royalists as allies of the Reich, he remained lifelong friends with Tito, whom he called 'an outstanding military and political leader, who had the greatest gift: of convincing people in total despair that everything was going to be alright'. Maclean was awarded the Partisan Star, First Class. Out of the Yugoslav war came more books: *Yugoslavia* and *The Battle of Neretva*.

Just as Tito's Yugoslavia became a bridge of sorts across the iron curtain, so Maclean became a bridge between the Marshal and western leaders, introducing Tito to Margaret Thatcher and Prince Charles. Maclean never lost his intrepid, debonair air. He loved to entertain at his house on the Adriatic island of Korcula, birthplace of Marco Polo. He was not averse to the good life; his despatches would occasionally mention his favourite drink, pink vanilla brandy.

As MP for Lancaster, serving in the Churchill and Eden governments, Maclean became Under Secretary of State for War and Financial Secretary to the War Office. But his personality was perhaps too large and open-minded for party political point-scoring. In 1959 he moved to become MP for Bute and North Ayrshire, which enabled him to play the Scottish squire more congenially, especially in farming his 5,000 acres bordering Loch Fyne, Strachur, and owning the Creggans Inn, where he often entertained in informal style. 'Being a Highlander myself,' he once said, 'I like mountain peoples. I like their love of freedom. I like their heroic approach.' One of Maclean's last campaigns was to defend the Polaris missile base at Holy Loch, near his home. 'I think [the CND campaign] is deplorable … It gives the impression that Scotland is not prepared to play its full part in the alliance.'

After Tito's death in 1980, Maclean wrote that his old friend had left Yugoslavs with an abiding sense of loss. 'But,' he added in a tribute: '[his death] has also left a keen sense of gratitude that he lived long enough to endow the new Yugoslavia with sufficient stability for it to be able to continue along the lines laid down in his lifetime…'

He leaves a wife and two sons.

HELLA PICK writes: Fitzroy Maclean was already a legend when I first met him in Belgrade in the late 1960s. Physically and mentally larger than life, his enthusiasm for Yugoslavia was infectious. Given his wartime exploits with Tito and his partisans, it was hardly surprising that he held the Yugoslav leader in deep admiration. They had become good friends, and met regularly. But Fitzroy was also convinced that Tito had succeeded in building a multi-ethnic nation; that the country was sufficiently united to endure beyond Tito's death. Yugoslavia's disintegration was not merely a bitter blow, but also one that Maclean had not anticipated.

He was one of only two or three foreigners who were allowed to own property in Yugoslavia: he had a beautiful house on the island of Korcula, now part of Croatia. I will always remember a magical summer's day when Yugoslav tourist authorities took a group of British journalists, uninvited, to attend the wedding of Fitzroy's son in Korcula. We arrived just as the bridal pair walked out of the church in procession through the old town. We were allowed to join the revels, which seemed to involve the island's whole population. Next morning, Fitzroy waved us off as we sailed away bleary-eyed and happy; and oh so sure that Yugoslavia was for ever.

No doubt, Maclean's death will revive arguments that he misled Winston Churchill about Tito's potential, and that Britain was wrong to give such unequivocal backing to communist Yugoslavia. But those who knew Yugoslavia well never doubted Maclean's judgement about the wisdom of backing Tito during and after the war. Revisionists should be seen off unceremoniously.

SIR FITZROY MACLEAN OF DUNCONNEL · *born* 11 March 1911 · *died* 15 June 1996 ·

17 March 1998

BENJAMIN SPOCK
Christopher Dodd and Sheila Kitzinger

For more than half a century, Dr Benjamin Spock, who has died aged ninety-four, author of *The Common Sense Book of Baby and Child Care* and prominent anti-nuclear campaigner, was the most famous name in the field of childcare and parenting. First published in 1946, his book was an immediate success. Through six editions it has sold more than fifty million copies, making it the twentieth-century's bestseller, second only to the Bible in publishing's all-time sales chart. *Baby and Child Care*, the product of reconciling concepts of psychoanalytic training with years of listening to mothers talking about their children, sought to reassure parents and apply commonsense to the rearing of their young. 'Trust yourself,' Spock wrote. 'You know more than you think you do ... Don't take too seriously what the neighbours say. Don't be overawed by what the experts say. Don't be afraid to trust your own commonsense.' It was a formula that worked.

The eldest child of a railroad lawyer, Benjamin Spock, and his wife, Mildred, the young Spock grew into a tall, gangly youth. He was tied closely to his mother's apron strings at their home in New Haven, Connecticut, until, in 1923, he escaped into rowing – and the Yale crew. He won a gold medal in the 1924 Olympic Games, in which Yale represented the United States in eights. Spock danced with Gloria Swanson on the liner taking the crew to France. The star addressed the tongue-tied young man in her arms as 'Big Ben but no alarm'.

Although he resented his mother banning the wearing of sneakers, keeping him in short pants well into his teens, and making him live at home in his freshman Yale year lest life in the dorm should be corrupting, Spock's mother's love of babies was one of the things that influenced him in becoming a paediatrician. After Yale, he specialized in paediatrics and psychiatry at Columbia University, New York, practised medicine and, while doing war service with the US Navy in California as a psychiatrist (he had also undergone analysis), worked on his book in the evenings with the help of his first wife, Jane Davenport Cheney. After the war, he taught at Western Reserve University.

Spock's family background was Republican, but his move from Yale to New York radicalized him. So did the New Deal and the Spanish Civil War. But his politics remained passive until a 1960 television appearance with Jacqueline Kennedy, who said, 'Dr Spock is for my husband, and my husband is for Dr Spock!' The resumption of nuclear testing by Khrushchev, and then by Kennedy, alerted Spock to the global peril of the nuclear arms race. He feared for the future of his army of children and began painfully to realize that, having set out with a mission to reassure mothers, he was now going to have to alarm them in order to save their children from radiation. His first real campaigning act was to draft a full-page advertisement in the *New York Times* for the National Committee for Sane Nuclear Policy (Sane). He backed the 'peace in Vietnam' presidential candidate, Lyndon Johnson, leading the Doctors for Johnson Committee, but was soon publicly denouncing the new president for betraying promises. Spock then took to the streets in his neat, blue consultant's suit, and tried to avoid being caught up in the internal politics of the peace movement. He continued to campaign hard, even in 1985, spending six months on the road, working for various peace groups.

In a Boston show trial, he was convicted of conspiracy, along with the Yale chaplain, the Revd Sloane Coffin Jr, and others, for inciting young Americans to burn their draft cards. The convictions were overturned on appeal because the judge had given the jury a ten-point loaded questionnaire in addition to the task of deciding innocence or guilt. Spock retired from teaching in 1967 but continued to write about aspects of childcare, and in 1970 published *Decent and Indecent: Our Personal and Political Behavior*, a careful and clear account of his own political experiences and philosophy.

At one stage, however, he had fallen foul of the women's movement. When he addressed the National Women's Political Caucus in 1972, Gloria Steinem told him: 'I hope you realize you have been a major oppressor of women in the same category as Sigmund Freud.' In the light of the women's movement, he revised some of the conservative views expressed in early editions, and in the 1976 version of *Baby and Child Care*, every pronoun was changed, and the advice for fathers to compliment their daughters on their pretty dresses had disappeared. Spock was, at one stage, hailed by *Ms magazine* as a hero of the women's movement.

In the 1980s, he became profoundly disillusioned with the materialism of the young, and what he called the Superkid phenomenon, in which 'parents get excited when they read that some kid has been taught to read at the age of two and immediately want their child of two or three to be taught to read', and of 'the proliferation of bowls' – the goal of winning, at all costs, in both sport and in life. The change came after the Vietnam conflict was settled, but Spock consoled himself that a generation could change its values again just as quickly.

The 1990s, however, brought him little comfort. In a new foreword to the sixth edition of the book, in 1992, he lamented the strains and stresses of American family life and blamed both men and women for being obsessed with work. 'Many women have, in a sense, joined the rat race,' he wrote. A seventh edition of *Baby and Child Care* will be published on his birthday in May.

Spock travelled widely to places like China and Nicaragua to further his political education. His recreation from 1924 onwards was sailing, mainly off Maine and the Virgin Islands. In 1976 he divorced Jane Cheney and married Mary Morgan Councille, and took up the oar again on the lake at the foot of her Arkansas garden, where they both went sculling. He had two sons by his first marriage.

SHEILA KITZINGER writes: Dr Spock was the first of the baby experts to make it clear through his writing that he respected women and treated them as intelligent adults. In *Baby and Child Care*, he told them that they could trust their feelings and their own experiences as they learn from their children and, unlike many experts, he nurtured their self-confidence.

He never talked down to his readers, and wrote in a warm, non-didactic, personal way, for fathers as well as mothers, that enabled them almost to enter into a dialogue with the author. It was as if he was not only talking, but also listening to them. Spock respected and delighted in children, and included anecdotes from his own childhood, his experiences of parenthood and of being a stepfather, and his own mistakes, sharing with his readers the adventure of being a parent, rather than setting himself up as an authority figure.

His view of love and sex, however, was firmly heterosexual. He clung to a view of the ideal family as a state of Janet-and-John calm and reasonableness, with a tender, concerned mother and a father who was a real pal. He believed that one of the main tasks of raising children was to prepare them to build such families themselves. He was strongly opposed to physical punishment, to the steady diet of television violence, and to the whole idea of raising children with the single goal of success in a selfishly acquisitive society.

It is often claimed that in later editions of his books, Spock ditched his earlier belief in tolerance and was horrified at the way in which he had encouraged relaxed child-rearing. But this is a caricature of his views. He never repudiated his earlier philosophy. There was, instead, an evolution.

The change came about with the horrors and the waste of human life of the Vietnam war, and his indictment by the Lyndon Johnson administration for his activities in opposing that conflict. The Rev Norman Vincent Peale, for instance, preached a much-publicized sermon, in which he denounced young men who refused to fight, claiming they were undisciplined because their parents had followed Spock's teaching and given them 'instant gratification'.

No longer just the understanding paediatrician who loved children, Spock became politicized, and in his 1969 edition warned parents not 'to keep their eyes exclusively focused on their child, thinking about what he needs from them and from the community, instead of thinking about what the world … will be needing from the child'.

Child-rearing is not merely a domestic matter, to be classified along with recipe books, flower-arranging and DIY. It is a political issue. Spock's values about society were not separate, but integral to how he thought good parenting should be.

BENJAMIN MCLANE SPOCK · *born* 2 May 1903 · *died* 15 March 1998 ·

JOHN HUNT
Jim Perrin

One of the very few negative things it is possible to say about Lord Hunt of Llanfairwaterdine, who has died aged eighty-eight, is that he was the man who did not climb Mount Everest. That fact only needs to be stated because of his indelible public association with the mountain, the British expedition responsible for the first ascent of which, as Colonel John Hunt, he led in 1953. His leadership of that undertaking will perhaps remain his memorial. It was the culmination of a campaign which had unfolded over more than thirty years: 'I was able to supply an element of military pragmatism,' he wrote later of his own role. But his achievement was considerably more than that. He took over the leadership of the expedition in quite singularly unfortunate circumstances.

Eric Shipton, the great mountaineer of the 1930s, had been appointed to lead, but a faction within the joint Himalayan Committee of the Alpine Club and the Royal Geographical Society – unimpressed by Shipton after the failure of his party on Cho Oyu in 1952 – had concluded that he was not a 'finisher'. In consequence, he was deposed in an incompetent and unworthy manner and the chalice was passed to Hunt, who accepted it with alacrity.

The loyalties of many members of the original team were thus severely tested. It redounds greatly to Hunt's credit that he led a happy and united expedition, news of the success of which seized the imagination of a country already revelling in the ascent of Queen Elizabeth II to the throne. It is even further to Hunt's credit, and testimony to his fairmindedness, that he bestowed due praise on Shipton for his work in pioneering and reconnaissance on Everest throughout the previous twenty years. In a late interview he observed that 'It has been an abiding sorrow with me that Eric Shipton must have carried this disappointment with him to the end of his days. I can only say that from the moment we got down I was concerned to pass the tribute he deserved back to him at every conceivable opportunity.'

John Hunt was the elder son of an Indian Army officer who was killed early in the First World War. He was educated at Marlborough and at the Royal Military College, Sandhurst, into which he passed first of his year and from which he passed as senior under-officer, with a gold medal and a special sword. In 1930 he was commissioned into the King's Royal Rifle Corps. During the Second World War he served with distinction in India, northern

Italy (where he won the DSO), and in Greece. After the war, he rose to the rank of honorary brigadier and assistant commandant of the staff college before his 1956 retirement from the army.

His record of public service after 1956 was exceptional. The fame which had been almost adventitiously acquired on Everest became entirely focused in the public interest. He was, variously, director of the Duke of Edinburgh's Award Scheme, rector of Aberdeen University, personal adviser to Harold Wilson during the Nigerian civil war, chairman of the Parole Board and of the Advisory Committee on Police in Northern Ireland, a member of the Royal Commission on the Press, president of the Council for National Parks, the Rainer Foundation, the Council for Volunteers Overseas and the National Association of Probation Officers. Nor was his concern in any of these areas merely token. If a cause caught at his belief, his involvement was whole-hearted. He was a man of very warm human sympathy, and a natural social democrat from the outset of his career. Indeed, in his early days in India he attracted frequent mutterings along the lines of 'young officers these days going native'.

He believed that if you were to come to terms with an adversary – a better policy, in his view, than war – you must, through association, learn about the workings of his mind. It was a view he put to service in the upper house after his ennoblement as one of Harold Wilson's peers in 1966. He found a congenial political home in the Social Democratic party in 1981 and frequently spoke from the crossbenches, particularly on environmental issues.

Within mountaineering circles, it is often forgotten that he came to Everest in 1953 with impressive credentials, despite having been outside the mainstream of Himalayan and Alpine mountaineering in the preceding decades. His attempt on the beautiful and difficult Peak 36 – now known as Saltoro Kangri – in the Karakoram in 1935, when he reached 24,500ft, and then sat out a storm for three days in a high camp, was among the more audacious Himalayan exploits of the 1930s. But for an adverse medical report – so much for heart murmurs! – he would have earned and been accorded a place on Ruttledge's 1936 British Everest Expedition.

By 1952, heart murmurs forgotten in the national interest, he had been recommended to the Joint Himalayan Committee by an influential alpine partner as a 'terrific thruster'. Even at the age of forty-two, on the 1953 trip he still felt himself to be in contention for the summit. With the sherpa Da Namgyal he carried loads in poor weather to 27,500ft, three days prior to Tenzing's and Hillary's ascent of the mountain, which he thus played a large part in enabling.

In the course of a mountaineering career and interest, which continued into old age, he climbed widely: in the Alps, where he was a potent force in the postwar renaissance of British alpinism; in the Caucasus and Pamirs, to which he led Anglo-Soviet expeditions in 1958 and 1962; in the Polish Tatras, the Pindos Mountains of Greece, the St Elias range in Alaska and the Staunings Alps in Greenland. He was never the most technically adept or graceful of rock-climbers, his build being perhaps too heavily powerful, but he greatly enjoyed this aspect of domestic mountain activity. He was as happy, too, tramping the gentler border hills above the Radnorshire village from which he took the title of his baronetcy. There was an enjoyment, a deep appreciation of wild regions which informed and brought calm to his character throughout his life. It was a crucial part of his life's project to convey that affection to others, and to preserve the landscapes which could stimulate it. Much of his work with the Duke of Edinburgh's scheme and the Council for National Parks was towards these ends.

John Hunt was a man of enormous charm, and by no means free from endearing hints of weakness, insecurity and susceptibility, which make the whole portrait more credible. He was engagingly vain, had a liking for flattery, an intense – and it should be added quite innocent – enjoyment of the company of attractive women, not least amongst whom were his wife, Joy (*née* Mowbray-Green, a Wimbledon player whom he married in 1936), and their four daughters.

He was also a man of great natural authority, judicious and kindly in its exercise. Physically impressive, his fine profile and bearing would have graced Augustan Rome or Periclean Athens as readily as present-day Westminster, the business of which preoccupied the later years of his life. As well as his life peerage, this fine old soldier-statesman was made CBE in 1945, knighted in 1953, and made a Garter Knight in 1979. He wrote or edited several books about mountaineering, including *The Ascent of Everest* (1953), which was a worldwide bestseller. A volume of autobiography, *Life is Meeting*, was published in 1978.

HENRY CECIL JOHN HUNT, BARON HUNT OF
LLANFAIRWATERDINE · *born* 22 June 1910 · *died* 7 November 1998 ·

ALIX MEYNELL
Fiona MacCarthy

Dame Alix Meynell, who has died aged ninety-six, was one of the great women of this century. She enlarged the possibilities open to women in both the public and private spheres.

In her public persona as Alix Kilroy she was a powerful civil servant. She entered the service in 1925, the year in which the administrative grade examination was opened to women for the first time. When she retired thirty years later, Dame Alix was one of the most senior civil servants in the country, an under-secretary heading her own department. Her most controversial wartime assignment was the utility furniture scheme, and in 1947 she spoke out against the wastage of national resources in adopting the full skirts and mid-calf hemlines of Christian Dior's 'New Look'.

Her private life was unconventional. Her long love affair and eventual marriage, in 1946, to Sir Francis Meynell, poet, distinguished typographer and founder of the Nonesuch Press, is described in her autobiography, *Private Servant, Public Woman*, with a candour that surprised and delighted women of a younger generation when it was published in 1988. Her insistence that emotional truthfulness meant more than technical fidelity was prophetic of later, more tolerant sexual attitudes. She was a woman of rare intellectual clarity and physical energy: in her time she was an expert ballroom dancer and good skier. In a sense she was an early 'having-it-all' woman, and her radiance lasted into a grand old age.

She was born into a large, clannish professional family in Nottingham. The four confident and clever Kilroy sisters, referred to by Francis as the 'Kilrush', were always to be close. To family and friends Alix, the second daughter, was always known as 'Bay'. The name was chosen by her mother, a fan of the actress Mrs Patrick Campbell, in the romantic belief that this was what she called her son. Alix Kilroy was brought up in provincial liberalism. Her father was a naval surgeon, often absent, and the influence of her mother and her mother's relations, the Dowsons, a well-known Midlands Unitarian and suffragist family, was paramount – Alix's mother was herself a highly original, determined, emotional woman, who had insisted on a career and trained as a professional nurse, volunteering to go out to Bombay in 1897, the year of the great plague.

Alix later recollected that she felt grown up at seven, shouldering responsibility in the largely fatherless family and nursing her mother, who had by then succumbed to recurring sick headaches and become a semi-invalid. The family fortunes fluctuated. She was sent to Malvern Girls' College, probably because the fees were lower than at Cheltenham, and disliked the torrid atmosphere of schoolgirl 'crushes': she blamed Malvern for her later inability to handle all-women gatherings. Meanwhile her mother and sisters were flitting around London and she was spending her holidays in a down-at-heel hotel in Earls Court.

Virtually expelled from Malvern, she won a minor scholarship to Somerville and arrived at Oxford in 1922, reading Modern Greats. In that year Somerville had only forty entrants, among them Evelyn (later Dame Evelyn) Sharp, who became a lifelong friend, almost an alter ego, and Agnes Headlam-Morley, destined to be Oxford's first woman professor. Another Somerville friendship, with Jane Martin, lasted until Jane married the ambitious young art historian Kenneth Clark.

Somerville was still in its separatist phase of high-minded conversation over the cocoa mugs. Undergraduates were not allowed out alone with a man unless they were carrying golf clubs. (Her friend Jane took up golf.) You could not go to a man's room except in twos, and then only with permission from the principal. Alix put up with these petty restrictions, loving the intellectual seriousness that Oxford offered. When her philosophy tutor, Professor John Macmurray, greeted her conventional essay on Descartes with the words 'Yes, but what do YOU think?' it was the most exciting question she had ever been asked.

A curious encounter at Oxford was with Aleister Crowley, aesthete and black magician. Jane Martin took her to tea in his gloomy panelled rooms, where she found the tall saturnine Crowley, made more sinister by a covering of purple face powder, surrounded by a group of undergraduates admiring the new Nonesuch Press *Genesis* with its superb Paul Nash woodcuts. This was seven years before Alix and Francis Meynell met.

She left Oxford with a disappointing second and intended to become a barrister. It was more or less by chance that she heard the examination for the administrative class of the Home Civil Service was now open to women. Candidates had to be over twenty-two and under twenty-four. She and her older sister Maud (alias Bimbi) decided to enter almost on a whim, arriving for their vivas at Burlington House on a sweltering summer day dressed in cotton frocks and sandals, with bare legs. She passed twelfth in order of merit, out of 200 candidates. Two other women were admitted: Enid Russell Smith, later Dame Enid, who eventually became deputy head of the Ministry of Health, and Mary Smeiton who, as Dame Mary, was head of the Ministry of Labour. Bimbi missed entry by just six marks.

On 25 October 1925, she took up her appointment as an assistant principal (lowest grade in the administrative class) at the Board of Trade. Every day on the way to the office she walked past the statues of Palmerston, Disraeli and Gladstone, men who had been held up to her not only by her teachers but, more importantly, by her suffragist grandmother and aunts as great men who had made history. She was not exactly nervous, but aware that with her entry to the Civil Service she was making a species of history herself.

She expected that her Board of Trade male colleagues would accept her and treat her as an equal. Her glamour was evidently a surprise to them. The following year, when Evelyn Sharp joined her at the Board of Trade, a colleague recalled 'two young ladies looking like a couple of film stars'. She was appalled when the fat, elderly chairman of the Committee of Inquiry into applications by the manufacturers of Buttons, Pins, Hooks and Eyes and Snap Fasteners seized her hand under the table. But her competence ensured that she was taken seriously, and by 1932 she had become the first woman ever appointed a principal in the Board of Trade.

Her department was a new one: Commercial Relations and Treaties, commonly known as CRT. It had been set up in the wake of the economic crisis of 1931 and the abandonment of old free trade policies. CRT was in charge of governmental policy on commercial and trade relations and negotiations over trade treaties. There were three other principals in the department. Her responsibility was initially for Sweden. Feeling rich after her recent promotion, she invited her Swedish opposite number to lunch at the Ivy, then (as now) one of London's smartest restaurants. Wanting to convince him of the good sense of the Board of Trade request for a reduced duty on small cars, she drove him to the restaurant in her own small British car. Much to her embarrassment, her guest had to crank-start it when it stalled halfway up St James's Street.

Her two bibles were Maynard Keynes's *The Economic Consequences of the Peace* and Virginia Woolf's *A Room of One's Own*. Through her work she had achieved an unusual independence for women of that period, able to keep herself in comfort and afford more than one holiday a year. Emotionally and sexually she had matured late. She was seventeen when she was first kissed and twenty-six when she finally lost her virginity to the sophisticated, hopelessly unstable Garrow Tomlin, brother of the sculptor Stephen Tomlin. Kenneth Clark referred to them as 'Beauty and the Beast'. Garrow introduced her to Bloomsbury circles and heady ideas of sexual experimentation. The first time they spent a weekend together, at the Bear in Hungerford, Alix's youngest sister, Mona, shared a double bed with them. 'A curiously innocent arrangement' as Alix later described it. But later the relationship developed into a more formal *ménage à trois* and they went on a camping holiday together feeling they were both 'married' to Garrow, camp-fire cooking, bathing naked. Alix wrote that 'There was none of the heart-burning I had feared.'

To her terrible grief Garrow was killed in a flying accident, just as his erratic love for her seemed to be steadying. She had meanwhile begun a new affair, believing that real love was non-exclusive. Her experience had taught her that 'more than one love can exist at the same time between men and women, just as can other forms of human love – for mother, siblings, friends. Why not?'

She had first met Francis Meynell in 1929. He was the son of a famous literary couple, Alice and Wilfred Meynell, and was already a considerable figure in the typographic world, friend and patron of Stanley Morison and Eric Gill. He was also a notorious political firebrand, a courageous supporter of the suffragettes, a conscientious objector in the First World War and founder, with Bertrand Russell, of the No Conscription Fellowship, and was actively in favour of the General Strike in 1926. He was briefly a member of the Communist party. Under his influence Alix's own politics moved further to the left.

The debonair Francis was a superb dancer. Their friendship began as a dancing partnership at a period when the 'graceful gliding romantic one-step' took over from the Charleston. Years later, she could still 'feel the sway of the slow foxtrot danced with Francis to the music of "Night and Day"'. Their relationship deepened after Garrow's death. But even then, and even after they were married, sexual possessiveness did not come into it. Francis's view mirrored hers: that 'the only prurient thing about sex is the mystery and pretence with which convention surrounds a natural function and delight'. They stipulated total honesty, evolving a system of unfaithfulness by consultation. Before sleeping with architect Wells Coates, Bay enquired of Francis if he minded. Her fellow civil servant Evelyn Sharp knew that Francis had Alix's permission for them to 'cement their friendship' by a long-running sexual relationship. Jealousy was not an emotion they admitted. She and Francis felt secure that they were 'one another's best'.

In the middle 1930s, Alix Kilroy, then a pacifist, found herself in charge of the Board of Trade section of the War Book, a day-to-day plan for action to be taken at outbreak of war. From her official vantage point she watched with a growing sense of dread as the three fascist dictators – Hitler, Mussolini and Franco – bestrode Europe's stage. Gradually her views changed, and when war was declared she felt 'total commitment and pride that at last we were confronting fascism'.

She stayed in London through the Blitz. This 'brilliant representative of women civil servants', as Sir Cecil Weir described her at this period, was now promoted to assistant secretary rank. Her first task in the Import Licensing Department was to draw up a preliminary list of food imports to be prohibited. Her superior advised her to start her list with all the things she most enjoyed eating. Alix Kilroy then moved to a new wartime department, the Control of Factory and Storage Premises. This was in effect an attempt to prevent Lord Beaverbrook, as newly appointed Minister for Aircraft Production, from slapping requisition orders on factories still needed for the production of exports and essential civilian goods.

Her most absorbing war work came when she took charge of IM4, one of the big Board of Trade departments responsible for introducing furniture rationing. All her senior staff were men and it was now, for the first time since joining the service, that she became conscious of male hostility. Male prejudice extended to Hugh Dalton, President of the Board from 1942, who defaced one of her minutes with his scribbled red ink comments: 'Rubbish', 'Nonsense', 'Absurd'. She stormed into his office. Dalton did not make the same mistake again.

Alix Kilroy was responsible for introducing the utility furniture scheme by which wartime furniture production was limited to approved designs at controlled prices. This was more sweeping than the regulation of utility clothing, which covered only a proportion of garments produced. The aim was to eliminate unnecessary material and labour in construction: claw feet, for example, were taboo. As it was evolved by the furniture committee chaired by Gordon Russell, utility was plain, functional and modernist. It reflected the ideals of rationalist living that Alix and Francis Meynell had developed for themselves.

Her next important assignment, in January 1943, was to take charge of the newly formed Reconstruction Department. Already, plans were being made for policies for the home market when the longed-for peace arrived. Her department made plans for the unscrambling of the many wartime controls imposed on industry, and policies to help revive the old and declining industrial areas, now designated development areas. Among her initiatives was the invention of the Institute of Management and the formation of the Council of Industrial Design.

She was linked, by chance, with Francis, who had been appointed the Board of Trade's adviser on consumer needs, in a department with responsibility for finding and reporting shortages of consumer goods of all kinds except food. Domestic crockery, for instance, was in such short supply that in some parts of the country people were reported to be drinking from sardine tins. Kilroy went to Stoke herself and helped develop a cup without handles, relatively quick and cheap to make. A shortage of wedding rings that was diagnosed because jewellery retailers were concentrating their reduced trade on more profitable goods. 'Utility' wedding rings were introduced.

The couple's long relationship had been an official secret. The Board of Trade congratulated itself on matchmaking when Alex Kilroy announced her forthcoming marriage to Sir Francis (as he had just become) in August 1946. She had to ask for special permission, as a civil servant, to get married: the service's ban on married women was not formally lifted until later that year. She also had to consult her employers about being named co-respondent in Francis's divorce from his previous wife, Vera. She wanted to be co-respondent, typically, because 'this was the true state of affairs'.

She campaigned for, and achieved, some other fundamental changes in women's status. When she joined the Civil Service, women could not enter the senior ranks of the diplomatic or consular services. They were finally ruled eligible equally with men in 1946. Women's scales of pay achieved parity with men's, after a long fight, in 1961. These victories were the result of the persistence of the Council of Women Civil Servants, of which Kilroy was on the executive and, for a time, served as chairman. But they must have been affected by her personal charisma, the shining example of integrity she set. She regarded herself as a pioneer. 'I want both to marry and to have children as a social experiment,' she wrote. She intended to show the Civil Service, and prove to other women that marriage, motherhood and demanding, worthwhile work were by no means incompatible. If, in the end, she solved only one part of the equation, since her failure to have children was a lasting sadness, her successful balance of work and love and living was an inspiration.

She was made a Dame in 1947, one year after a damehood was bestowed on her old friend Evelyn Sharp, then deputy secretary in the Ministry of Town and Country Planning. 'Two Dames in one house is better than any panto,' wrote Sir Dick Plummer, an old friend of both. After a somewhat unwelcome secondment to be secretary of the first Monopolies Commission, she returned to the Board of Trade in 1952 at her own request. Feeling she was being passed over for further promotion, Dame Alix retired early in 1955. She retreated with Francis to their beautiful Norfolk pink Cobbold's Mill in Suffolk where they farmed and tended pigs. Now began her active involvement in Meynell's Nonesuch Press as well as her initiative in founding an employment bureau for voluntary work by retired professional people. She called this the Company of Professional Elders, shortened to COPE.

She joined the protest against Suez in 1956 and campaigned energetically for CND. In March 1962, she led a formidable deputation of the CND women's committee to protest to Prime Minister Harold Macmillan at the renewed use of Christmas Island for nuclear bomb testing. Faced with such a galaxy of grand dames, including Professor Dorothy Hodgkin, Diana Collins, Jacquetta Hawkes, Marghanita Laski, Dr Antoinette Pirie and Mary Stocks, Macmillan was heard to say that the opinions of knowledgeable women should not be underestimated.

Francis died in 1975 and, in old age, for the first time, Dame Alix was drawn into party politics. She was a founder member of the SDP and stood, albeit unsuccessfully, as SDP candidate in the Suffolk county council elections at the age of eighty-three. To those who did not know her, her brisk manner could be off-putting. But her capacity for affection was enormous, and the length, breadth and zest of her experience made her a joy to talk to. She never lost her curiosity. Her asperity and wisdom lives on in Francis's love poems, with their tender period quality. For Christmas 1933 he sent her his first draft of a poem on lending a wristwatch, of which the last line is: 'Time stays his flight. Look, Time is on your wrist.'

DAME ALIX (HESTER MARIE) MEYNELL · *born* 2 February 1903 · *died* 31 August 1999 ·

13 November 1999

VIVIAN FUCHS
Anthony Tucker

Famous as the leader of the Commonwealth Trans-Antarctic Expedition of 1957–8, during which he met Sir Edmund Hillary at the South Pole and carried out research which established the existence of a huge continental land mass beneath the polar ice cap, Sir Vivian Fuchs, who has died aged ninety-one, was one of the great adventurers, scientist-explorers and expedition organizers of our time. He was director of the Falkland Islands Dependencies Survey from its creation in 1947 and, from 1958to 1973, the continuing direc-tor of its successor, the British Antarctic Survey (BAS). His life spanned a period of massive transition in the nature and purposes of exploration.

Although science lay behind the early expeditions of which Fuchs was a member, experience and triumph over difficulties – both physical and intel-lectual – were of greater importance to him. Forty years on, priorities had reversed. Under his direction the BAS eschewed adventure and self-indulgence, concentrating instead on carefully planned scientific research in the most difficult working conditions on earth.

Physically strong and striking in appearance, Fuchs's compulsion for adventure emerged in 1929, the year he completed the first part of the natural history tripos at St John's College, Cambridge, where the dour but caring James Wordie was his tutor. Wordie had been Shackleton's senior scientist on the famous *Endurance* Imperial Trans-Antarctic expedition of 1914–16, and from Cambridge he encouraged and joined his students on expeditions to Greenland and elsewhere. On 2 July 1929, Fuchs and three other students set out with Wordie from Aberdeen aboard a Norwegian sealer heading for the Arctic.

Fuchs later acknowledged that this journey into the shimmering caverns of the polar regions, with its assault on the highest known Arctic peak under conditions of such stress and privation that all the members of the team were taken to the extremes of physical tolerance, was a revelation which shaped his future. His journal, although marvelling at the scale and beauty of what he saw, makes it clear that he possessed an extraordinary inner calm and clarity of perception, even in the most difficult situations.

It was to be almost twenty years before Fuchs returned to polar regions. Instead, in June 1930, he joined the Cambridge expedition to the East African lakes, studying the fresh-water biology, geology and history of the lakes in the eastern and western rift valleys. He contracted malaria, but despite great difficulties the expedition achieved all its goals – and had the bonus of meeting Sir Alan Cobham who, attempting the first flight from Cairo to the Cape, landed his seaplane on a nearby lake channel to refuel.

Fuchs's interest in Africa and, in particular, in its geology, cultural history and archaeology, had also been triggered at Cambridge by the great Dr Louis Leakey, then a research fellow at St John's. In 1931 Leakey was planning an expedition to the Olduvai Gorge, Tanzania, with the German explorer Professor Hans Reck. Reck had discovered the Tanganyikan gorge fossil beds and, in 1915, unearthed an apparently ancient – yet obviously human – skeleton among the fossils of extinct animals. Although it could not be dated, he claimed that the skeleton belonged to one of the earliest phases of human existence. Leakey planned to extend the investigation with Reck and, in need of an expedition-hardened geologist, invited Fuchs to join him.

The expedition reached the site in October 1931 in an exceptionally dry season. The larder was raided nightly by leopards. In addition to the dig and the geological mapping of the gorge, game specimens were being collected for the British Museum – although in his autobiography of 1990 Fuchs stressed that animals were shot only for essential food or scientific collections.

Although it yielded a mass of fossil material, the dig revealed that Reck's 'early human' find was, in fact, only a few thousand years old. Reck, who suffered from heart problems, promptly set off to investigate higher levels of the gorge, with Fuchs delegated to look after him. In the end, in total darkness, Fuchs had to nurse and carry his German colleague down a 2,000ft chasm-ridden escarpment.

But in that amazing and largely uncharted wilderness, Fuchs had found his feet and his vocation. When Leakey packed up and took his scientific team home in December 1932, Fuchs stayed on. In less than three months, working with three bearers and one vehicle, he mapped and carried out a geological survey of the Njorowa Gorge, Kenya. Back in England, broke but very happy, he made two proposals: one was marriage to his cousin, Joyce Connell, a world traveller in her own right; the other was for an East African rift valley expedition of his own.

Both proposals were accepted. In 1934, accompanied by Joyce and a substantial scientific team, Fuchs carried out the first scientific survey of Lake Rudolf and the northern sector of the Kenyan rift valley, a region then barely known. Ostensibly for mapping and geological survey, the expedition's studies embraced everything from anthropology to zoology, including the locust life-cycle. It was the first of a series of expeditions which, by the Second World War, had established Fuchs as a world-class expedition organizer and leader and, in particular, as the outstanding young expert in African exploration.

The war changed everything. Fuchs joined the Cambridge Regiment, then transferred to an African regiment during the North African campaign, from where he was selected to return to staff college at Camberley. He took part in the Normandy invasion, heading a small civil affairs unit, which moved forward behind the tanks, and whose role was to set up civil administration in shattered towns and villages. He ended the war as a major in Schleswig-Holstein, where he served as acting magistrate and set up the foundations of an education system.

Towards the end of 1946, Fuchs turned down promotion and returned home. An old friend told him that the colonial office was recruiting scientists for the Falkland Islands Dependencies Survey (FIDS), which itself had been born out of the Royal Navy's secret Operation Tabarin, set up to ensure that Britain's Antarctic bases and dependencies were protected during war. Fuchs applied for a geologist's job and was amazed to be offered the post of overall field commander on the survey. Assigned to the ship *John Biscoe*, he was given generous resources and told to carry out as much geology, minerology and meteorology as possible. The overtones, tilted towards permanent occupation and mineral discovery, were political rather than scientific, but he had a free hand – and used it.

Across a decade, Fuchs established a highly organized and efficent network of research stations, whose scope extended into ecology, biological resources, fossil history, and, eventually, into the science needed for conservation. By 1957 he felt confident to move further south, to carry out a double transect of the Antarctic ice cap itself. The outcome, driven through with determination, was the triumphant Commonwealth Trans-Antarctic Expedition. Fuchs entered the limelight, gained a knighthood and, when FIDS evolved into the British Antarctic Survey (BAS), stayed on as director, overseeing the transition from a partly political organization into one dedicated wholly to scientific research. The BAS long-term studies later revealed the sinister holes in the earth's ozone layer.

Vivian Fuchs retired in 1978 and wrote *Of Ice and Men* (1982), the history of the FIDS and the BAS. When asked whether adventure, comradeship or the urge for discovery had been his most important driving force, he explained that in exploration or scientific research in remote regions, the three were indivisible. 'My only regret is that it has meant spending so much time away from my family,' he would say.

Fuchs was born on the Isle of Wight, to an English mother and a German father. He spent his childhood in Kent, where his parents worked a small-holding, and developed a natural respect for animals and the integrity of living systems. Family life was shattered in 1914 with the internment of his Anglophile father as an alien and the official confiscation of all land and property. There followed years of hardship on the Isle of Man, where his father was in prison camp, and difficulties which continued long after the war ended. In 1917 his father was allowed to return, as a gardener under supervision, to his own former smallholding.

Fuchs was educated at Asheton preparatory school, near Tenterden, and Brighton College. The year he went up to Cambridge, the government returned his father's money and property and the family moved to Heatherdene, a large house with farmland and woods in Surrey. Here, often alone, Fuchs's first wife, Joyce, who died in 1990, raised their son and daughter (another daughter died), and kept numerous huskies, among other pets. In 1991 Fuchs married his BAS personal assistant, Eleanor Honnywill. She survives him, as do the two children from his first marriage.

VIVIAN ERNEST FUCHS · *born* 11 February 1908 · *died* 11 November 1999 ·

NOEL ANNAN

Douglas Johnson

Lord Annan, who has died aged eighty-three, was a remarkable man. His qualities had a completeness that made him the spokesman of more than one generation. To his intellectual flair and imagination was added considerable experience. After distinguished war service he became a leading academic, a fellow of King's College, Cambridge, and a university lecturer in politics. He went on to become a university leader and administrator, as provost of King's from the early age of forty (1956–66); as provost of University College London (1966–78); and the first full-time vice-chancellor of the University of London (1978–81). He held these responsibilities at crucial periods in the history of British universities. He knew periods of expansion and prosperity, as he knew years of stringency and uncertainty. He sat on innumerable committees and chaired most of them. His decisiveness and affability were valuable assets, but much more than this, he was one of the few who sought both to understand and to explain what was happening. He strove to find a philosophy of education.

Annan was also a public figure. Once again he presided over councils and committees. He was a director of the Royal Opera House, Covent Garden, chairman of the board of trustees of the National Gallery, a trustee of the British Museum, and president of the London Library. There were government bodies, such as the public schools commission, and private bodies, notably the Gulbenkian Foundation. He was therefore much in the public eye. At times he attracted attention by making statements which were deliberately resonant. In 1970, for example, he forcefully expressed his opposition to the plans of the Conservative government of Edward Heath to allow public museums and galleries, which had hitherto been free, to charge for admission. Why, Annan asked, should someone who worked in a shop be unable to spend some of the lunch break looking around the British Museum or the National Gallery? The Prime Minister angrily claimed that this was a small matter which had got completely out of hand, and there were those who mocked – Annan encountered many such in the course of his career – by asking how many shopgirls did Lord Annan know? But the protests succeeded. And for Annan this was not a small matter. His indignation was part of a process in which he devoutedly believed: that of civilizing people.

He was an accomplished speaker. As an orator fulfilling his duties as provost of King's, when giving the Hobhouse lecture at Bedford College (1958) or the Romanes lecture at Oxford (1965), speaking on the television Brains Trust in the 1960s, or performing as the Dimbleby Lecturer on the BBC some years later, he was always impressive. He became a life peer in 1965, and his speeches in the Lords were always carefully prepared and listened to with respect. He often took the chair at public lectures and would frequently conclude proceedings with an anecdote that was better than any of those which the speaker had produced. This always delighted the audience, and sometimes the speaker.

Noel Annan was educated at Stowe and King's College, Cambridge. He wrote the biography of Stowe's first headmaster, J. F. Roxburgh (published in 1965), who was also his headmaster. Annan believed that it was during the 1920s that the intelligent public began to doubt seriously whether the accepted principles of the public school were adequate and right. Roxburgh, whom Annan admired, had tried, in his own way, to deal with these demands. And at Cambridge Annan pursued these considerations. After the war, in the days of Attlee's 1945–51 Labour government, he thought that the university had not paid sufficient attention to what had been happening in schools and in education. He wanted Cambridge to change its attitude. He believed in grammar school boys, and as they adapted themselves to fit into their new surroundings, they discovered that brains and originality opened doors. Annan believed that in the 1950s it was the manners of the grammar schools that came to predominate. Both public and grammar school boys came to dislike the upper classes and their ways.

As provost of King's, Annan made an effort to attract boys from the maintained grammar schools. Thirty years later he noted that 54 per cent of the entry to King's came from the comprehensive system and 15 per cent from the few maintained grammars schools that still existed. He believed that comprehensive school students had a greater potential than their public school contemporaries.

But, of course, Annan himself belonged to the gilded elite. His own description of how he was recruited, in the war years, and became a member of MI14, a small unit of the military intelligence division of the War Office, could not be bettered. It was in December 1940. 'I was lunching with my father at our club, when he introduced me to a member called Carl Sherrington. He was the son of a famous Cambridge physiologist who had won the Nobel prize.' As a result of this meeting, 'I got a letter telling me to report to a Captain Sanderson at the War Office.' This captain believed that Annan was an expert on railways. He was not, but his father had been associated, some time before 1914, with the Chesapeake and Ohio railway. Hence, Annan was given an important job in operational intelligence studying the movement by rail of German forces. Then, after Germany's surrender, a chance meeting with Bill Cavendish-Bentinck (the future 9th Duke of Portland) led to Annan's appointment to the political division of the British control commission, eventually stationed in Berlin.

This is surely the old public school account of how we won the war, a story which accords with Correlli Barnett's view of the British upper class supporting each other as they muddle through. But Annan shows us in his account, *Changing Enemies* (1995), how the machinery became professional and worked. His book is very far from the traditional story of a man at war. It is the essential Annan. Who else would have begun with a quotation from *Troilus and Cressida*? Who else would be able to recall a return to Berlin in 1948, when the East Germans were beginning their blockade of the city, and to tell of how he had renewed his student acting days? The Marlowe Society were producing Webster's *The White Devil* and they invited Annan to play the part of Cardinal Monticelso.

Annan enjoyed Cambridge hugely. He was at the centre of social and intellectual life. He always remained a King's man. E. M. Forster had been given a set of rooms in King's from 1953 (to his death in 1970) and Annan constantly referred to him as 'my guru'. Forster sometimes thought that King's was a bit too ostentatious, and that its buildings had a tendency to say 'look at me'. Annan's critics would say that it was not surprising that he did not think this. They suggested that Annan was too smart and sophisticated. But if Annan defended that which was exclusive, he was sometimes only being sensible. It was absurd to accuse the Apostles, a club that existed to discuss a variety of subjects, as being the centre for homosexuals or for becoming traitors, as certain hostile critics did.

He was very active as a critic. It was during these years that he wrote two influential articles, one on 'Kipling's Place in the History of Ideas' (*Victorian Studies* 1959–60) and the other, 'The Intellectual Aristocracy', on the emergence of that group in England (published in *Studies in Social History*, a tribute to G. M. Trevelyan, 1955). Both have been endlessly quoted. It was during these years that he developed his views on sociology, and proposed that it be taught as an undergraduate subject in Cambridge. 'Nothing marks the break with Victorian thought more decisively than modern sociology' was his dictum. His work *Leslie Stephen: His Thought and Character in Relation to His Time* (1951) on Stephen as a literary critic raised the question of literature and its relation to society.

It was here (as well as over C. P. Snow's ideas of the two cultures, the scientist and the humanist) that he came into conflict with F. R. Leavis (and his wife, Q. D. Leavis). This became a classic antagonism, with Leavis denouncing Annan as a key member of the establishment and ridiculing him because he supposedly thought of a university as an industrial plant, for ever humming away in ceaseless training of the hapless young. Annan had little difficulty in pointing to the contradictions and inadequacies of Leavis's arguments and denouncing him as callous and dismissive. He once wrote, 'all public controversy is dispiriting; controversy with Dr Leavis is degrading'.

Annan's activity in promoting widespread educational reform was considerable. He hosted more than one important conference on the subject, and it was widely rumoured that when Labour returned to power, as expected in 1964, he would be given a ministerial post. But this was not to be. And when he left Cambridge in 1966 it was to take over the direction of University College London, 'that university within a university' as he called it.

It was ironical that he should have chosen University College. In Cambridge, Leavis and others had attacked him for being at the centre of the supposed Bloomsbury–King's cult (King's had been described as Bloomsbury-on-Cam) and now Annan was within a few hundred yards of Bloomsbury Square and his new college occupied many houses where the Bloomsbury set used to live in Gordon Square, and where Maynard Keynes's widow was still to be seen walking her dog in the mornings. Outside his office was another of Leavis's hates, Jeremy Bentham, whose clothed skeleton occupies a box. One day Annan emerged from his office, with a number of Japanese visitors, to discover the French Marxist philosopher Louis Althusser trying to break into the case to prove that it was not Bentham.

He found much at University College to surprise him. He could not understand that the first college to admit women with full status should have a senior common room from which women were excluded. They had their own common room, which was small. And there was a joint senior common room, universally known as the 'joint'. When a vote was held, the women preferred the existing system. The exclusion only ceased when a number of women simply started to use the senior common room as a matter of convenience.

He was also surprised by the power of the professors, but accepted with joviality the information that they spent only three to four hours teaching in some weeks of the term. He was sure the students learned a great deal during that time. And the same professors feared Annan's innovatory intentions and were uneasy over new appointments, since he had a wide range of friends and contacts.

For a time, expansion continued and new subjects were introduced. The last major building in Annan's time was the School of Architecture and Planning, the Wates building, which was opened in 1975. For the first time Annan encountered student unrest and new developments in the organization and role of the college's non-academic staff. Annan had made a careful study of the literature of student unrest and had a good understanding of the phenomenon, as he later showed in the report that he wrote on student protests in the University of Essex, which was a model of discernment. At University College his attitude was essentially personal. He would meet student leaders and talk and socialize with them. The saying among staff was 'as long as Noel doesn't run out of glasses, we're all right'. On one occasion students occupied part of the main building and caused considerable inconvenience. Annan pursued a policy of discussion and waiting. Some members of staff thought that this was too weak, and the professors of history, for example, with one exception, signed a protest demanding strong action. But before the protest had reached the provost, the student action collapsed. He showed some sympathy towards the exhausted and depressed young men and women, and some irritation towards the professors.

At University College he enjoyed helping with syllabuses. To give one example, he devised the degree course in Latin American studies and Spanish. But he was the first to say that he was not skilful in raising money. And he thought increasingly that many of University College's problems were part of the general problem of the University of London. He was very careful that his many other activities did not interfere with his duties as provost, whether it was his role in the Lords or whether it was as the author of the committee on the future of broadcasting report, always known as the Annan Report (published in 1977).

But he sensed that these activities were at times resented by members of the college. He was, as was not always realized, a sensitive man. It was this hostility that was one of the reasons why he chose to become the first full-time vice-chancellor of the University of London. There he endeavoured to rationalize the university, by grouping together certain colleges. He found himself dealing even more with civil servants, and it was with feeling that he coined the phrase 'the memo is more deadly than the demo'. He always looked back to the ideal which he had had when in Cambridge. 'The intellect. That is what universities exist for. Everything else is secondary.' He realized this ideal was always being questioned. He questioned it himself, but always came back to it in some form.

Noel Annan lived life to the full. He played tennis until he was quite elderly. When preparing his report on the future of broadcasting, he would rise very early and go for a swim in Hampstead. He was alert to the intellectual scene, as he showed with the panoramic display of his generation in his remarkable book *Our Age* (1990). In this he was ably helped by his wife Gabriele, herself a distinguished and incisive writer. All of Annan's many activities, centred as they were on education, literature and philosophical history, were devoted to the one subject: culture, and 'enclosing the wilderness of an idea within a wall of words' (Samuel Butler). His last book, *The Dons: Mentors, Eccentrics, and Geniuses* (1999), was full of perceptive academic comment.

His wife and two daughters survive him.

NOEL GILROY ANNAN, BARON ANNAN · *born* 25 December 1916 · *died* 21 February 2000 ·

12 January 2001

DENYS LASDUN
Diana Rowntree and Fiona MacCarthy

The architect of the Royal National Theatre, Sir Denys Lasdun, who has died aged eighty-six, was already an impressive figure as a student at the Architectural Association (AA) in the 1930s. His upright carriage, the sculpted head and commanding eyes, perfectly expressed the sureness with which he was to chart his way through an embattled profession.

At coffee time in Ching's Bar, Denys would not be engaged in noisy debate. He would sit with one other person, honing his architectural beliefs. Tradition for him – as for the rest of us – was the modern movement. He saw classicism as a constant, discreetly hidden in every revolution, and recognized the paradoxical link between the desire for total renewal in art and a deep attachment to the past.

Although the principal, E. A. A. Rowse, was a lifelong influence – along with Maxwell Fry and Berthold Lubetkin – Lasdun left the AA early, without a diploma, to work with Wells Coates, a member of the MARS Group, the intellectual sounding board of modernism. Two years later, he joined Tecton, Lubetkin's practice, on which all modern eyes were turned. Before war put a stop to such things, he built a house, 32 Newton Road, Paddington, strictly following Le Corbusier's domino principle. Later, Ronald Searle bought it and dreamed up the awful girls of St Trinian's there. From 1939 to 1945,

Lasdun served with the Royal Engineers, and was awarded an MBE before returning to Tecton as a partner. When the firm was dissolved in 1947, he set up in practice with Lindsay Drake, and continued to work on a Paddington housing scheme, the Hallfield estate.

Links with the London County Council architect's department, a centre of excellence, brought them the commission for Hallfield primary school, on which they were able to demonstrate, they believed for the first time, that a primary school should appear physically as the centre of an area. This was a generation of architects excited by the possibilities offered by reinforced concrete, and powered by social commitment. Next came the chance to build cluster blocks for Bethnal Green, east London. This innovative idea consisted of four fourteen-storey stacks of flats linked to a central stair and lift tower. It allowed for piecemeal renewal on bombed sites, and was probably the most interesting built example of Le Corbusier's 'streets in the air'.

Art was endemic in the Lasdun family. His father, an engineer and businessman who died when Denys was only five, was a cousin of the artist Leon Bakst, who worked with the Ballets Russes. His mother was a pianist, so his childhood was spent among music and musicians. He was educated at Rugby school.

His marriage to Susan Bendit in 1954 continued the artistic tradition. She had been at Camberwell Art School, and went on to study graphics, and to write. Their honeymoon was spent visiting the classic modern buildings of America. Susan understood the nature and the problems of architecture, and later worked on the interiors and colour of the National Theatre, among other buildings.

Late in the 1950s – and a far cry from Bethnal Green – a stunningly simple block of flats arose overlooking Green Park, in the West End of London, and gracefully took its place between two classical buildings without a single expression of outrage. Twenty-six St James's Place was London's first experience of strata, though the idea had been fermenting in Lasdun's mind for twenty years. He said that 'strata express the visual organization of social spaces in geometrical terms; they recall the streets and squares of the city and contour lines of the hills; and, at a more profound level, they bear witness to the roots of an architectural language inspired by natural geological forms'. When fighting his corner against the derangement of strata at the National Theatre, Lasdun claimed, 'strata have given the Thames back to London'.

The 1950s ended triumphantly for Lasdun with the commission for the Royal College of Physicians (RCP), on a site in the circle of Nash's terraces overlooking Regent's Park, north London. I believe that the prestige of the college, and the honour of designing for such a site, gave this son of Russian Jewry a place he had desired in Britain's establishment – and the Royal Institute of British Architects' 1992 trustees' medal.

I remember Lasdun saying that he regretted not having been to university, and wondering what a man of such presence, with such marvellous command of English, and of so philosophical a bent, imagined a university could do for him. The RCP became his favourite among his buildings: 'It accorded with the Nash terraces without imitating them.' And thirty years later, a meeting room he added to the building turned out to be one of the three 'entirely satisfactory spaces' of his *œuvre*.

The National Theatre was a live project in the office, by then Denys Lasdun and Partners, for thirteen years. The architect was appointed in 1963. While other contenders faced the board as a multi-professional team, Sir Peter Hall has recalled the drama – amounting to pathos – of Lasdun's solo performance. Any building called upon to accommodate three theatres (one seating 1,100 people), their audiences, scenery, props, workshops, foyers, restaurants and bars, is bound to provoke controversy. At the National, admiration tends to centre on the magic of the foyers and the Olivier Theatre, which was inspired by the ancient amphitheatre at Epidaurus – the largest of Lasdun's 'entirely satisfactory' spaces. Criticism is mostly of backstage arrangements, the lack of signposting and, of course, the concrete. This material enabled Lasdun to open up the public spaces of the building to the public view. He likened the project to planning a small city.

Lasdun was very skilled in the use of concrete. He told Sir Peter Hall: 'Concrete is a very intractable material, but it can be a beautiful material if it is used in the way its own nature intends it to be used … It is a sort of sculpture that you can only do with reinforced concrete, but you need to work to a certain scale … It is not a cosy little material.'

In 1976 Lasdun's long struggle to reconcile the wishes of a many-headed client with his own highly disciplined vision was marked by a knighthood. I think the award of the Royal Gold Medal for Architecture represented a consensus of British architects in acknowledging his stature. With such architects' work, the question repeatedly arises: should the key buildings of an architectural epoch be altered as their use continually demands? The fact that user requirements change was the reason why modern theory favoured lightweight and demountable buildings. At the National Theatre, the absence of weight-bearing walls is conducive to change, but the reinforced concrete strata are not. Is the masterpiece in reinforced concrete on the South Bank not as worthy of preservation as Somerset House, that earlier masterpiece on the north bank? At Christ's College, Cambridge, Lasdun's superb, stepped residential building met with disaster, when the college, pressed for more accommodation, allowed a lesser building to be tacked onto the street façade, and so prevent the terraced block from being seen ever again in its entirety. He was luckier at the University of East Anglia, where the architects who succeeded him as master planner have respected his plan and its intentions. Chief among these is the protection of the site's natural form. The Teaching Wall, which follows a contour line, is still the dominating presence, and the sheen produced by skilled casting is still visible.

Like other architects, Lasdun designed many projects that never got built. Among these is a powerful, geometric design, defined by four pairs of towers, for the ancient site of the Hurvah synagogue in Jerusalem. After Louis Kahn's death in 1974, it looked as though it might go ahead, but this now seems unlikely.

I do not know when Lasdun wrote, 'Every building has, at its heart, a generating idea, which must express itself through every part and in every detail.' Looking back at the Hallfield school, its plan now appears overdesigned. With each building of his since then, the details, still lovingly designed, seem to merge more smoothly into the impression of the whole, which is of ever-increasing scale.

The latest, and largest, of the stratified designs is the European Investment Bank in Luxembourg. The spacious, woodland site has allowed a simpler plan, which may adapt more readily to change than more condensed buildings. At the centre of this cruciform plan is the Water Room, one of the spaces that Lasdun found 'entirely satisfactory'. William Curtis has the last word on the Luxembourg building: 'It reaffirms,' he has said, 'that it is understatement that makes powerful art.' Art of this kind demands a lifetime's dedication of working and thinking.

Denys Lasdun is survived by his wife and three children, all of whom work in the arts; Louisa as a composer, James as a writer and William as a sculptor.

FIONA MacCARTHY writes: Denys was in ebullient mood, greeting his friends with bear hugs, when I saw him last month at the opening of the British Museum great court. As a fellow architect, who loved to work on the grand scale, he was full of admiration for Norman Foster's scheme. He dismissed the controversy over the new stone portico as irrelevant, mean-minded criticism of a kind to which he had himself become all too accustomed in a lifetime of architectural slings and arrows. We planned to visit him and Susan in their house in Hammersmith as soon as the builders (yes, the builders) had moved out.

Denys's enthusiasms had always seemed unstoppable. He was, more than anyone, my architectural mentor. I first got to know him well on holidays in southern Tuscany, staying with our shared friends, Sally and Graham Greene. My perceptions of Grosetto and its hill towns, of Massa Maritima and the Etruscan tombs, will always be entwined with my memories of Denys's affectionate lucidity. His friendships crossed the generations; my young daughter Clare adored him. All Companions of Honour should be forced to take a Lasdun test in lack of pomposity and openness of mind.

Those who think of Lasdun as an architectural brutalist get him wrong completely. They miss out on the imaginative richness of his buildings. He was a subtle, deeply knowledgeable man. His feeling for the ebb and flow of cities, the disconcerting beauties of modern urban life, transmitted itself in a strange way to his son James, whose success delighted Denys. My favourite late Lasdun building, the meeting room at the Royal College of Physicians, seems energized by the traffic circulating frenziedly around Regent's Park.

The retrospective at the Royal Academy in 1997 confirmed Lasdun as the most important British architect of the last half century. A detail that entranced him was the peephole through from his exhibition to the late Braque show beyond it. These were the sorts of juxtapositions Denys loved.

DENYS LOUIS LASDUN · *born* 8 September 1914 · *died* 11 January 2001 ·

23 August 2001

FRED HOYLE
Bernard Lovell

Sir Fred Hoyle, who has died aged eighty-six, will be remembered as one of the most distinguished and controversial scientists of the twentieth century. Soon after the end of the Second World War he became widely known both by scientists and the public as one of the originators of a new theory of the universe. He was a fluent writer and speaker and became the main expositor of this new theory of the steady state, or continuous creation, according to which the universe had existed for an infinite past time and would continue infinitely into the future, as opposed to what Hoyle styled the 'big bang' theory.

As a young man during the Second World War, Hoyle had worked in the Admiralty Signals Establishment and during that period he became friendly with Hermann Bondi and Thomas Gold. The ideas that led to the continuous creation theory were born at that time, and in 1948 their historic papers on the theory were published. Although the names of Bondi, Hoyle and Gold are associated with that revolutionary theory, Hoyle's paper was published separately, two months later than the joint one of Bondi and Gold. The latter had stressed the philosophical aspect of a perfect cosmological principle in which the universe would have a high degree of uniformity not only in space but also in time, thereby evading the scientific problem associated with a beginning in a finite past time. Hoyle dealt with the continuous creation of the primordial hydrogen that would be essential to maintain the steady state, and placed the concept within the framework of general relativity.

The detailed presentation of the theory in the journal of the Royal Astronomical Society in 1948 was not a cooperative effort. The evidence is that Hoyle had sent his paper to an American journal, where it was rejected. Its eventual publication, two months after the Bondi–Gold paper, was a coincidence that formed an impenetrable phalanx for nearly two decades. The conflict with the conventional idea that the universe had a specific origin billions of years in time past was absolute. Until the discovery of the cosmic microwave background in 1965, the observational evidence was inconclusive and the emotive feelings aroused led to one of the bitterest scientific divisions of the century. Hoyle never accepted the complete defeat of the continuous creation theory, and long after the 'big bang' universe had become conventional scientific wisdom he continued to probe its defects.

Although Hoyle was most widely known for this cosmological theory, there is little doubt that his most lasting and significant contribution to science concerns the origin of the elements. This theory of nucleogenesis (the build-up of the elements in the hot interiors of stars) was an outstanding scientific landmark of the 1950s. In the development of this theory Hoyle collaborated with W. A. Fowler of the California Institute of Technology in Pasadena, and with Geoffrey and Margaret Burbidge. Hitherto, the general belief was that all the elements must have been produced in the hot primordial universe. The new paper, on the contrary, showed that the elements could be produced from the primordial hydrogen by nucleosynthesis in the hot interior of stars. The theory gave a satisfactory account of the relative abundances of the elements, provided an explanation of the direction of stellar evolution and gave an objective basis for calculation of the internal constitution of stars. The theory also confirmed a prediction of Hoyle's that there must be an excited state of the carbon twelve isotope – at the energy he had predicted from a consideration of the evolution of red giant stars.

This, incidentally, was agreeably consistent with the steady state cosmological theory, since there was no necessity for an initial hot condition of a primordial universe.

The paper, published in an American journal in 1957, has been described as monumental, and the theory has had a cardinal influence on astrophysics. Although there were four authors, it is widely known that the Burbidges contributed the data from their stellar observations and that the core and essence of the paper was the work of Fowler and Hoyle. Fowler was awarded the Nobel prize for physics in 1983, and why Hoyle was not included in this award remains a mystery hidden in the confidential documents of the Royal Swedish Academy. The editor of the scientific journal *Nature* suggested that the academy did not wish to be associated with any endorsement of another idea then being promulgated by Hoyle.

This was linked to Hoyle's belief that life must be of frequent occurrence in the universe. He argued that the primeval molecules from which life evolved on Earth had been transported from elsewhere in the universe. In itself this idea would not necessarily be rejected as absurd by the scientific community, but Hoyle had publicized a further argument that influenza epidemics were associated with the passage of the Earth through certain meteor streams, the particles of which conveyed the virus to Earth. This was dismissed as fictional by nearly all members of the biological and physical scientific disciplines. Indeed, the idea belonged more to Hoyle's activity as a writer of science fiction for over three decades. His most famous novel was *October the First is Too Late*, and several, such as *The Black Cloud* (1957) and *A For Andromeda* (1962), which was made into a television serial, achieved a wide circulation. Another, *Rockets in Ursa Major* (1962), was also produced as a play.

Hoyle played a prominent part in the scientific affairs of the UK. He served on the council of the Royal Society as vice president from 1969 to 1971 and was president of the Royal Astronomical Society 1971–3. As a member of the Science Research Council from 1967 to 1972 he was active in the assessment of the astronomical facilities in the southern hemisphere, which led to the creation of the 150-inch Anglo-Australian telescope at Siding Spring in New South Wales. He was a member of the joint policy committee from 1967, during the planning stage for the telescope, became chairman of the Anglo-Australian telescope board in 1973, and presided at the inauguration of the telescope in 1974 by the Prince of Wales.

Hoyle was born at Bingley in Yorkshire, the son of a wool merchant, and by the age of ten could navigate by the stars. From Bingley grammar school he went up to Emmanuel College, Cambridge, to read maths: he was the

Mayhew Prizeman in the 1936 Cambridge Mathematical Tripos. In his immediate postgraduate years he was Smith's Prizeman, Goldsmith Exhibitioner and was awarded a senior exhibition by the Commission for the Exhibition of 1851. He was elected to a fellowship at St John's in 1939.

During these years he first became associated with R. A. Lyttleton on problems of accretion of dust and gas around large bodies. Thereby began his shift of interest from mathematical physics to astronomy and, in later years, it led to his work on the formation of planetary systems and to his conviction that life must be of frequent occurrence in the universe. In a broadcast talk in the early 1950s, at a time when Australia was dominating England at cricket, he remarked that he would wager that somewhere in the Milky Way there was a cricket team who could beat the Australians. During the war he was engaged in technical projects, such as radar for the Admiralty, where he found himself working with Bondi and Gold. Hoyle returned to Cambridge after the war as university lecturer in mathematics. In 1958 he was appointed the Plumian professor of astronomy and became the first director of the Cambridge Institute of Theoretical Astronomy in 1967.

Although the occupant of two such distinguished offices, he became immensely unhappy with his life in Cambridge. The crisis came over a dispute concerning the election to a professorial chair and he tendered his resignation as Plumian professor from 1972 and as director of the Institute from 1973.

For many years I had been closely associated with Hoyle in astronomical and policy matters, and his attitude to Cambridge was epitomized in his explanatory letter to me. 'I do not see any sense in continuing to skirmish on a battlefield where I can never hope to win. The Cambridge system is effectively designed to prevent one ever establishing a directed policy – key decisions can be upset by ill-informed and politically motivated committees. To be effective in this system one must for ever be watching one's colleagues, almost like a Robespierre spy system. If one does so, then of course little time is left for any real science.'

At the age of fifty-seven, Hoyle retired from his formal appointments in the UK, residing first in the Lake District and then on the south coast. He held honorary research professorships at the University of Manchester and University College, Cardiff, from which he published extensively, with N. C. Wickramasinghe, on the biological aspects of his astronomical concepts. He did much of his work in the United States, particularly in the California Institute of Technology, where he was appointed visiting associate in physics in 1963, and at Cornell, where he held a visiting professorship for six years after he retired from Cambridge.

Hoyle was awarded numerous honorary doctorates, medals and prizes. His many books included *Frontiers of Astronomy* (1955), *Men and Materialism* (1956), *Star Formation* (1963), *Galaxies, Nuclei and Quasars* (1965), *The Relation of Physics and Cosmology* (1973), *Ten Faces of the Universe* (1977) and *On Stonehenge* (1977). His autobiography, *Home is Where the Wind Blows,* was published in 1994. He was elected a Fellow of the Royal Society in 1957 and was knighted in 1972. In 1974 he was awarded the royal medal of the Royal Society, and on that occasion the president said that Hoyle was one of the most original minds in present-day astronomy and that his 'enormous output of ideas are immediately recognized as challenging to astronomers generally … his popularization of astronomical science can be warmly commended for the descriptive style used and the feeling of enthusiasm about his subject which they succeed in conveying'. Indeed, Hoyle packed the lecture rooms wherever he spoke in the world.

He is survived by his wife, Barbara Clark, whom he married in 1939, and by his son and daughter.

FRED HOYLE · *born* 24 June 1915 · *died* 20 August 2001 ·

16 January 2002

MICHAEL YOUNG
Malcolm Dean

Michael Young, Lord Young of Dartington, who has died aged eighty-six, was a man of many parts: educator, author, academic, consumer advocate, policy-maker, political activist – and rebel. Over and above these were two other roles, inventor and entrepreneur, which made him a unique figure in British twentieth-century social reform. He was the country's great seedsman of social ideas and institutions. The new paths he hacked out in education, consumer rights and health services have helped millions of people. Some of his ideas – like the Open University and the Consumers' Association – have become world famous, but there were numerous other projects of which even his friends were unaware, like the do-it-yourself garage in Milton Keynes.

Skilled at using the media to promote his schemes, Young always shrank from personal publicity. He hated the idea of profiles in the newspapers, and was determined there would be no biography. The majority of his projects were simple and practical, meeting an obvious need: brain trains, on which commuters teach each other; Linkage, bringing together older people without grandchildren, and young people without grandparents; Language Line, a telephone interpreting service for doctors and ethnic groups; health advice lines and a hospital waiting list guide. Others were of a more challenging nature: Asset, the study of time; the Argot Venture, to set up a (still pending) space museum; even a project to test living in space. Those of us sucked into some of these schemes could only admire the breadth of Young's personal network, the skill with which he handled the various prima donnas he brought together, and the boyish charm which made it impossible for even the busiest people to turn down his appeals for help.

His energy was phenomenal. So was his never-flagging ability to discover new needs and come up with new institutions, even in the most stressful situations – like the College of Health, a pressure group for patients, which emerged from his first spell in hospital for cancer in 1982.

Michael Young was born in Manchester. His father was an Australian violinist turned music critic, his mother a Bohemian painter and actor. His early years were spent in Melbourne, but he returned to England at eight, shortly before his parents' marriage broke up. There was not much money. By the age of fourteen, he had been through four schools, where he was 'hunted and harried by rules, regulations and corporal punishment'. Relief came in 1929 with his transfer to Dartington Hall, a new progressive school in Devon for twenty-five children of the intelligentsia.

This was the start of Young's long association with Dartington. The founders, Leonard Elmhirst, an agricultural economist, and his American wife, Dorothy, who had inherited part of the Whitney fortune, used to take him on visits to the United States, where some journeys were made by private train. He became a Dartington trustee in 1942, deputy chairman in 1980 and, two years later, his account of the school, *The Elmhirsts of Dartington: The Creation of a Utopian Community*, was finally published.

By the start of the Second World War, Young had picked up an economics degree at London University and qualified as a barrister at Gray's Inn. By the end of the war – asthma blocked him from military service – he had served five years as director of Political and Economic Planning, a think-tank that brought together policy-makers and practitioners, and become director of research for the Labour party. He was twenty-nine. He prepared a vast speakers' handbook for the 1945 general election, and singlehandedly wrote the Labour manifesto, which he described as 'nothing very visionary, but very detailed because we had had so much time to plan'. Various themes, such as a social science programme and a child-centred society, were vetoed by Herbert Morrison, soon to become deputy prime minister. So was Young's idea of an empty chair at cabinet meetings to represent the unknown constituent, akin to the unknown warrior.

None the less, his readiness to challenge sacred cows from the inside did not take long to surface. In 1947 he was almost sacked for criticizing the Trades Union Congress in a pamphlet on the need to restrain wages. In the same year he called for a social science research council, and became its first chairman when he eventually persuaded Tony Crosland to set it up seventeen years later. He left his Labour research job in 1950 'because the party had run out of ideas'.

Young's interest in sociology had begun during the Second World War, and in 1952 – at the age of thirty-seven – he returned to the London School of Economics, and switched his Ph.D. research from a political voting study, under Harold Laski, to housing conditions in London's East End, under Richard Titmuss. Setting up his base in Bethnal Green, he was shocked at the extent to which local Labour leaders had lost touch with their communities. 'The local councillors heard the complaints, but did nothing about them because they were captured by the officials.' This was what led Young to set up, in 1952, the Institute of Community Studies, the base from which so many of his later ideas were launched. From the beginning, he was concerned with giving people more say, improving the rights of housing tenants and NHS patients, and fostering neighbourhood councils 'to reduce the scale of government'. The Institute was an ideal base for such an inventive man. It was never burdened by a large bureaucracy, although it did require him to search endlessly for funds. One of his first studies, *Family and Kinship in East London* (1957), which he wrote with Peter Willmott, forced planners to reassess the fashion for sweeping urban redevelopment.

Within academic sociology, Young was criticized as romantic, unscientific and too ready to draw sweeping conclusions. None of this perturbed a man who put more faith in the methods of Victorian reformers like Mayhew, Booth and Rowntree than in postwar sociological techniques. His approach was to listen to ordinary people, put down in lucid prose the problems they set out, and produce practical solutions. He was invited by Cambridge University to set up its sociology department, but quickly became disillusioned by the dons who refused to accept his radical idea of expanding facilities to increase the intake. One heretical idea was to use the lengthy vacations to take in a second shift.

Instead, Young started a dawn university on Anglia Television, which became the prototype for the Open University, launched by Harold Wilson in 1964. In between these initiatives, he started the National Extension College, providing distance learning courses for thousands of British Students and, in 1972, the International Extension College for Third-World students. A decade later, he joined forces with Peter Laslett to launch the British version of the University of the Third Age. Young's other educational inventions include the Advisory Centre for Education (ACE), set up in 1960 to give parents and communities more information on education issues; the Open College of the Arts (1988), which confounded the experts who thought the practical arts could not be taught by correspondence; and the Open School (1989), which used distance-learning techniques to help teachers become familiar with the new National Curriculum.

Like all good entrepreneurs, Young picked up ideas from a wide variety of sources. For example, he first thought of the Consumers' Association on reading a report about American consumer unions before the war – although he had to wait until 1957 to launch its British version. He protected the association's magazine *Which?* from libel risks by persuading Gerald Gardiner, the future Labour Lord Chancellor, and then the country's foremost defamation lawyer, to let his name appear on the masthead.

Three years after the Consumers' Assocation was launched, Young published *The Chipped White Cups of Dover*, which set out detailed ways in which public services could give their clients a better deal. He accurately predicted that 'politics will become less and less the politics of production, and more and more the politics of consumption'. His solution was a new consumers' party, an idea so heretical that the Fabian Society refused to publish his pamphlet, and Young was forced to finance it himself. Later, he was to become the first chairman of the National Consumer Council, set up to improve public services.

Young's only period of affluence was thanks to another iconoclastic essay, an attack on equal opportunity, which the Fabians also refused to publish. Written in a satirical form – as a supposed Ph.D. dissertation by a Manchester grammar school graduate in 2034 – it was expanded to book length and rejected by eleven publishers before it appeared as *The Rise of the Meritocracy*, published by Thames & Hudson in 1958. In the end, it coined a new word for the language, sold 500,000 copies in twelve languages, helped to abolish the 11-plus examination, made the left think more carefully about equal opportunities, and widened support for a pluralistic society.

Young was married three times: first, in 1945, to Joan Lawton, with whom he had two sons and a daughter (and who died in 1989); and then, in 1960, to Sasha Moorsom, the novelist, sculptor and painter, with whom he had a son and daughter. He worked closely with Sasha on many projects, and gamely took part in family painting exhibitions. Visiting South Africa together, they found a new role for distance-learning schemes among young black dropouts from township schools. After Sasha's death in 1993, Young married Dorit Uhlemann, with whom he had a daughter.

Young inspired loyalty and exasperation in equal amounts from the staff of his many projects – loyalty for his kindness, sense of fun and gentleness, exasperation at the iron determination with which he pursued his ideas. He loved ruffling feathers. It was Young who named his SDP think-tank the Tawney Society to irk his Labour friends, and christened his new policy journal *Samizdat* to irritate the right.

There was one final paradox: he was the egalitarian who accepted a life peerage in 1978. Why? It coincided with his almost filial attachment to Dartington. His other projects required regular journeys to London, but he had run out of money. The peerage offered him free rail travel, plus attendance allowances in the House of Lords. Taking Barbara Wootton's advice, he reluctantly – and 'guardedly' – accepted. It never changed the man.

He is survived by his children and his third wife.

MICHAEL YOUNG, LORD YOUNG OF DARTINGTON ·
born 9 August 1915 · *died* 14 January 2002 ·

19 April 2002

THOR HEYERDAHL
Jo Anne Van Tilburg

Thor Heyerdahl, who has died of cancer aged eighty-seven, was one of the great individualistic standard-bearers of mid-twentieth-century adventure. In 1947 he and his five-person crew climbed aboard *Kon-Tiki*, an experimental balsa raft, and swept atop the Pacific's Humboldt current from Peru to the Tuamotu Islands – and into history. His achievement, Heyerdahl announced to the world, proved that New World mariners from the east might have sailed into Polynesia, contradicting the general assumption that it had been populated from the west.

Today, there is no question that *Kon-Tiki* demonstrated, in the words of archaeologist Glyn Daniel, the possibility – but not the actuality – of entering the Pacific from east to west on a balsa raft. The project lay at the heart of

Heyerdahl's life-work – trying to prove his conviction that the cultures of the ancient world were sometimes linked by sailors who could cross oceans.

To establish the dryland archaeological support for this hypothesis, in 1952–3 Heyerdahl travelled to the Galápagos Islands, lying on the equator 500 miles to the west of Ecuador. Shards of what were suggested to be pre-Incan pots challenged the view that there had been no pre-European visitors there.

This was just the prelude to his expeditions to Easter Island (Rapa Nui), set remotely apart to the south-east of the Tuamotu archipelago. Following that venture, he became interested in the feasibility of crossing the Atlantic in reed boats, and then in the possibility of ancient feats of seafaring in the Arabian Sea and Indian Ocean.

Streaming through all the extensive body of published work that Heyerdahl produced is the complex, contradictory persona of a man who thought like an outsider, but not an outcast. Demanding, opinionated, but sensitive and kind, throughout his career he stubbornly cast himself in steady counterpoint to academia. He refused to play by the most basic rules of academic interchange, yet bristled when faced with criticism, and promptly took his case to the welcoming court of public opinion. There was, he said in a recent interview, a 'shocking extent of ignorance' on the part of those who 'call themselves authorities and pretend to have a monopoly of all knowledge'. None the less, every archaeologist who ever worked with Heyerdahl liked and respected him.

Born in Larvik, Norway, Heyerdahl was the lonely, only son of unhappy, estranged parents, who divorced during his early childhood. Entering Oslo University to study zoology and geography, he changed to anthropology while living in Fatu-Hiva in the Marquesas Islands of French Polynesia, having become fascinated by the question of where its inhabitants had come from. There he shed the conventions of normal life – including the completion of his degree course – and, like so many earlier South Seas travellers, artists and poets, embarked on his own internal journey. As Pacific historian Gavin Daws put it, Heyerdahl was determined to turn his personal quest 'into accomplishments that the world will pay attention to'. And this he did.

The next step, from 1939 to 1940, was to pursue his theory of native American movements into the Pacific by looking for a 'missing link' in British Columbia. He believed that an early Stone Age people from south-east Asia had crossed the Pacific to north America, and had set off again for Polynesia at some point before AD 1000. Certain artefact and language characteristics suggested to him that there might be a connection between peoples in Malaysia, Polynesia and – at the apex of this distended and still unproven theoretical triangle – some of the native American tribes of British Columbia.

From 1941, Heyerdahl fought in the free Norwegian military forces in Finnmark, at Norway's northernmost extremity. He then conducted further research in Europe and the US from 1945 to 1947.

The *Kon-Tiki* expedition took its name from a mythical seafarer king who, in a legend of the Aymara Indians of Lake Titicaca, in modern Bolivia, had set off across the seas with his followers and disappeared: such folk memories formed yet another strand in Heyerdahl's radical view of ancient technology and enterprise. A bearded face, representing the early ocean sailor, adorned the sail of the modern craft. From Callao, Peru, to the island of Raroia, in Polynesia, it covered 4,300 miles in 101 days.

In 1948, the day after his second marriage had taken place in Santa Fe, New Mexico, Heyerdahl met the American archaeologist Edwin N. Ferdon Jr. At the time, Heyerdahl was lecturing and raising funds to support his book *American Indians in the Pacific: The Theory Behind the Kon-Tiki Expedition*, a controversial tome published in 1952. One of his chief interests was to trace the origins of Rapa Nui's megalithic sculpture, and to seek evidence of the relationship he believed it had to South American traditions. Ferdon joined the Norwegian expedition to Rapa Nui at Heyerdahl's invitation, and the two men embarked upon a rewarding friendship that, in spite of distance and differing opinions, endured for fifty years. William Mulloy (who told an amused Heyerdahl, 'I don't believe a damn thing you've published'), Arne Skjolsvold and Carlyle S. Smith made up the rest of the archaeological team.

Very soon after the expedition landed on the island, Heyerdahl called the other archaeologists into the expedition's base tent. 'You know my theories,' he said, and then instructed them to go their own ways without fear of interference. He was open-minded and always fair, even when their results failed to prove his theories.

In 1958 Heyerdahl published *Aku-Aku: The Secret of Easter Island*, an imaginative, even fanciful, but engrossing yarn of 'secret caves' and 'ghostly' ceremonies, woven around the island's imposing sculptures, and stories of a mythical conflict between long- and short-eared people. It became immensely popular mainstream reading, and encouraged a welcome upsurge in modern tourism to the island. Those interested in more solid information turned to the expedition's formidable formal report. Edited by Heyerdahl and Ferdon in 1961, it is a landmark in Pacific studies and a monument to the project.

The presence of the sweet potato, an indigenous South American plant, in south-east and central Polynesia by AD 1000 remains the best and most convincing evidence of human contact between the two regions. In 1919 Katherine Routledge, who with her husband William Scoresby had been a pioneering predecessor of Heyerdahl's, had written that reaching Rapa Nui from South America was 'out of the question'. More recent investigations, summarized by New Zealand scholar Roger Green, suggest a more cautious evaluation. Green, who met Heyerdahl for the first time at the Pacific science congress in Honolulu in 1961, differed from him on many issues. Perhaps the most important of them was the raft as a means of contact between South America and Polynesia. Heyerdahl, Green said, 'just had things backward'. The contact, most Pacific scholars believe, had been from south-east Polynesia to the northern South American coast and then back again.

The two men held other contradictory opinions, but each regarded the other as a colleague and good friend. Thus, the question that *Kon-Tiki* first posed so dramatically more than fifty years ago is still open, and current archaeology is pursuing it according to the agenda that Heyerdahl advanced.

In Peru, Heyerdahl had become acquainted with the use of small reed boats on Lake Titicaca. Excavations on Rapa Nui had uncovered images of what he believed were three-masted reed boats, and this led Heyerdahl to speculate whether such vessels, apparently known in ancient Egypt and still constructed by the Buduma people from Lake Chad, could have crossed the Atlantic. His 1969 voyage from Morocco in *Ra I* proved that a papyrus ship could survive ocean conditions for a long time, though its stern threatened to disintegrate after covering 3,000 of the 4,000 miles to Barbados.

However, Heyerdahl and his collaborators came to appreciate that the inwardly curled stern they discerned in some ancient Egyptian pictures was not ornamental. It was essential to a vessel's elasticity, and so Heyerdahl enlisted the aid of four Aymara Indians from Bolivia. The second attempt, in *Ra II* a year later, reached Barbados. The *Tigris* expedition of 1977–8 built on the knowledge gained during the course of the *Ra* voyages. Heyerdahl sought to prove that Mesopotamian berdi reed could equally well have provided the material for Sumerian boat-builders to get to the Red Sea and Egypt, to the west, and to the ancient civilizations of the Indus Valley, to the east. In the course of building *Tigris*, Heyerdahl introduced his Aymara Indian comrades to their Iraqi Marsh Arab counterparts: despite the language barrier, the two groups worked together to build a ship that was, at more than fifty feet, Heyerdahl's largest. But when wars in the Red Sea region confined it to Djibouti harbour, he burnt it in protest.

His expeditions to the Maldive Islands in 1983 and 1984 followed, blossoming out of his belief that these coral reefs had been known to seafarers long before their discovery by Arabs in 1153. Then, in 1986, 1987 and 1988, he returned to Rapa Nui with two main objectives. A story told in the early 1900s claimed that the island's great statues were capable of 'walking'. Working with a Czechoslovak engineer named Pavel Pavel, Heyerdahl tied ropes to the top and to the bottom of a small, upright statue, and then crews pulling on the ropes wriggled it back and forward, moving it about four feet. The method was impractical in the island's rugged terrain, and Heyerdahl did not pursue it, or other land-based theories, with the passion he brought to sea voyage experimentation.

His other aim concerned the toromiro tree, which is endemic to Easter Island. In 1956 he had taken seeds from a dying specimen and had them planted in the Gothenburg botanical garden. While the tree was not extinct, its numbers had been greatly diminished. He encouraged conservation efforts by re-establishing seedlings in the plant nursery of the island's national park.

Among the pyramids of Tucume, Peru, from 1988 to 1993, Heyerdahl found what he believed was proof of his original *Kon-Tiki* hypothesis: 'images of reed ships crewed by mythical men with bird heads' – symbolic motifs similar to others found in petroglyphs on Rapa Nui. In 1990 more pyramids took him to Guimar, Tenerife, in the Canary Islands, where he met his third wife, Jacqueline, and bought a house in which the couple married in 1996. He theorized that the Tenerife pyramids had an astronomically oriented temple function, and took them to have been left by the Guanche people, who had surrendered to the Spaniards. In one of the final examples of the sweeping, global connections that he loved to make, he described their king as 'the last of the white and bearded seafarers that were only kept alive in the legends in Mexico and Peru'.

Heyerdahl published extensively, lectured widely, made documentary films – the 1951 Oscar-winning *Kon-Tiki* left an indelible impression – received numerous awards and was granted several honorary degrees. He encouraged conservation and environmental awareness, had a wide public that he was very conscious of, and enjoyed the undisputed celebrity status of world figure and Norwegian national treasure.

In the field of Polynesian studies he made three significant and enduring contributions: the notion of the sea as connector not a barrier, the now indisputable fact of contact between South America and Polynesia, and his generous support of modern archaeology. Heyerdahl and the Kon-Tiki Museum in Oslo (founded in 1949 with his wartime colleague and radio operator on the raft, Knut Haugland) have initiated, raised money for, or published the results of, projects in Rapa Nui, Pitcairn, the Marquesas Islands, South America and, most recently, in Western Samoa. His thirst for knowledge and experience provided the driving force for new archaeological discoveries.

When Heyerdahl revisited Rapa Nui in 1984, the islanders put on an enormous welcome, and he graciously attended dozens of public and private affairs in his honour. I was there as an archaeology graduate student, and held a special dinner at the house I was renting in the village, complete with Rapa Nui children in dancing costume. Heyerdahl came and, as I recall, danced with abandon with my then eight-year-old daughter. Over the following years, we had heated differences of opinion over issues related to the statues, but we also had marvellous, stimulating conversations.

Rapa Nui people are grateful to him for bringing their history to the attention of the world, and archaeologists Sonia Haoa and Sergio Rapu, like many other colleagues, appreciated his love of tackling big, complex questions, and encouraging others to do the same.

Kon-Tiki and Heyerdahl's other larger-than-life adventures were all, in the words of Robert Louis Stevenson, 'a voyage to a further goal'. The growth of knowledge, Heyerdahl knew, is never neatly linear. He took us all on a magnificent, exploratory sail, tacking restlessly from one direction to another, but always heading towards a new island just over the horizon, and always before the wind.

Heyerdahl was married three times. He had two sons from his first marriage to Liv, whom he married in 1936. His second wife was Yvonne, whom he married in 1948; they had three daughters, one of whom predeceased him. His third wife, Jacqueline, survives him, along with his two sons and two daughters.

THOR HEYERDAHL · *born* 6 October 1914 · *died* 18 April 2002 ·

THE MEDIA

...

TOM HOPKINSON
Alan Rusbridger and David Mitchell

Sir Tom Hopkinson, who has died aged eighty-five, will be chiefly remembered as the editor of the most successful picture magazine ever to have been published in Britain. In its twelve years (1938–50) it invented a form of photojournalism which combined a distinctive photographic style with sharp, literate and challenging reportage. He was sacked at the height of its success, but went on to edit *Drum*, an equally pioneering magazine for South African black people before returning to Britain to found Britain's first university course in journalism.

Hopkinson was one of nine children of a classical archaeologist. He grew up on the *Manchester Guardian*, and from an early age aspired to work for it. 'I thought all *Guardian* leader writers wore tweed suits, smoked pipes and had terriers,' he recalled later in life. 'But I was prepared to undergo all those hardships if I could realize the height of my social and journalistic ambition.'

In fact he started life on the *Westminster Gazette*, sold advertising and hawked encyclopaedias, but was propelled back into journalism by anger at unemployment and frustration at the general political climate of the 1930s. Edward Hulton had intended *Picture Post* to be a sixpenny Conservative paper, and watched impotently as its maverick Austrian editor, Stefan Lorant, and Hopkinson turned it into a hugely successful anti-appeasement, pro-Labour magazine.

The list of photographers who worked on *Picture Post* under his editorship is a Who's Who of the craft: Bert Hardy, Bill Brandt, Kurt Hutton, Grace Robinson among them. Robert Kee, Jill Craigie and James Cameron were among the young reporters who first made their mark with Hopkinson. '*Picture Post* was successful because it was bang on its time,' Hopkinson told the *Guardian*'s picture editor, Eamonn McCabe, last month. 'When it came out in October 1938 there were other picture magazines, but they were all aimed up-market at the huntin', fishin' and shootin' set. The real idea of the magazine was to bring to ordinary people something which had hitherto been the prerogative of the well-to-do. It also took seriously the achievements of ordinary life. We ran seven pages, for example, on a charwomen's outing to Southend. No one had ever thought of photographing something like that.'

The magazine was so critical of the Government during the war that distribution to the troops was blocked by the Ministry of Information. But Hopkinson's editorship combined combativeness with a rare sensitivity. He would never shock for shocking's sake. He recalled of one particularly harrowing picture: 'It was a stunning photograph, but it was pointless horror because it told you nothing about the war.' From 1941 to 1946 he managed to edit both *Picture Post* and its baby sister, *Lilliput*, in tandem. But Hulton's refusal to print a Cameron/Hardy exposé of atrocities committed by South Koreans in 1950 led to Hopkinson's departure from the magazine and ultimately to the death of the magazine itself. Television has, in conventional wisdom, been blamed for its demise. Hopkinson thought otherwise. 'I think it should have re-cast itself instead of committing suicide.'

His third wife, Dorothy, persuaded him to make a fresh start in Johannesburg after a brief spell as features editor of the *News Chronicle*. Ian Berry's coverage of the Sharpeville massacre was the most notable scoop achieved during his three years on *Drum*. Writing about the event in the *Guardian* this year Hopkinson recalled: 'One picture in particular, showing a policeman on top of a tank reloading his weapon while his companions still fired into the fleeing crowd, effectively demolished the government case that the police had been forced to fire in self-defence.'

It was Hopkinson's conviction of the need to promote African journalists that first led him into training, in Nairobi. He then pioneered Press Studies at Sussex University and for five years directed the Centre for Journalism at University College, Cardiff.

DAVID MITCHELL writes: In 1944, having been discharged from the forces 'on psychiatric grounds' as an incorrigible misfit, I laboriously typed an article, my very first about that farcical period in uniform, and posted it to *Lilliput*. It came back with an encouraging, neatly written note from Tom Hopkinson, then editing *Lilliput* as well as, almost miraculously, keeping *Picture Post* freshly alive with a skeleton staff despite censorship problems and paper rationing.

Three years later, in the Hulton Press offices in Shoe Lane, facing a blitz-cleared, wildflowered wilderness, I was interviewed by Tom soon after history finals at Oxford. Though I had taken no part in undergraduate journalism, I was given a trial run and soon felt mightily privileged to have joined what Tom described as 'some kind of enlarged family, but a family I had myself largely chosen, not one provided for me'.

After harrowing years with his first wife, the spectacularly unstable Antonia White, and with his second marriage to Gerti Deutsch unravelling, that Shoe Lane family was Tom's true home. A manically conscientious editor, he was already engaged in a bruising struggle with Edward Hulton to preserve the crusading just-left-of-centre tone of *PP* which had made it something of a national institution. Rumours of this ongoing skirmish added to the tension of weekly 'ideas' conferences at which everyone, from the office boy to such distinguished writers as James Cameron and Robert Kee, was expected to make a contribution and, democratically, to call Hopkinson 'Tom'.

I did so in a tentative mumble, for though slight in stature he was a formidable father figure with a *Noli-me-tangere* space around him. Awed to know that he had contributed to *Horizon*, I sometimes wondered whether he was wrestling with the problems of a short story or a novel. More likely he was planning how to avoid yet another dinner party with the Hultons, for as he admits in his autobiography, *Of This Our Time*, he was essentially a loner for whom social contacts were an ordeal. Vividly blue, hypnotically protruberant eyes, the 'level, earnest voice' inherited from his father, an Anglican archdeacon, the forward-tilted stance of a scrum-half impatient for the ball to be heeled (he had played rugger for Lancashire), an invariably dapper appearance: all this, behind a desk of awesome neatness, gave the impression he longed for any 'intruder' to tidy himself away.

He had seriously considered entering the Sudan Political Service, and at *PP* fashioned a paternalistic ethos with some resemblance to that of Sir John Reith at the BBC. His briefing was that words, which were to be aimed at an intelligent fifteen-year-old, came second to photographs and he insisted that, whatever their background and status, the magazine's human subjects should always be treated with respect. The result was that, as the photographer Grace Robertson puts it, 'the name *Picture Post* opened doors which were often closed to other sections of the press ... You were not from "the press" and nobody mistook you as such.'

There were occasional parties at the elegant Hopkinson house in Cheyne Row (rented for £175 a year): at one of them I recall jiving strenuously with Barbara, the jolly copper-headed wife of *PP*'s assistant editor, Ted Castle. When, less than a year after joining Tom's family, I was hospitalized with TB, he kept me on the payroll during a long absence. My loyalty extended to sporting a bow-tie, Tom's habitual neck-wear (which according to some made him look like a rather cross pussy-cat) and when in September 1950 he was sacked after a clash with Hulton over Cameron's allegedly pro-communist despatches from Korea, I, like the rest of the staff, was ready to resign in sympathy. But Tom, who thought that 'consciences require some degree of stifling if life is to go on at all', told us to reconsider. Most of us did.

It seemed outrageous that because of his unorthodox scale of priorities – first came the readers and the 'character' of the magazine, then the staff, then, finally, and grudgingly, the proprietor – he should have been driven from a publishing phenonemon which he, even more than the mercurial Stefan Lorant, had created, and which, as he says, soon 'lost its way and wandered off into the fog'.

At eighty-four, during a 150th-anniversary-of-the-invention-of-photography conference in Bradford, he held the stage for one and a half hours. There's a room named after him at the Photographers' Gallery in London and in 1987 *Shady City*, a novel set in Nigeria, was published upon which (he said in a letter) he had been working since 1964. *Much Silence*, co-authored with his beloved third wife, Dorothy (Hugh Kingsmill's widow), is an account of their devotion to the spiritual teachings of the Indian seer Meher Baba, and the only other Hopkinson title in print.

He is survived by two daughters from his first marriage and two from his second.

HENRY THOMAS HOPKINSON · *born* 19 April 1905 · *died* 20 June 1990 ·

15 November 1990

MALCOLM MUGGERIDGE
A. J. P. Taylor

Malcolm Muggeridge, who has died aged eighty-seven, and I became friends when we were in Manchester more than fifty years ago: he as a leader writer on the *Manchester Guardian*, I as a lecturer at the university. The Muggeridges had the ground floor of a converted Didsbury house; my wife and I had a flat in the attic. It was very much a communal life. Thereafter our ways parted, but the deep affection Malcolm and I felt for each other never dimmed. He wrote not long ago that though we had never agreed about anything, we had never quarrelled: a rare tribute for Malcolm to pay.

I can best characterize Malcolm Muggeridge by taking the title of one of his books, *In a Valley of This Restless Mind*. I have never known a man so restless, physically and in his thinking. He could not write a leader or a chapter in a book without jumping up half a dozen times to pace around the room or rush out for a walk along the bank of the Mersey.

His life was the same on a larger scale. Malcolm never stayed in one job or even in one town for long. When I first knew him he was still under thirty. Yet he had already managed to fit in three years at Cambridge, then a spell teaching English at a Christian university in Travancore, and after that three years teaching at Cairo University. Malcolm liked India and did not like Egypt, from which he escaped to the *Manchester Guardian*. (Arthur Ransome, then the *Guardian's* correspondent in Egypt, recommended him to C. P. Scott, and he joined the paper as a leader writer in 1930.) In outlook Malcolm was a birthright Fabian, accustomed from his earliest years to Fabian summer schools with their sandals and homespun tweeds (though his father combined managing a shirt-making business in Croydon with Labour politics). His Fabianism was reinforced by marriage to Kitty Dobbs, the ravishing niece of Beatrice Webb.

Fabianism suited well the *Manchester Guardian* of the time. Difficulties came with the financial crisis of 1931. Crozier and Wadsworth, the two senior figures on the paper, were for supporting the National Government. Malcolm was for opposing it, and he triumphed when Ted Scott, the editor, returned from holiday. I remember the victor's mien that Malcolm brought back with him from the editorial office. He had a vision of leading the *Manchester Guardian* on some great campaign of liberation. Some months later the vision turned to dust when Ted Scott was drowned in Lake Windermere. Crozier, Ted's successor, set the *Guardian* on a staider course.

Malcolm soon developed a new enthusiasm: the Soviet Union. He sought a Utopia and like others at the time was convinced that he would find it in Moscow. I warned him that he would be disappointed. He would not listen: 'The only danger is that I shall be unworthy. Soviet Russia will be too good for me.' Off he went, leaving his worldly possessions, and incidentally his family, behind him. Malcolm arrived in Moscow when the Stalinist tyranny and the great famine which Stalin induced were just beginning. Within a couple of weeks he was disillusioned. Not only did he lose his faith in communism, he also turned sharply against all the left-wing ideas that he had acquired in his youth. This was the greatest crisis of his younger life. Many years were to pass before he discovered a faith again. Until then he gave the appearance of being an embittered cynic. This was not really true: Malcolm was a cynic who got great fun out of it.

Once escaped from Moscow, he had to put his life together again. Once more it was astonishing how much he fitted in during the six years before the war: a stretch on the *Evening Standard,* a year or so as assistant editor of the *Calcutta Statesman,* and then back to reviewing novels for the *Daily Telegraph.*

He also wrote some novels himself. *Winter in Moscow* was an account half fancy, half fact of that terrible time: the best account, I think, ever written. *Picture Palace* displayed Malcolm's idealistic lack of commonsense. The book was a very funny and reasonably fair picture of life on the *Manchester Guardian* when Malcolm was there. Unfortunately it contained highly libel-lous portraits of leading figures on the paper, easily identifiable. The book had to be withdrawn and has never been published. It was much the same with a biography of Samuel Butler, author of *Erewhon,* which Jonathan Cape com-missioned. Cape hoped to revive Butler's flagging sales. Malcolm saw in Butler a hero of his youth, and produced a version so scathing that Butler must have sunk into even deeper obscurity. Yet all I can now remember of these disap-pointments and setbacks is the gaiety they provoked.

The world changed again for Malcolm when the Second World War broke out. Once more he had found a cause. 'This war,' he told me, 'will be a crusade against evil things.' Of course among the evil things Malcolm included the Soviet Union, and there was not much of the crusade left for him when Soviet Russia became our ally. However, if Malcolm did not find a crusade for long, he found entertainment when he became an intelligence officer in MI6. This culminated in the remarkable arrangement whereby he directed British intel-ligence on the east coast of Africa and Graham Greene directed it on the west, which illustrates the Muggeridge law that real life always surpasses in fantasy the wildest products of the imagination. (However, a colleague recalled that he was able, from his Lourenço Marques [now Maputo, Mozambique] lair, to tap quite effectively the Nazis' communications with the South African national-ists. 'I know what they're after,' Muggeridge said to a friend when the police raided the War Office at Pretoria and carried off a load of files: 'My dossier on Malan.') Malcolm finished the war as an intelligence officer in Paris, where he performed the incomparable service of getting P. G. Wodehouse out of France to the security of Switzerland.

After the war Malcolm became among the first in words of the cold war-riors. Discerning in the Labour government unwitting tools of Moscow, he even spoke for Conservative candidates at by-elections. His more serious task was to put his journalistic career together again. He was by now a first-rate and very experienced leader writer. Over the years he was sometimes in Fleet Street, sometimes in Washington, sometimes in New York. He liked all three places. Perhaps it would be more correct to say that he liked least of the three the one where he happened to be at the moment.

The climax of this period was reached when Malcolm became editor of *Punch*. This was then a prestigious appointment, and for this reason he disliked it from the first. 'How absurd' was his favourite phrase, and he now applied it to himself. Besides, he liked writing; he did not like administration, particularly the routine which goes with the work of an editor. He regarded the readers of *Punch* as being as absurd as himself, not an endearing characteristic to them. Malcolm left *Punch* with great relief. Once more there was a change in his life. He withdrew increasingly from London and enjoyed his country house in Robertsbridge, Sussex. Here he could walk out into the fields whenever he wanted. He could write what he wanted, and still got great enjoyment from this.

Television was a great emancipation for him, as it became for some others, including myself. It even took him back to India thirty years later. No more Raj; no more sahibs; no more viceroy. With what enjoyment Malcolm seated himself on the throne of the deserted vice-regal palace at Simla. As a television debater I thought him less good, being inclined to repeat the same idea over and over again. I did not regard him as a formidable television antagonist. Perhaps I was disarmed by my abiding love for him.

Malcolm's puritanism suited him as he grew older. It was really a flashback to his early Fabianism, where teetotalism and vegetarianism had prevailed. Malcolm had never liked good cooking and dismissed vintage wine as 'merely alcohol, dear boy'. This had not prevented him from drinking to excess in his younger days.

The greatest change in him was his discovery of God and Jesus Christ. All religion is to me a buzzing in the ears, and I cannot explain or even describe what happened to Malcolm. All I know is that he was utterly sincere. Sometimes he had full faith in a future life. Sometimes he believed only in 'that of God that makes for righteousness'. Sometimes he gave the impression of wishing that his faith went deeper. Certainly religious faith enriched his later years without making him in any way sanctimonious. I suspect he understood little of theology and perhaps cared little also. (In 1982 Muggeridge surprised his friends by being received into the Roman Catholic Church, after bringing Mother Teresa to the attention of the world through the medium of television. He wrote an account of this sea-change, after years of atheism, in *Conversion: A Spiritual Journey* (1988).

The one fixed point in Malcolm's life was his marriage with Kitty, a marvellous woman as beautiful in old age as in youth. They often quarrelled, as was inevitable with Malcolm's restlessness. But they always came together again. On one occasion Kitty ended a quarrel, which had lasted three weeks, by saying: 'You had better stick to me. You'll never find anyone who loves you so much.' This was true. Malcolm and Kitty were as much in love at the end of their lives as they had been when they married.

MALCOLM THOMAS MUGGERIDGE · *born* 24 March 1903 · *died* 14 November 1990 ·

14 December 1998

LEW GRADE
Dennis Barker

Lew Grade, who has died of heart failure aged ninety-one, was unusual even among showmen in being able to turn a flair for wheeler-dealing into a genuinely creative art. As an agent who imported American stars into the dreary austerity days after the war as well as developing local talent, as an impresario, as a television tycoon with the common touch, he was adept at matching ideas to personalities. That was the flair that enabled him to dominate his world, in a uniquely hands-on way, for more than sixty years. Even his forays into feature film production had their successes. There was *On Golden Pond* and *The Muppet Movie* to compensate for British cinema's most expensive disaster, *Raise the Titanic*, which cost $36 million and grossed only a derisory fraction of that. 'It would have been cheaper,' he famously observed, 'to lower the Atlantic.'

Grade was pear-shaped, 5ft 5ins tall, with piercing and honest blue eyes. He had nerve and cheek, chutzpah – and incurable optimism. He was the eldest of the three showbusiness brothers, alongside Bernard Delfont and Leslie Grade, and was the leader and trail-blazer. This meant he got on better with Leslie, an introverted figures man, than with Delfont, a showman himself whose acceptance of a peerage from Harold Wilson in 1976 was slightly marred by the discovery that Lew, who had been knighted seven years before, had got one too.

'Wealth,' said Grade, 'is about relationships, not money.' This did not prevent Grade being worth £45 million, but the money, he insisted, was a by-product. His life, he maintained, had been made by relationships; and if, at worst, that might have boiled down to scratch-my-back-and-I'll-scratch-yours, it was not only his adored wife Kathie – who he consulted often about his deals – who noted his capacity to light up a room. The journalists he cultivated succumbed not to his Christmas lunches, his bottles of champagne or his expensive cigars, but to the promise of exciting ventures. He could marry talent to willing, or even unwilling, finance. A typical persuasive victory came when Roger Moore, after seven years as the television *Saint*, told Grade he would never do another TV series. But Grade wanted him for a new vehicle, *The Persuaders*. American financiers didn't, claiming that Moore was over-exposed. They would only back the series if Grade could get Tony Curtis as the other Persuader. Curtis had vowed never to do television but ninety minutes with Grade changed his mind. Grade then offered Moore a cigar and an already made-out cheque. *The Persuaders* was a success.

Grade was born Louis Winogradsky to Olga, a very determined mother, and Isaac, a rather feckless father, in the Ukrainian town of Tokmak, near Odessa. When Louis was six, the family made the move from impoverishment and pogroms within the Tsar's empire to poverty in London's East End. In his first three months in London Isaac lost almost all his capital. He then took over management of a small cinema – later Raymond's Revue Bar – in Soho's Brewer Street before gravitating to the rag trade. Meanwhile, the young Louis went to the Rochelle Street school in Shoreditch where he displayed an extraordinary knack for figures. Showbusiness exerted its pull early – he preferred Saturday-morning cinema to the synagogue.

Destined for accountancy, he was instead noticed by the man who lived opposite, Alfred Goldstein, an agent who booked artists for the Savoy Hotel's cabaret and who suggested going for a job as agent for a local clothing firm. At fifteen, Grade took the job, quickly grew out of it, and set up his own firm with his father. It soon had eight machines, operating twenty-four hours a day.

But then there was dancing at the East Ham Palais. It was the 1920s and he shone at the Charleston. 'Louis Grad' won the 'world solo Charleston championship' at the Albert Hall in 1926, with the showman C. B. Cochran and Fred Astaire as judges. He sold the clothing firm and became a professional dancer, 'the man with the musical feet'. He joined a dance band, expanded his act, and met the agent Joe Collins, father of Joan and Jackie, who got him a job at the Ambassadeurs club. Gradually Grade – he had taken the name after a French paper misspelt Grad as Grade when he appeared at the Moulin Rouge – got drawn into Collins's agency. But by 1934 the Charleston was passé, he had water on the knees, and it was time to move on and up. He wanted to be an agency partner, which Collins initially resisted, making him an employee. Grade went to the Continent to get artists, met them at ports with cars, and filled out their tax forms. It was at this point, with war approaching, that Grade met – as a client – Kathleen Moody, a petite singer for whom he deliberately did not get a part in a show, deeming it too lewd and *risqué* for her. After she remonstrated he arranged for her to appear on an early television show. In 1942 they married at Caxton Hall – the best deal he ever made, said Grade.

During the war Grade became an implausible soldier in the Royal Signal Corps but was invalided out by the knees again. He also arranged for Mrs Churchill an Aid to Russia show at the London Coliseum. After the war, at around the time his wife suggested he offer his clients cigars, he began smoking them himself. This was, he said, 'the real moment Lew Grade was born'. He found that a cigar in his mouth or hand gave him confidence and it became his trademark – though, like Winston Churchill, he tended to smoke cigars mostly when cameras were present.

After a row with Collins – by now they were partners – Grade formed his own agency with brother Leslie. Unlike other agents, they put together complete shows. In 1947 they went to the United States to recruit acts, but as unknowns from England managed to capture just one client. Subsequent visits were more successful: he brought over the singers Lena Horne and Johnny Ray, the comedian Jack Benny and the film actress Dorothy Lamour. Grade set up offices in New York and California and by the early 1950s his was the biggest agency in Britain.

Then in the mid-1950s came commercial television. Grade responded by investing in ATV, which made an initially disastrous start, after which he moved in full-time and made another fortune. It became one of the dominant original television companies – and Grade the dominant figure in popular commercial TV. Shows such as *Robin Hood, Sunday Night at the London Palladium* and *Emergency Ward 10* came to rule the TV top ten.

When, rather later, Grade televised a National Theatre production of *Long Day's Journey Into Night* – and sold it to the US NBC network – he remarked that the Americans badly needed quality programmes among all their populist shows. This observation was as often to be true of his own ATV schedules, before the Independent Broadcasting Authority broke the group up.

By the 1970s, as head of the giant ACC company, which brought live shows and TV under one umbrella, he decided to climb the highest mountain – feature films. His brother Bernard Delfont had just tried and failed to revive Elstree Studios. Grade decided he would do better and for a time he did.

It was curious that the films made by Grade, normally a believer in sweetness and light, were dark-hued and by no means pro-establishment. *The*

Cassandra Crossing had Burt Lancaster as a US Army officer trying to run a train full of passengers with a terrible contagious disease into a chasm; *Capricorn One* dealt with a US government agency's attempt to fake a supposed landing on another planet in a top secret film studio; *The Boys From Brazil* had Laurence Olivier as a hunter of escaped Nazi war criminal Dr Mengele (Gregory Peck) in New England; *The Eagle Has Landed* was about German paratroopers landing in Britain to assassinate Churchill. The two highly lucrative *Pink Panther* comedy movies he made and the series *Jesus of Nazareth*, made after he visited the Pope, were the exceptions.

All these had been medium-budget movies, in line with his view that small British films wouldn't sell abroad and that really big budgets were for the US studios. But then, in 1980, came *Raise the Titanic*. This was to be his 'James Bond' movie and used a model of the sunken liner that itself cost as much as many modest film budgets, and a tank said to be the biggest in Europe. The film sold well – in Japan. The flop threatened not only Grade's leadership but the very existence of ACC. At this time, Jack Gill, his accountant and number two, started his own film production company, a move which Grade saw as an insult and a threat. Grade moved Gill's eviction from the board, which was carried. The two men ended up in a shouting match, with a weeping Gill embracing his old colleague and giving him six months.

In fact he would last a year. Enter the Australian, Robert Holmes à Court. He bought 25 per cent of ACC's non-voting shares and expressed his affection and respect for Grade, who welcomed him into his office to watch him conclude telephone deals. Grade also took him to the US to watch him do business there. His description of all this in his autobiography *Still Dancing* (1987) read like a rather sick comic novel of impregnable self-deception: even when Holmes à Court, on Grade's recommendation, was sold 51 per cent of the voting shares, Grade did not sense the stiletto half an inch from his back. He saw it only when the younger man sacked all Grade's personal office staff, including the veteran tea lady, a move which finally made Grade realize he had been gulled. But then the usurper, Holmes à Court, died prematurely. With very rare Old Testament severity, Grade commented: 'He died quite a young man for all his millions.'

Grade, meanwhile, worked first for the US Embassy Communications group as its London chief before establishing his own company, and setting up deals in films and TV. He even bought up 450 of Barbara Cartland's romantic novels and started making films of them. He also rejoined the International Television Corporation, the company he had founded forty years previously.

Grade was still at work, the bearer of several honours, including the

Fellowship of the British Academy of Film and Television Arts, in his nineties. He is survived by Kathie, an adopted son and two grandchildren.

LEW GRADE, BARON GRADE OF ELSTREE · *born* 25 December 1906 · *died* 13 December 1998 ·

3 September 1998

LORD ROTHERMERE (VERE HARMSWORTH)
Roy Greenslade and Peter Preston

Vere Harmsworth, Lord Rothermere, the last of the old-style newspaper barons, who has died aged seventy-three, was a mass of contradictions. He enjoyed the power of an autocrat but preferred to delegate. He knew what his papers should contain but had little clue how to achieve it. He proclaimed his love for Britain yet lived abroad to save paying British taxes. He was a passionate advocate of family values yet lived openly, until his first wife's death, with his mistress. He believed in the need for privacy yet did nothing to discourage his editors from intruding into other people's. He paid lip service to respect for shareholder democracy while revelling in a stock arrangement which gave him total control of the company. He acted like a Tory and ensured his papers supported the Tories, but declared recently that he had never been a Tory and last year decided to take the Labour whip in the Lords.

Even by the standards of his extraordinary family and the eccentricities we have come to expect from members of his class, the flamboyant third Viscount Rothermere was a remarkable character. At turns he was courteous and cold, charming and infuriating, cunning and naive. Most of all, he loved to make mischief, and it was this which concealed the answer to the question which so many posed about him: was he a very smart man who pretended to be otherwise, or a very stupid one who got lucky? As the journalist Lynn Barber memorably pointed out in one of the rare interviews he gave, the 'common verdict is that he is twice as clever as he looks, but only half as clever as he thinks'. Certainly, it was obvious to everyone that Rothermere owed a great deal of his success to the man whose death he was still mourning when he died himself: Sir David English.

Rothermere was devastated at English's unexpected death in June. He regarded his former *Daily Mail* editor not only as a colleague but as a close friend. The secret of their many accomplishments lay in the complex dynamics of their partnership and it was to Rothermere's credit that he recognized that fact. Many other powerful proprietors, lured by giant egos into believing their empires depend alone on them, have been too ready to jettison equally talented people.

Vere Harmsworth was born into newspapers. His great-uncle, Lord Northcliffe, and his grandfather, the first Lord Rothermere, between them had created a mighty Fleet Street empire with a string of titles, including the *Daily Mail, Daily Mirror, The Times*, the *Sunday Pictorial* and the *London Evening News*. These two Harmsworth brothers, very different in interests and character, were the founders of Britain's most enduring family newspaper dynasty.

It was against this background of glittering success that Vere (named after his father's brother, who died on the battlefield in the First World War) grew up. He was educated at Eton and, by his own account, did not shine. His only happy time, he later recalled, was the year he spent at Kent School, Connecticut, when he was evacuated in 1940. He had been badly disturbed by his parents' split, when he was three, and still more upset by the divorce five years later, which was the subject of a lengthy and somewhat scandalous court case.

He was one of the very few Eton boys to fail the Army officer selection board and was compelled to do his four years' national service as a private. But he evidently enjoyed the experience of mixing with the other conscripts, the majority of whom came from Glasgow's Gorbals, and was renowned for his prowess as a boxer. It gave him, he said, an invaluable insight into 'people', a euphemism for the working class. He went to Canada in 1948, to work in a paper mill producing newsprint, before joining the family firm in Fleet Street in 1952. The great days of Northcliffe were long past.

In 1940 his father, Esmond, had inherited the viscountcy and the papers, but little of his father's and uncle's magic touch. He had been a Conservative MP and had shared, with his father, an admiration for Hitler's prewar regime. His poor political vision was matched by his grasp of newspapers. With *The Times* and *Mirror* long gone from the stable, he soon found his flagship *Daily Mail* out-gunned by Lord Beaverbrook's much more entertaining *Daily Express*. Attempts to buy other titles, such as the *Daily Graphic*, renamed the *Daily Sketch*, proved disastrous.

The son watched unhappily as the father made mistake after mistake. But in 1956 he forged the friendship that was to be the key to his future good fortune. He helped the *Daily Sketch's* features editor, David English, to launch a win-a-pub competition. Meanwhile Vere fumed on the sidelines as his father, even when suffering from Alzheimer's, refused to relinquish his hold. *Mail* editors were coming and going at the rate of one every two years, a merger with the *News Chronicle* failed to lift sales, and he was forced to close the loss-making *Sunday Dispatch*. Vere finally took control in 1971, seven years before his father's death, and immediately set about reversing the *Mail*'s decline. He had already engineered English's appointment as *Daily Sketch* editor two years before. Then, in one of the boldest and riskiest of ventures, he merged the *Sketch* and the previously broadsheet *Daily Mail*, put English in the chair and decided to relaunch the new paper in a tabloid format.

At the time, many commentators thought Vere would come a cropper; sales were slack in the first few years. But the dream of a right-of-centre, middle-class paper for a mythical Middle England gradually became a reality, with English as the driving force. Rothermere's first ambition was to overtake the *Daily Express*, then selling 1.6 million more. It took fifteen years to achieve. Now the *Mail* is 1.2 million ahead. Once confident of the *Mail*'s success, Rothermere launched the *Mail on Sunday* in 1982. He was immediately unhappy with his initial choice of editor, fired him, and put his faith in English once again as temporary editor. That paper, in just sixteen years, has become the most successful in its field, eclipsing the *Sunday Express* and over-taking two red-top rivals.

One of Rothermere's greatest joys was to wrest control of the London *Evening Standard* from the old Beaverbrook stable in 1986, six years after being forced to close Northcliffe's beloved *Evening News*. Despite continual sales problems, by holding a monopoly in London, the *Standard* has continued to contribute healthy profits to the company. When that monopoly was threat-ened in 1987 by Robert Maxwell's launch of the *London Daily News*, Rothermere pulled off an outrageous counterstroke. He revived the *Evening News* at 10p, half the cover price of both the *Standard* and the new paper. Maxwell followed suit with the London *Daily News*, so Rothermere cut the *Evening News* to 5p. The *coup* worked, helping to drive Maxwell's paper off the streets within months.

Meanwhile, at a more serious level, Rothermere had built his media empire, known as the Daily Mail and General Trust (DMGT), into a formidable £2.8 billion company with profits last year of £143.7 million. There are five divisions aside from Associated Newspapers, which produces the national papers. Northcliffe is one of Britain's leading regional publishers with seven-teen daily papers and fourteen paid-for weeklies, while Harmsworth Publishing runs lucrative educational businesses. Harmsworth Media, with a large stake in Teletext and various radio stations in Australia and Sweden, makes money. DMGT also owns 71 per cent of *Euromoney*, the hugely successful market leader in international financial publishing with 100 magazines worldwide. Even the company's small Hungarian division, dating from the days when Vere's grandfather was offered that country's throne, provides profits.

But City eyebrows have lifted over the company's dual share structure. Since Rothermere ensured that his family owned most of the voting stock, he could do as he wished. Analysts argue that this increasingly rare anachronism is an affront to shareholder democracy. Not that it mattered when Rothermere produced continuous profits and behaved so benignly.

His private life was just as colourful as his commercial one. In 1957 he married Patricia Brooks, a Rank starlet known to everyone (except Rothermere) as Bubbles. They had two daughters and a son. But by the late 1970s, they were leading separate lives. While she stayed in London, he moved to Paris in 1978 with a Japanese-born Korean, Maiko Lee, who had previously worked as a hand model. But Rothermere resolutely refused to divorce and did not marry her until a year after Bubbles died of a heart attack in 1992. It was Maiko Lee who drew him towards Buddhism and a belief in reincarnation.

In recent years, Rothermere spent less and less time in Britain. He moved between homes in Paris, the south of France and New York. It is generally believed that his personal riches far surpassed those of all the other newspaper owners, but when asked by an interviewer how often he spent time in London, he chided him for behaving like a tax inspector. Despite his many charitable gifts, his recent conversion to New Labour had not made him keener to contribute more of his money to the public purse.

PETER PRESTON writes: The *Daily Mail* exists, by design, to be loved or loathed: but the owner who remade it for modern success – and turned a struggling inheritance into business triumph along the way – was a gentler soul.

He was silvery and round and oddly self-deprecating, as though Eton and a hereditary title had turned him into the very model of an English aristocrat. His working colleagues at Associated Newspapers sometimes appeared as courtiers, clucking over this unworldly figure. And, like landed gentry with death duties on their mind, he had come increasingly to operate from abroad: from a villa in the hills above Kyoto, a Paris flat on the Isle St Louis, a château in the Dordogne. The *Mail*'s patriotic trumpets were sounded far away.

But, though the jibes were sometimes easy, the man himself was no carica-ture. He was less of a toff than a Tory knight of the shire (in the old, pre-Thatcher mode). Rothermere's papers may have been dry, but he himself was always a little on the wet side, anxious that the middle-class values his editors championed were becoming too hard in their edge.

He wished to be kind, as he himself was in private life: the flirtation with New Labour at the end was no aberration. But most of all he wished to hand over the group that an accident of birth had thrust upon him in flourishing financial health. He did not want it to be his generation that fumbled and failed. The fate of the Beaverbrook empire was always with him.

Rothermere worked his passage through the more mundane departments of Associated so that he knew every stick of the newspaper industry. He delighted in lordly lectures to newer members of the Newspaper Publishers Association (like Rupert Murdoch), which had their sting in his mastery of detail. His greatest gifts, though, were as a picker of people and a deviser of strategy.

Journalists liked him because he liked them, and paid them well. The part-nership he formed with David English was a rock upon which much else was based. He supported his editors in a jam and gave them the time and freedom to set their own paths. He would call English from wherever he was once or twice a day. He was always in touch and ready to put himself on the line. The death of the *Daily Sketch*, the tabloiding of the *Mail*, the launch and relaunch-ing of the *Mail on Sunday*, the defeat of Robert Maxwell in the battle of the London evenings – they were all his call and his risk.

Most of his wishes in business came true. He aspired to be a success out of duty and did, on any count, far more than that. But his last and greatest wish was a smooth transition to the next generation. He had carried that burden and he knew its weight. Without him and English, both dead within months of each other, the final test of his stewardship begins.

VERE HAROLD ESMOND HARMSWORTH, VISCOUNT
ROTHERMERE OF HEMSTED · *born* 27 August 1925 ·
died 1 September 1998 ·

ALASTAIR HETHERINGTON
Geoffrey Taylor

Alastair Hetherington, who has died aged seventy-nine, was one of the fore-most journalists of his generation. He was editor of the *Guardian* for nineteen years (1956–75), which included a period in the 1960s when he had to struggle for its survival. He wrote with vigour and required the paper to serve high purposes at home and abroad. He showed in his person and his writing fairness and frankness. He brought physical stamina as well as intellectual precision to his work. He loosened up, and made less stratified, the internal workings of the paper. When he made mistakes, he acknowledged them. His quirks either mildly irritated or, more often, mischievously endeared him to his staff. They saw in him a straightforward and generous man and a chief they could follow, respect and, especially in his fighting moods, admire.

The transition from Manchester to London, after his first five years in office, was not only one of geography but of attitude. It involved, over time, big changes in editorial content, notably in the number and style of features and other material. At the time, Hetherington defined the paper's first concern as 'government in the widest sense' – that is, the shaping of public policy and the influences on it. His *Guardian* took a highly informed outsider's part in all the arguments which beset the governments of Eden, Macmillan, Home, Wilson, Heath, and Wilson again. Its comments were read in President Kennedy's White House. At the same time it coped with – and became identified with – all the social changes of the time. It now seems that virtually every question Hetherington and his paper came to tackle was one never met before on the same scale: CND, the Pill, the Beatles and all that came in their train, large-scale immigration from the Commonwealth, the satire industry, the 'death of God', fear among the young.

By 1975 Hetherington's vigour was still unimpaired, but his time and attention were increasingly taken up by worries at the fringe of editing. Those included a difficult, though polite, argument with the National Union of Journalists' chapels about worker participation (which he favoured, and on which his record was already in advance of anyone else in Fleet Street); Michael Foot's closed shop rules for editors; a threat by Denis Healey's Treasury to the continuation of the Scott Trust, the independent owners of the *Guardian*; and a nasty little attack on him by detractors in the Central London NUJ.

In addition, he was due to retire in four years and would need something to do. He had already rejected a safe Labour parliamentary seat in Glasgow, a government post under Wilson and at least one university vice-chancellorship. He took the job of controller of BBC Scotland. He and the BBC, however, found they were by no means temperamentally attuned, and in 1982 he began a third career in Scottish academic life, where his origins lay.

He was born the second son of Hector and Alison Hetherington. His father was professor of logic and philosophy at University College, Cardiff, and, as Sir Hector, became principal at Glasgow University from 1936 to 1961, chairman from 1943 to 1947 and 1949 to 1952 of the committee of vice-chancellors and principals, and a key figure in the links between Commonwealth universities.

After Gresham's School, Holt, Alastair Hetherington's studies at Corpus Christi College, Oxford, were interrupted by the war. On volunteering in 1939 he failed the eyesight test, but was called up to the Royal Army Pay Corps ('dreary work, with no prospect', he wrote in a letter) in August 1940. The following year a change in Army Council policy provided that anyone in a non-combatant unit who applied for active service could not be refused. This enabled him to join the Royal Armoured Corps in 1941. After various regimental transfers he was sent to the 2nd Northamptonshire Yeomanry ('snobbish and incompetent lot – didn't know how to handle their tanks and never learned'). With the rank of captain, he was serving as part of 11 Armoured Corps shortly after the Normandy landing, during an advance towards Vire, when his tank was destroyed; one crew member was killed and two wounded. As Major Hetherington, he took part in the relief of Antwerp and completed his military career in 1945 by writing the 100-page *Military Geography of Schleswig-Holstein*, of which about 100 copies are said to be located as classified documents in the vaults of the Ministry of Defence.

In 1940 Hetherington had spent three months in the sub-editors' room at the *Glasgow Herald*. On the strength of this experience he was, to his surprise, asked by the British Control Commission in Germany to become editorial controller of *Die Welt*, the first nationwide newspaper to be produced in the British zone in 1945. 'Those months at the old Broshek plant in Hamburg,' he wrote many years later, 'were tremendous experience, with otherwise an almost wholly German staff. A vital thing was to get them enough food, so that they could work at night, since Hamburg was not far from starvation.'

After Hamburg, Hetherington went back to the *Glasgow Herald*, joined the *Guardian* from there in 1950, and was foreign editor and defence correspondent from 1953 to 1956. On the retirement, and almost immediate death, of

A. P. Wadsworth in the autumn of 1956, he was the successful candidate from four possible choices as editor. The paper was still small enough for the editor to assimilate all of it, but as it grew, Hetherington increasingly sub-contracted the features department to a succession of later famous journalists – John Rosselli, Brian Redhead, Christopher Driver and Peter Preston. He, meanwhile, concentrated on its political direction in home affairs. In one area, down-to-earth social reform, Hetherington's radicalism told him the paper had much new work to do. He promoted several series of articles about the gap between rich and poor, and north and south, and directed much of the paper's energy into exposing bad living conditions, shortcomings in the social services, and industrial inefficiency. His reporters joined in these campaigns with a will and, from 1957, they found a powerful exponent in John Cole as labour correspondent.

Politically, Hetherington's closest contact was Harold Wilson (before him Gaitskell) and his closest friend Jo Grimond. This balance was reflected throughout his time in the support given to the two parties. In 1959 he wrote in his eve-of-poll leader: 'We should like to see Labour in office and the Liberals strengthened,' and that remained substantially true until 1974. But the *Guardian* was not to be taken for granted. Before the first 1974 general election, Hetherington raised at meetings with his senior staff the prospect of supporting Heath, whom he thought had been right in his conflict with the miners. By the time of the second election of 1974, a formidable band of Labour stalwarts on the paper – John Cole, Ian Aitken, Jean Stead, Keith Harper – got together to keep him strictly in line.

Hetherington, however, was determined to bring up to date a cause he had spent many leading articles in promoting: Lib–Lab cooperation to defeat the Tories. Coalition, even a government of national unity, was preferable, in his view, to continued Tory hegemony, with a disunited and squabbling left. In spite of the tug of history – and of his staff – he wanted to preserve the paper's freedom of action. He advised a Liberal vote and would have been happy with a government of the three major parties or a Lib–Lab–Scot Nat coalition. In foreign affairs and defence, bipartisanship was generally accepted as the norm. Perhaps Hetherington's yearning for domestic consensus owed something to that experience.

Consensus in foreign affairs was emphatically not, though, the way his editorship began. The Suez explosion in October 1956 happened at the moment of his taking office. With no hesitation, he launched the *Manchester Guardian* into total opposition to that 'act of folly, without justification in any terms but brief expediency' – and maintained the attack day after day. The assumption was that the paper lost circulation at Suez. Both the proprietor, Laurence Scott, and Hetherington thought it was doing so, and to Scott's credit he told his new editor not to worry but to do what he thought was right. When the figures came in at the end of November, the circulation had gone up, not down. Hetherington's leaders were written with high passion certainly, but more importantly, they were written with the knowledge supplied by his foreign correspondents about the effects of Anthony Eden's actions in the United States, at the UN, and in the Middle East. Hetherington's strict observance of the facts and the avoidance of self-delusion or polite pretence in assessing either Britain's new role in the world or the actions of his natural allies at Westminster were crucial to the paper's standing.

When he went to Vietnam and switched the paper's policy line – arguing that having committed itself America should stay to finish the job – he did so out of commitment to the facts as he had discovered them. His loneliness in the face of strong opposition – inside and outside the office – spoke of his courage in taking an unpopular line. In his memoirs, he half-apologized; he had no need. If he was wrong on that occasion, his error did credit to his honesty.

Hetherington was in at the founding of CND, or at least at preparatory meetings held at the house in Didsbury of Lord Simon of Wythenshawe, with Bishop Greer, Sir Bernard Lovell and Bertrand Russell. He did not, however, go along with CND, thereby causing one of his not infrequent confrontations with a bevy of hard left leader-writers. Instead, he put forward plans for what he called a non-nuclear club. Britain would give up the bomb in exchange for an undertaking by the other nuclear powers not to export their technology, and a renunciation of the bomb by all the countries not then (1957–8) possessing it. Labour and the TUC were enthusiastic, but the club perished with the return of a Conservative government in 1959. Hetherington later wrote that the idea was one of the most creative acts of journalism in his time.

Hetherington might have been content if all he had to do was edit a national newspaper. In 1959 the paper had dropped Manchester from its title, and in 1961 the printing operation in London began. But the scale of the change, and particularly the culture of Fleet Street newspaper production, had been misjudged. The editorial staff, particularly in the middle ranks, lost its self-confidence. Editions were missed. Circulation was sluggish. The high hope of competing with its rivals on equal terms had to be put aside. In 1965 Laurence Scott lost heart and decided to merge the paper with Lord Astor's *Times*. Talks began, but they came to nothing because of the obvious incompatibility between the two papers. The next year, however, Lord Thomson bought *The Times*, and Scott, in a desperate attempt to keep his old idea alive, set up a consortium to oppose Thomson before the Monopolies Commission and put in a rival bid. Then, while Hetherington was making a quick trip to Israel, Scott carried out a *coup*. He convened a meeting of the Scott Trust, under his cousin Richard, which agreed to give him a free hand in negotiating a merger. It was Hetherington's furious reaction on returning to London and insisting that the Trust (of which he was not a member) be reconvened and the decision reversed that saved the *Guardian* from, at best, humiliation and, at worst, submergence in a triumphant *Times*.

The upshot was a reorganization of the company and the arrival of a new and highly competent set of managers. The two sides enjoyed working together and the rejuvenated paper went on to succeed editorially and commercially. In 1971 Hetherington was named Journalist of the Year in the National Press Awards. He rarely missed an opportunity to say how much of the paper's success depended on the *Manchester Evening News*, whose profits had for so long kept it afloat.

Alastair Hetherington lived an ascetic life – plain food, no tobacco, alcohol only when to abstain might appear conspicuous, never a taxi for a mile or two if there was time to walk. He spent long days walking the Lake District and Scottish mountains, and long evenings making full notes of his political conversations, running into millions of words, to be circulated to senior staff. His Downing Street notes often included a tally of how much Harold Wilson had had to drink.

These predilections, his academic upbringing, and his membership of the intellectual establishment evidently persuaded him that he didn't know much about ordinary people. Yet when the 1960s burst open he showed no doubt about how the *Guardian* should respond to each new wave of liberty, license or frivolity; he took it to be what people wanted and therefore, provided Lord Wolfenden's horses didn't mind, should have. He gave evidence for the defence at the Lady Chatterley trial and became the first editor to allow the word 'fuck' into his paper.

And so to his quirks. The clock in his office was on the wall opposite his desk; his eyes constantly flicked to it over the left shoulder of whoever was talking to him. He made a point of bounding upstairs to the third floor while others took the lift; he assumed that everyone else shared his enthusiasm for racing up hillsides. He refused cream at lunch because he was on duty that night and needed a clear head. He once tried to organize a London–Manchester meeting at Watford Gap on Boxing Day on the grounds that those concerned had already had Christmas Eve off. He liked to have the last word in an argument. He found personal relations difficult and used hearty language to disguise that fact.

But the irritants were far outweighed. Hetherington did not put people down. He never publicly issued a rebuke. He made suggestions rather than issued orders, and, although the effect was the same, there was room for discussion. He ran the paper as a corporate enterprise. He and his wife, Miranda, whom he married in 1957, were generous hosts.

The *Guardian* he left in 1975 had been relaxed and informal. Scottish television, he soon found, was very different, full of hierarchies and procedures. The thing he most enjoyed was learning new techniques and applying them. Two programmes which he was proud of promoting were a series about the deprived Lilybank area of Glasgow and another about walks on Scottish mountains, including those on Arran, where he eventually retired in 1989.

But he fell foul, mainly about the permissible degree of devolution, both of the director-general, Charles Curran, and of his own predecessor, then managing director of BBC-TV, Alasdair Milne. The new DG, Ian Trethowan, reluctantly sacked him. Like a deposed Soviet minister, Hetherington was sent to be station manager for Highland Radio at Inverness. His last five working years were spent as research professor in media studies at Stirling University.

He retained a close link with the *Guardian* through membership of the Scott Trust, of which he became chairman from 1984 until his retirement. He brought a new style to that office as a hands-on and interventionist chairman, giving critical support to his successor as editor, Peter Preston. He also played a substantial part in the appointment of his successor as chairman, Hugo Young.

Hetherington's *Guardian* was the pioneer of the modern quality broadsheet. All of them – *The Times, Independent, FT*, even *Telegraph* – owed a debt to him. He transformed the very worthy, very civilized but, it must now seem, anachronistic *Manchester Guardian* into a type of paper new to English readers. But he knew how far he wanted to carry this revolution and where he wanted it to stop. He still liked a degree of decorum.

His marriage to Miranda Oliver, with whom he had two sons and two daughters, was dissolved in 1978, and the following year he married Sheila Janet Cameron, with whom he inherited three stepchildren.

HECTOR ALASTAIR HETHERINGTON · *born* 31 October 1919 · *died* 3 October 1999 ·

ROBIN DAY
Dick Taverne

Sir Robin Day, who has died aged seventy-six, was the most outstanding television journalist of his generation. He transformed the television interview, changed the relationship between politicians and television, and strove to assert balance and rationality into the medium's treatment of current affairs.

Day was the youngest of four children. His father, a Lloyd George Liberal, was on the administrative staff of the Post Office. Robin was educated at Bembridge School, had an uneventful war in the Royal Artillery, became a captain, and went on to St Edmund Hall, Oxford, in 1947 at the age of twenty-four, to read law. He made his mark as a memorable president of the Oxford Union.

After two years at the bar, he decided that the prospect of success was too distant. He spent one year with the British Information Services in the United States, was briefly employed, on a temporary basis, by BBC Radio and, at its launch in 1955, joined Independent Television News, as one of its new breed of newscasters. ITN made him. It gave him, by his own account, his happiest four years in television – though he was not an instant success. It was originally felt that he was too unsympathetic and harsh in manner, but this view changed as he developed an entirely new style of interviewing.

In the pre-Day era, television interviews were almost always respectful, generally dull and stiff, often insipid. Day asked the direct question pointed like a dagger at the jugular. The turning point in his career was an interview with Sir Kenneth Clark, then chairman of Independent Television, at a time when proposals were mooted to cut ITN's airtime and money. Day asked him questions about the station's future which dumbfounded colleagues and critics by their directness. It was unprecedented that the person in ultimate charge should be questioned about his responsibilities by one of his own employees – and the impact was dramatic.

There followed a number of historic interviews that established Day's reputation: with Egypt's President Nasser after the 1956 Suez crisis, when Day sought to pin him down on whether he accepted the existence of the state of Israel; with ex-President Truman – 'Mr President, do you regret having authorized the dropping of the atomic bomb?'; and notably with Prime Minister Harold Macmillan in 1958, in what the *Daily Express* called 'the most vigorous cross-examination a prime minister has been subjected to in public'.

This interview turned Macmillan into a television personality, and was probably the first time that television became a serious part of the political process. Day also made Parliament come alive with his unscripted reports of the heated debates during the Suez débâcle.

In 1959 Day moved to the BBC and *Panorama*, then the most prestigious current affairs programme. The corporation never really made the best use of his talents, except at elections and, eventually, on *Question Time*, between 1979 and 1989. The fashion turned against 'talking heads' and 'government by debate', with which he, above all others, was identified. He was gradually sidelined, as a chairman figure who simply opened and closed programmes. He described his pre-*Question Time* period as 'ten years in the wilderness'. There was even a spell of nearly two years when he did not appear at all.

In the early 1970s, Day became more deeply involved in radio, where he proved an innovator with *It's Your Line* from 1970 to 1976. This was a national phone-in programme that enabled the general public, for the first time, to put questions directly to the Prime Minister and other politicians (it later spawned *Election Call*). He also presented *The World At One* from 1979 to 1987, but never felt that radio was his *métier*. He was not at his best reading from a script, and it is significant that in his memoirs he dismisses his eight-year contribution to the programme with a single sentence.

General elections, however, were the time when all the grand inquisitor's talents as cross-examiner came on full display, when the television public saw 'the scowling, frowning, glowering' Robin Day 'with those cruel glasses' (Frankie Howerd's description), as well as the relieving shafts of humour. His most satisfying role in television came with *Question Time*. At last, he was given his own show, with an audience – which he had long asked for – albeit late at night, as a temporary, six-month 'filler', and mainly as a way of giving him something to do. Its success in becoming, under his chairmanship, the most popular and effective current affairs programme on television reveals a great deal about his talents. Why did Robin Day become a national institution, one of the most immediately recognized people in the land, outshining in reputation and respect other television stars whose shows commanded far larger audience figures and, as he much resented, far higher salaries?

It was because he had a unique combination of qualities. He was a very big personality in the true sense, with immense authority. He was extraordinarily witty. A collection of good Day jokes would fill a minor anthology. *Question Time* also brought out his charm and showmanship. He was inordinately proud of his music-hall gifts, and would insist on showing visitors to his flat videos of his appearances on the *Morecambe and Wise Christmas Show* and (especially) his Flanagan and Allen rendering of 'Underneath the Arches' on the *Des O'Connor Show*, in which he outstarred and outsang O'Connor. But above all he was one of the most well-informed, widely read and serious political figures in public life.

Day imbibed politics almost with his mother's milk. His father brought him up to revere Parliament and great parliamentarians. As a nine-year-old, he was taken to hear Churchill speak, in the rain. Respect for Parliament and the traditional institutions of British life, such as the monarchy and the legal profession, was at the heart of his philosophy all his life. It might be said that his interests were somewhat conventional and narrow. He was almost fixated by Parliament, and seemed to think that if someone had made a great parliamentary speech, they had won a great battle, when, in fact, it was events outside parliament that were transforming British politics. His world was one of party politics and current events, rather than long-term trends. He was not particularly interested in industrial affairs or economics, or developments in European countries.

Gradually, his private views became more and more conservative, at times rather narrowly nationalist, although he did not allow his personal prejudices to show in public or influence his professional performances. But within the boundaries of his particular interests he applied his formidable powers of argument and his extensive knowledge to devastating effect, in private as well as public. He believed passionately in 'government by debate' and in the need for television to balance pictures of current events with reasoned analysis. Otherwise, the powerful visual impact of television would distort and trivialize. He was equally dedicated to the principle that the interviewer had a duty to be well informed.

Many observers commented on his careful preparation; few realized just how assiduous he was. He would read every current biography and autobiography, and nearly every government White Paper. Without research assistants to supply him with background briefings, he would generally be better informed than the many Cabinet ministers he interviewed. No wonder Prime Ministers treated him as their equal, and lesser mortals on the political scene regarded him with awe.

Day's contribution to British public life was not confined to the media. For twenty-five years he campaigned tirelessly, and eventually successfully, for the televising of Parliament – not in the interests of television, but of Parliament itself. He claimed that he was the first to present the detailed arguments in favour, in a Hansard Society paper in 1963. He also played a major part in the establishment of the National Lottery. When the Rothschild Commission on

Gambling was set up in 1979, he wrote a letter, arguing in detail for the kind of lottery we have today. Lord Rothschild wrote back, questioning his arguments. Day replied, refuting all criticisms; his arguments prevailed and the eventual report recommended the scheme Day had originally proposed. He followed up with endless letters to successive ministers with relevant responsibilities.

In his private life, Day had two personalities. To those who did not know him, he could, at times, appear aggressive and insensitive, seemingly interested only in those who were important because of their fame, public success or wealth. He sometimes found it difficult to talk naturally to intelligent women. He might, to some, have seemed the quintessential member of the all-male Garrick Club, one of his favourite haunts.

To those who knew him well, however, he was the most stimulating, amusing, convivial and warmest of companions. He was one of those rare people who was genuinely loved by his friends. He was prepared to take infinite pains on their behalf. He was also surprisingly modest; despite his obvious success in public life, he frequently talked of his career as a relative failure, because he had not achieved anything solid.

He regretted that he had never entered Parliament – although he ran as a Liberal at Hereford in 1959 – and contributed to the real world of politics, instead of playing a secondary role through television. He thrived on his public fame and was proud to be the first television star to be knighted, but privately seemed to feel that his achievements did not compare with those of others who had made their mark in the more traditional professions, especially the law, or by writing learned books.

In 1965 he married Katherine Ainslie, an Australian law don at St Anne's College, Oxford, and had two sons. The marriage was dissolved in 1986. One of the tragedies of his life was that his elder son never fully recovered from the effects of multiple skull fractures he sustained in a childhood fall.

Some years ago, Day had a coronary bypass, and he suffered from breathing problems that were often evident when he was on the air. He had always fought against a tendency to put on weight. As an undergraduate, he weighed seventeen stone, and claimed that, in the course of his life, he had succeeded in losing more weight than any other person. He is survived by his two sons.

ROBIN DAY · *born* 24 October 1923 · *died* 6 August 2000 ·

MARY STOTT
Lena Jeger and Fiona MacCarthy

Mary Stott, who has died aged ninety-five, was the first – and longest-serving – editor of the *Guardian* women's page. One of the great campaigning journalists of the twentieth century, in her fifteen-year tenure, from 1957 to 1972, she invented a platform for women's voices and concerns, and used it to further such causes. Part of her strength – and perhaps why so many men read her page – was her belief that discrimination, in any form, was a total sin. She cared about poverty, unemployment and disability, wherever lives were diminished. She tried hard to win equality for women, but not as an isolated problem. She could be combative in all her campaigns, but never a bigot.

Naturally, she encouraged women writers – often beginners, urgent with something they wanted to tell. The 'Mainly For Women' title of her page gave way, in 1969, to 'Woman's *Guardian*', which ran until 1973. After a two-year change of tack as '*Guardian* Miscellany', '*Guardian* Women' re-emerged, with Mary still a contributor. It was, throughout, a conduit for ideas, and her social antennae were uncannily sensitive. She once told me that if she could open some doors 'even a crack', it might be useful. There seemed an inevitability about Mary's newspaper life. For nearly half a century, almost unbroken, she worked in the medium. And she loved it. 'I have lived all my life with the smell of newspapers,' she wrote. 'The sharp smell of the ink and the warm smell of the paper.'

Born and brought up in Leicester, she was the only daughter of two journalists, Robert and Amalie Waddington (*née* Bates), and had two older brothers. Her uncle Henry Bates was also a local journalist. Years later, she recalled being 'a most dislikable child'. She felt that she was 'plain and charmless, with disastrously straight hair and thick glasses'. They stayed, but she grew out of her gawkiness and developed an uncontrived charm. Her face kept its lived-in look. I never heard her voice raised shrill in dissent but it could sharpen in emphasis, the tone more detergent than caustic. Mary's early social awakenings emerged from her mother, who took her to meetings of local women Liberals, charity fundraising events and 'comfort-making' parties during the First World War. Her first memory was of being driven around with a green ribbon in her hat, campaigning in the 1911 general election. 'I have no recollection of ever being bored or restless,' she later recalled.

At the age of seventeen, she went straight from Wyggeston grammar school in Leicester to the *Leicester Mail*, where she was 'tolerated as a temporary copyholder'; she was unable to join either the Typographical Association or the Correctors of the Press Association because neither accepted women members. When, at nineteen, she was asked to take over the women's page, she said: 'It nearly broke my heart – I thought my chance of becoming a real journalist was finished.'

Of course, it wasn't. By way of the *Bolton Evening News*, in 1933 she moved to the Co-operative Press in Manchester, where she edited the two pages of the weekly *Co-op News*, devoted mainly to reports of the women's co-operative guild, and children's publications. In 1945 John Beavan offered her a sub-editing job on the *Manchester Evening News*; she found him and his staff 'totally devoid of sex prejudice, and there was no discrimination in the allocation of work'. She felt a real journalist.

None the less, in 1950 she was sacked in order to protect the male succession to the post of chief sub-editor. She spent the next seven years mainly in 'domesticity'. Mary had, in 1937, married a real journalist too: Ken Stott, of the *News Chronicle*, always known to her simply as 'K'. Until his premature death in 1967, at the age of fifty-six, they shared a marriage of true minds in a decorous, unshowy Edwardian semi in Heaton Moor, Cheshire, with trim lawns, herb beds, Scandinavian furnishings and a rather overbearing Bassett hound named Ben.

It was Mary Stott's background in 'real' journalism that led her to think hard when the then *Guardian* editor Alastair Hetherington asked her to edit the paper's women's page in 1957. In fact, she was never, even during the heyday of the women's movement, always at one with feminist thinking. She had no time for the term 'Ms', and later regarded the Labour party's compulsory quota system for women candidates as sexist, discriminating and patronizing. 'I do not believe,' she wrote – and often said – 'that the mind has a gender.' This was not acceptable to all her friends, but none could fault her industry and dedication as she held down a responsible job, ran a home (she took only a short time off when her daughter was born) and breathed life into many voluntary organizations.

One of them was always Women in Media, for whom Mary led a march to Downing Street in February 1973. They were not received at No. 10, but the duty policeman, Sergeant Garnham of Cannon Row, said that two of them could deliver a written message. Uncharacteristically for media women, they had pens but not a sheet of paper between them. The sergeant tore a page from his notebook for their missive to Ted Heath. 'Sometimes,' said Mary, 'the British way of life is very endearing.' We hoped the Prime Minister agreed.

But for all her happy and fulfilling life, darkness fell with the death of her beloved 'K'. It was never bright morning again. She wrote a brave and painful autobiography, *Forgetting's No Excuse* (1973), which confronted her own experience of widowhood, because she thought it might help others to live as the left-over half of the couple they had been. Her second volume of memoirs, *Before I Go* (1985), contained reflections on both the problems and compensating joys of old age.

Fortunately, Mary also had a rich hinterland. She loved serious music, and often said it made life worth living – she believed in Addison's 1694 song for St Cecilia's Day: 'Music, the greatest good that mortals know/ And all of heaven we have below.' She took lessons from Elizabeth von Hedervary, a professional singer, and they sang with the Hallé Orchestra under Henry Wood, Thomas Beecham and Malcolm Sargent. She would travel far and wide to sing madrigals in schoolroom concerts. Almost to the end, she played piano duets with friends at her flat in Blackheath, south London. Her other transport of delight was painting, mostly watercolours from holidays to hang on the walls of her home; she said it gave her tranquil memories. As a subject, she sat with her *Guardian* colleagues Polly Toynbee, Jill Tweedie, Liz Forgan and Posy Simmonds for a group portrait by Sarah Raphael, commissioned by the National Portrait Gallery in 1994. The idea came from the writer Claire Tomalin, and the painting was unveiled by the first woman Speaker, Betty Boothroyd, who called herself one of Mary's 'admiring readers'.

Academic honours came with an honorary fellowship from Manchester Polytechnic in 1972, an honorary MA from the Open University in 1991, and an honorary doctorate from De Montfort University, Leicester, in 1996. She was made an OBE in 1975.

I last saw Mary Stott in Blackheath, busy fixing contemporary family photos into old albums so that 'the grandchildren will be able to look at three generations'. She is survived by her journalist daughter Catherine, who observed, of both her mother's homes: 'This place smells of newsprint.'

FIONA MacCARTHY writes: I arrived in Manchester in 1964, as Mary Stott's assistant on the *Guardian* Women's page she had, by then, been editing for seven years. It would be no exaggeration to say she had invented a page whose content had previously been in the remit of the night editor, along with letters, travel and obituaries.

Mary set out to create a page which 'depended mainly on warmth, sincerity and personal involvement'. With extraordinary speed, it established its identity, reflecting, to an uncanny degree, the attitudes and personality of Mary herself. I can think of no other editor who built up such direct rapport with her readers, or who saw such possibilities in them as contributors. At a time when feminism in Britain was just dawning, Mary was acute in her judgement that what women cried out for was the sharing of experience, the sense of real people writing on her page.

How did she get away with it? Here, in a national newspaper (the *Guardian* had recently dropped 'Manchester' from its masthead and was expanding its London operation), Mary established her own power base, an influential and idiosyncratic female sub-state. She knew from her own experience the struggle women had in balancing love, family and their professional lives, and she ran her page with a dogged sense of purpose in opening out the possibilities for women, forming supportive networks, creating solidarities.

It operated as a community notice board on a giant scale. Mary believed in the special authenticity of amateur contributors, arguing that readers could often identify more closely with a non-professional writer. She backed her hunch – with sometimes riveting results – from the stack of more than fifty unsolicited manuscripts that arrived every week. Betty Thorne describing life in a Sheffield two-up, two-down; Betty Jerman on being 'squeezed in like sardines in suburbia': these were classics of their time. Such missives from the coalface of female deprivation drew an enormous correspondence, and started the whole journalistic genre of personal unburdening. Mary's women were the first of the Women Who Told All.

At her best, she was also a first-class columnist. But she preferred a more self-effacing role, proud of her page make-up skills and working hard to build up a nucleus of trusted contributors, who inevitably also became her friends. Sometimes, you could accuse her of an excess of loyalty to columnists whose day was done. But the calibre of her regular writers in the 1960s – Shirley Williams, Lena Jeger, Marghanita Laski, Taya Zinkin, Gillian Tindall, Margaret Drabble – made the *Guardian*'s weekly 'Women Talking' one of the most widely read and avidly discussed newspaper features of its period.

Mary encouraged her writers to sound off on the whole human condition: ways of living, relationships and morals; education, social services, and gaps in the welfare state. One of her great crusades was for women's financial independence, as the basis of real equality. For her, the most successful of all 'Women Talking' articles was E. Margaret Wheeler's case history of a woman's dependence on her husband, the 'Tale of a five-bob-a-week wife'.

The voicing of a social problem often led to direct action. In 1961 the Housewives' Register was formed after a letter pointed out the social and intellectual isolation of so many 'housebound housewives with liberal interests and a desire to remain individuals'. The Pre-school Playgroups Association was launched when another reader, Belle Tutaev, drew attention to the total inadequacy of nursery education. Ann Armstrong's vivid account of life as a responaut, paralysed from the neck down, led to the formation of the Invalids at Home Trust. Then there was Single Women and their Dependents, the Welfare of Children in Hospital, and the Disablement Incomes Group – the potential good causes, and Mary's enthusiasm for them, seemed unlimited. By the end of the decade, the term 'Guardian women' had entered national consciousness, soon to spawn the less respectful 'Guardian wimmin'.

An interesting development was the eagerness of readers to parody themselves. An article by John and Elizabeth Newson suggested that, in primitive societies, the problem of sleepless babies did not exist 'because the baby sleeps snugly against his mother's body, and so allows her to sleep too'. A famous spoof reader's letter claimed that her bed was capacious enough to hold her family of seven, and very often did. Mary delighted in the female clubbishness her pages generated. But her success was rooted in her moderation. In feminist terms, she was never an extremist; she found the aggressiveness of Betty Friedan's *The Feminine Mystique* baffling. Until the Lady Chatterley trial enlightened her, she did not know the meaning of the word 'fuck'.

The 1960s Women's page was an onslaught on old-time suburban female values from within. The silence of women in those days was pervasive in a way incomprehensible to women living now.

Mary's zest for discussion was what made her a great editor. She provided a platform for all ages, classes and persuasions. By giving us encouragement and space, she helped an awful lot of women – myself, gratefully, among them – to acquire the confidence to say the things we wanted. Her subversive brilliance was in persuading women other choices were available. Gradually, women talked, and even men began to listen. Mary Stott created a new climate of argument and restlessness. She helped a generation find its voice.

CHARLOTTE MARY STOTT · *born* 18 July 1907 · *died* 16 September 2002 ·

THE GREAT AND THE GOOD

...

LAURENS VAN DER POST
J. D. F. Jones

Laurens van der Post, who has died aged ninety, was a man of many achievements, public and private. He was an Afrikaner and, by long residence and cultural familiarity, also a European. He had been a soldier – and a prisoner of war who discovered and preached forgiveness for his enemies. He was a farmer who became a writer, a journalist and also an internationally successful novelist and film-maker. He was a traveller who explored Africa, a philosopher who embraced psychoanalysis, a secret diplomat, the confidant of princes and – said his critics – a South African liberal who became a bit of a reactionary (but that wasn't really true...). His life always brought together literature and public affairs.

He was born in the Orange Free State, the thirteenth of fifteen children of a distinguished Afrikaner family; his father was Dutch, a prominent lawyer, his mother a member of one of South Africa's oldest Huguenot families. Van der Post was to return again and again in his books to this upbringing on the edge of the Kalahari Desert: he often explained his Bushman nurse was a seminal character in his life. At seventeen he became a journalist in Durban – again, he wrote frequently about this period of his life. At twenty he was briefly associated with Roy Campbell and William Plomer on a literary magazine called *Voorslag* which, although only three issues appeared, has since acquired an exaggerated significance for its role in South Africa's inter-war literature.

More interestingly, 1926 was also the year when he first visited Japan in the company of William Plomer, and as guest of the magnificent Captain Katsue Mori, a mercantile officer whom van der Post met by accident and protected from racial unpleasantness. Japan was to be more important in van der Post's life than he could have imagined, and both he and Plomer later wrote about that journey – with fascinating discrepancies in the reportage.

Thereafter, the prewar period appears to have been difficult. Van der Post married Marjorie Wendt in South Africa in 1928. They had two children. He came to London, then returned to South Africa to work on the *Cape Times*, then came back to Britain, where he combined farming in Gloucestershire with freelance journalism. He also wrote his first novel, *In a Province*, which was published by Leonard and Virginia Woolf's Hogarth Press in 1934. This was one of the earliest fictional indictments by an Afrikaner of what was to become apartheid – worthy of comparison with Plomer's Turbott Wolfe – and it was well received; but van der Post had not yet come into his own. When war broke out, he immediately enlisted and was soon commissioned. He served first in Ethiopia (an experience that he would write about only many years later in *The Voice of the Thunder*, 1993), then in the Western Desert and Burma, finally in Java, where he was captured by the Japanese, to be held – sometimes under threat of imminent execution – for three years. Many of his subsequent books refer back to his experiences as a prisoner of war.

It was the turning point of his life. *The Seed and the Sower* (1963) eventually became the film *Merry Christmas, Mr Lawrence*; *The Dark Eye in Africa* (1955), a meditation which he had begun to write before the war, signalled his renewed interest in the problems of his own continent. Van der Post's writings, so often autobiographical, cover only some of the episodes in his long life: for instance, only in his ninetieth year did he write about his experiences in Indonesia after the war. In *The Admiral's Baby* (1996), an autobiographical sequel to *The Night of the New Moon* (1970), he described the brief British involvement in Java, 1945–7, when he worked in a senior role for Lord Mountbatten during the difficult period when the Dutch prepared, mistakenly, to resume their colonial role.

Eventually – long after the war had ended – he returned to Britain, collected an OBE and a CBE 'for gallant and distinguished services in the field', quit the army (where he was a full Colonel), and set off again for Africa and for a new career as writer-explorer. In 1949 he married again to Ingaret Giffard, a Jungian analyst whom he had met on a sea journey before the war. She introduced him to Carl Gustav Jung in Zurich. Van der Post's literary reputation took off with the publication of *Venture to the Interior* in 1952, his account of a journey to Nyasaland investigating for the British government. The book continues to attract plaudits for its poetic sensibility and profound insights into Africa, even as it is criticized for its inflation of a simple central African journey. Van der Post never looked back. He produced colourful and (for those in sympathy) magnificent novels set in an Africa frequently borrowed from his childhood, their themes tending to the adventurous: for example, *The Face Beside the Fire* (1953), *Flamingo Feather* (1955), and later, when he had become famous for his expertise on the Bushmen of Bechuanaland/Botswana, *A Story like the Wind* (1972) and *A Far-Off Place* (1973).

In the 1950s he had made journeys to the Kalahari (*The Lost World of the*

Kalahari, 1958, *The Heart of the Hunter*, 1961), with spin-off television documentaries. These were later to attract criticism from professional anthropologists, though laymen better remembered van der Post's love of these doomed people. He went on to travel in, and report from, Russia and Japan and even managed an engaging cookery book called *First Catch Your Eland* (1977).

But this was his role as writer. Van der Post was also a man of public affairs, which he conducted very privately. His contacts – his friendships – in southern Africa were considerable, as they were in London and elsewhere, and this brought him roles in the dramas of the past thirty years, many of which still remain unreported. For example, we now know that he was awarded his knighthood in 1981 because of his role as intermediary in the London–Johannesburg negotiations over a Rhodesian settlement – and not because his friend Margaret Thatcher appreciated his literary gifts.

He often chose to conceal his continuing fight against apartheid in its darkest days, just as he was totally discreet about his role as sage and counsellor to the Royal Family: that he was godfather to Prince William was the only public clue. (*Private Eye* never really understood how important he was to Prince Charles, however they mocked the relationship in the wickedly funny serial 'Heir of Sorrows'.)

As the years passed – he had based himself in London and in a converted lighthouse in Aldeburgh – van der Post's books became increasingly autobiographical, reflective and mystical. *In Yet Being Someone Other* (1982) and *About Blady* (1991), the nearest he got to straightforward autobiography, van der Post was writing about long-lasting memories, recent friendships and urgent concerns. He became an influential and active leader of the world-wide 'wilderness' concept, and a foundation has been set up to support his pioneering work. He followed events in South Africa intensely, and continued to be a frequent visitor: his sympathies – for Chief Gatsha Buthelezi, for instance – were rarely in line with current fashion, just as his opposition to sanctions (and his likely influence in this on Margaret Thatcher) did not assure him the approval of many *Guardian* readers. None of this should suggest that he ever had the slightest sympathy for apartheid: on the contrary, he was from his youth, as his books confirm, a passionate and instinctive enemy of racialism. But he was born a member of the Afrikaner Establishment and could never resign.

He was for ever a White African – he was honoured to be dubbed a 'White Bushman' – yet he spent most of his life outside South Africa. In his later years, his energies undiminished by age, he continued to write and to nurse his wife Ingaret (to whom many of his books were dedicated). He always found the time to respond, unfailingly, to the people, strangers as well as friends, who applied to him for support and wisdom. He was greatly loved by old and young: he had a natural courtesy which he offered, indiscriminately, to princes or waiters, statesmen or students.

His friendship with Jung had been very important in his life (and his biography of Jung was one of the books he was happiest to have written), though he never felt the need to undergo analysis. In old age he was increasingly drawn to the ultimate masters of literature – Homer, Shakespeare and Dante – and his writing shows his growing preoccupation with them. He had discovered and developed to a fine art a wonderful African gift for public story-telling; the sessions when he could be persuaded to hold forth, with never a note, were invariably crowded, as he led his listeners through Bushman or Homeric tales to ponder the laws and the wisdom of the soul. He had become the wise old man of Africa – a Jungian – and also universal – archetype, and as such he, and his memory, will survive the occasional sceptic and his – very few – detractors. He is survived by his wife, Ingaret, a daughter, Lucia, and six grandchildren.

LAURENS JAN VAN DER POST · *born* 13 December 1906 · *died* 15 December 1996 ·

6 September 1997

MOTHER TERESA
Peter Hebblethwaite

One of Mother Teresa's most signal journeys in recent years was to Tirana, capital of Albania. After years of isolation the most systematically atheist state ever seen signalled its desire to rejoin the human race by inviting home the world's most famous Albanian.

Her heart, sustained by a pacemaker inserted in December 1989, finally gave out at the age of eighty-seven yesterday. Though she received the Nobel Peace prize in 1979, she was best known for her work among the poor and destitute of Calcutta. No doubt one day she will be known as St Teresa of Calcutta.

She had the distinction of being unofficially canonized in her lifetime. The *annus mirabilis* was 1975: she made the cover of *Time* magazine with the caption 'Living Saints – Messengers of Hope for our Time,' and Malcolm

Muggeridge made a gushing television programme about her. She became a familiar international figure in her white sari with blue edgings, the sandals and the crucifix over the left shoulder. She was a conscience-prodding reminder of death in the streets of Calcutta and Third World poverty.

She carried the message to high places. A fund-raising lunch presided over by Britain's Prince Philip tactfully consisted of one meagre course. At Downing Street she upbraided Margaret Thatcher about Londoners reduced to living in what she called 'cardboard coffins'. She found the poverty of the First World even more incomprehensible than that of the Third. It was the sign of a callous society that had lost all sense of human community. As staunchly anti-communist as Pope John Paul II, she responded to former President Mikhail Gorbachev's invitation to open a house in Moscow. Her sisters, known as the Missionaries of Charity, were among the first to arrive in Yerevan, Armenia, after the earthquake of 1988.

It was a far cry from the hill-top village near Skopje, then in the Ottoman Empire, where Agnes Bojaxhiu was born four years before the outbreak of the First World War. At eighteen she left for India to become a nun in the Congregation of Loreto. For fifteen years she taught geography and history to middle-class girls at St Mary's High School, Entally, Bengal. She became headmistress and was also put in charge of a group of Indian sisters known as the Daughters of St Anne. They wore blue saris. Then in September 1946, with communal strife plaguing India, she heard her 'call within call' while on a train to Darjeeling. 'The message was clear,' she explained, 'I was to leave the convent and help the poor while living among them. It was an order.' But that was easier decided than done.

The local archbishop was soon convinced of her sincerity and determination. Always a practical woman, she learned nursing and dispensary work in Patna on the banks of the Ganges and began to gather her first helpers. The Vatican proved harder to persuade. Because there are too many already, new religious orders of women are discouraged. Mother Teresa had to prove that she could gather recruits and keep them. For the first ten years she was not allowed to work outside her own diocese, Calcutta. The work developed in three directions.

First, Kalighat, a hospice for the dying, was set up in the grounds of a Hindu temple. So as not to be overwhelmed, the sisters took in only those brought by the police – the most abandoned. More than 30,000 have passed through Kalighat and been helped to die well. Next came the Sishu Bhavan or children's home. Stories about babies being rescued from dustbins are not false. But more usually they were found abandoned in doorways or outside convent gates. Then a home for lepers was opened. It can take 200 – admittedly a mere fraction of India's two million lepers.

After 1960 the work began to expand throughout India to Ranchi, Jhansi, Delhi and Bombay. In Delhi she got in touch with government leaders. A garlanded Prime Minister Jawaharlal Nehru came to visit her children's home. 'Shall I tell you about my work?' she asked. 'No,' said Nehru, 'I know about it – that is why I have come.' She became a figure on the national scene. Although life was being made hard for expatriate Christian missionaries, Mother Teresa seemed to transcend religious divisions and to belong to everyone. She never used denominational tests for anything. She was given a free travel pass on Indian railways and on Indian Airways. Pope Paul VI's visit to Bombay in 1964 marked another stage in her progress. Paul heard about her work and donated to her the car he had used in India, a white Lincoln. It was raffled off. Her name was made. Mother Teresa was launched on the international scene.

But she had failures and disappointments. The sisters were thrown out of Colombo and Sri Lanka and snubbed in Belfast. They have worked in Africa, Jordan, among the Aborigines of Australia and the suburbs of Rome. But they did not 'take' in Latin America. Mother Teresa blamed this failure on liberation theologians who thought they should deal with the unjust structures of society and not just tinker with the works. This was always the most basic objection to what she was doing: one should deal with the causes as well as the effects of poverty, and proclaim justice as well as charity. Mother Teresa's reply was that the sisters were 'outside politics' and that to change society, one had to begin somewhere. She began on the pavements of Calcutta, where there were 100,000 homeless. To her mind, a single act of love and gratitude was sufficient justifi-cation for all her work. She wanted to do – in the phrase picked by Muggeridge – 'something beautiful for God'.

In 1976 the Missionaries of Charity celebrated their twenty-fifth anniversary. They numbered 1,133 and had 200 novices. In addition, there was the male congregation, the Missionary Brothers of Charity, who numbered about 160. For canonical reasons, they are independent, but they acted under Mother Teresa's inspiration. No less important in her eyes were the hundreds of thousands of lay people known as 'co-workers' – the term comes from Mohandas Gandhi. There are 30,000 in Britain alone. They pray for the Missionaries of Charity and send them bandages and medicines. The circles expand still more to embrace the sick who offer their sufferings for the work and contemplatives who pray for it.

In 1976 Mother Teresa spoke at the Eucharistic Congress in Philadelphia to mark the American bicentennial. She appeared on the platform alongside

Archbishop Helder Camara of Recife, north Brazil, the other contemporary Catholic folk-hero. Although she was not a great speaker, her tiny figure radiated great energy, dynamic, rugged charm and an indefinable sense of God's presence.

In the pontificate of Pope John Paul II, she began to be exploited as 'the good nun'. She was invited to the 1980 synod on marriage to denounce abortion and contraception. She told an Oxford conference in 1988 that she would never allow a child entrusted to her care to be adopted by a woman who had had an abortion or used contraceptives because, she said, 'such a woman cannot love'. Liberal she was not.

She went to Beirut in 1983, but could hardly do more than contemplate the ruins. She visited troublespots and famine areas on behalf of the Pope, and was cast in the role of spokeswoman for papal causes. Feminist she was not.

She had a spirit of Franciscan poverty and a low opinion of herself. She compared herself to 'God's pencil – a tiny bit of pencil with which he writes what he likes'. Asked, 'What next after Mother Teresa?' she answered simply: 'After Mother Teresa, the Missionaries of Charity.'

Mother Teresa resigned as Superior General on the grounds of health on 11 September 1990. This was accepted by the Vatican. However, the electoral college was deadlocked, and there were fears of an Indian breakaway if English Sister Priscilla were elected. A saint is a hard act to follow.

MOTHER TERESA (AGNES GONXHA BOJAXHIU) ·
born 27 August 1910 · *died* 5 September 1997 ·

21 April 1998

TREVOR HUDDLESTON
Eric James

It is one of the most remarkable facts of our time that it was a white bishop whom the African National Congress asked to open their first conference in freedom in 1991. His return to South Africa as a hero, after an absence of thirty-five years, was the measure of the stature of Bishop Trevor Huddleston, who has died aged eighty-four.

After all that Huddleston had achieved in South Africa, when he was recalled to England by the Community of the Resurrection in 1956 at only forty-three, that might have been the end of his story. It proved to be just the beginning. He grew in stature as, successively, Bishop of Masasi, of Stepney, of Mauritius and, finally, Archbishop of the Indian Ocean. From 1983, in so-called retirement, he was president of the Anti-Apartheid Movement and chairman of the International Defence and Aid Fund. His repute in the black community in South Africa was undimmed.

If a man is known by the company he keeps, there were those Father Huddleston knew as promising young men in Johannesburg – Oliver Tambo, Nelson Mandela, Desmond Tutu – who grew to be great men, of the stature of his later friend Julius Nyerere in Masasi. But most of his company never became names, and his top priority each day was to 'keep company' with God in prayer.

Huddleston was born in Bedford, the son of Captain Sir Ernest Whiteside Huddleston, eventually commander of the Indian Navy. Captain Huddleston was absent in India, and father and son did not meet until he was seven. Trevor's mother, too, was often absent in India, and he was brought up in Hampstead by a wealthy widowed aunt. His devout Anglo-Catholic home and the local church were powerful influences upon him.

Early in his childhood, he began to think he was called to the priesthood. Later, Lancing College was a huge influence. At Christ Church, Oxford, Trevor felt the call to be a monk as well as a priest. To have read history at Oxford under the tuition of J. C. Masterman and Keith Feiling was to stand him in good stead for the rest of his life. After Oxford, he spent an invaluable year in Ceylon, up the Irrawaddy river, in India, and in Palestine, in the steps of Charles de Foucauld. He returned for two years at Wells Theological College, and then, in 1936, was ordained to a curacy in the railway town of Swindon at the height of the Depression.

In 1939, aged twenty-six, Huddleston went to Mirfield to test his vocation to join the Community of the Resurrection. Fr Edward Keble Talbot, the Superior, warned him that having no children would prove the most costly demand of the religious life. Huddleston's wartime reclusive years at Mirfield, when most able-bodied men were being called up, were testing. None of his fellow novices saw in Trevor a future leader. He was the last person they could imagine defying authority.

When Raymond Raynes returned from South Africa to be Superior of the Community, Huddleston happened to be on kitchen and front-door duty. Raynes was clearly sick and was put to bed. Huddleston took Raynes's meals up for a week and was ordered to stay and talk. Soon it was announced that Raynes had decided Huddleston should succeed him as priest-in-charge of

Sophiatown and Orlando Anglican Missions, Johannesburg. His ship sailed for Cape Town in convoy in 1943, but the convoy was bombed, and the ship in which Trevor was sailing was narrowly missed.

Within days of his arrival, Huddleston was immersed in the beginnings of his onslaught on apartheid, in Church as well as State, the story of which he would eventually recount in his bestseller *Naught For Your Comfort* (1956). His outstanding gifts of leadership and courage were soon apparent. He learnt to communicate powerfully both as a speaker and writer. He had the voice of a visionary and a handsome and commanding face. He worked not only with like-minded Anglicans but with Jews, Hindus, Muslims and agnostics. People like the mining magnate Sir Ernest Oppenheimer began to follow his lead.

Everything Huddleston wrote or said was the product of his experience. Where apartheid was concerned, he was totally uncompromising – which led him into conflict with the bishops of his church, especially with Geoffrey Clayton, Bishop of Johannesburg, later Archbishop of Cape Town. The Archbishop of Canterbury, Geoffrey Fisher, also said to him: 'You are entirely wrong in the methods you are using to fight this situation.' Huddleston begged to differ.

Huddleston's ministry in Sophiatown was movingly described by Alan Paton in *Cry, The Beloved Country* (1948). Huddleston was Provincial of his Community in South Africa from 1949 to 1955. He was given the ANC's highest award, the title Isithwalandwe, the Courageous Warrior. When his Community recalled him in 1955, only his vow of obedience made him obey: he would almost certainly otherwise have been arrested. His Superior judged that a South African prison was no place for a diabetic like Huddleston. In South Africa, those who depended on him, like Oliver Tambo, were dumb-founded.

There followed four unhappy years. Trevor, coping with his bereavement of Africa and with correspondence and invitations to speak that flowed from the bestselling *Naught For Your Comfort*, was for a time guardian of novices at Mirfield and then prior of the CR house at Notting Hill Gate. People close to Trevor were clear he should return to Africa. Evelyn Baring, in his days as High Commissioner to South Africa, had come to know Trevor well. Baring, in 1960, was chairman of the Universities Mission to Central Africa, and agreed that Trevor was just the man to be bishop of a diocese in Tanganyika: the fourth poorest country in the world, then on the verge of independence under the leadership of Julius Nyerere.

Huddleston was Bishop of Masasi from 1960 to 1968. Nyerere, a Roman Catholic, called him 'our bishop'. They worked together as partners. In 1963

Trevor returned to Oxford to conduct a memorable Mission to the University, delivering addresses published as *The True and Living God*. It was Robert Stopford, Bishop of London, who, in 1968, invited Huddleston to be Bishop Suffragan of Stepney. He was again bereaved of Africa, and often found priorities like pastoral reorganization frustrating. Yet, at a time when east London was witnessing a considerable increase in the immigrant population and a growing mass hysteria against the Pakistanis, there could hardly have been a wiser appointment. The Asian and West Indian communities held Huddleston in high esteem, but so too did ordinary churchgoers, not least children. The simplicity of life and austerity of his home at 400 Commercial Road were the opposite of a prelate's palace.

It was Gerald Ellison, Bishop of London, who realized that, at sixty-five, Huddleston needed to be relieved of the pressures and responsibilities of Stepney, that he still had it in him to be a very considerable bishop overseas, and caused him to be both Bishop of Mauritius and Archbishop of the Indian Ocean from 1978 to 1983. He grew in understanding of the faiths of Muslims, Hindus and Buddhists. This new ecumenism became central to what he believed and practised. In Mauritius, he acted as host to the inter-faith consultation which prepared for the Sixth Assembly of the World Council of Churches in Vancouver.

If anyone imagined the septuagenarian Huddleston would sit back they were much mistaken. When he retired, he became provost of the Selly Oak colleges, president of the Anti-Apartheid Movement, chairman of the International Defence and Aid Fund, and a Trustee of the Runnymede Trust – a massive expenditure of time and energy.

No one who knew Trevor Huddleston intimately could deny that he remained to the end, in a rather old-fashioned sense, a man of God. Living his last years in a few rooms at the top of the vicarage of St James's, Piccadilly, there was still much of the monk about him. He went back regularly to Mirfield and the Community of the Resurrection. Prayer remained the very centre of his life. But close to Piccadilly Circus – he undoubtedly liked being 'at the centre' – he was available to the media, and leaders like Julius Nyerere, Nelson Mandela, Abdul Minty, Sonny Ramphal. And, if they pressed him, he would fly to the ends of the earth. Not only important people sought him out. It was as often the unknown and, very often, young children.

When one asks why Huddleston remained such a hero, Archbishop Tutu probably provides the best answer. He says: 'I was in hospital for twenty months with TB, and, if Father Huddleston was in Johannesburg, he made it a point to visit me at least once a week. I was just a nonentity, thirteen years old, and yet he paid so much attention to me.' And he adds: 'And you could have knocked me down with a feather, when this man doffed his hat to my mother. I couldn't understand a white man doffing his hat to a black woman, an uneducated black woman.' Trevor was the first white man who accepted them. If Trevor Huddleston seemed sometimes a man with a cause – to the point of obsession – it was only because he was, first, a man with compassion for individual children of God.

ERNEST URBAN TREVOR HUDDLESTON · *born* 15 June 1913 · *died* 20 April 1998 ·

DONALD SOPER
Dennis Barker, Leslie Griffiths and John Gittings

With his black cassock, his soap box on Tower Hill and Hyde Park Corner, his socialism, pacifism, teetotalism and practical work for vagrants and alcoholics, Lord Soper, who has died aged ninety-five, was the Nonconformists' nonconformist, a Christian socialist of a breed now almost extinct, a preacher who grew up without microphones. Alcohol, fox-hunting, gambling, apartheid and meat-eating were among the many targets of his resonant and often disarmingly humorous strictures.

Donald Soper's Methodism derived from his family background: his father, a prosperous loss-adjuster, was a devout Wesleyan who campaigned against alcohol as the result of seeing his own father drunk. But the other touchstone of his long life – pacifism, which he maintained throughout the challenge of Nazism – originated from accident, not aggression. As a star cricketer at Aske's School, he bowled the first ball of a cricket match on a hard pitch and saw the ball hit the batsman over the heart and kill him.

It was a formative, if illogical, experience – as was encountering so many war veterans when he was at Cambridge – in a life which had been one of comfortable certainties. Handsome, with a powerful voice that was to help make him famous, and a photographic memory that made academic learning easy, he had been captain of the school team and head prefect, and was secure in his or his father's beliefs. But even in his certainty he was fair-minded. When in 1920 the son of a communist refused to observe the minute's silence on the second, profoundly emotional Armistice Day, Soper was expected, as head prefect, to make the boy conform; instead he defended his right to his views. He claimed that it was at this moment that he learned tolerance – a quality that always informed even his most pugnacious views.

He was only thirteen when he decided to become a minister. His Sunday school superintendent father told him that God's son had been a minister; he wanted his son to become one too. He went up to St Catharine's College, Cambridge, to read history as a different and chastened being – almost, as he said later, in a state of nervous breakdown. The death of the batsman, though it was proved he had a defective heart, haunted Soper; he also had been a big fish in the small pond of his school and now found himself a very small fish. He volunteered his services to the Sunday school superintendent at Cambridge, but after reading Lecky's *History of the Rise and Influence of the Spirit of Rationalism in Europe* had to confess to the man that he was now an atheist. He suffered from boils and on one occasion cut part of his chin off; he admitted to being a psychological mess. But he carried on playing the Sunday school piano, which he thought helped him recover his faith.

After St Catharine's, he moved on to Wesley House in Cambridge, where he was one of its first students. There, under the influence of Alex Wood, the dedicated socialist fellow of Emmanuel College, and Edward Woods, later Bishop of Lichfield, Soper blossomed. He was later to take his doctorate at the London School of Economics. Soon he was lecturing in the open air. To attract a crowd outside a stocking factory in Derby, he played Gilbert and Sullivan on a whistle. It was his first sight of how industrial wage-slaves lived, and it converted him to socialism.

By twenty-three, the Methodist Church made him a probationer minister in the South London Mission, Old Kent Road, where he was faced with a disappointingly small audience. His typically forceful response was to start speaking more outdoors rather than in the mission itself. It was the beginning of a progress towards his regular Sunday soap-box sessions at Hyde Park Corner and Wednesday midday sessions on Tower Hill, which he began in 1926. He played hecklers like the skilled musician he was. A very small man once ridiculed his pacifism: 'If I'm attacked, shouldn't I defend myself?' 'In your case,' retorted Soper, 'I would advise against it.' He had one of the most formidable repertoires of debating put-downs since George Bernard Shaw.

In 1929 he moved to Islington and remained there until 1936. But the main core of his life's work, as superintendent of the West London Mission, based on the Kingsway Hall, lasted for forty-two years. He saw the Mission battling with the problems of alcoholics, unmarried mothers, the elderly and its own money difficulties (latterly much of the hall was rented out and his speaking was done in the smaller of the two halls).

He remained a staunch enemy of alcohol, though he always saw the alcoholics at his Mission shelter as victims rather than culprits. Though he was a vegetarian for much of his life 'with occasional lapses', he ate meat again in later life on medical advice. In his latter years, with one of his good-natured compromises, he would say that if we ever reached the Kingdom of Heaven, light wines might just be permissible. But he did scourge Toryism, and Thatcherism in particular, which he insisted was incompatible with Christianity. Herself, he once argued, was an example not of degradation but of original sin. Taxed with the sins of communist regimes, he would reply – quick debater that he was – that these regimes were not socialism but state capitalism.

His admission that the only real friends he ever had were his brother Ross, who died early, and his wife Marie, opened him to the criticism of being more interested in debates than people. But in fact, though he did not socialize in the corridors of power, he had several long-standing friends who never reached the public eye. And he radiated human decency, even towards people who did not share his views, often arguing that many Tories were better people than their precepts and many socialists worse than their principles. His four daughters, he admitted with good humour, all enjoyed a drink.

He was a flamboyant president of the Methodist Conference in 1953, though pledging himself to represent the denomination as a whole rather than his own views. In 1965 he accepted a life peerage, soon after the London County Council, on which he was an alderman, was abolished on the creation of the Greater London Council, ending his local government career. He was a member of the Labour party and saw the House of Lords as yet another platform from which to air his views. He also thought his presence there might 'keep the bishops in order'. One of his first observations was that the House of Lords was itself 'proof of the reality of life after death'.

He was the author of many books, of which his best was probably *All His Grace* (1957). He will be remembered also as an early Aldermaston marcher, and as the recipient of several honorary doctorates. He was a gifted media performer, so much so that during the war his pacifism got him banned from the radio; later he became a star performer on Radio 4's *Any Questions*. He was the creator of a media record: three appearances on the BBC's *Terry Wogan Show* in a year.

In 1929, he married Marie Dean, by whom he had four daughters.

LESLIE GRIFFITHS writes: Donald Soper always described himself as being of the 'high chapel' party in Methodism. The main ingredient of this stance was his sacramentalism. He had a high doctrine of Holy Communion long before the 'rediscovery' of the sacrament in the Church at large. He often said he couldn't go out into Hyde Park on a Sunday afternoon unless he'd first presided at the Lord's Table. He was, of course, merely reverting to the practice and teaching of the Wesley brothers and the spirituality of the earliest generation of Methodists. Similarly, he followed the Wesleys' custom of preaching in the open air. How he loved rounding off what he always called the 'fellowship of controversy' with G. K. Chesterton's words: 'Remember,' he'd say, 'Christianity hasn't been tried and found wanting; it's been thought too hard and never tried.'

Such was the impact Soper made on the world beyond his church that most non-Methodists continued to think of him as the prototypical representative of the Methodist Church. When a public inquiry was held recently to establish whether an Eruv should be created to give orthodox Jews certain benefits on the Sabbath, it was to Soper as a former president (forty years previously) that one party turned for support, even though the current president was living within the area to be included within the Eruv. He was heard regularly on radio and television, his clear thinking and gravelly voice rarely failing to make a strong impact on his hearers.

There is no doubt that he was desperately saddened at the failure of Anglican-Methodist conversations in 1969. He had always had special warmth of affection for the Church of England and was prepared to be re-ordained in order to exercise a wider ministry in a united church. What a splendid bishop he would have made. In his mind the Methodists were a preaching order (sometimes he called them 'the missionary arm') of the Church of England. Unity would enhance the mission of both bodies. But that was not to be.

Although he used to anger many of his fellow believers by his more outrageous remarks ('It's impossible to be a Conservative and a Christian'), everybody came to love him in old age. I once asked him how he'd best like to be remembered. Without hesitation he replied: 'As one of John Wesley's preachers.'

JOHN GITTINGS writes: Pitching a platform near Donald Soper at Speakers' Corner was always a mistake: he was the crowd's favourite and impossible to compete with. The time was 1958–60, the platform we had belonged to the Combined Universities Campaign for Nuclear Disarmament. After crossing Marble Arch – there were no crush barriers to stop us in those days – we could instantly see if Soper was there by the size of the crowd and the recurring laughter. He was very skilled at dealing with the really abusive heckler: his short-haired muscular appearance helped. God (whom he did not mention too often) was not going to take any nonsense.

We would set up pitch some way off, call on Britain to stop this madness, ban the bomb and give the world a lead. Our partners and friends tried to look like an audience. When the light faded and so did we, Soper was still entertaining and disputing with a real crowd at his feet.

Earlier, as an eighteen-year-old RAF cadet adrift in London on a Chinese course, I had attended his lectures in the Kingsway Methodist Hall. They steered me away from West Sussex C of E Christianity towards an ethical socialism, which seemed, and was, much more relevant. The only question those days for learner speakers was whether to model ourselves on Donald Soper or Michael Foot. Both combined passion, strength, humour and socialism – not an easy mixture to sustain on cold Sunday afternoons. Soper kept going much longer than just after lighting-up time. He was still going strong thirty-five years later when we had long since abandoned the platform.

THE REVEREND DONALD OLIVER SOPER, BARON SOPER OF KINGSWAY · *born* 31 January 1903 · *died* 22 December 1998 ·

6 March 1999

LORD DENNING
Stephen Sedley

The death of Alfred Denning, Lord Denning of Whitchurch, at the age of 100, marks the passing of one – perhaps the last – of a sparse succession of major judicial figures who have succeeded in shaping areas of the law into conformity with a strongly held world view.

Denning's most abiding and probably least deserved reputation was as a liberal. He adhered throughout his life to a conservative set of personal and public values, and he gave effect to them in his private life in rural Hampshire, in his judgments and in his numerous public pronouncements off the bench. It was these values that led him, as a newly appointed judge in the 1940s, to devise a legal doctrine which lawyers regarded as revolutionary, but which performed the elementary moral task of holding people to their promises – something which the commercially-oriented common law had found it expedient not to do.

His trail-blazing continued with the deserted wife's right to salvage a home from the ruins of a marriage, and the liability of advisers for negligent advice. These were issues on which the law had got entrenched in indefensible moral positions, and it was a mark of Denning's greatness that he had the scholarship, the courage and the sense of opportunity to restore the credit of the common law when the chance came his way.

By 1949, in spite of a prosecution of some Jewish businessmen in which his summing-up to the jury had given some signs of unwholesome prejudice, he had been promoted to the Court of Appeal. He took with him his distaste for interference with individual enterprise, whether by the state or by trade unions, and his paternalistic, and sometimes simplistic, views on social questions. These had a long lineage. Sir Edward Coke's dictum, in the days of the early Stuarts – 'At the common law no man can be prohibited from working at any lawful trade, for the law abhors idleness, especially in young men' – repeatedly found echoes in Denning's judgments: 'Many a married woman seeks work. She does so ... to fill her time with useful occupation, rather than sit idly at home waiting for her husband to return. The devil tempts those who have nothing to do.'

Denning went on for four decades to mould law to his perceptions of private and public morality, rarely hesitating to torture precedent until it yielded the desired result. His enormous popularity was a combination of the appeal his pronouncements made to popular commonsense, or at least to conventional wisdom, and the simple and comprehensible prose in which he made them. His literary style, in fact, is perhaps his most underrated achievement. While in his many books the simplicity is studied and sometimes embarrassingly overdone, Denning's judgments in case after case performed the feat, achieved by no other judge, of speaking directly and compellingly to ordinary people in well-constructed and lucid prose. Concepts which lawyers had struggled to articulate, clashes of doctrine which seemed insoluble, would emerge in his judgments as crystalline statements of principle. For all the professional smirks generated by Denning's famous opening line in a judgment about an appalling motor accident ('It was bluebell time in Kent'), this accessibility of language was the rock on which his popularity and influence were built. When, not long after his retirement, he appeared in full wig and gown on *Jim'll Fix It* and tried Little Noddy for knocking down PC Plod, what stuck in the mind was not the incongruity but the homogeneity of it – the same benign moralism as the legal profession had known for forty years, in prose begotten by Samuel Smiles upon Enid Blyton.

Such was his authority that lawyers now believe that Lord Mansfield, giving judgment in favour of the slave James Somersett, said: 'The air of England is too pure for any slave to breathe: let the black go free.' But the line appears in no contemporary report of Mansfield's judgment: the phrase has a long lineage, but the attribution originates, so far as is known, in Denning's celebrated 1949 Hamlyn Lectures, *Freedom under the Law*.

But Denning's simple language went with a penetrating mind. The son of a draper, he was born in Whitchurch, Hampshire, and educated at the village school and Andover Grammar, before going on to Magdalen College, Oxford. Of his four brothers, one became a general, another an admiral. After war service in France – where two of his brothers died – Denning began his university life as a mathematical scholar, took honours in that subject and then in law, and went on to shine at the Bar. His marriage to Mary Harvey, in 1932, produced one son, Robert, a professor of inorganic chemistry and fellow of Magdalen College, Oxford; Mary died in 1941, and Denning's marriage to his second wife, Joan Start, in 1945 lasted until her death in 1992.

In 1929 Denning produced an edition of Smith's *Leading Cases* which is a collector's item. His compendious memory for law never deserted him; in judgment after judgment he would refer to authorities which counsel had not produced, sometimes predicating his decision on them. It led to some rancour on occasions, partly because it meant that cases were being decided on unargued points, but partly also because the cases he cited tended not to support the propositions for which he invoked them. The result was always more important to him than how he got there.

Denning's personal image was part of his jurisprudence. The half-smile to be seen in every picture of him never left his face. People felt they were in the presence of a benign judge with a ready ear for their problems. But while he could be readily influenced by the underlying agenda or the emotive side-issues of a case – 'I just want to get the feel of it,' he would say, as he probed to and beyond the margins of relevance – he would rarely display hostility to those cases which, in his court at least, did not stand a chance. Instead, he would help the destined loser to articulate his or her argument: 'I expect you'd say that … Yes, you'd put it this way, wouldn't you…' Losers, especially litigants in person, went away feeling that they had gained something, and Denning's court got through a lot more work by avoiding protracted arguments.

But there were limits to his tolerance, and these became increasingly well known as the years went by and as his confidence grew. It became notorious that the hate-figures of the popular press – students, trade unions, squatters, prisoners – rarely won in Denning's court. His reputation was also sullied by his views on race, which were believed finally to have precipitated his retirement in 1982. A new book of his contained derogatory remarks about black jury members which descended to the 'alien presence in our midst' level. The book was withdrawn and the passages rewritten, and Denning expressed his regret; but he had gone too far, and his departure from the bench after nearly forty years as a judge, twenty of them as Master of the Rolls, took place under a shadow. It was a shadow which lengthened in the succeeding years, with racial indiscretions on the record.

It would be as wrong, however, to remember Denning as a judicial Alf Garnett as it would be to remember him as a beacon of judicial virtue. He was complex in his strategic views, and in many ways a vigorous modernist. In the 1950s he helped to clear the path for the re-establishment of judicial review of executive and local government, a process which has today changed the face both of law and of government in Britain. It was he who coined the concept of legitimate expectation as a new shield for the citizen against the State.

For Denning, this protection often appeared to be the supreme goal. Yet he was perfectly ready to abdicate in favour of an unaccountable executive where he believed the political stakes were too high. It was typical that when, in 1977, he made the U-turn in the case of the journalist Mark Hosenball, deported without being able to learn – and therefore answer – the case against him, he did so by asserting his faith in the infallibility of the security services: 'In some parts of the world national security has been used as an excuse for all sorts of infringements of individual liberty. But not in England.'

Then came his judgment in 1980 on the attempt by the Birmingham Six to sue the police for beatings they had suffered before five of them made confessions: 'If the six men win, it will mean … that the convictions were erroneous. That would mean that the Home Secretary would either have to recommend they be pardoned or he would have to remit the case to the Court of Appeal … This is such an appalling vista that every sensible person in the land would say it cannot be right that these actions should go any further.' Seven other judges shared Denning's conclusion; yet it is on him, as usual, that history's unforgiving eye has come to rest. He could not complain, for it was what he constantly courted, and the peroration of his judgment in the Birmingham Six case – 'This case shows what a civilized country we are' – will remain an ironic epitaph not on them but on him.

At other times Denning's ends and his means coincided. In his 1963 report on the Profumo affair, a strongly authoritarian approach to public affairs marched with a rigorous view of private morality and a patrician attitude to individuals, as he chronicled the dealings of 'Mr Profumo' with 'Mandy' and 'Christine'. But neither xenophobia nor opportunism obstructed Denning's response when the great issue on which his lead was awaited came before his court (for Denning generally diverted the most tempting cases into his division of the Court of Appeal): was the new body of EEC law, overriding both the common law and the sovereignty of Parliament, going to be welcomed and assisted by the judges, or cribbed and confined by restrictive judicial interpretation? Denning surprised everybody who thought they knew his foibles. In a 1974 judgment, which ranks among the great passages of English judicial prose, he avoided both grudging acquiescence and overt welcome by using as an image the great forces of nature, which an island people had traditionally coped with and survived: 'The treaty is like an incoming tide. It flows into the estuaries and up the rivers. It cannot be held back.' On these great issues of political power, Denning was a realist in his stewardship of the law. Later, as a crossbench peer, he proclaimed himself a traditional constitutionalist and tried vainly to stem the same tide as he saw it threatening to burst the banks of Westminster.

Denning was made a law lord in 1957. But he welcomed his transfer back to the Court of Appeal as Master of the Rolls five years later because, in a three-judge court, he needed only one ally to get a majority; and although the repeated oversetting of his judgments by the Lords became notorious, it is probable that Denning felt much freer to innovate and take chances, knowing that if his decisions were considered wholly impolitic the Lords would incur the odium of upsetting them and his own standing would be undiminished.

Where he found himself without allies, his dissents sometimes won the day in the Lords; and even where they did not, some have acquired their own legitimacy – for example, his notable dissent giving priority to the right of peaceful civic demonstration over the rights of estate agents and property speculators. (He happened to perceive the contest as charity versus trade; if he had been persuaded to regard it as militancy versus free enterprise, it is unlikely that the result would have been the same.)

If there is a label for Lord Denning's stance as a lawmaker, it is radical conservatism. The emergence of just this as the dominant mode of the political state during Denning's later years is perhaps an index of his prescience and a confirmation of his status, not merely as a judge, but as a historic figure of enduring importance.

ALFRED THOMPSON DENNING, LORD DENNING OF WHITCHURCH · *born* 23 January 1899 · *died* 5 March 1999 ·

6 August 2001

LORD LONGFORD (FRANK PAKENHAM)
Peter Stanford

Though conducted simultaneously, the two crusades that made Frank Longford, who has died aged ninety-five, a household name in Britain were an odd combination. The first, launched in the early 1970s, aimed to outlaw pornography and presented him as a prurient reactionary and a shameless hypocrite touring the sex clubs that he wanted to close down. The second, which continued for the last three decades of his life, attempted to win parole for the Moors murderess, Myra Hindley. Here Longford was at his most liberal, Christian and naive, building on a lifetime of interest in prison reform, to argue that Hindley, and indeed all offenders, could be rehabilitated if society was prepared to forgive.

Of the two, it was his lonely battle to help Hindley that revealed the true man. The pornography escapade was an aberration, embarked upon against the advice of old friends and under the influence of Mary Whitehouse and anti-libertarians. From the day his report came out, Longford rarely returned to the subject.

It was in the area of penal reform that he made his most lasting contribution. A Labour politician, who spent a record twenty-two years on the Lords frontbench, held junior office under Clement Attlee in the 1940s and later sat in Harold Wilson's cabinets, Longford could, when he resigned in 1968, have rested on his laurels. But he was not a conventional politician, and retirement gave him the freedom to take up the unpopular cause that was closest to his heart, without fear of damaging his party.

It was not only his appearance – noble cranium and mad scientist's tonsure – that set Longford apart from his government colleagues. Though a committed Labour party member, and a regular attender of PLP meetings and annual conferences well into his nineties, he saw politics less as a career and more as part of a moral crusade. Conscience came before party loyalty, heart before the head.

Such a stance belonged more to the nineteenth-century philanthropic tradition than to twentieth-century Westminster. And, in many senses, Longford was a nineteenth-century figure, struggling, often with humour, to deal with the problem of being born too late. Like William Wilberforce and Lord Shaftesbury, his was a privileged upbringing; like them, he was a devout Christian determined to translate faith into action; like them, he was an unpredictable combination of political savvy and childlike clear-sightedness.

The essential difference between the three was that while Wilberforce reformed the slave trade and Shaftesbury the factories, Longford only aspired to alter the penal system. His failure could not be put down only to the changed climate of the twentieth century. His own character played a part; never one to manage a concerted campaign, to push and cajole friends to a cause that many cabinet colleagues regarded indulgently as 'Frank's hobby', he was too much the individualist, too fond of argument for argument's sake – an effect of his 1930s time as an Oxford politics don – and, ultimately, too light-weight in Whitehall to carry the day. With his knack for making people laugh, and his tireless enjoyment of socializing as well as socialism, it was too easy to ignore the fact that Longford was way ahead of his time in questioning the direction of prison policy. Though his prophecy of the failure of the punishment-oriented system of mainly Conservative postwar governments was repeatedly borne out, he never managed to translate his vision into work-able reform.

That is not to say he was without substantial achievements; it was just that the goals he set himself remained outside his grasp. He dreamed of being a reforming home secretary, an ambition that prompted his old friend Evelyn Waugh to remark 'and then we would all be murdered in our beds'. A prison visitor since the 1930s, Longford was still going, two and three times a week, to visit the abandoned and despised in jail until close to the end of his life. Though the tabloids portrayed him as a man who got a kick out of contact with infamous killers – a throwback to the 'Lord Porn' caricature – such 'names' made up only 1 per cent of those Longford journeyed to see.

An example: in the late 1980s, he was contacted by the solicitor for a young Dutchman, convicted of a drugs offence, sent to Albany prison on the Isle of Wight, suffering from Aids and cut off by his family. Longford was the only person to visit this dying man, a gesture repeated in countless episodes that never made headlines but which brought succour and relief.

He also initiated practical measures to ease offenders' reintegration into society. He founded the New Bridge in 1955, the first organization dedicated to ex-prisoners' welfare. In 1970 he established, in New Horizon, the first drop-in centre for homeless teenagers. Until the end, he spent time at New Horizon's offices, oblivious to its users' sometimes rough teasing, anxious to understand what had alienated them from the mainstream. He also con-tributed a series of learned reports on penal reform during Labour's period out of office between Attlee and Wilson. He chaired the committee which, in 1963, recommended the setting-up of the parole system, still the bedrock of the current system.

Attlee admired Longford's passion for society's outcasts and tried, often against his colleagues' advice, to harness it. In the 1945 Labour landslide, Longford – then Frank Pakenham – stood for Oxford, but was defeated by Quintin Hogg, later Lord Hailsham. Attlee was persuaded to elevate him to the peerage, and bring to Labour's sparsely populated Lords benches a youthful thinker who had been Sir William Beveridge's right-hand man on his landmark welfare state report. Longford was tempted to decline the offer and await a suitable by-election, but feared that, since his childless elder brother was in poor health, it was inevitable that he would soon become the Earl of Longford. But acceptance effectively relegated him to the role of also-ran in Labour politics. Without a Commons seat, he remained an enigma to his colleagues, outside the mainstream and, for some, a figure not to be trusted.

Initially, however, he won rapid promotion. In 1947, Attlee made him, as Chancellor of the Duchy of Lancaster, responsible for the British zone of occupied Germany. It was Longford's finest hour as a minister. For a year, he worked tirelessly to stop the Germans starving to death. He reopened schools and hospitals, and worked with American and French counterparts on the currency reform that would bring stability to West Germany. He fought the Foreign Secretary, Ernest Bevin, for a reappraisal of the industrial dismantling of the occupied zone under the reparations policy, but Bevin refused. On the ground, Longford saw sooner than his superior that cooperation with the Soviets was impossible, and that partition was inevitable. Konrad Adenauer, the father of West Germany, came to regard him as his people's one true friend in London. This tribute was prompted perhaps by Longford's optimistic avowal to the Germans that the British had forgiven them the wartime excesses. His remarks caused a storm of outrage in a country still suffering rationing. Attlee was persuaded to move him to the Ministry of Civil Aviation, where he proved a successful minister, save for the mishandling of the report from a crash inquiry that almost cost him his job. Attlee stuck by him, and later raised him to First Lord of the Admiralty, just outside the Cabinet.

In opposition after 1951, Hugh Gaitskell, who had shared rooms with Longford at Oxford and referred to him as his 'oldest friend', kept him at the centre of Labour affairs, even when he became chairman of a City clearing bank. The appointment caused some raised eyebrows in the square mile, where Longford was blackballed from at least one financiers' club.

After Gaitskell's death in 1963, however, Harold Wilson had no time for such an unpredictable figure. Though included in the 1964 Cabinet as leader of the Lords, Longford knew he was only there as a sop to the Gaitskellites. Wilson treated him with personal kindness but professional contempt, remarking that Longford – who had got a double first at Oxford – had a mental age of twelve. By his own admission he was 'ineffective' in the treacherous atmosphere of Wilson's Cabinets. Even as Colonial Secretary in 1966, he was so dispirited that he failed to master his brief and was quickly removed.

He had talked with Gaitskell in the early 1960s of taking up Tony Benn's Disclaimer Act and renouncing his peerages – both the inherited title which finally came his way in 1961, and the barony awarded by Attlee. Then he would be free to seek a Commons seat at the 1964 general election and, if successful, a Cabinet post as head of a major department. Gaitskell had given qualified support; Wilson, however, pooh-poohed the idea. It was a deeply frustrating period. In terms of prestige, Longford had reached the pinnacle of his career, but in practice he was impotent, and often resorted to playing up to his image as the Cabinet jester.

Wilson talked often of sacking Longford, so when he resigned from government in January 1968 over the abandonment of a commitment to raising the school-leaving age, it was a matter of jumping before being pushed. If Benn, Richard Crossman and Barbara Castle all recorded their relief at his departure in their diaries, the Queen continued to hold him in high esteem. In 1972 she made him a Knight of the Garter.

After 1968 Longford devoted himself to his campaigns and to publishing. He had already produced several volumes of autobiography and one book – *Peace By Ordeal*, on the background to the 1921 Anglo-Irish treaty – that was regarded as a classic. But his later efforts, while tackling ambitious subjects like humility and forgiveness, were politely, though unenthusiastically, received.

From the floor of the House of Lords, as well as continually pushing the government on prisons policy, he spoke often on Ireland, a country he regarded as his home. It was a claim – dubious since he spent the vast majority of his life on this side of the Irish Sea – that occasionally got him into trouble. While still in Wilson's cabinet, he attended the fiftieth anniversary celebrations of the Easter Rising, and was photographed next to his old friend President de Valera. Though he remained sentimentally attached to Ireland, Longford broke every tradition of his Anglo-Irish ascendancy family. He was born into a military, Protestant, Conservative and Unionist clan, and educated at Eton and New College, Oxford. As an adult, he embraced the Roman Catholic Church and Irish nationalism. His failure to follow his soldier father, who was killed at Gallipoli when Longford was nine, remained an open wound. In 1940 he was invalided out of the forces after a nervous breakdown.

He regarded the episode as the ultimate humiliation, but came to believe that it gave him some insight into the degradation of those sent to prison and shunned by society.

In Elizabeth Harman, whom he married in 1931, Longford found the emotional warmth and love denied him as a child by a difficult, and often cruel, mother. Made painfully aware of his insignificance in her eyes, next to his elder brother, he only recovered a sense of self-esteem while at Oxford. At a summer ball, he was asleep on a couch when spotted by Elizabeth, one of the most beautiful and sought-after undergraduates of her generation. 'The face was monumental beauty,' she later wrote, 'as if some Graeco-Roman statue … had been dressed in modern clothes.' Two years later, when they were both lecturing for the Workers' Educational Association in Stoke, at the height of the 1930s Depression, love blossomed.

It was Elizabeth, a great-niece of Joseph Chamberlain, who convinced Longford to join the Labour party. In return, having been converted to Catholicism while at Oxford by the Jesuit Father Martin D'Arcy, he persuaded her to join him in the Church of Rome. He found great strength in the moral certainties of Catholicism. The Longfords enjoyed an extraordinarily happy marriage, touched by tragedy with the death, in 1969, of their daughter Catherine in a car crash. They remained active in their various political, literary and campaigning activities well into their nineties, relaxing only to enjoy their countless grandchildren and great-grandchildren at their cherished Sussex home, Bernhurst. Longford gave the family seat, Tullynally Castle in Co. Westmeath, to his son and heir in 1961 upon inheriting it.

With friends and family, his razor-sharp wit could flourish, while in public he felt he had to restrain it in the interests of being a better Christian. All the best stories about his eccentricity – and there were many – were first told, and no doubt embellished, by Longford himself.

Myra Hindley became part of his extended family, the large group of writers, politicians and activists who satisfied his continuing need to be in touch with what was going on in the world. Such consultations would usually take place over lunch at the House of Lords. His conviction that Hindley would one day be his guest there went unfulfilled. She was, in many ways, an unworthy recipient of his concern. He ransomed his good name for her, but, once convinced he was no longer the key to her release, she moved on to other advisers. He knew what was happening, but saw it as natural and inevitable, and continued to strive for her freedom.

Longford's memory will live on, if not for the scale of his achievements then certainly because of his courage, tenacity and nobility in trying. He was a man of great intelligence and moral strength. He is survived by his wife, four sons and three daughters.

FRANCIS 'FRANK' AUNGIER PAKENHAM, 7TH EARL OF LONGFORD · *born* 5 December 1905 · *died* 3 August 2001 ·

ONE-OFFS

...

ROBERT MAXWELL
Dennis Barker and Christopher Sylvester

Robert Maxwell, who has died aged sixty-eight, was one of the most mercurial postwar operators not only in the British media but British commerce generally, a self-made individualist who managed – just – to keep a fitful peace with the mores of a British corporate scene notoriously unaccepting of flamboyant personalities.

He left his native Czechoslovakia as a youth to escape Nazi persecution of the Jews, had a distinguished war that brought him the Military Cross for bravery, set up his own publishing company, Pergamon, shrewdly buying the copyrights of books by academics who wanted reputation more than money, survived being proclaimed in a Board of Trade report as a person unsuited to head a public company and then went on to own the Daily Mirror Group and the *New York Daily News*.

All this was due to the essence of his assertive character forged in his early years. He was born to peasant parents, Michael and Ann Hoch, in Slatinske Doly, a village near a salt mine on disputed territory near the border of Rumania. He always described himself as self-educated. In an obscure period of his life, he acquired at least a smattering of several languages, came to Britain and joined the British army under a series of aliases – du Maurier and Jones as well as Maxwell – because the War Office insisted that refugee soldiers should have false names in case they were captured.

As he was to do later in life in entirely different contexts, Maxwell agitated to get himself towards the centre of the stage, this time in the form of membership of a crack fighting regiment. He joined the 6th Battalion, the North Staffordshire Regiment, in 1943. He landed with his regiment on the beaches of Normandy shortly after the D-Day invasion of the Continent and distinguished himself not only by his bravery but by his skills as a fixer, once exciting admiration and envy by returning to the battlelines with bottles of Calvados.

The bravery was real enough. In January 1945, when the war was in its final months, he was on the Maas River in Holland with some other soldiers, who charged a block of flats in an attempt to retake them from the Germans. A few days previously he had been promoted from Corporal to the commissioned rank of 2nd Lieutenant. Maxwell charged straight across the Germans' line of fire, a perfect target. Large numbers of bullets pinged around him, but all missed. For this heroism he got his Military Cross.

When the fighting stopped, there was anticlimax. He was a man built for battle. He interrogated German prisoners at Iserlohn in the Rhineland, then went to the Control Commission, the Allies' organization quickly set up to manage the industry, economy and life of the defeated Germans. He rose through the Public Relations and Information Services Control, both as an army officer and as a demobbed civilian. His skill as an entrepreneur was finely honed in these circumstances. Keeping the permitted newspapers going meant that the various sections of the services had to bid to the Control Commission for supplies, since none were available on the open market. Maxwell emerged as an organizer extraordinary.

At the same time he was a shareholder in a London import–export company set up by a German. It eventually became Maxwell's company for distributing scientific literature. Maxwell left the Control Commission two years after the end of the war, and started to sell scientific literature to Britain and the US from an office off Trafalgar Square. A deal with the German publishing giant Springer helped establish him in the market. He launched his own company, Pergamon, in 1949.

In 1959 Maxwell began his political career in earnest by being adopted Labour candidate for Buckingham. He won the seat when the Labour government came to power in the 1964 general election and held it until 1970. His relationship with the House of Commons, given his high degree of self-will, was predictably cool. Becoming chairman of the Refreshment Committee of the House of Commons in 1967, he encountered a past year's loss of £33,000 and a bank overdraft of £61,000. He brought in professional advisers from Forte, sold off the wine stocks to raise cash and privatized the liquor, a personally characteristic rather than socialist step. He did not produce the profits he hoped for and after disagreements with other committee members resigned in April 1969.

After losing his parliamentary seat in 1970, he fought twice for Labour at Buckingham in February and October 1974, but his political career, unlike his business career on more than one occasion, did not rise from the ashes, leaving his great energies available for newspaper publishing.

'Notwithstanding Mr Maxwell's acknowledged abilities and energy, he is not in our opinion a person who can be relied upon to exercise proper stewardship of a publicly quoted company.' These words, from the conclusion of the interim report by two Department of Trade inspectors in 1970, were to dog Maxwell for the rest of his business career. Years later, when most people had forgotten the details, he would claim in interviews that a judge had cleared him of all charges. This was disingenuous. What had happened was that Maxwell had complained about the way in which the inspectors had conducted their investigation, arguing that it was a breach of natural justice that their interim report should have been published. A judge had agreed with him, but the Court of Appeal had overruled the judge and castigated Maxwell for his impertinence in attacking the inspectors. Indeed, Lord Justice Lawton praised one of the inspectors for 'the way he dealt with a witness [Maxwell] who tended to be verbose and irrelevant'.

Today, knowing what we do of Maxwell's business resurgence, the inspectors' report still provides fascinating insights into the man's character. Among those who have worked with Maxwell in the newspaper and publishing business, even those who were his admirers, few could disagree with the following judgement: 'He is a man of great energy, drive and imagination, but unfortunately an apparent fixation as to his own abilities causes him to ignore the views of others if these are not compatible.' The DTI inspectors' report was the most damaging setback Maxwell ever suffered. But he demonstrated that resilience for which he later became famous, bouncing back within a few years. This quality may have been only one of the reasons why he was nicknamed the Bouncing Czech, but it was certainly a powerful one.

What was the essence of the charges against Maxwell in the Pergamon–Leasco affair? In 1969 Maxwell's Pergamon opened negotiations with the American entrepreneur Saul Steinberg, whose Leasco Data Processing Corporation was interested in making a bid for Pergamon. At that time, Pergamon (a name which has had many different incarnations under Maxwell's direction over the years) was the publisher of scientific journals and the owner of a subsidiary, ILSC, which published encyclopaedias. During the negotiations, which lasted several months, Maxwell represented to Steinberg that the encyclopaedia business was extremely profitable. This picture proved false. Steinberg withdrew from the deal, and under the old takeover code, the DTI appointed inspectors to investigate the matter. Steinberg's company commenced legal proceedings against Maxwell in the US. What the DTI inspectors found was that Maxwell used transactions between his private family companies and his Pergamon to inflate Pergamon's share price. In July 1974 it was announced discreetly in the *New York Times* that Steinberg had collected $6.25 million from Maxwell and his UK merchant bankers. By 1977 the Director of Public Prosecutions had decided not to bring criminal charges. Maxwell was the fortunate beneficiary of a laxer age in business regulation.

Maxwell later claimed to have turned Pergamon around himself, but a more accurate appraisal would pay tribute to the work of Sir Walter Coutts, the chairman of Pergamon appointed by Grindlay's Bank after the Leasco deal collapsed. Coutts later wrote that because of the hard work that was done by himself, three independent directors, and the company's dedicated staff, 'Mr Maxwell was handed on a plate in 1974 a firm base on which to build the business about which he now (in 1986) boasts.' Sir Walter later offered a scathing analysis of Maxwell's personality to a couple of Maxwell biographers: 'Maxwell has an ability to sublimate anything that stops him getting what he wants. He's so flexible he is like a grasshopper. There is no question of morality or conscience. Maxwell is Number One and what Maxwell wants is the most important thing and to hell with anything else.'

The late 1970s and early 1980s saw Maxwell cutting a new swathe through the British business world, acquiring the British Printing and Publishing Corporation and turning it around from deficit to profit. He was adept at trimming waste, slashing excess manpower, and releasing locked-up assets. One of the key profit centres in his public companies was that of treasury transactions, a sophisticated form of gambling in which he used shareholders' funds to turn a quick profit on international currency dealings and short-term investments in the stock market.

However, Maxwell's ambition had always been to become a national newspaper proprietor, and sixteen years after his first stab at it (his abortive bid for the *News of the World*), he succeeded in purchasing Mirror Group Newspapers from Reed International for £113 million on 13 June 1984. This marked the beginning of the most fascinating period in Maxwell's career, during which he was rarely out of the headlines. Maxwell tried to solve the problem of famine in Ethiopia, he 'rescued' the Commonwealth Games (which was later found to be insolvent), he patronized Neil Kinnock and other Labour politicians, he sued *Private Eye* (successfully) for suggesting that he had tried to buy a peerage, he launched Britain's first twenty-four-hour newspaper (the *London Daily News*), he launched *The European*. He became another Fleet Street legend, notorious for his treatment of editors and journalists as well as print workers.

He took America by stealth rather than by storm, acquiring the prestigious Macmillan Inc. publishing business and the *Official Airlines Guide*, and later the *New York Daily News*. His much-vaunted ambition of a few years ago – to build a business empire in the field of media and communications that would be comparable to one of the seven major multinational companies which dominate the world oil market – foundered on an excess of appetite. Although Maxwell often argued that his global strategy was equity led, not debt led like Rupert Murdoch's, it all amounted to the same thing once the share price of Maxwell Communications Corporation (MCC) began to slide last year. This year the pressures began to pile up, with criticisms in a BBC *Panorama* documentary (which inevitably drew forth libel writs) echoing the judgement of the DTI inspectors in 1970. He had been up to his old trick of using transactions between his private companies, registered in secretive tax havens such as Lichtenstein and Gibraltar, and MCC to bolster MCC's share price.

There was always something rather ridiculous about Maxwell's constant need to prove himself. He was criticized and mocked for his sycophancy towards the satraps of eastern Europe, where Pergamon had done business since the late 1940s. He published the speeches of Husak, Kadar, Ceausescu, Brezhnev, Andropov and Chernenko. A recent interview with Maxwell in the magazine *Playboy* demonstrated the Walter Mittyish aspect of his character. He virtually claimed that he, above all others, had been responsible for persuading the Israeli premier Yitzhak Shamir to show restraint in the teeth of Saddam Hussein's scud attacks during the Gulf War. When asked whether he was more powerful than most politicians, the former Labour MP said: 'Yes, except for the two or three highest people in an administration.'

But if Maxwell was less powerful than he himself believed, he was none-the-less an effective bully. When two hostile biographies were published in early 1987, Maxwell the litigant went on the rampage, seeking injunctions and firing off libel writs to high-street booksellers. The first book, *Maxwell: A Portrait of Power* by Peter Thompson and Anthony Delano, was withdrawn. The second, *Maxwell: The Outsider* by Tom Bower, sold out its hardback print run, but got no further. Maxwell even bought the publishing company, Sphere, which had acquired the paperback rights. Yet when Tom Bower and his publishers, Aurum Press, filed a weighty defence to Maxwell's libel action eighteen months ago, Maxwell decided that discretion was the better part of valour and discreetly allowed the action *Maxwell v. Bower* and others to go to sleep.

Robert Maxwell will be sorely missed as a public figure. Whatever he did, he always made waves. *Private Eye* has created a whole mythology around Cap'n Bob, and will be hard-pressed to find a substitute for his elemental personality. However, many of those who had dealings with him, whether as employees or otherwise, were relieved when they could escape his embrace. Lady Coutts, whose husband picked up the pieces at Pergamon in the early

1970s, had the best parting shot. Following a dinner at Headington Hill Hall, Maxwell's home and business headquarters, the tycoon was saying goodnight to his guests in various of the nine languages which he professed to speak fluently. When it came to Lady Coutts, she spoke to him in Swahili, a language that not even the bombastic Maxwell claimed to understand. She said: Kwaheri ashante sana sitaki kukuona tena. Translated, this means: 'Goodbye. Thank you very much. I don't wish to see you again.'

IAN ROBERT MAXWELL · *born* 10 June 1923 · *died* 5 November 1991 ·

23 May 1992

ELIZABETH DAVID
Christopher Driver

Elizabeth David, who has died at the age of seventy-eight, has been identified with food and cookery for over forty years, and as a researcher and writer in these fields she has been unsurpassed in English since such 'kitchen receipts' were first printed.

Yet she came to her craft and art almost by accident, long after her taste had been formed by significant friendships and early exposure to the whole spectrum of Mediterranean civilization, with Norman Douglas as her mischievous guide. Among her own sex and literary generation, she belonged not with 'cookery writers' but with, say, Sybille Bedford or the late Doris Langley Moore, equally at home in a theatre, a restaurant or an art gallery. (It was Sybille Bedford who remarked memorably that Escoffier's maxim, *faites simple*, does not mean *faites slapdash*.)

The singularity of Elizabeth David was that at the trough of a grin-and-bear-it decade, she saw in postwar British cookery a fossilized shell of unexamined culture, like the wreck of a hotel Stilton, and found the right words for the future: 'Look, taste, anywhere but this.' In 1950 a young Barnsley miner with a broken leg, trying to keep warm in the public library, picked up *A Book of Mediterranean Food*, just published by John Lehmann. As he put it forty years later, 'I did not even bother to look for olive oil, garlic or aubergines – I knew they weren't in the shops. Instead I waited until the plaster came off my leg and travelled to the places Elizabeth David wrote about. I have never been back to Barnsley.'

When her great sequence of palate-looseners – especially *Italian Food* (1954) and *French Provincial Cookery* (1960) – had fired the British middle-class imagination, it was possible for her to sink shafts into the food we have lost in our own tradition, richer by far than the cowed natives supposed. The 'English' books – *Spices, Salt and Aromatics* (1970) and *Bread and Yeast Cookery* (1977) – have never had the same popular appeal, partly because the historian overtook the journalist in the author's temperament: the passion for certainty and comprehensiveness left longer and longer intervals between books, to the alarm of her patient publisher, friend and latterly protector, Jill Norman.

A single life is too short even for the subjects she has made her own. (Her book on ices is probably still incomplete at the time of her death.) But two marks of a great scholar are visible in her work: nothing that she touched will ever have to be redone for want of care, and by breaking so much untilled ground, she left plenty of worms for younger academic blackbirds. Besides, although her astringent critical throwaways in print and conversation could leave people examining their scars for years, serious enquirers could depend on a corresponding generosity with her time and her learning. Her belittling in honours lists disgraced a philistine, ungrateful establishment. On to Westminster Abbey...?

Her human foibles took their own place in that context: not only her sallying forth to dinner with her own bread tucked under her arm but her notorious microphone and camera shyness and her biographical self-effacement, so different from the brazen new world of the food-writing 1990s. One guide editor, brave enough to take her out to lunch at a restaurant he recommended, enquired about her time as an actress. 'How do you know that?' she replied, shocked to find her past penetrated.

However, her occasional pieces, collected in *An Omelette and a Glass of Wine* (1984), and other references build up the profile of a reluctant rebel, slow to find her *métier*, reserved to prickliness, but fiercely loyal to her real friends and their memories. She was one of four daughters born into a Conservative family: her father, Rupert Gwynne, was MP for Eastbourne, and in her mother's family there was a Victorian Home Secretary (Viscount Ridley). Inevitably, she was educated in a girls' school of superior manners and inferior food. But her schooling included a good history teacher, and her capricious mother sent her to learn French in a greedy *famille bourgeoise* in Paris.

At eighteen she left home for the theatre, including the Open Air Theatre in Regent's Park. But her mother, a friend of Marcel Boulestin, also intro-duced her to Lett Haynes and his partner Cedric Morris, the painter and gardener, who at Benton End created one of those odd artistic communities that British culture spawns unpredictably like chanterelles, usually in revulsion from the metropolis, materialism or machinery, or all three. She learnt not only painterly values there but the glories of English country house gardening and cookery, exemplified by Haynes and Morris and, in books, by Mrs C. F. Leyel. Later, when she sought illustrators for her own books, she went to John Minton and Renato Guttuso.

When she met Norman Douglas she was twenty-four and he was seventy-six, but she must already have been good company in Capri. After Capri and the Cyclades the war found her in Cairo, running the Ministry of Information library, marrying a soldier (hence her exploration of British India's culinary colonialism), and exchanging ideas with her Sudanese cook. This gastronomic catholicity was unusual in her background, and if anything in her first book was calculated to horrify an American audience, it was a sentence on the first page: 'Anyone who has lived for long in Greece will be familiar with the sound of air gruesomely whistling through sheep's lungs frying in oil.'

Much of this work suggests a person operating at a certain remove from the daily realisms of London shopping and cooking. This would be misleading, although she needed a stimulus, initially from Anne Scott-James in 1947. She took to food journalism like an Athene, fully armed. Apart from her aesthetic sensibility, her scholarly precision and her delight in eating and drinking, above all she knew how to write a recipe – an exacting form. Throughout a lifetime of domestic cookery, I could always rely on Elizabeth. She would never permit her readers to neglect or scamp a crucial point. There is no room here for her lucid prose and the scope of her allusion, but here is the egg virtuoso passing on the best practice for *œufs en cocotte*:

> …Put the little dishes into the oven (Regulo 5) and take them out as soon as the butter has melted, slide an egg into each, pour a large tablespoon of cream on to the egg, avoiding the yolk, return them to the oven. They will take 4–5 minutes to cook, allowing perhaps ½ minute less for those on the top shelf … Experience and knowledge of the idiosyncrasies of one's own oven [determine] success. No pepper or salt should be added, except at table, but a very little cut fresh tarragon when they come out of the oven is an acceptable addition.

Her influence has been incalculable, and not just because of her repertoire, authority and practicality. She even opened her own kitchen shop in Pimlico, as original as everything she did. Alas, originality and perfectionism are dangerous in commerce, and she was outwitted, her precious name now 'owned' by a concern she no longer controlled: that wound never healed.

In the year of her first book, a British kitchen designer wrote: 'It is important to plan the kitchen well so that you need spend as little time in it as possible, as my women readers will agree ... The sink is undoubtedly the focal point of the room.' Ten years later, Elizabeth wrote for a readership by then in hundreds of thousands: 'Some sensible person once remarked that you spend the whole of your life either in bed or your shoes. Having done the best you can by shoes and bed, devote all the time and resources at your disposal to the building of a fine kitchen. It will be, as it should be, the most comforting and comfortable room in the house.'

Norman Douglas was surely present behind her pen there, for he had a favourite maxim: 'To be miserly towards your friends is not pretty; to be miserly towards yourself is contemptible.' Elizabeth's memory of her friend resulted in a surprise for many a haughty maitre d'hotel and patronizing wine waiter, expecting a lone woman to order the cheapest dish and most humble wine. There is a Bateman-like vignette, some time in the 1950s, of the steward on the Edinburgh–London Express, who yelled at that quietly formidable customer across the rattling crockery and two bemused passengers, 'A bottle, madam? A whole bottle? Do you know how large a whole bottle is?'

ELIZABETH DAVID · *born* 26 December 1913 · *died* 21 May 1992 ·

10 January 1995

PETER COOK
Barry Humphries, Jonathan Miller, Paul Foot and Barry Fantoni

Peter Cook, who has died aged fifty-seven, was pivotal to British satire and comedy. He was educated at Radley College and Cambridge, had two revues running in the West End while still an undergraduate, and became internationally famous at the cusp of the 1960s when the Edinburgh Festival revue, *Beyond the Fringe*, played in the West End and on Broadway. Across thirty-five years, he was quicksilver through films, TV, stage and publishing.

BARRY HUMPHRIES writes: Peter Cook was an anomaly in the world of comedy. He was a romantic figure. Both men and women had enormous crushes on him. Like most true artists of comedy, he was obsessive in his hatreds. He would pursue a joke or the idea for a joke relentlessly until it yielded another and another.

He was a bracing influence for sanity in the sloppy 1960s and his *Private Eye* and its satellites were extensions of his wit and of his scorn. He was a moralist, yet he reserved a special derision for those who made edifying distinctions between destructive and constructive humour. For Peter, it was funny or it wasn't.

Peter's generosity was unusual in a profession notoriously self-seeking and fraught with petty jealousies. The spectacular renaissance of Frankie Howerd was due solely to his fervent advocacy and financial encouragement. My own early (unsuccessful) cabaret efforts in London were sponsored by him, and David Frost's first appearances in the West End were under Peter Cook's aegis. He was the *deus ex machina* of the so-called satire movement of the 1960s and can now be credited with having reinvented British comedy. Cook, a master of improvisation even when drunk, elevated scatology to a lyrical plane. In his later years, he seemed to be careless of his gifts and indifferent to his health: even to life itself. He became inaccessible to those who loved him and sought to help him with his alcoholism.

JONATHAN MILLER: In 1959 a meeting was convened in a Euston Road restaurant by John Bassett, who was putting the revue *Beyond the Fringe* together for the Edinburgh Festival. Dudley Moore, Alan Bennett and I were immediately overwhelmed by the astonishing improvisational productivity of Peter Cook's imagination, which seemed to come from some source completely alien to the person in front of us.

Peter was much more elegant, assured and good-looking than us, which was quite at odds with his disruptive surrealism. When we saw our costumes – uniform grey flannel suits – he was the only one who looked good in it. He was very puzzling to confront. I had seen him in the *Footlights* – an astonishing, strange, glazed, handsome creature producing wierd stuff, the like of which I'd never heard before. I remember his first line when I was shot upright in my seat by him. He was playing some person in a suburban kitchen concealed behind a newspaper. He didn't say a word. But all eyes were drawn to him. Then he rustled the newspaper and simply said, 'Hello, hello, I see the *Titanic*'s sunk again.' One knew one was in the presence of comedy at right angles to all the comedy we'd heard.

I have no idea where it came from. Peter himself, I think, was mystified by it. He ought to have been an extremely successful young diplomat. You felt you were with somebody from the Foreign Office who had suddenly gone completely bananas. He was like one of those discreet people shadowing Douglas Hurd. His father was a colonial diplomat, so that was the world Peter came from. He was a master of linguistic paradox, phrases which you can't invent. I don't think he ever set himself the task of being disruptive. He saw strange obsessional people, and in a strange, almost ventriloquial way, they took possession of him. He had a grasp of a character's idioms, so that people like E. L. Wisty or these mad upper-class judges are memorable in exactly the same way as some of the great Dickens characters.

Peter was always rather distant from us. Later there were reunions, when we would sit at a table and laugh and joke. He was always interested in this strange world of showbiz, celebrity golf, football. Yet he had this phoenix-like capacity to re-emerge. There was that revival when he did those four wonderful and inspired pieces with Clive Anderson a year ago. He hadn't had his time. If anyone could come up with what he did for Anderson, at a time when he was said to have not fulfilled his promise, they would be very grateful.

The fulfilment that he did give was so much greater than what has been given by most people, and at such a level, that it would be rancorous discontent to complain of a lack of other things that he might have done. He gave a great gift to British theatre, and the British comic idiom. There was no one quite like him.

PAUL FOOT writes: As a most unusual and unlikely gloom settles on *Private Eye*'s offices, my memory skips back thirty years to the table at the Coach and Horses pub where the staff of the new magazine gathered each lunch-time. 'This is Peter Cook,' Richard Ingrams was saying, and we shook hands. The conversation was stilted, almost formal, until suddenly something quite mundane seemed to click in Peter's mind and he said something ridiculous. We all laughed. The laughter seemed to jolt him out of his reverie. His eyes sparkled, his face broke into a mighty grin and he was off, leaping from one glorious fantasy to another, while the laughter grew, sucked in the entire pub, inspired him yet again and grew again. I was working for the *Sun* up the road. Every morning I scuttled through my work in the hope that I might inhale another gale of that infectious laughter.

The infectious and collective nature of that laughter explains a lot about *Private Eye*'s success. People still ask: 'Who writes that stuff?' There must, it is assumed, be one author, a single genius. The answer is always the same: 'They all do.' 'They' write collectively, sparking each other off with their laughter. We socialists are always told: 'You can't write by committee'; yet from long happy years revelling to the laughter of this most productive committee, I know you can.

Just as Peter Cook was at his best when others were laughing at him, so the *Eye*'s best satire developed out of communal laughter. Peter made his name on TV and film, but he was funniest when he was unrehearsed. At a rather sombre *Eye* banquet to say goodbye to Richard Ingrams in 1986, Cook rose at the end with nothing in his hand but the menu. He proceeded to read the menu out, commenting at length on the origin of the potatoes and the sprouts, and before long all of us were weeping with laughter.

Peter was a keen observer of what was going on in the world. He was suspicious of rulers of every description, but in particular he detested the secrecy, pomposity and hypocrisy which sustains them. His portrait of Harold Macmillan in *Beyond the Fringe* set the tone for the irreverence of the time, the impatience with old values and dithering, greedy Tory politicians.

When I asked him tentatively if he would open an Anti-Nazi League sports afternoon, he jumped at the chance. After a gracious – rather too gracious – opening speech, he spent the afternoon trying, without success, but with all the fanaticism which he invested in a lifetime's support for Tottenham Hotspur, to win a five-a-side football competition. Peter was also that rare creature – indeed in my philosophy the creature does not exist, so he proved me wrong – the enlightened proprietor. He saved and sustained *Private Eye* more than once, but never gorged himself on it, still less interfered in it.

I recall one dreadful evening where Ken Tynan and Jonathan Miller savaged us for our connections with *Private Eye*. Many of their angry criticisms were justified, but they didn't seem to understand, as Peter Cook did, that *Private Eye* is free publishing; indeed, it is perhaps the only genuine example of regular free publishing in postwar Britain. Peter stuck to his guns, constantly rebuffing his friends' demands to curb the *Eye*'s more unfair attacks.

They are meeting now downstairs to decide what to write in the *Eye* about the death of the real Lord Gnome. But I am quickly comforted by the certainty that if Peter Cook had been asked to comment on his death, he would have made a joke about it.

BARRY FANTONI writes: I first met Peter Cook in autumn 1963, when *Private Eye*'s circulation seemed to have drifted into an irreversible decline from 95,000 to around 15,000. Against this background, Peter Cook re-emerged as a central figure, and one who was, in some senses, to singlehandedly alter the *Eye*'s history. He had just been in America with his hugely successful review *Beyond the Fringe*, and was bristling with self-assurance and full of what seemed to me, as I was then a very junior satirist, an endless stream of extraordinarily original ideas. I confess I was in awe of Peter at the time and remained in awe of him to the day he died. No other satirist I know had the ability to take an idea, no matter how mundane, and develop it into quite wonderful fantasy, while at the same time never losing the point. Peter's contribution to the *Eye*'s revival is specific, and there is a precise moment when this change came about.

Pieces at the *Eye* are always written in concert, with two, three and even more contributors throwing in jokes, while someone writes them down in longhand. On this one occasion, Peter sat down at a typewriter – the only machine in the office, as I recall – and off the top of his head, typed with one finger the opening chapter of a feature called 'Tales of the Seductive Brethren'. Over the months that the *Eye* ran the feature, Peter invented a range of characters (my favourite was a figure called The Clintisorit of Wintistoring) which gripped the readers' imagination, and the 'Tales' became compulsive.

At the same time, Peter introduced the team of Barry Humphries and Nick Garland to the *Eye*. Barry wrote, and Garland drew the 'Adventures of Barry McKenzie', which traced the adventures of an innocent Australian in Swinging London. This strip was an enormous hit and, perhaps more than the tales, became the instrument in *Private Eye*'s resurrection.

I became a close friend. Peter himself said that I was the only member of the editorial staff, besides himself, who knew what a football looked like and had any interest in the world of popular culture. During a big fight or cup match on TV, he would ring me, or I him, and we'd watch the contest in our own homes, while at the same time amusing each other with personal observations. This would have a particular poignancy, and more jokes, if Spurs were playing – Peter was an avid Spurs fan.

It was during such TV phone-ins that more general jokes would come about. The only time I drew a cartoon with a caption by Peter, it arose from such a bout of casual banter. Two men are talking in a pub. One says: 'I'm writing a book.' The other says, 'Neither am I.'

I last saw Peter just before Christmas. We had lunch and he spoke with tears in his eyes about his mother, who had died last summer. He was in many ways more human than I had seen him at any other time. Naturally we laughed a great deal and there was plenty of Cookish humour. But against that he seemed to be harbouring something very deep and personal – perhaps it was a portent, perhaps he knew then more about the condition that was to kill him a month later.

I can't remember his last words to me, but he did say something I did not expect. In public, he was a vital and witty man, with a brain as sharp as a surgeon's, but what he said did not fit this image. He told me that he had no bad friends. He hated no one and to his best knowledge, no one hated him. On the day he died, I think he would be astonished to know the deep love so many continue to feel for him as a man and for his towering genius as a satirist.

PETER EDWARD COOK · *born* 17 November 1937 · *died* 9 January 1995 ·

22 November 1999

QUENTIN CRISP
Veronica Horwell and Estelle Holt

His favourite line was from *A Streetcar Named Desire*: that frail flower Blanche Du Bois saying: 'I never lied in my heart.' How true. Quentin Crisp's honesty, about everything and with himself, made his life valuable. He was emotionally far tougher than butchissimo guys in leathers at the bar, 'carrying their helmets,' as he said, 'even though they've come by bus'.

He had been through and seen through love, sex, gender, fame, failure, poverty, sixty years of deep-pile dust carpeting bedsits, and John Hurt approximating his life in five wigs, mouse to mauve, in the televised version of Crisp's memoir, *The Naked Civil Servant*. And had proved his belief that even if you only lean limply against a wall, but live a very long time (he was ninety when he died), it will give way.

This was all much more than Dennis Pratt, born an Edwardian in Carshalton, Surrey, could have hoped. Miserable boarding-school years longing to vamp not pupils but teachers were followed by a useless journalism course and art school; useless because he already knew what he wanted to do in life, and that was not to do, but to be. He wanted to be celebrated for being himself.

'Blind with mascara and dumb with lipstick,' Crisp stalked brazenly about London, stylized in gesture as a supermodel and as haughty, walking fast, at least when barefoot – his shoes were a hobbling several sizes too small. Martyrdom he expected, and was seldom disappointed: he was slapped across the face without a warning word; followed by crowds; beaten up. 'Who do you think you are?' the scornful hissed. He did not think. He knew. He was proud of being homosexual, which by his definition meant living as a dream of a woman, though without the aesthetic insult of travesty cross-dressing ('My ankles look all wrong in a gown'). He did not come out of the closet. He had never been in one.

There were few sources then to fund a life as an object of art or scandal, and from the day when his father told him not to spread so much butter on his bread, finance was problematic. He worked as a map tracer only until he had been employed long enough to draw 15s 3d. dole weekly, on which he repined in a rented room. It was easier to 'starve supine than erect'. Thereafter, in various decades, he hawked bad commercial art and wrote a treatise on window-dressing; stayed long enough in the art department of a publishers to stash pound notes in drawers to pay for a year off writing a novel as unpublished as his play and, later, musical; and put the faces on 4,000 dolls for shop display units.

Late in the Second World War, when his arty friends were in camouflage (painting it, dear, not wearing it) and he had been totally excluded from call-up on the grounds of 'suffering from sexual perversion', he did find a near-*métier*. The dearth of able-bodied men, any men, meant his country needed him as a freelance art-school model. In a posing pouch cut down from a pair of pants, he performed with vigour, 'as Sistine as hell', crucifying himself on a curtain rail. Crisp returned to modelling, on and off, and in the end demoted to face only, well into his bus-pass years. Explaining its mad ordinariness – he had been no more than a civil servant, although a naked one – he hit on the title for the autobiography.

There was plenty of content for it because making a living had never impeded him from having a life. Nor had any of the usual mortal activities. His clothes were hand-me-downs, jauntily worn. His solitary-by-choice rented rooms were at first frequently changed. Then he settled in a Chelsea boarding house where he left the dust heroically undisturbed through decades: in his whole renegade life, no statement was more outrageous than his 'after the first four years the dirt does not get any worse'.

Physically, he decided as a boy that masturbation granted the intellect freedom from the body. Philosophically, he made a choice to be happy. Happiness was the state of those who lived in the continuous present. That was a state not then part of the British Empire.

Crisp had earlyish intimations of happiness when the fleet was in at Portsmouth, summer of 1937, a carnival of uniforms. Shortly after, with the help of Hitler ('When war was declared I went out and bought two pounds of henna'), six years of happy present followed. It wasn't the sex, although 'as soon as the bombs started to fall, London became like a paved double-bed' and Uncle Sam sent over supplies of lend-lease Americans in deliciously tight kit. It was more that those Americans proved that their nation really did pursue happiness. When they ran short after D-Day ('Here's a GI,' said a party-giver, 'he's a bit small but they're getting difficult to find') Crisp felt deflated. He was nearly forty and changed the henna for a blue rinse, hence his crack about being one of the stately homos of England. He had been before the courts on a charge of soliciting, which he gracefully disproved, thus causing the police to dislike him enough to ban him from Soho and Fitzrovia. (Once, he had been on the game for six months, but was hopeless at it – looking for love, not loot.)

He took to leading a 'rich full life by proxy' in the 'forgetting chamber' of the cinema stalls and not coming out again until driven forth by a dislike of the New Wave, and the sudden realization of liberalization in the 1960s, when his old urban playgrounds were declared 'a safari park for hooligans'. Crisp found himself a rare survival, a media trophy.

First came the Third Programme to tape his Crisperanto aphorisms. Then, in 1968, Jonathan Cape accepted *The Naked Civil Servant*, worth 3,500 copies and £300. As ever ahead of his time, Crisp had realized that most publishing was about personality, not words on pages (though his words were funny and profound), so the publication gave him access to audiences, starting with a *Late Night Line-Up* show. Even better was the TV documentary shot in his room, so small the camera crew had to lurk in the bathroom lest they upset Quentin's cup of Complan. Dramatist Philip Mackie laboured on scripting *Civil Servant* for the movies but could find no production money. Crisp wrote *How to Have a Life Style* and practised tentative live lunch-time theatre performing, also picking up a few pounds in the public-speaking racket. Mackie's script was finally directed by Jack Gold for Thames TV in 1975, and made the rest of Crisp's life. John Hurt became Crisp's representative on earth, and Crisp became 'part of the fantasies of total strangers'. What was beginning to be the official gay community hated his pronouncements, accusing him of being the Martin Luther King of the movement in youth and Uncle Tom in age: he replied that his crusade was for identity and individuality, rather than the lesser right to sexual freedom.

His individuality was in demand. His second theatrical season was packed, and he upgraded himself to a later hour with *An Evening with Quentin Crisp*. He took advice from Harold Pinter and Bette Midler ('That's right, baby: smile') and was perfectly patient about playing in Chipping Norton, Mold, and major cities of Australia. And then he crossed the Atlantic. First to Toronto for a day to publicize *Civil Servant*. Then to New York, same mission;

he opened his arms to the skyscraperscape like a child towards a Christmas tree. He returned there to stage *An Evening* at the Player's Theater. 'Am I illegal?' he asked a cop who approached him in the street; 'No,' said NY's finest, 'we just wondered how the show was going.' 'Americans want you to want something so they can give it to you,' Crisp wrote. He wanted NY. They gave it him. The airport immigration official said to him quietly: 'Is it nice to be vindicated at last?'

At the age of seventy-two, in 1980, he became NY's oldest runaway in a rooming house on the Lower East Side, just up the block from the Hell's Angels: a place for forgetting. Not a second childhood, but the adolescence he could barely have imagined – making sure, as he wrote, that when they laid him in his coffin there was not anything inside him he had not unpacked.

Crisp was candid about the 'fatuous affability of celebrity', otherwise known as the smiling and nodding racket, told Jay Leno he could live on hospitality peanuts and champagne, graciously accepted his official Queen's Birthday parties hosted by friends and invitations to almost anything. His occasional movie journalism remained horribly shrewd, since he had always understood the rules of onscreen games of pretence and desire, and he was a wicked descant voice at gay events – drag acts wore 'fishnet tights through which whole haddocks could have escaped' he noted, wondering what happened if innocents at the bar asked chaps clad in chaps how their ranch was doing.

He began to be paid to perform in films he called festival cinema, 'never to be shown to real people', going into servitude to publicize them nationwide at art cinemas. There was Jonathan Nossiter's documentary *Resident Alien*, also the title of Crisp's NY journal, and Sally Potter's *Orlando*, in which his Elizabeth I was an icon beyond sex who had, however, not quite outlived flattery. He also failed to dance the Madison in the Hollywood movie *Philadelphia* and wrote about location shooting with Tom Hanks with the same surprised thankfulness he felt about having a day out with Sylvester Stallone's mother in full diamonds.

He feared intimacy – and yet adored company, investing to the end much of his energy performing for strangers. He did not deny the occasional dark *après-midi* of the soul, when his deafness made it harder to receive pleasurable and frightening phone-calls; or when he was ambulanced suddenly and handled as though his body were already dead. But he had known very much worse times for the spirit and would prove it in two quotes.

During his early TV fame, he had kept a modelling appointment at a suburban art school. His old employer taunted him that he had not managed to escape real life: 'You were a nine days' wonder, weren't you?' 'Yes, madam,' he had said, hearing again the echoes of 'Who do you think you are?' But in the New World, a black passer-by reacted to Crisp's face in fullest slap with an enthusiastic: 'Well, my, you've got it all on today.'

He claimed not to fear dying alone. 'If you die with people,' he explained, 'you have to be polite. You have to say give my love to Monica.'

ESTELLE HOLT writes: When I first met Mr Crisp in 1939 his hair was red and I thought he was like a character in a Victorian children's story, supernatural, supercilious, all-wise. Since then people have likened him to a dotty aunt, a Victorian lady explorer, Lady Diana Cooper and a Siamese cat. He did often sound like Mrs Thatcher. Lots of Victorian values, self-reliance. He would go, he said, from his cradle to his grave without a debt. His only worry was that he might not keep up with the cost of living, however simple his needs.

To go around as he did took courage. Other people declared it exhibitionism or masochism. But I think it was really a cussed refusal to compromise. 'To refuse to compromise is a form of insanity,' he once said to me. Yet it led him to startling sanity.

He wrote most of the material for an intimate review, never staged because the money ran out, but a lot of which I can still quote; a play, *Man With a Sword*, set in the Trojan wars, that he found years later had been up for a treatment at a Hollywood studio; and a play, influenced by Pirandello, wholly brilliant and playable. When I asked him once what he would like in his obituary, he said: 'Mr Crisp thanks the world for letting him stay so long.'

QUENTIN CRISP (DENNIS PRATT) • *born* 25 December 1908 • *died* 21 November 1999 •

8 January 1999

HENRIETTA MORAES
Tim Hilton

Henrietta Moraes, who has died at the age of sixty-seven, was one of those people whose life was divided into two periods: the first devoted to drink or drugs (both, in her case), while the second half was clean and sober. Her autobiography, *Henrietta*, published in 1994, surveyed her dissipated past and ends with the brave, contrite sentence 'My grandchildren and my dog have never seen me drunk, and I trust and pray that they never will.'

This dog, Max, who survives her, is a long-haired dachshund of equable temperament, who accompanied his volatile mistress in the routines of her later life. Henrietta, infirm and poor, lived in one room in Chelsea. Rising later than many of her neighbours, she and Max would set off for the King's Road in search of the *Daily Mail* (the only paper she liked) and three packets of Camels. Charity shops were monitored for her gorgeous, dowdy clothes, which she sometimes stole, on the grounds that she herself deserved charity. In various chemists' shops, pills were bought, not of the dangerous variety. She simply liked taking pills. In her last illness there was a horrible professionalism in the way she shook open the various packets of painkillers and swallowed them down.

She was born Audrey Wendy Abbott in Simla in 1931. Her father, who was in the Indian Air Force, deserted her mother. Little Audrey was brought up in England by a horrific grandmother, who disciplined her with a leather strap. There was an education, of sorts, then a spell at a secretarial college. She thought of becoming an actress, but by 1950 was working as a model in various London art schools.

In this year she met her first husband, the film-maker Michael Law, who gave her the name Henrietta. They set up home in an attic in Dean Street. Now began her career as the queen of Soho's artistic life. Her haunts, besides many others, were the Carlisle (nowadays the Nelly Dean), the Café Torino, the French Pub (which also functioned as her bank), the Gay Hussar and the Gargoyle Club. At the Gargoyle, where she was always the youngest person present, she mixed with such notables as Cyril Connolly, Brian Howard, her best friend Francis Wyndham, Philip Toynbee and Donald Maclean; but was more at home in the company of artists, who included Michael Wishart, 'Johnny Minton and twenty sailors', Francis Bacon and Lucian Freud. She drank all day and her love life was uninhibited.

Henrietta was close to Minton, who financed her in many ways and introduced her to his friend the body-builder Norman Bowler, whom she shortly married. Bowler was the father of Henrietta's children, Joshua and Caroline, who survive her. During their childhood she was intermittently employed running a coffee bar in David Archer's bookshop in Greek Street. It was through Archer, always interested in young writers, that she met the elfin Indian poet Dom Moraes. This was in 1956, when her marriage to Bowler ended. Moraes was eighteen, and on his way to Oxford.

In 1957 the rich, generous, alcoholic Minton bequeathed Henrietta a house in Chelsea, just off Cheyne Walk. Here she seduced Moraes, to give him a good start to his undergraduate career, and began the short, best years of her life. She was often in Oxford and (Ved Mehta's autobiographical *Up At Oxford* tells us) was an alarming visitor to the university. The Bohemia of Soho and Chelsea was her true home, and perhaps she was the muse of that society. Certainly she is commemorated in many paintings, particularly in canvases by Francis Bacon.

Henrietta sat for Lucian Freud in the early 1950s. He painted slowly: there may not be more than three of her portraits from his brush. Bacon worked quickly. Henrietta thought that he painted her eighteen times. When she told me this, she could not remember clearly, and in any case the situation is confused. For Bacon's portraits were derived from pornographic photographs of Henrietta taken by their mutual friend John Deakin. Though he used these photos, Bacon also needed Henrietta's naked presence in the studio, for reasons apparent to anyone who ever met her. Some models inspire painters by their looks, others by their personality. Henrietta was foul-mouthed, amoral, a thief, a violent drunkard and a drug addict. Yet she was witty, wonderfully warm and lovable. Her presence in any room immediately told you that life is more thrilling than we dull folk imagine. She had a good heart. Never was a woman less demure, but other women liked Henrietta and often got her out of scrapes. And her aura of danger must have helped the mood of Bacon's paintings.

Henrietta married Dom Moraes in 1961, and lived with him, on and off, until he left the Chelsea house one day to buy cigarettes and never returned. In the early 1960s she began to take drugs, as though the immense intake of booze was not enough to satisfy the cravings of her addictive personality. Normally forthcoming, she was quiet about the origin of her drug habits. From odd remarks I gathered that it began after the Eichmann trial in Jerusalem in 1961. *The Times of India* had sent her new husband there to report. Every day she sat with him in the courtroom. A more devastating honeymoon can scarcely be imagined. Henrietta, not by nature a political person, was a great hater of prejudice and of people in power. In the next years she moved from the art world to the hippy scene. Every drug, except heroin, was eagerly consumed. The Chelsea house was lost. There were long expeditions in gypsy caravans to New Age shrines in the Celtic West Country. In the late 1960s Henrietta and some companions took four years to travel from London to Wales. She enjoyed life in Ireland, where there were young, upper-class addicts in ramshackle mansions. For a time – she could not remember how long – Henrietta was a general assistant to Marianne Faithfull. Many other things about these times were forgotten.

Back in London, her head buzzing with amphetamines and Carlsberg Special Brew, she had an unsuccessful career as a cat burglar. After her release from Holloway prison she settled down somewhat. She became sober, with only one or two backslidings, when doctors found cirrhosis of the liver. Alas, she did not write enough in recent times. Short stories remain unpublished. A further volume of memoirs was to be called *Encore Henrietta*. Another putative title was 'Fuck Off, Darling', her famous catchphrase from the old Soho days. She spent last Christmas Day with her agent and helper Alexandra Pringle. She was as exciting and as beautiful as ever, also very kind to all the children. Max is safe with Maggi Hambling.

HENRIETTA MORAES (AUDREY WENDY ABBOTT) ·
born 22 May 1931 · *died* 6 January 1999 ·

28 February 2002

SPIKE MILLIGAN
Stephen Dixon

Spike Milligan, who has died aged eighty-three of kidney failure, was once talking about Eccles, his favourite *Goon Show* character:

> 'Eccles represents the permanency of man, his ability to go through
> anything and survive. They are trying to get off a ship on the Amazon
> and lower a boat. When they get to the shore Eccles is already there.
> 'How did you get ashore?'
> 'Ho hum, I came across on that log.'
> 'Log … that's an alligator!'
> 'Ooh. I wondered why I kept getting shorter.'

That brief exchange, recognizable instantly as something only Milligan could have written, does tell us something about this troubled, gifted man, with his unique mind and puzzled pity for humanity. Jimmy Grafton, who co-wrote many of the early shows, maintained that Eccles was the nearest thing to Milligan's own id – a very simple, uncomplicated creature who doesn't want to be burdened with any responsibility and just wants to be happy and enjoy himself. Grafton added: 'Spike achieved a reputation for eccentricity and has become, by his own choice, a sort of court jester. You begin to wonder to what extent in some circumstances the eccentricity is involuntary and to what extent it is deliberate. He can always get out of trouble by going a little mad.'

Milligan never achieved Eccles's simple dream of happiness, and comedy is richer for his failure. He lived his life at the end of his mind's tether and was always a man of seemingly irreconcilable contradictions: an anarchist with a passion for conservation, a vulnerable and acutely sensitive exhibitionist, a sophisticated person who preferred to retain a vision of childlike purity. He was often distinctly unsettling, both offstage and as a writer/performer. The writer and jazz singer George Melly, while admitting that Milligan was not the sunniest person all the time, added that his was 'the greatest mind in what is loosely called comedy'.

George Orwell's assertion that 'whatever is funny is subversive' was never truer than in the case of Milligan. He didn't invent surrealistic radio comedy – nor did he ever claim to – but he opened up the medium with his uncluttered anarchic vision, and his influence since the early 1950s has been vast. It took its toll: 'I was trying to shake the BBC out of its apathy. I had to fight like mad and people didn't like me for it. I had to bang and rage and crash. I got it right in the end, and it paid off, but it drove me mad in the process ... I'm unbalanced. I'm not a normal person, and that's a very hard thing to have placed upon you in life.'

Milligan was born in Poona, India. He was the son of an Irish captain in the Royal Artillery, and Irishness, represented by his contempt for authority and his free-wheeling humour – one thinks of the novelist Flann O'Brien – always ran through his work. His father was a frustrated entertainer who did impressions of G. H. Elliott, the 'Chocolate-Coloured Coon', at camp concerts, but never had the confidence to turn professional, and Milligan appeared at such concerts from an early age. 'I wasn't consciously aware of it,' he said, 'but I had had enough of the British Empire. *The Goons* gave me a chance to knock people my father and I had to call "Sir". Colonels. Chaps like Gritpipe-Thynne with educated voices who were really bloody scoundrels.'

Milligan was educated at the Convent of Jesus and Mary, Poona, and, after his father was posted to Rangoon in 1929, at the Brothers de La Salle; the family stayed in Burma until 1933, when they returned to England to what Milligan described as a fairly impoverished life and where his education continued at the South East London Polytechnic in Lewisham. He worked in a nuts and bolts factory, but had already decided to become an entertainer, and learned to play the ukulele, guitar and trumpet. At one point he won a Bing Crosby crooning competition at the Lewisham Hippodrome.

When the war broke out he joined his father's old regiment and served in North Africa, where he first met Harry Secombe. He began to organize music and comedy shows for the armed forces entertainment organization ENSA with Secombe and others, and was wounded in Italy. His war experiences later formed the basis for a number of bestsellers, including *Adolf Hitler, My Part in His Downfall* (1971), *Monty, My Part in his Victory* (1976) and *Mussolini, His Part in my Downfall* (1978).

Back in civvies in 1946, he formed a trio and started the weary round of agents and audition rooms. The act failed to generate any enthusiasm, and when it broke up Milligan 'sort of wandered around'. It was during these wanderings that he renewed his friendship with Secombe, who had been struggling along as a comic at the Windmill Theatre in London's West End which, in a pre-strip club era, provided static nude tableaux. He also made the acquaintance of another young hopeful, Peter Sellers, and the wild-haired and equally anarchic Michael Bentine. All gravitated to Jimmy Grafton's pub in Westminster, where they would do turns in the backroom to entertain each other. And it was there that the seeds of the *Goon Show* were sown.

Grafton was writing jokes for the radio comedian Derek Roy and, impressed by Milligan's unique view of the world, asked him to co-write some material. In this way Milligan wrote for several top comics of the day – Bill Kerr, Alfred Marks and even Frankie Howerd. He also wrote for Secombe and Sellers, who had started to become established, in a modest way, as radio performers. Sellers had the best contacts and first put the idea for the *Goon Show* to the BBC ('Goon' came from a strange being in the Popeye cartoons which Milligan loved).

The corporation was lukewarm, but agreed to give the show – starring Sellers, Milligan, Bentine and Secombe – a trial run under the title *Crazy People*. Thus it began in May 1951, swiftly changing its title and losing Bentine, whose surreal style clashed with Milligan's. It ran, with twenty-six shows a year, for nine years. It toured the variety theatres as a stage show in the early 1950s, and it was on this tour that Milligan's emotional imbalance began to assert itself. In Coventry his solo spot went badly and he strode to the footlights and raged at the audience: 'You hate me, don't you?' Receiving an affirmative, he threw his trumpet to the stage and stamped on it, and when this was greeted with appreciative applause, left the stage and locked himself in his dressing room. Knowing about their friend's mental instability, Secombe and Sellers broke down the door, fearing that he had tried to kill himself. He hadn't, but it was an omen of unhappy times to come.

Milligan, with or without Grafton or Larry Stephens, wrote all the shows, with Eric Sykes drafted in to help on occasion. Although the show could hardly have existed without Milligan's participation, his difficult behaviour kept him at constant loggerheads with the BBC. However, it was when the programmes ended – at Milligan's instigation – in 1960 that his personal demons started to dominate his private and professional life. 'When the Goons broke up I was out of work,' he said. 'My marriage ended because I'd had a terrible nervous breakdown – two, three, four, five nervous breakdowns, one after other. *The Goon Show* did it. That's why they were so good.'

Because of the 'difficult' label, he almost had to beg for work, and the first to respond was the actor-manager Bernard Miles, who asked him to play Ben Gunn in *Treasure Island* at the Mermaid Theatre on the edge of the City of London. It was during its successful run that Milligan and John Antrobus wrote the bleak comedy *The Bed-Sitting Room*, which was set in the aftermath of the third world war. It, too, opened at the Mermaid, in 1963, with Milligan appearing as a sort of disruptive 'chorus', and then went to the Duke of York's Theatre and the Comedy Theatre. In 1970 the play was made into a film.

His next piece, *Oblomov*, was just as successful, opening at the Lyric Theatre, Hammersmith, in 1964. It was based on the Russian classic by Ivan Goncharov, and gave Milligan the opportunity to play most of the title role in bed. Unsure of his material, on the opening night he improvised a great deal, treating the audience as part of the plot almost, and he continued in this diverting manner for the rest of the run, and on tour as *Son of Oblomov*.

In the late 1960s he did a number of television series, notably the *World of Beachcomber* and *Q5*. He also became a favourite on TV chat shows, although it was with some trepidation that the host – be he Michael Parkinson, Eamonn Andrews or Terry Wogan – would introduce him. Milligan rarely had much of an inkling of what he was going to do, even at far more formal, scripted occasions. 'I turn up on the day,' he said. 'They point me at the audience and I do it.'

He also turned his attention to the cinema. His films included *The Magic Christian* (1971), *The Devils* (1971), *The Three Musketeers* (1973), *The Last Remake of Beau Geste* (1977) and *Monty Python's Life of Brian* (1978). On the the big screen there was not marked success, for it was impossible to get near the essence of Milligan in short, carefully rehearsed takes.

He worked harder than almost any entertainer one can think of, but seemed to have an imperfect grasp of what was good and what was dashed-off self-indulgence in his prolific output – a *Private Eye* cartoon in 1984 had a bookshop with a sign in the window: 'Spike Milligan will be here to write his latest book at three o'clock.' Novels, memoirs, verse – words gushed from him in a torrent.

He seemed to mellow in later years, but there was always a hint of the dangerous spark that had brought him to the brink of despair so many times and lit beacons of laughter to cleanse us all. In 2000, to a clutch of awards was added an honorary knighthood. It was honorary because – and earlier the cause of considerable furore – his father's Irish background meant that he was denied automatic British citizenship and thus the official title.

His first marriage, to June Marlowe, ended in divorce. His second wife, Patricia Ridgeway, died in 1978. He is survived by his third wife, Shelagh Sinclair; they were married in 1983. He leaves two daughters and a son from his first marriage, and a daughter from his second.

TERENCE ALAN (SPIKE) MILLIGAN · *born* 16 April 1918 · *died* 27 February 2002

6 March 2003

HARDY AMIES
Colin McDowell

It is not so much that the couturier Hardy Amies lived a fraction too long to do his reputation any good; it is more that he gave in to the vanity that so frequently afflicts the aged survivor. And certainly, he was a survivor. Reaching the age of ninety-three was remarkable enough, but even more amazing was the vigour the man commanded right to the end: past the age of eighty he was active enough to go sailing, and was still playing tennis. And his capacity to down a Bloody Mary was awe-inspiring.

All the sadder, then, that he allowed himself to be betrayed by the news media. As his judgement slipped, Amies became prey to ruthless editors who encouraged him to say sloppy things, exposing his envy of the young and displaying in public his understandable resentment and bewilderment that fashion had moved on, leaving him stranded, surrounded by nothing other than the shreds of his belief in the past excellences of the glory days of *haute couture*.

His attack on the modern British couturiers John Galliano and Alexander McQueen, published in the *Spectator* in 1997, was just silly – appearing as the ramblings of a vain old man, determined not to acknowledge that the fashion world had undergone a radical change since his day. Any editor worthy of the name would have spiked it. That year he was similarly betrayed in the *Sunday Telegraph*, in an interview in which a journalist egged him on to be indiscreet about the Queen – he, who had always been so punctilious in not giving any details of what went on during the fittings at the palace. And he, who kept his comments, often hilarious in their waspish observation of HM and her entourage, for only his closest and most trustworthy friends. And yet the piece was published.

Such manipulation of an old man was distressing, especially as those in the know were aware that they were the cry of a man frustrated and hurt by the fact that he had been removed from all control of the firm which, after all, he had founded and brought to triumphant maturity, keeping it going when all about him London couture houses were closing, never to open again. He was a man who, for all of his life, had been a control freak, but whose business acumen was poorly rated by the new shareholders at Hardy Amies – they all but banned him from the premises bearing his name.

His observations were also the late-flowering self-indulgence of a man who, it seems, had always rather fancied himself as a writer – and had, in his youth, hoped to be a journalist. He could not resist the flattery of being in print.

But all of that was Hardy Amies past his prime. The man who was famed as the Queen's dressmaker was of different clay. Witty, sharp and alert to everything happening in society and the arts, Amies in his prime was a marvellous companion – provided you could stomach his snobbishness. After a queen, Hardy Amies dearly loved a duchess and considered a duke not only a cynosure but the arbiter of all things which mattered – which, in his view, were to do with dress, deportment and manners, dominated by the standards of a class long past its prime. Middle-class to the tips of his talented fingers, Hardy was in great awe of the aristocracy and tried to ape them as much as he dared. Although he frequently referred to himself as a 'humble shopkeeper', he in fact fooled nobody. Amies was consumed with arrogance, and confident in the position which he had carved for himself both socially and creatively.

To anyone who did not know him, all of this must have made the man sound unsympathetic. Despite the fact that he could be monumentally difficult – a trait shared with every couturier I have ever met myself – nothing could be less true. All was redeemed by a quick intelligence, a sharp wit and a sparkling sense of humour.

He was born in Maida Vale, west London. His father was a civil servant working for the London County Council, and his mother was a saleswoman who, until her marriage, had worked at a court dressmaking establishment in the capital's Bond Street. He had a sister, and also a brother, who had Down's syndrome. Amies was educated at Brentwood School, Essex, where he made a name for himself in school theatricals playing female roles. He left in 1927, and was interviewed for a job by the editor of the *Daily Telegraph*, who advised his father to spend money on sending him abroad, rather than to university. Amies worked in France and Germany and returned home fluent in the language of both countries.

Although he had no experience in fashion – his job in Germany was with the weighing-machine firm Avery's – a letter he sent to an aunt, describing a fellow guest's dress at a dinner party, ended up landing him his first job in fashion. The dress described was worn by the wife of the owner of the fashionable sportswear firm Lachasse, whose designer, Digby Morton, had left to set up his own fashion house. Amies – totally untried – took over his role, although what he was to do was never actually spelled out to him. The year was 1933.

His early experiences at Lachasse, a firm which specialized in tailoring, never left him: the Amies name was always based on his tailored clothes rather than on his dressmaking. Amies was ambitious and, by 1935, he had become Lachasse's managing director as well as design supremo. But his success at Lachasse left him chafing at the fact that the firm was not his, and he could therefore never exert full control. He determined to rectify the situation, but his plans were scuppered by the outbreak of war in 1939.

Lachasse closed and Amies joined up with the services. His linguistic skills proved valuable, and he moved up the ranks in the Intelligence Corps to Lieutenant Colonel. He did not give up designing. The Government allowed couturiers time off to continue work in fashion, specifically for its own Utility scheme, launched to produce well-designed clothes in accordance with its imposed wartime restriction, and to create luxury couture to sell abroad for dollars to help the war effort.

In 1946 Amies was demobilized, and set about realizing his interrupted dream of having his own fashion house, which would give him absolute control over everything. He bought a bombed-out Georgian house, 14 Savile Row, which had once belonged to the dramatist Sheridan, and began repairing it while recruiting staff. Despite crippling postwar shortages of materials and workers, he knew he was back in business.

It was an amazing time to be a young couturier. In February 1947 Christian Dior showed his first collection, which introduced the New Look – long, wide skirts underpropped by petticoats, and tiny waists constricted by corsets. Its impact was huge, and it instantly put couture back in the fashion lead, making it newsworthy as well as desirable, even to women who could never hope to afford it. All designers swung behind such a powerful statement and produced their own versions of the look, but Hardy Amies had been there a little earlier than Dior. His 1946 collections had emphasized exactly what were to become the components of the New Look, but they lacked Dior's impact because shortages made it impossible for Amies to give his designs the extravagance which characterized those of the French house.

However, they brought Amies a loyal North American following, which he cannily capitalized on by going there, visiting the great stores and captivating customers by his very English looks and also his extreme English voice. He was not only a couturier, he was also a social catch in the way in which Cecil Beaton was in North America – and for the same reasons.

In 1955 Amies became one of the Queen's dressmakers, 'By Appointment', a post considered at that time to be a great accolade. He had been supplying her with clothes since her Canadian tour of 1950. Whereas Norman Hartnell, the doyen of royal dressing at the time, concentrated on her evening dresses, Hardy provided the royal back with beautifully cut suits and coats in the manner of Balenciaga and Givenchy. It is a moot point whether or not the royal connection vitiated Amies's design output. Certainly, all royal clothes were subject to stringent rules and regulations, but it must be remembered that London fashion in the 1950s was largely dominated by couturiers who were all creating clothes in the style chosen by the Queen. There was none of the extravagance of imagination or richness of ideas to be found in Paris. Quite simply, the French capital led and the London couturiers followed. The last thing their clients wanted was any sort of originality, at least until it had been seen and sanctified across the Channel.

Amies had been creating a ready-to-wear line since 1950, and in 1959 he added a range of men's wear. He became design adviser to the men's multiple tailoring firm Hepworth's and was a huge success, having an influence on how men dressed in every high street in Britain. He was also beginning to build up a strong group of licensees, who paid for the privilege of marketing his lines for men and women across the globe, including the highly lucrative Japanese market, where the 'By Appointment' label made him a hot property.

His business skill only once let him down. The late 1960s and early 1970s, when fashion was besotted with the casual dress of youth, were especially taxing times for couture houses. In 1973 Amies sold his company to Debenhams, in order to generate capital and to ensure expansion in an increasingly difficult financial climate. It was a disaster, although he always maintained that the experience was not entirely unhappy. On one side, the problem was that Debenhams never really understood the subtleties of running a couture house and all its ancillary components, and on the other, Amies's psychological difficulties in not having the reins in his hands alone. It was a great relief to both sides when he bought back control of his company in 1980. In May 2001 he finally sold the firm to the Luxury Brands Group.

In addition to the normal areas of design, Amies was frequently asked to design uniforms and special clothing for groups ranging from the Oxford University Boat Club to the Stock Exchange guides. He dressed many West End productions and designed for films, most notably for Stanley Kubrick's *2001: A Space Odyssey*. An inveterate traveller, he frequently visited Tokyo, Sydney, New York (where he kept a flat on the upper east side of Manhattan) and most big cities in North America. But his greatest joys were to be found in England. He was a passionate opera-goer with a lifelong devotion to Covent Garden and to Glyndebourne. His happiest days were spent in the garden of his Oxfordshire home, a converted village school with nothing pretentious about it but everything perfect to the last detail.

Amies lived an admirably smooth-running life, which was a testament to his business acumen, organizational ability and creative energy. He had the zest to enjoy his work and the common sense not to allow it to get in the way of his play. He appreciated the good things in life and was a connoisseur of good food, fine wines and firm male flesh – all of which he enjoyed to the full in his long and distinguished life. And, of course, he wrote. His autobiography was published in two parts: *Just So Far* appeared in 1954, and *Still Here* came out thirty years later.

Amies received several honours during his life. In 1946 Belgium recognized his war work with the Ordre de la Couronne. In 1977, the year of the royal jubilee, he was made a commander of the Royal Victorian Order and, in 1989, knight commander of the Victorian Order. His fashion awards included a *Harper's Bazaar* award in 1962, the *Sunday Times* Special Award in 1965, and the British Fashion Council Hall of Fame Award in 1989.

EDWIN HARDY AMIES · *born* 17 July 1909 · *died* 5 March 2003 ·

DIANA, PRINCESS OF WALES

Charles Nevin

Her life, it was often said, although not so much of late, was like a fairy-tale. She was, it was often said, though not so much of late, a fairy-tale princess. And although this was one of those typically lazy Fleet Street labels, you could see the truth in it when the young Diana Spencer first emerged blushing and blinking into this lens and that lens, and all those lights and clicks and whirrs and shouts.

For the young prince had been seeking a bride; but, as with princes, a pure bride of noble breeding. And these were in such short supply in the kingdom that some despaired of his ever finding one. Until, suddenly, she was there.

Our first proper view was the one of the nursery assistant, shyly pretty, caught in the playground, innocent of the sunlight and the lenses and clicks and whirrs and friendly shouts and guile that would make her skirt entirely diaphanous. It was a fairy-tale moment; but a twentieth-century fairy-tale moment, with a knowingness among the smiles. And, as we all ought to know by now, twentieth-century fairy-tales do not end happily.

No, they spin faster and faster, whirligigs powered by the pursuit of fame and profit and every last detail, a conspiracy of interests heavy with the inevitability of tragedy, large or small, but never underplayed or undersold, and always with the lights and the headlines.

None other has come close to matching the life and death of Diana Spencer. And not only in its twists, turns, heroes, speculations, confirmations, villains, stark reliefs and immense, unrelenting profile in which every quality, every event was endlessly exaggerated and simplified for the century's easier digestion. Here, also, the century met the monarchy in a collision that may in time prove as fatal as the desperate event in Paris: a collision between the light and the magic that royalists had long warned against but in the end proved powerless to prevent, and even helped to fix. But, despite all our cynicism and countless hindsights, it still did not seem quite like that as Lady Diana Spencer stood in the nursery playground on that day in 1980, posing for that photograph.

Then, in royal terms, it seemed a happy, clever, almost perfect match. A public tiring of an endlessly energetic bachelor prince who nevertheless seemed to be achieving little, publicly or privately, was delighted with Lady Diana, as were the photographers and their editors. She was fresh, unknown, beguilingly shy, already with the appealing and trademark upward glance.

And, most importantly for the photographers and their editors, and unlike many another royal or would-be royal, she was genuinely pretty and in possession of that most vital of twentieth-century qualities: she was very, very photogenic. Good news, then, for Fleet Street, especially at the lower end, where Rupert Murdoch and his *Sun* newspaper in particular were increasingly alive to the attractions for readers of royalty, of a young and fresh royalty.

Buckingham Palace's more traditional concerns were equally satisfied. This might be the first English woman to marry an heir to the throne for over 300 years. But this was no common English woman. Lady Diana's father, the eighth Earl Spencer, had been an equerry to both George VI and the Queen. Her maternal grandmother, Ruth, Lady Fermoy, was a close friend and lady-in-waiting to the Queen Mother.

Diana was born on 1 July 1961 at Park House, on the Sandringham estate, in the same room in which her mother, Frances, had been born. In her childhood, she had played regularly with Prince Andrew and Prince Edward. This was a girl who knew the form. But also a girl unaffected by the hauteur and distance that usually go with the form.

Journalists who spent a lot of time in the early days of her courtship with the Prince of Wales on the doorstep of the ungrand flat she shared in Coleherne Court in Kensington were surprised to find how approachable, how friendly she was. If it is easy to see the seeds of future troubles in this now, it would have been much easier then to see other seeds in other parts of her background. But such was the enthusiasm, high and low, for Diana; and such was the shortage of other supposedly suitable mothers for a future monarch that little attention was paid to a childhood that had been anything but stable or happy. She had been only six when her mother left to take up with the lively and witty Peter Shand Kydd, a businessman and something of a contrast to her father, whose friends and pursuits she found dull. By accounts, Lady Fermoy was determined that custody would remain with Diana's father, the then Viscount Althorp, and not with her daughter, irrevocably deemed, even in the 'swinging sixties', a 'bolter'.

Diana's fall from a horse while in her mother's care formed part of the custody proceedings. She was later to recall rows and violence between her parents. When her mother left, she would later recollect, she and her young brother Charles, now Lord Spencer, cried themselves to sleep together; she could remember, she said, the crunch of the gravel under her mother's shoes as she left. Thus, classically, and beneath that appealing freshness, was to emerge the bulimia that was, by her own frank admission, to so plague her.

She was sent to Riddlesworth Hall, a boarding school near Diss, Norfolk, at the age of nine. She did not shine academically, either there or when she moved on to her mother's old school, West Heath, near Sevenoaks, although her former teachers did speak loyally of sporting prowess, particularly at swimming. She failed all her O levels, twice, leaving school at sixteen. She spent a brief time at the Institut Alpin Videmanette, a Swiss finishing school, before moving to the London flat, bought for her by her father.

Initially, before becoming an assistant at the Young England nursery in Pimlico, she had had various temporary jobs cleaning, acting as waitress at cocktail parties and nannying. Not the form thing, either. Her elder sister, Jane, had followed a rather more conventional route by marrying Robert Fellowes, an assistant private secretary to the Queen, later to become principal private secretary. Her eldest sister, Sarah, had been an earlier girlfriend of the Prince of Wales.

These connections, and Lady Fermoy's close interest, combined to bring Diana to the attention of the Prince and the Palace. In the summer of 1980, one of the early royal-watchers discovered her through his binoculars, poised attractively on the banks of the Dee at Balmoral, looking up admiringly at a fishing Prince of Wales. And so to the Coleherne Court doorstep, the nursery playground and, in February 1981, the announcement of the engagement.

The couple were haltingly, stiltingly, interviewed on television, Diana doing much upward looking, displaying her engagement ring, hiding chewed nails and much else, if probably not as much as her fiancé. In a segment endlessly replayed throughout the tortuous doings that were to follow, they were asked if they were in love. 'Of course,' replied Diana, in an embarrassed rush. 'Whatever love is,' replied the Prince, in an embarrassed rumination.

Much has been made of the contrast, particularly in the light of the revelation that the Prince of Wales was conducting at the time, and continues to conduct, a relationship with Camilla Parker Bowles, an old girlfriend who had, for the usual complicated reasons, married someone else. Not so much has been made of other subsequent revelations about Diana's worries about the match, even up to the eleventh hour, when she had to be persuaded to go ahead by her sisters, with their only half-joking warning that the souvenir tea-towels were already on sale. Duty did not play its part only on the Prince's side.

Even less has been made of how significant it was that an interviewer should have dared in the first place to ask the question of whether they were in love. It is hard, for example, to imagine it being asked of Princess Elizabeth and Philip Mountbatten. It was also a question that prepared the way for the even more intrusive questioning of the couple years later by Jonathan Dimbleby (of Charles) and Martin Bashir (of Diana).

But the nation, buoyed up by the earlier celebration of the royal jubilee, remained in the mood for pageantry, and the wedding, on 29 July 1981, was carried off with style amid genuine public interest and happiness. Their long kiss on the balcony at Buckingham Palace was judged a great success, although observant lip readers had seen the Prince asking for permission. The differences between the couple in ages and interests did not excite much comment. Royal marriages had never dwelt overmuch on compatibility. Duty remained the watchword.

But so absolute a concept was becoming increasingly isolated in a Court that had taken a conscious and determined decision to modernize itself. Only by revealing more of itself, argued the modernizers, led by the Duke of Edinburgh, could the monarchy be made more easily understood, its use more easily recognized. The Victorian constitutional theorist, Walter Bagehot, had warned that letting light on to the monarchy would destroy its mystique. The modernizers were more confident. But they reckoned without a society which, influenced by an ever more irreverent media, was rapidly discarding deference. More particularly, they neglected to note how attractive newspapers and their readers were finding royalty as soap opera. The threat was both within and without.

Diana, with her beauty, her youth, her genuinely winning manner, her seeming unstuffiness, her artlessness, her clear and unforced compassion, was prime fascination. Any amount of pop psychology has been devoted to the effect of this on a young woman from an unhappy and insecure background, but in truth she was facing new pressures that no amount of royal training could have prepared anyone for. But clearly, too, Diana enjoyed the attention, whether or not, as the pop psychologists argue, this was to compensate for the lack of attention she suffered as a child. Clearly, too, what she saw as a lack of private attention from her husband contrasted cruelly with the unending public attention.

Outwardly, at first, all seemed well with the royal marriage. Prince William was born in 1982; Prince Harry in 1984. A spare and heir achieved; popularity across the world, a leader of fashion, a patron of charities, another week, another magazine cover, another month, another triumphant foreign tour. Later, though, the Princess was to declare that her marriage was dead in three years, effectively ending after the birth of Prince Harry. The Prince, unhappy in his marriage, took refuge in his old round of holidays and country pursuits, and in his old mistress. The Princess, as with any princess, took refuge in her children and her charities. But, this being modern times, there was also her Walkman and an extensive range of advisers and consultants, including a psychotherapist, an aromatherapist, a reflexologist and an astrologer.

Rumours about the state of the marriage continued to emerge, usually in the Sunday newspapers, and usually dismissed as 'downstairs gossip'. They were further fuelled by a number of public incidents, endlessly speculated on, first starting with the Prince's early return on his own from a summer holiday in Majorca in 1986, through various foreign tours where she asked for separate rooms, turned her head away just as he was about to kiss her, and posed alone and forlorn in front of the Taj Mahal.

Then, in 1992, came publication of Andrew Morton's *Diana: Her True Story*, much of which seemed, even given the previous years of whisper and rumour, incredible. Morton alleged that the Princess suffered from bulimia nervosa; that she had thrown herself down the stairs at Sandringham while pregnant with Prince William; that she had slashed at her wrists with a razor blade, a penknife and a lemon slicer, and that she had once thrown herself against a glass cabinet. It also disclosed that the Prince kept in touch with Camilla Parker Bowles even while on honeymoon on the royal yacht *Britannia*, a disclosure allied to the one that Diana had found an inscribed gold bracelet intended as a gift from the Prince to Parker Bowles only days before the marriage. A fairy-tale romance, indeed.

Once again, Buckingham Palace threw doubt on the allegations. But Morton claimed that the information had all come from close friends. And three days after the first extract from the book had been published in the *Sunday Times*, Diana made a public and tipped-off visit to one of them, her former flatmate and bridesmaid, Carolyn Bartholomew.

In its way, this use of the media to put her case was as startling as the more sensational allegations. It followed earlier private briefings by the Prince and Princess to newspapers and marked a significant step beyond any previous contact between the press and royalty, but also a determination by Diana not to be crushed by the Court. The modernizers suddenly discovered that they were being rather outplayed at their own game by someone for whose intellect they had not previously shown an immense amount of respect.

But the gift for public relations displayed by the incident, and particularly its timing, is one of the more compelling aspects of a much misunderstood and complex personality. Certainly, the Prince and the Palace were perpetually on the back foot thereafter, which is where, after yesterday, they will perpetually remain. In December of that year, the Prince and Princess announced their formal separation. This brought no respite from the line of allegation and disclosure, growing ever more public and ever more tawdry as the opposing sides, authorized or not, attempted to create two hard, clear and opposing images. The Prince was portrayed as a weak, heartless, hidebound figure, bullied by his father, overwhelmed by his responsibility, dominated by his selfishness. For her part, the Princess was to be seen as neurotic, unbalanced, frivolous, flighty, in sway to fame and frocks.

There was something in both characterizations. But there was rather more to the Princess. A surprisingly steely resolve, a gift for friendship, certainly; but also something more elusive. That early artlessness, openness and friendliness, that which in more formal days had been usually described as the 'common touch' had become translated into a quality of compassion, a gift of ease, and had been put to apt work, with children, with Aids victims, and in areas where, as with her recent land mines campaign, a high-profile example or a large amount of publicity could be more use than any amount of earnest cajoling and lecturing.

Thus, despite the sneers, Saint Diana. But, also, uncomfortably for times where the simplicity of the message is the most prized, it went hand-in-hand with, and fed off all those sessions with consultants, all those meetings with celebrities, all those frocks and smiles.

It was also, sadly, inextricable from the accompanying tawdriness of the commonplaces of a broken marriage made extraordinary by the married. In 1994 the Prince told Jonathan Dimbleby in a television interview that he had been unfaithful. In Dimbleby's biography, published the same year, the Prince conceded he had been bullied into the marriage by his father; he had, he said, never loved his wife.

The Princess responded by arriving for a dinner in Hyde Park on the night of the Prince's adultery confession in an outfit so black and daring as to capture a good proportion of the front pages and raise more doubts in the public mind about the tastes and good sense of its future monarch. In the same year, Diana was linked with the England rugby captain, Will Carling. They had met at one of the public gyms used by Diana, whither and whence she was to be seen most days when she was in London, and whither and whence she was, most days, photographed.

It was a curious relationship, that between Diana and her photographers. She could be at turns friendly or distant. That distance was frequently misjudged, vividly this year in the case of a long-time freelance pursuer of her who found himself being attacked by a member of the public at her behest. The sneerers claimed it was all part of a need for publicity which had become unbalancing, and claimed to see much piquant irony in the affair in 1993 when the *Daily Mirror* published photographs of her exercising taken clandestinely by a gym owner.

Similar doubts were raised in 1993, when the Princess announced that she intended to reduce her official engagements and become more of a private figure. Four months later, she was back. But, once again uncomfortably for the stereotype of a fame junkie, it was to a role, as Red Cross roving ambassador, where she would be able to point out real achievement in the face of a sceptical and lukewarm government. Her supporters claimed that the very public gym trips and the lunches were vital to maintaining some sort of normal life, and that the relationship she cultivated with the press and the paparazzi was also vital to maintaining that normality, even if it did have its explosions and inconsistencies. Whatever the faults on whichever side, it was a relationship that was eventually to kill her.

Her part, in the public eye, as the innocent party in the marriage break-up was felt to be a crucial part of the Princess's popularity. When, before the separation, the 'Squidgygate' tape recording had surfaced, allegedly detailing a telephone conversation between Diana and a lover, the story was widely disbelieved as a malicious invention, much more so than the so-called 'Camillagate' tape, in which the Prince of Wales, inter alia, appeared to be favouring reincarnation as a tampon. The most clear response to Squidgygate was that the Princess of Wales's Royal Regiment began proudly, if unofficially, to refer to itself as 'Squidgy's Own'. In 1994, too, the publication of Anna Pasternak's book *Princess in Love*, supposedly detailing her five-year affair with a former army officer, James Hewitt, was similarly derided.

But, in another extremely shrewd piece of PR, timed for its influence on the couple's possible divorce and its custody implications, Diana gave an interview the next year, 1995, to the BBC *Panorama* programme that held the nation gripped with its combination of intensity and artlessness assisted by an artifice that by now seemed second nature. It had a candour clearly influenced by the pyschotherapeutic treatment the Princess had been receiving.

Asked by Martin Bashir 'were you unfaithful' with Hewitt, the Princess replied 'Yes'. She agreed that the Squidgygate tape was genuine, and that she had made a series of phone calls to a married friend, Oliver Hoare. The interview, which attracted fifteen million viewers, was as clear an example as exists of the contrasts in the Princess's personality. For, as well as these concessions, there were references to her husband's staff as 'the enemy', the questioning of his suitability to become king, and the clear declaration that she had no intention of seeking a divorce.

There was the winning, telling sound-bite: 'We had three of us in this marriage, it was a bit crowded.' And there was the typically overblown sound-bite, that she would never be Queen of the country, but she would like 'to be a

Queen of people's hearts, in people's hearts'. She continued, tellingly: 'I don't think many people will want me to be Queen. Actually, when I say many people I mean the establishment that I married into because they have decided that I'm a non-starter … because I do things differently, because I don't go by a rule book, because I lead from the heart, not the head. That's got me into trouble in my work, I understand that. But someone's got to go out there and love people and show it.' Any member of the Prince's party listening to it all would have concluded, as did Nicholas Soames, that Diana was in the 'advance stages of paranoia'.

This, though, was a complete misjudgement of the public's mood. For it was perhaps the greatest mark of the Princess's many and curious gifts that she continued to remain personally immune from the republican mood in the country that she had done almost as much as anyone to foster. This again in contrast to all the other troublesome young members of the royal family, in particular the exuberant and ultimately very silly Sarah Ferguson.

After the *Panorama* appearance, the divorce could not be long delayed; and was, indeed, urged by the Queen, at last, but far too late, disturbed by all this media manipulation. In February 1996, three years after the separation, the princess, after a private meeting with her husband at St James's Palace, once again wrongfooted the Court by releasing a statement to the Press Association that she had agreed to a divorce shortly after breaking the news to the Queen by telephone. Negotiations began between respective solicitors, with the Princess's lawyer, Anthony Julius, of Mishcon de Reya, himself being touched by media celebrity as discussions continued until July on the size of the settlement, access and custody, the Princess's role and future title, much royal magic being considered invested in the dignity of Her Royal Highness, the title withheld from the Duchess of Windsor at the behest of the Queen Mother.

On 12 July 1996, the terms were announced: a settlement believed to be around £15 million (the Princess had been reported to be asking for nearer £50 million), equal responsibility for the upbringing of their children, and the demotion in title to Diana, Princess of Wales.

It is almost impossible to resist the temptation to see the period since then as one of acceleration towards the horror of yesterday. The Princess's behaviour, in the way it was highlighted, at least, seemed to be at once a little more erratic, and its reception a little less respectful.

The narrowness of the public role she had agreed and chosen was another danger. The number of the charities she actively supported was drastically cut at the time of her divorce settlement. The controversy that had first greeted her entry into the land mine debate earlier in the year had only last week been resurrected in an interview with a French journalist in *Le Monde*, where she was alleged to have described the Tory government's policy on land mines as 'hopeless'. There had also been more sideswipes at the press. A feeling that Diana's PR, formerly so successful, if famously erratic, needed more control was fuelled by the row that followed when her office denied that she had so described the Tories, thus extending and exaggerating a row which would have quietly deflated on its own.

But there could be no doubt about the sincerity and the worth of her work for charity in areas normally carefully skirted by royalty and the establishment. Turning Point, the national drink, drugs, mental health and learning disabilities agency, an unfashionable charity with which she was involved for ten years, is a good example of this.

But her habit of doing good by stealth, the clandestine hospital visits, the charity auction of her wardrobe: such things were treated increasingly as eccentric rather than saintly, while such events as the charity auction of her old outfits was seen, unfairly, as having more to do with her fascination with the world of *Hello!* magazine celebrity, a feeling strongly reinforced by one of the year's strongest images, her red-eyed appearance earlier in the summer at the funeral of Gianni Versace, consoling a weeping Elton John. And strongly reinforced, too, by the long summer of Dodi Fayed, the posing and the confrontations, the promises of a 'big surprise', retracted but soon fulfilled in the shape of the Egyptian.

We will now never know whether this decline in the immunity of her public popularity was temporarary, and, indeed, whether it would have survived a lengthy liaison with Dodi Fayed and, more particularly, his - controversial father, certain to become only more controversial. As Jackie Kennedy discovered, immense private wealth and privilege has a way of corroding the affection and admiration gained in the attractive exercise of public wealth and privilege. But the consolation of such a horrible, twentieth-century, twisted-metal, senseless kind of death, if there is any consolation, is that the reputation of Diana, Princess of Wales, as a beautiful, winning, intriguing woman, unfairly treated by fate but touched with a rare compassion and influence for good, will remain forever frozen in time, inviolate.

DIANA, PRINCESS OF WALES, LADY DIANA FRANCES SPENCER ·
born 1 July 1961 · *died* 31 August 1997 ·